The Complete
Best of Bridge
Cookbooks

VOLUME 2

All 350 Recipes from
Winners and *Grand Slam*

Robert
ROSE

The Complete Best of Bridge Cookbooks, Volume 2
Text copyright © 2010, 1988, 1984 Karen Brimacombe, Mary Halpen, Helen Miles, Valerie Robinson
and Joan Wilson
Photographs copyright © 2010 Robert Rose Inc.
Cover and text design copyright © 2010 Robert Rose Inc.

The recipes in this book were previously published in *Winners: More Recipes from the Best of Bridge*,
published in 1984 by Best of Bridge Publishing Ltd., or in *Grand Slam: More Recipes from the Best of
Bridge*, published in 1988 by Best of Bridge Publishing Ltd..

For complete cataloguing information, see page 372.

Disclaimer
The recipes in this book have been carefully tested by our kitchen and our tasters. To the best of
our knowledge, they are safe and nutritious for ordinary use and users. For those people with food
or other allergies, or who have special food requirements or health issues, please read the suggested
contents of each recipe carefully and determine whether or not they may create a problem for you.
All recipes are used at the risk of the consumer.

We cannot be responsible for any hazards, loss or damage that may occur as a result of any
recipe use.

For those with special needs, allergies, requirements or health problems, in the event of any
doubt, please contact your medical adviser prior to the use of any recipe.

Cover design and page layout: PageWave Graphics Inc.
Indexer: Gillian Watts
Photography: Colin Erricson
Associate Photographer: Matt Johannsson
Food Styling: Kathryn Robertson
Prop Styling: Charlene Erricson

Cover image: Sweet and Spicy Cashew Chicken (page 156)

We acknowledge the financial support of the Government of Canada through the Book Publishing
Industry Development Program (BPIDP) for our publishing activities.

Published by Robert Rose Inc.
120 Eglinton Avenue East, Suite 800, Toronto, Ontario, Canada M4P 1E2
Tel: (416) 322-6552 Fax: (416) 322-6936

Printed in China

1 2 3 4 5 6 7 8 9 PPLS 18 17 16 15 14 13 12 11 10

CONTENTS

FOREWARNING 4

I BRUNCH BUFFETS
BRUNCH DISHES 6
MUFFINS AND QUICK BREADS 23

II LUNCH AND DINNER BUFFETS
DIPS AND SPREADS 44
BREADS 51
APPETIZERS 62
SALADS AND DRESSINGS. 93
SOUPS. 122
FISH AND SEAFOOD 138
CHICKEN, DUCK AND PHEASANT 149
BEEF AND VEAL. 169
PORK AND LAMB 184
PASTA 198
SIDE DISHES 216
SAUCES, CONDIMENTS AND SEASONINGS. 261

III GOODIES
COOKIES, SQUARES AND CANDIES 277
CAKES. 302
PIES AND TARTS 322
JUST DESSERTS 345
BEVERAGES. 364

INDEX 373

FOREWARNING

WHO ARE THOSE BEST OF BRIDGE WOMEN, AND WHERE DID THEY GET THAT GOOFY NAME?

IN 1975, AT A WEEKEND GETAWAY, EIGHT BRIDGE-PLAYING FRIENDS DECIDED TO WRITE A COOKBOOK AND CALL IT *THE BEST OF BRIDGE*, BECAUSE THE BEST PART OF BRIDGE IS THE FOOD. THESE YOUNG KITCHEN-COUNTER ENTREPRENEURS TURNED A GOOD IDEA INTO A GREAT BOOK AND SET THE STAGE FOR THE PHENOMENALLY SUCCESSFUL BEST OF BRIDGE COOKBOOK SERIES.

FROM THE OUTSET, "THE LADIES," AS THEIR CHILDREN NAMED THEM, HAD AN UNCONVENTIONAL BUSINESS SENSE AND AN UNCONVENTIONAL SENSE OF HUMOR. THEIRS WAS A PARTNERSHIP OF EQUALS AND A CELEBRATION OF FRIENDSHIP. THEY DID EVERYTHING (AND ANYTHING!) WITH ENTHUSIASM: RECIPE TESTING, WRITING, MARKETING, SHIPPING, PROMOTING AND EVEN PRODUCING A TV SERIES. THEY'VE SOLD OVER 3 MILLION COOKBOOKS, AND THEY'RE STILL BEST FRIENDS!

IN *THE COMPLETE BEST OF BRIDGE COOKBOOKS, VOLUME 2*, ALL OF THE RECIPES FROM *WINNERS* (THE GREEN BOOK) AND *GRAND SLAM* (THE BLACK BOOK) ARE COMPILED INTO ONE VOLUME SO THE NEXT GENERATION OF COOKS CAN ENJOY THE LADIES' FAMOUS COLLECTION OF RECIPES. THEY'RE EASY TO READ, EASY TO UNDERSTAND, WRITTEN WITH A SENSE OF HUMOR AND, BEST OF ALL, GUARANTEED TO WORK.

YOU'RE GOING TO LOVE THIS BOOK!

PART I
BRUNCH BUFFETS

BRUNCH DISHES

EGGS OLÉ!. 6

EGGS FLORENTINE. 7

WEEKENDER SPECIAL 8

SUNDAY EGGS AND HAM 9

CRUSTLESS QUICHE. 10

QUICHE LORRAINE. 11

SWISS APPLE QUICHE. 12

BAKED CHEESE AND
    TOMATO STRATA. 14

ZUCCHINI CHEESE PIE 15

THE UTMOST GRILLED
    CHEESE 16

MIDNIGHT FRENCH
    TOAST. 17

POTATO LATKES 18

SAUSAGE 'N' JOHNNY
    CAKE. 19

SAUSAGE PIE 20

SENSATIONAL SAUSAGE
    ROLL. 22

MUFFINS AND QUICK BREADS

SUNSHINE MUFFINS. 23

HEALTH NUT MUFFINS 24

MINCEMEAT MUFFINS 25

BANANA MUFFINS. 26

MANDARIN ORANGE
    MUFFINS. 27

PHANTOM RHUBARB
    MUFFINS. 28

CARROT AND RAISIN
    MUFFINS. 29

JALAPEÑO CORN
    MUFFINS. 30

CREAM CHEESE MUFFINS. . . 31

CHEDDAR DILL MUFFINS 32

CHEESE AND BACON
    MUFFINS. 33

GOING BANANAS. 34

BEST-EVER BANANA
    BREAD. 35

BLUEBERRY BANANA
    BREAD. 36

PINEAPPLE LOAF 37

STRAWBERRY BREAD. 38

EGGS OLÉ!

EASY, COLORFUL AND, OF COURSE, DELICIOUS! CARAMBA!

12	EGGS	12
1/4 CUP	WATER	60 ML
	SALT AND BLACK PEPPER TO TASTE	
6 TBSP	BUTTER, DIVIDED	90 ML
1 CUP	SLICED MUSHROOMS	250 ML
1/2 CUP	CHOPPED GREEN ONION	125 ML
1/2 CUP	COARSELY CHOPPED GREEN BELL PEPPER	125 ML
1/2 CUP	COARSELY CHOPPED RED BELL PEPPER	125 ML
1/2 CUP	COARSELY CHOPPED ZUCCHINI	125 ML
1/2 CUP	COARSELY CHOPPED TOMATOES	125 ML
1/4 CUP	GREEN CHILES (OPTIONAL)	60 ML
8 OZ	MONTEREY JACK CHEESE, SHREDDED	250 G
	SALSA, MILD OR HOT	

BEAT EGGS AND WATER TOGETHER. SEASON WITH SALT AND PEPPER. MELT HALF THE BUTTER IN A FRYING PAN AND ADD EGG MIXTURE. SCRAMBLE JUST UNTIL MOIST. PLACE IN A LARGE OVENPROOF DISH; KEEP WARM IN 150°F (70°C) OVEN. MELT THE REMAINING BUTTER IN FRYING PAN; SAUTÉ ALL VEGGIES TILL TENDER. SEASON WITH SALT AND PEPPER. SPOON OVER EGGS, SPRINKLE WITH CHEESE AND BAKE AT 300°F (150°C) UNTIL CHEESE MELTS. SERVE WITH LOTS OF SALSA. SERVES 6.

EGGS FLORENTINE

I	PACKAGE (10 OZ/300 G) FROZEN CHOPPED SPINACH	I
2 TBSP	BUTTER	30 ML
2 TSP	LEMON JUICE	10 ML
1/4 TSP	CELERY SALT	I ML
	SALT AND BLACK PEPPER TO TASTE	
2 TBSP	ALL-PURPOSE FLOUR	30 ML
2 TBSP	BUTTER	30 ML
I CUP	MILK	250 ML
1 1/2 TSP	GRATED ONION	7 ML
PINCH	GROUND NUTMEG	PINCH
6	EGGS	6
I CUP	SHREDDED SWISS CHEESE	250 ML
3	ENGLISH MUFFINS, HALVED AND TOASTED	3

COOK SPINACH AND DRAIN WELL. SEASON WITH BUTTER, LEMON JUICE, CELERY SALT, SALT AND PEPPER. IN A DOUBLE BOILER COMBINE FLOUR, BUTTER, SALT AND PEPPER TO TASTE. ADD MILK SLOWLY; STIR AND COOK UNTIL THICK, ABOUT 10 MINUTES. ADD SAUCE, ONION AND NUTMEG TO SPINACH MIXTURE AND MIX THOROUGHLY. PLACE IN SHALLOW BAKING DISH. BREAK EGGS OVER SPINACH MIXTURE. SPRINKLE CHEESE OVER EGGS. BAKE AT 325°F (160°C) FOR 15 TO 20 MINUTES OR UNTIL EGGS ARE SET. SERVE ON HALVED ENGLISH MUFFINS. SERVES 6.

WEEKENDER SPECIAL

BECAUSE YOU DON'T HAVE TO SPEND YOUR MORNING IN THE KITCHEN.

10	SLICES BACON	10
1/2 CUP	CHOPPED GREEN BELL PEPPER	125 ML
8	GREEN ONIONS, FINELY CHOPPED	8
1 LB	MUSHROOMS, SLICED INTO T'S	500 G
3 TBSP	CHOPPED PIMENTO	45 ML
3 TBSP	SHERRY	45 ML
12	EGGS	12
1 1/2 CUPS	MILK	375 ML
1 TSP	SEASONED SALT	5 ML
1 TSP	DRY MUSTARD	5 ML
1 TSP	DRIED THYME	5 ML
4 CUPS	SHREDDED GRUYÈRE CHEESE	1 L

FRY BACON UNTIL CRISP. DRAIN AND CHOP. IN SAME PAN, SAUTÉ GREEN PEPPER, ONIONS AND MUSHROOMS UNTIL LIMP. ADD PIMENTO AND SHERRY, HEATING UNTIL SHERRY EVAPORATES. IN A BOWL, BEAT EGGS, MILK, SALT, MUSTARD AND THYME. ADD BACON, MUSHROOM MIXTURE AND 3 CUPS (750 ML) OF CHEESE. POUR MIXTURE INTO EITHER A GREASED 13- BY 9-INCH (33 BY 23 CM) BAKING PAN OR TWO GREASED 8-INCH (20 CM) SQUARE BAKING PANS. COVER AND REFRIGERATE OVERNIGHT.

BAKE UNCOVERED AT 350°F (180°C) FOR 40 MINUTES. SPRINKLE REMAINING CUP (250 ML) OF CHEESE AND BAKE FOR 5 MINUTES OR UNTIL CHEESE MELTS AND AN INSERTED KNIFE COMES OUT CLEAN. LET STAND FOR 20 MINUTES BEFORE SERVING. SERVES 8.

SUNDAY EGGS AND HAM

24	EGGS	24
1/2 CUP	MILK	125 ML
1/2 CUP	BUTTER	125 ML
2 LBS	CANNED HAM	1 KG
1	CAN (10 OZ/284 ML) SLICED MUSHROOMS	1
2	CANS (EACH 10 OZ/284 ML) CREAM OF MUSHROOM SOUP	2
1/2 CUP	SHERRY	125 ML
8 OZ	SHARP (OLD) CHEDDAR CHEESE	250 G

BEAT EGGS; ADD MILK. MELT BUTTER IN A FRYING PAN AND SCRAMBLE EGGS. PLACE EGGS IN 13- BY 9-INCH (33 BY 23 CM) PAN. CHOP HAM AND SPRINKLE ON EGGS. NEXT, LAYER THE MUSHROOMS ON TOP OF HAM. WARM THE MUSHROOM SOUP WITH SHERRY AND SPREAD OVER ALL. GRATE CHEDDAR CHEESE ON TOP. COVER WITH FOIL AND REFRIGERATE UNTIL REQUIRED. BAKE AT 250°F (120°C) FOR 50 MINUTES, UNCOVERED. GREAT WITH COFFEE CAKE OR FRESH FRUIT. SERVES 12.

IF YOU'RE SUCH A GOOD COOK, WHY DO WE HAVE TO PRAY BEFORE EVERY MEAL?

CRUSTLESS QUICHE

REAL MEN LOVE THIS ONE!

10	EGGS	10
1/2 CUP	ALL-PURPOSE FLOUR	125 ML
1 TSP	BAKING POWDER	5 ML
1/2 TSP	SALT	2 ML
1/4 CUP	BUTTER, MELTED	60 ML
1 CUP	CHOPPED GREEN CHILES	250 ML
1 LB	MONTEREY JACK CHEESE, SHREDDED	500 G
2 CUPS	LOW-FAT COTTAGE CHEESE	500 ML

BUTTER A 13- BY 9-INCH (33 BY 23 CM) GLASS DISH. IN A LARGE BOWL, BEAT EGGS UNTIL FROTHY. ADD FLOUR, BAKING POWDER AND SALT AND BLEND WELL. MIX IN MELTED BUTTER, CHILES AND CHEESES. POUR INTO BUTTERED DISH AND BAKE AT 400°F (200°C) FOR 15 MINUTES, THEN LOWER HEAT TO 350°F (180°C) AND BAKE FOR 40 MINUTES LONGER. CUT INTO SMALL SQUARES. SERVE WARM WITH SALSA OR CHILI SAUCE AND CORNMEAL MUFFINS. SERVES 12.

YOU CAN'T HAVE EVERYTHING — WHERE WOULD YOU PUT IT?

QUICHE LORRAINE

*YOU DON'T HAVE TO BE A PASTRY CHEF
TO MAKE A PERFECT QUICHE.*

1/2	PACKAGE (14 OZ/400 G) FROZEN PUFF PASTRY	1/2
2 TSP	BUTTER	10 ML
1	LARGE ONION, CHOPPED	1
12	SLICES BACON, CHOPPED	12
4	EGGS	4
2 CUPS	WHIPPING (35%) CREAM	500 ML
1/2 TSP	SALT	2 ML
PINCH	GROUND NUTMEG	PINCH
PINCH	BLACK PEPPER	PINCH
PINCH	CAYENNE PEPPER	PINCH
1 CUP	SHREDDED SWISS CHEESE	250 ML

ROLL OUT PASTRY TO FIT A 9-INCH (23 CM) DEEP PIE PLATE. IN A FRYING PAN, MELT BUTTER AND SAUTÉ ONION UNTIL SOFT. FRY BACON UNTIL CRISP. COMBINE EGGS, CREAM AND SPICES IN A LARGE BOWL AND BEAT UNTIL WELL MIXED. SPRINKLE PIE SHELL WITH ONION, BACON AND CHEESE. CAREFULLY POUR EGG MIXTURE ON TOP. BAKE AT 425°F (220°C) FOR 15 MINUTES. REDUCE HEAT TO 300°F (150°C); BAKE FOR ABOUT 40 MINUTES OR UNTIL KNIFE INSERTED IN CENTER COMES OUT CLEAN. SERVES 6 TO 8.

SWISS APPLE QUICHE

FULL MARKS! YOU CAN TAKE THIS ONE TO THE BANK.

PASTRY SHELLS

1 CUP	ALL-PURPOSE FLOUR	250 ML
1/2 CUP	WHOLE WHEAT FLOUR	125 ML
1 1/2 TSP	GRANULATED SUGAR	7 ML
1/2 CUP	BUTTER	125 ML
1	EGG YOLK	1
3 TBSP	ICE WATER	45 ML

FILLING

3	MEDIUM TART GREEN APPLES, PEELED AND FINELY CHOPPED	3
8	GREEN ONIONS, THINLY SLICED	8
1/4 TSP	GROUND NUTMEG	1 ML
1/2 TSP	CURRY POWDER	2 ML
2 TBSP	BUTTER	30 ML
4 CUPS	SHREDDED GRUYÈRE CHEESE	1 L
1 CUP	WHIPPING (35%) CREAM	250 ML
4	EGGS, LIGHTLY BEATEN	4
1/2 CUP	DRY VERMOUTH OR DRY WHITE WINE	125 ML
1/4 TSP	COARSELY GROUND BLACK PEPPER	1 ML

PASTRY SHELLS: SIFT TOGETHER THE FLOURS AND SUGAR; CUT IN THE BUTTER UNTIL MIXTURE RESEMBLES COARSE MEAL. BEAT EGG YOLK WITH ICE WATER AND STIR INTO FLOUR MIXTURE UNTIL DOUGH IS FORMED, ADDING ADDITIONAL WATER, 1 TSP (5 ML) AT A TIME, IF NEEDED. FORM DOUGH INTO TWO BALLS AND FLATTEN SLIGHTLY. WRAP IN WAXED PAPER AND CHILL FOR 1 HOUR.

CONTINUED ON NEXT PAGE...

PREHEAT OVEN TO 425°F (220°C). ROLL OUT DOUGH ON FLOURED SURFACE. PLACE IN TWO 9-INCH (23 CM) PIE PLATES OR QUICHE PANS AND CRIMP EDGES. PRICK BOTTOMS LIGHTLY WITH A FORK AND BAKE ON LOWER RACK OF OVEN FOR 15 MINUTES. CHECK AND COVER EDGES WITH FOIL IF TOO BROWN. RETURN TO OVEN AND BAKE AN ADDITIONAL 5 MINUTES. REMOVE FROM OVEN AND COOL.

FILLING: PREHEAT OVEN TO 375°F (190°C). COMBINE APPLES, GREEN ONIONS, NUTMEG AND CURRY. SAUTÉ IN BUTTER FOR 3 TO 5 MINUTES, OR JUST UNTIL SOFT. COOL. SPOON INTO COOLED PIE SHELLS AND TOP WITH CHEESE. COMBINE CREAM, EGGS, VERMOUTH AND PEPPER. POUR SLOWLY OVER CHEESE. REDUCE HEAT TO 350°F (180°C). BAKE QUICHES ON MIDDLE RACK FOR 35 TO 45 MINUTES OR UNTIL FIRM AND GOLDEN. WATCH THAT PASTRY EDGES DON'T GET TOO BROWN. COVER IF NECESSARY. REMOVE FROM OVEN AND COOL ON A RACK FOR 15 MINUTES. MAKES 2 QUICHES; EACH SERVES 8.

IF YOU WANT TO FEEL GUILTY, CALL YOUR MOTHER.

BAKED CHEESE AND TOMATO STRATA

2/3 CUP	SOFT MARGARINE	150 ML
1	CLOVE GARLIC, MINCED	1
1 TSP	DRY MUSTARD	5 ML
1	LOAF ITALIAN STYLE WHITE BREAD, SLICED	1
12 OZ	SHREDDED SWISS CHEESE (OR HALF CHEDDAR, HALF SWISS)	375 G
3 TBSP	GRATED ONION	45 ML
1 1/2 TSP	SALT	7 ML
1 TSP	PAPRIKA	5 ML
PINCH	BLACK PEPPER	PINCH
1/3 CUP	ALL-PURPOSE FLOUR	75 ML
3 CUPS	MILK	750 ML
1	CAN (19 OZ/540 ML) STEWED TOMATOES	1
3	EGGS, BEATEN	3

IN A SMALL BOWL, CREAM 1/3 CUP (75 ML) MARGARINE, GARLIC AND 1/2 TSP (2 ML) MUSTARD. REMOVE BREAD CRUSTS AND SPREAD ONE SIDE OF EACH SLICE WITH MARGARINE MIXTURE. LINE A 13- BY 9-INCH (33 BY 23 CM) BAKING DISH WITH BREAD TO COVER BOTTOM AND SIDES, MARGARINE SIDE DOWN.

IN A LARGE BOWL, COMBINE CHEESE, ONION, SALT, PAPRIKA, PEPPER AND REMAINING MUSTARD. TOSS UNTIL WELL BLENDED. IN A MEDIUM SAUCEPAN, MELT REMAINING MARGARINE. REMOVE FROM HEAT AND STIR IN FLOUR, THEN GRADUALLY STIR IN MILK. HEAT TO BOILING, THEN

CONTINUED ON NEXT PAGE...

STIR IN TOMATOES. ADD A LITTLE HOT MIXTURE TO EGGS, STIRRING, AND POUR BACK INTO SAUCEPAN. STIR.

SET ASIDE 1/2 CUP (125 ML) CHEESE MIXTURE. IN THE LINED DISH, ALTERNATE LAYERS OF REMAINING CHEESE MIXTURE AND BREAD, MARGARINE SIDE UP. POUR TOMATO SAUCE OVER ALL. SPRINKLE WITH REMAINING CHEESE. REFRIGERATE, COVERED, OVERNIGHT. PREHEAT OVEN TO 375°F (190°C). BAKE FOR 45 MINUTES OR UNTIL PUFFY AND GOLDEN ON TOP. SERVES 8.

ONE OF THE HARDEST DECISIONS IN LIFE IS WHEN TO START MIDDLE AGE.

ZUCCHINI CHEESE PIE

A GREAT CASUAL DISH FOR BARBECUE OR BRUNCH. SERVE WITH A SALAD ON THE SIDE.

1/2 CUP	SHREDDED CHEDDAR CHEESE	125 ML
3 CUPS	SHREDDED ZUCCHINI	750 ML
1 CUP	BISCUIT MIX	250 ML
1/2 CUP	VEGETABLE OIL	125 ML
1 TBSP	CHOPPED FRESH PARSLEY	15 ML
4	EGGS	4
	SALT AND BLACK PEPPER TO TASTE	

MIX CHEESE, ZUCCHINI, BISCUIT MIX, OIL AND PARSLEY TOGETHER. IN A BOWL, BEAT EGGS, SALT AND PEPPER AND MIX WITH OTHER INGREDIENTS. POUR INTO 9-INCH (23 CM) PIE PLATE AND BAKE AT 375°F (190°C) FOR 40 MINUTES. CUT INTO WEDGES. SERVES 6 TO 8.

THE UTMOST GRILLED CHEESE

1	LOAF FRENCH BREAD	1
2 TBSP	PREPARED MUSTARD	30 ML
1 CUP	SHREDDED CHEDDAR CHEESE	250 ML
1 CUP	SHREDDED MONTEREY JACK CHEESE	250 ML
1/4 CUP	BUTTER OR MARGARINE, SOFTENED	60 ML
1/2 TSP	WORCESTERSHIRE SAUCE	2 ML
1	EGG	1
4 TO 6	SLICES BACON, COOKED CRISP AND CRUMBLED	4 TO 6
2	GREEN ONIONS, CHOPPED	2

HALVE LOAF LENGTHWISE AND SPREAD CUT SIDES WITH MUSTARD. MIX CHEESES, BUTTER, WORCESTERSHIRE, EGG, BACON AND ONIONS IN A BOWL UNTIL WELL COMBINED. SPREAD MIXTURE ON BREAD. PLACE ON A BAKING SHEET AND BROIL TILL LIGHTLY BROWNED AND PUFFED (USUALLY 5 MINUTES). CUT INTO STRIPS AND SERVE IMMEDIATELY. GREAT FOR LUNCH OR DINNER WITH A STEAMING BOWL OF SOUP. IT'S HARD TO SAY HOW MANY THIS SERVES, SO WE DIDN'T!

MIDNIGHT FRENCH TOAST

WHAT A WAY TO END THE DAY — AND START THE NEXT!
SERVE WITH FRUIT OR MAPLE SYRUP.

12	EGGS	12
$\frac{1}{2}$ CUP	CREAM	125 ML
$\frac{1}{2}$ TSP	VANILLA EXTRACT	2 ML
	GRATED ZEST OF 1 ORANGE	
2 TBSP	ORANGE LIQUEUR OR ORANGE JUICE	30 ML
1	LOAF FRENCH BREAD, SLICED 1 INCH (2.5 CM) THICK	1

MIX EGGS, CREAM, VANILLA, ORANGE ZEST AND LIQUEUR IN 13- BY 9-INCH (33 BY 23 CM) PAN. PLACE SLICED BREAD IN PAN, MAKING SURE SLICES ARE WELL COATED. COVER WITH LID OR PLASTIC WRAP. PLACE IN FRIDGE OVERNIGHT.

NEXT MORNING, PLACE BREAD SLICES ON A WELL-GREASED COOKIE SHEET. BAKE AT 375°F (190°C) FOR 20 TO 25 MINUTES. SERVES 6.

TREAT HER LIKE A THOROUGHBRED AND
YOU WON'T END UP WITH A NAG!

POTATO LATKES

OY VEY! POTATO PANCAKES AND TASTY TOO! CAN BE MADE THE NIGHT BEFORE AND REFRIED OR MICROWAVED FOR BRUNCH. IF YOU HAVE LEFTOVERS, JUST FREEZE BETWEEN LAYERS OF WAXED PAPER.

3	LARGE POTATOES, PEELED AND GRATED	3
1/2	MEDIUM ONION, GRATED	1/2
	JUICE OF 1 LEMON	
6	EGGS	6
1/2 CUP	ALL-PURPOSE FLOUR	125 ML
1/2 CUP	VEGETABLE OIL	125 ML
2 TBSP	CHOPPED FRESH PARSLEY	30 ML
1 TSP	SALT	5 ML
1/2 TSP	BLACK PEPPER	2 ML
1/8 TSP	GARLIC POWDER	0.5 ML
	APPLESAUCE AND SOUR CREAM	

PLACE POTATOES AND ONION IN A BOWL AND TOSS WITH LEMON JUICE; COVER WITH COLD WATER. BEAT TOGETHER EGGS, FLOUR, OIL, PARSLEY, SALT, PEPPER AND GARLIC POWDER. ADD WELL-DRAINED POTATO MIXTURE AND MIX WELL. BATTER WILL BE SOUPY! DROP BY TABLESPOONS ONTO A LIGHTLY BUTTERED FRYING PAN, SPREADING OUT SLIGHTLY. FRY OVER MEDIUM HEAT UNTIL GOLDEN BROWN ON EACH SIDE. SERVE WITH APPLESAUCE AND SOUR CREAM. DEE-LISH! MAKES AT LEAST 30.

SAUSAGE 'N' JOHNNY CAKE

GREAT BRUNCH DISH!

16	LINK PORK SAUSAGES	16
1 CUP	CORNMEAL	250 ML
2 CUPS	BUTTERMILK	500 ML
1 1/3 CUPS	ALL-PURPOSE FLOUR	325 ML
1/2 TSP	BAKING SODA	2 ML
2 TSP	BAKING POWDER	10 ML
1/4 CUP	GRANULATED SUGAR	60 ML
1/2 TSP	SALT	2 ML
1/3 CUP	LARD	75 ML
1	EGG	1
1/2 TSP	VANILLA EXTRACT	2 ML

COOK SAUSAGES AND DRAIN FAT. ARRANGE IN PINWHEEL FASHION IN BOTTOM OF A WELL-GREASED 10-INCH (25 CM) ROUND PAN. SOAK CORNMEAL IN BUTTERMILK FOR 10 MINUTES. SIFT FLOUR, BAKING SODA, BAKING POWDER, SUGAR AND SALT. CUT IN LARD TO FORM A CRUMBLY MIXTURE. BEAT EGG AND VANILLA AND STIR INTO CORNMEAL MIXTURE. ADD TO DRY INGREDIENTS, STIRRING JUST TO MOISTEN. POUR OVER SAUSAGES AND BAKE AT 400°F (200°C) FOR 30 MINUTES. SERVE WARM WITH BUTTER AND MAPLE SYRUP. THIS RECIPE FREEZES WELL. SERVES 8.

I LIKE TO DO ALL THE TALKING MYSELF.
IT SAVES TIME AND PREVENTS ARGUMENTS.

SAUSAGE PIE

ONCE AGAIN, IT'S AN EASY MAKE-AHEAD. LOOKS FANTASTIC AND, BEST OF ALL, IT'S DELICIOUS! SERVE WITH A SALAD.

1	CAN (28 OZ/796 ML) TOMATOES, WELL DRAINED AND PRESSED (NO IRONING BOARD NECESSARY)	1
1/2 TSP	DRIED BASIL	2 ML
1/4 TSP	BLACK PEPPER	1 ML
1 LB	SAUSAGE MEAT	500 G
1/2 TSP	CHILI POWDER	2 ML
1/2 TSP	DRIED OREGANO	2 ML
1/2 TSP	DRIED BASIL	2 ML
1 1/2 CUPS	SHREDDED MOZZARELLA CHEESE	375 ML
3	GREEN ONIONS, THINLY SLICED	3
1/2 CUP	FINELY CHOPPED RED BELL PEPPER	125 ML
2	PACKAGES (EACH 8 OZ/235 G) REFRIGERATED CRESCENT DINNER ROLLS	2

PREHEAT OVEN TO 350°F (180°C). IN A BOWL, COMBINE TOMATOES WITH BASIL AND BLACK PEPPER. SET ASIDE. BROWN SAUSAGE MEAT, STIRRING WITH A FORK TO KEEP SEPARATED. DRAIN OFF FAT. ADD CHILI POWDER, OREGANO, BASIL, 1/2 CUP (125 ML) CHEESE, GREEN ONION AND RED PEPPER. STIR AND SET ASIDE. THE NEXT PART IS EASY!

OPEN ONE PACKAGE OF DINNER ROLLS AND UNROLL. CUT RECTANGLE OF DOUGH IN HALF ALONG THE PERFORATED LINE. MOLD HALF IN THE BOTTOM OF A 9-INCH (23 CM) SPRINGFORM PAN, COVERING THE BASE COMPLETELY. PINCH TOGETHER ANY SECTIONS THAT HAVE SEPARATED.

CONTINUED ON NEXT PAGE...

DIVIDE THE REMAINING SQUARE OF DOUGH ALONG THE PERFORATED LINES AND FIT THESE AROUND THE SIDES OF THE PAN, TRIMMING OFF ANY EDGES THAT PROJECT ABOVE TOP OF PAN. PINCH ALL SEAMS TOGETHER. SPOON SAUSAGE MIXTURE OVER DOUGH AND PRESS DOWN FIRMLY. SPREAD TOMATO MIXTURE OVER MEAT AND SPRINKLE WITH REMAINING CUP (250 ML) OF MOZZARELLA CHEESE. USING THE SECOND PACKAGE OF ROLLS, SEPARATE DOUGH INTO TRIANGLES AND CUT INTO 1/2-INCH (1 CM) STRIPS. FORM THESE INTO A LATTICE PATTERN OVER TOP OF THE FILLING. DON'T WORRY ABOUT "JOINS"; IT ALL BAKES TOGETHER. GENTLY ROLL THE DOUGH ALONG THE RIM DOWN TO COVER THE EDGES OF THE LATTICE STRIPS. BAKE FOR 35 TO 45 MINUTES, OR UNTIL GOLDEN BROWN. REMOVE FROM OVEN AND COOL 5 MINUTES. RUN A KNIFE AROUND THE EDGE TO LOOSEN CRUST. REMOVE FROM PAN. CUT INTO WEDGES. SERVES 8.

IF YOU WANT TO BE SEEN, STAND UP.
IF YOU WANT TO BE HEARD, SPEAK UP.
IF YOU WANT TO BE APPRECIATED, SIT DOWN AND SHUT UP!

SENSATIONAL SAUSAGE ROLL

AN EASY MAKE-AHEAD. NEVER FAILS, LOOKS FANTASTIC AND, BEST OF ALL, IT'S DELICIOUS! SERVE WITH A SALAD FOR BRUNCH OR LATE-EVENING ENTERTAINING.

1	PACKAGE (14 OZ/400 G) FROZEN PUFF PASTRY	1
8	SLICES BACON	8
1/2 CUP	FINELY CHOPPED ONION	125 ML
2 CUPS	FINELY CHOPPED MUSHROOMS	500 ML
1 LB	PORK SAUSAGE MEAT	500 G
1	MEDIUM TOMATO, SLICED	1
	BLACK PEPPER TO TASTE	
1	EGG, BEATEN	1

REMOVE PACKAGE OF PUFF PASTRY FROM FREEZER 2 HOURS BEFORE COOKING TIME. CUT A PIECE OF PARCHMENT PAPER TO FIT AN EDGED COOKIE SHEET. POKE PAPER WITH A SHARP KNIFE TO PROVIDE DRAINAGE HOLES. FRY BACON UNTIL CRISP; DRAIN, COOL AND CRUMBLE. COMBINE BACON, ONION AND MUSHROOMS IN A LARGE BOWL. ADD COLD, UNCOOKED SAUSAGE MEAT TO BOWL AND MIX WELL. ROLL OUT PUFF PASTRY TO EDGES OF FLOURED BROWN PAPER.

SPREAD THE MEAT MIXTURE DOWN THE MIDDLE OF THE PASTRY. PLACE TOMATO SLICES ALL ALONG THE TOP AND SPRINKLE WITH PEPPER. CUT THE EXPOSED PASTRY ON EACH LONG SIDE INTO 1-INCH (2.5 CM) WIDE STRIPS (THEY SHOULD BE ABOUT 3 INCHES/7.5 CM DEEP). FOLD EACH END UP OVER FILLING, THEN LAY THE STRIPS FROM EACH SIDE ALTERNATELY OVER THE TOP TO PRODUCE A BRAIDED

CONTINUED ON NEXT PAGE...

EFFECT. BRUSH PASTRY WITH BEATEN EGG. BAKE ON BROWN PAPER ON RACK ON COOKIE SHEET AT 375°F (190°C) FOR 1¼ HOURS. SERVES 6.

SUNSHINE MUFFINS

SO QUICK YOU WON'T BELIEVE IT!

1	ORANGE	1
½ CUP	ORANGE JUICE	125 ML
1	EGG	1
¼ CUP	VEGETABLE OIL	60 ML
1½ CUPS	ALL-PURPOSE FLOUR	375 ML
¾ CUP	GRANULATED SUGAR	175 ML
1 TSP	BAKING POWDER	5 ML
1 TSP	BAKING SODA	5 ML
1 TSP	SALT	5 ML
½ CUP	RAISINS (OPTIONAL)	125 ML
½ CUP	CHOPPED NUTS (OPTIONAL)	125 ML

CUT ORANGE INTO 8 PIECES. PUT CUT-UP ORANGE (THAT'S RIGHT, THE WHOLE ORANGE), ORANGE JUICE, EGG AND OIL IN BLENDER. BLEND UNTIL SMOOTH. ADD FLOUR, SUGAR, BAKING POWDER, BAKING SODA AND SALT. BLEND. ADD RAISINS AND NUTS (IF USING). BLEND JUST UNTIL MIXED. POUR MIXTURE INTO GREASED MUFFIN TINS AND BAKE AT 375°F (190°C) FOR 15 TO 20 MINUTES. MAKES 16 MEDIUM MUFFINS.

UPDATE: TRY THIS RECIPE WITH DRIED CRANBERRIES.

HEALTH NUT MUFFINS

1 1/2 CUPS	VERY HOT WATER	375 ML
1/4 CUP	LIGHT (FANCY) MOLASSES	60 ML
1/2 CUP	ALL-BRAN	125 ML
1/2 CUP	ROLLED OATS	125 ML
3 TBSP	GRANULATED SUGAR	45 ML
3 TBSP	BROWN SUGAR	45 ML
3/4 CUP	WHOLE WHEAT FLOUR	175 ML
1/2 CUP	SKIM MILK POWDER	125 ML
3 TBSP	WHEAT GERM	45 ML
1 TSP	BAKING POWDER	5 ML
1/2 TSP	BAKING SODA	2 ML
1 1/2 TSP	SALT	7 ML
1/3 CUP	VEGETABLE OIL	75 ML
2	EGGS	2
2 TSP	VANILLA EXTRACT	10 ML
1/2 CUP	CHOPPED WALNUTS	125 ML
1/2 CUP	SUNFLOWER SEEDS (OPTIONAL)	125 ML
1 CUP	RAISINS	250 ML
1/2 CUP	CHOPPED DATES	125 ML
1/2 CUP	CHOPPED DRIED APRICOTS	125 ML
1/2 CUP	COCONUT (OPTIONAL)	125 ML

IN A LARGE BOWL, COMBINE WATER AND MOLASSES. ADD
BRAN AND OATS AND SOAK 15 MINUTES. MEANWHILE, IN
ANOTHER BOWL, COMBINE SUGARS, FLOUR, SKIM MILK
POWDER, WHEAT GERM, BAKING POWDER, BAKING SODA
AND SALT. TO THE SOAKED BRAN AND OATS, BEAT IN OIL,
EGGS AND VANILLA. ADD DRY INGREDIENTS AND COMBINE
THOROUGHLY. BATTER WILL BE RUNNY — DON'T PANIC! STIR

CONTINUED ON NEXT PAGE...

IN NUTS AND FRUITS. BAKE AT 350°F (180°C) FOR 20 TO 25 MINUTES. REMOVE FROM OVEN AND COOL ON CAKE RACKS. MAKES 3 DOZEN.

A KISS IS A PLEASANT REMINDER THAT TWO HEADS ARE BETTER THAN ONE.

MINCEMEAT MUFFINS

1 CUP	BROWN SUGAR	250 ML
2	EGGS	2
1 1/2 CUPS	ALL-PURPOSE FLOUR	375 ML
1 1/2 CUPS	WHOLE WHEAT FLOUR OR GRAHAM FLOUR	375 ML
2 TSP	BAKING POWDER	10 ML
2 TSP	BAKING SODA	10 ML
1 TSP	SALT	5 ML
1/2 TSP	GROUND CLOVES	2 ML
1/2 TSP	GROUND GINGER	2 ML
2 CUPS	MILK	500 ML
3/4 CUPS	VEGETABLE OIL	175 ML
1 CUP	MINCEMEAT	250 ML

CREAM SUGAR AND EGGS. USE MIXER FOR THIS ONLY; DO THE REST BY HAND. SIFT DRY INGREDIENTS AND ADD TO CREAMED MIXTURE WITH MILK AND OIL. DO NOT OVERMIX. ADD MINCEMEAT LAST. SPOON INTO GREASED MUFFIN PANS OR BAKING CUPS, THREE-QUARTERS FULL. BAKE AT 350°F (180°C) FOR 15 TO 20 MINUTES. MAKES 28 LARGE MUFFINS.

BANANA MUFFINS

ANOTHER RECIPE FOR ALL THOSE OVERRIPE BANANAS.
VERY MOIST. GREAT FOR THE LUNCH BOX!

1/2 CUP	BUTTER OR MARGARINE	125 ML
1 CUP	GRANULATED SUGAR	250 ML
2	EGGS	2
1 CUP	MASHED RIPE BANANAS	250 ML
1 1/2 CUPS	ALL-PURPOSE FLOUR	375 ML
1 TSP	GROUND NUTMEG	5 ML
1 TSP	BAKING SODA	5 ML
2 TSP	HOT WATER	10 ML
1 TSP	VANILLA EXTRACT	5 ML

CREAM BUTTER AND SUGAR. ADD EGGS AND BANANAS. MIX
WELL. STIR IN FLOUR AND NUTMEG. DISSOLVE SODA IN
HOT WATER; ADD TO BANANA MIXTURE. STIR IN VANILLA.
FILL GREASED MUFFIN TINS HALF FULL. BAKE AT 350°F
(180°C) FOR ABOUT 20 MINUTES OR UNTIL GOLDEN BROWN.
MAKES 12 MEDIUM MUFFINS.

WHEN YOU SEE A LIGHT AT THE END OF THE TUNNEL,
IT MEANS THERE'S A TRAIN HEADED YOUR WAY.

MANDARIN ORANGE MUFFINS

1½ CUPS	ALL-PURPOSE FLOUR	375 ML
1¾ TSP	BAKING POWDER	8 ML
½ TSP	SALT	2 ML
¼ TSP	GROUND ALLSPICE	1 ML
½ TSP	GROUND NUTMEG	2 ML
½ CUP	GRANULATED SUGAR	125 ML
⅓ CUP	BUTTER	75 ML
1	EGG, SLIGHTLY BEATEN	1
¼ CUP	MILK	60 ML
1	CAN (8 OZ/227 ML) MANDARIN ORANGES, JUICE RESERVED	1

TOPPING

¼ CUP	MELTED BUTTER	60 ML
¼ CUP	GRANULATED SUGAR	60 ML
½ TSP	GROUND CINNAMON	2 ML

SIFT FLOUR WITH OTHER DRY INGREDIENTS. CUT IN BUTTER. COMBINE EGG AND MILK; ADD ALL AT ONCE TO DRY INGREDIENTS, MIXING ONLY UNTIL MOISTENED. FOLD IN ORANGES AND ¼ CUP (60 ML) RESERVED JUICE. FILL GREASED MUFFIN TINS THREE-QUARTERS FULL. BAKE AT 350°F (180°C) FOR 20 TO 25 MINUTES. REMOVE FROM MUFFIN TINS WHILE STILL WARM. DIP TOPS IN MELTED BUTTER AND SUGAR-CINNAMON MIXTURE. MAKES 12 LARGE MUFFINS.

PHANTOM RHUBARB MUFFINS

WHAT DO YOU MEAN THEY'RE GONE? AGAIN?

RHUBARB MUFFINS

1/2 CUP	FAT-FREE SOUR CREAM	125 ML
1/4 CUP	VEGETABLE OIL	60 ML
1	EGG	1
1 1/3 CUPS	ALL-PURPOSE FLOUR	325 ML
1 CUP	DICED RHUBARB	250 ML
2/3 CUP	BROWN SUGAR	150 ML
1/2 TSP	BAKING SODA	2 ML
1/4 TSP	SALT	1 ML

BROWN SUGAR CINNAMON TOPPING

1/4 CUP	BROWN SUGAR	60 ML
1/4 CUP	CHOPPED PECANS	60 ML
1/2 TSP	GROUND CINNAMON	2 ML
2 TSP	MELTED BUTTER	10 ML

MUFFINS: BLEND TOGETHER SOUR CREAM, OIL AND EGG. SET ASIDE. IN ANOTHER BOWL, STIR REMAINING INGREDIENTS TOGETHER AND COMBINE WITH SOUR CREAM MIXTURE. MIX JUST UNTIL MOISTENED. FILL 12 LARGE GREASED MUFFIN CUPS TWO-THIRDS FULL.

TOPPING: COMBINE ALL INGREDIENTS AND SPOON ONTO EACH MUFFIN. BAKE AT 350°F (180°C) FOR 25 TO 30 MINUTES. MAKES 12 MUFFINS.

AGE IS A HIGH PRICE TO PAY FOR MATURITY.

CARROT AND RAISIN MUFFINS

1 CUP	ALL-PURPOSE FLOUR	250 ML
1/2 CUP	WHOLE WHEAT FLOUR	125 ML
2 TSP	BAKING POWDER	10 ML
1/2 TSP	SALT	2 ML
1/2 TSP	GROUND CINNAMON	2 ML
1/4 TSP	GROUND NUTMEG	1 ML
1/2 CUP	BROWN SUGAR	125 ML
1	EGG	1
1/2 CUP	MILK	125 ML
1/3 CUP	VEGETABLE OIL	75 ML
1 CUP	GRATED CARROTS	250 ML
1/2 CUP	RAISINS	125 ML

GREASE MUFFIN TINS. PREHEAT OVEN TO 400°F (200°C). COMBINE DRY INGREDIENTS IN A LARGE BOWL. BEAT TOGETHER EGG, MILK AND OIL. POUR INTO DRY INGREDIENTS. STIR JUST UNTIL INGREDIENTS ARE MOIST. FOLD IN CARROTS AND RAISINS. FILL TINS TWO-THIRDS FULL. BAKE AT 400°F (200°C) FOR ABOUT 20 MINUTES. SERVE WITH ORANGE BUTTER. MAKES 12 MUFFINS.

ORANGE BUTTER

1/2 CUP	SOFT BUTTER	125 ML
1/4 CUP	SIFTED ICING SUGAR	60 ML
1 1/2 TBSP	GRATED ORANGE ZEST	22 ML

CREAM BUTTER UNTIL FLUFFY. BEAT IN SUGAR AND ORANGE ZEST. SERVE WITH MUFFINS. MAKES ABOUT 3/4 CUP (175 ML).

JALAPEÑO CORN MUFFINS

½ CUP	ALL-PURPOSE FLOUR	125 ML
I TBSP	BAKING POWDER	15 ML
½ TSP	SALT	2 ML
I½ CUPS	YELLOW CORNMEAL	375 ML
2	EGGS	2
I CUP	FAT-FREE SOUR CREAM	250 ML
I CUP	SHREDDED LIGHT CHEDDAR CHEESE	250 ML
I	CAN (10 OZ/284 G) CREAMED CORN	I
¼ CUP	CHOPPED SEEDED JALAPEÑO PEPPERS	60 ML
½ CUP	BUTTER OR MARGARINE, MELTED	125 ML

SIFT FLOUR, BAKING POWDER AND SALT TOGETHER. ADD CORNMEAL, EGGS, SOUR CREAM, CHEESE, CREAMED CORN, JALAPEÑO PEPPERS AND BUTTER; MIX WELL. SPRAY MEDIUM MUFFIN TINS OR USE PAPER LINERS AND FILL WITH MIXTURE. BAKE AT 450°F (230°C) FOR 15 TO 20 MINUTES. MAKES ABOUT 18 MEDIUM MUFFINS.

DON'T WORRY ABOUT TEMPTATION — AS YOU GROW OLDER, IT WILL AVOID YOU.

CREAM CHEESE MUFFINS

1 3/4 CUPS	ALL-PURPOSE FLOUR	425 ML
1 TSP	BAKING POWDER	5 ML
1/2 TSP	BAKING SODA	2 ML
1/4 TSP	SALT	1 ML
1/2 CUP	BUTTER, MELTED	125 ML
8 OZ	CREAM CHEESE	250 G
2	EGGS	2
1/4 CUP	MILK	60 ML
1 TSP	VANILLA EXTRACT	5 ML
1/4 CUP	RASPBERRY JAM	60 ML
1/4 CUP	BUTTER, SOFTENED	60 ML
1/4 CUP	ALL-PURPOSE FLOUR	60 ML
1/4 CUP	BROWN SUGAR	60 ML
1 TSP	GROUND CINNAMON	5 ML

PREHEAT OVEN TO 350°F (180°C). GREASE 12 MUFFIN TINS. IN A LARGE BOWL, COMBINE FLOUR, BAKING POWDER, BAKING SODA AND SALT. IN ANOTHER BOWL, CREAM TOGETHER BUTTER AND CREAM CHEESE WITH AN ELECTRIC MIXER. ADD EGGS ONE AT A TIME AND BEAT WELL AFTER EACH ADDITION. BEAT IN MILK, VANILLA AND RASPBERRY JAM. MIX WITH DRY MIXTURE AND STIR UNTIL MOIST BUT STILL LUMPY. FILL MUFFIN TINS COMPLETELY WITH BATTER. MIX LAST FOUR INGREDIENTS UNTIL CRUMBLY AND SPRINKLE OVER TOP OF MUFFINS. BAKE FOR 20 TO 25 MINUTES. MAKES 12 LARGE MUFFINS.

CHEDDAR DILL MUFFINS

DILL MAKES THE DIFFERENCE.

2 CUPS	ALL-PURPOSE FLOUR	500 ML
1 TBSP	BAKING POWDER	15 ML
3/4 TSP	SALT	3 ML
2 TBSP	GRANULATED SUGAR	30 ML
1/4 CUP	FINELY CHOPPED FRESH DILL	60 ML
1	EGG	1
1 CUP	PLAIN YOGURT	250 ML
1/2 CUP	MILK	125 ML
3 TBSP	MELTED BUTTER	45 ML
1/2 CUP	SHREDDED SHARP (OLD) CHEDDAR CHEESE	125 ML

SIFT FLOUR WITH BAKING POWDER, SALT AND SUGAR. STIR IN DILL. COMBINE EGG, YOGURT, MILK AND MELTED BUTTER. GENTLY STIR LIQUID MIXTURE INTO FLOUR MIXTURE JUST UNTIL BLENDED. FOLD IN CHEESE. USING AN ICE CREAM SCOOP, FILL BUTTERED MUFFIN TINS THREE-QUARTERS FULL. BAKE IN PREHEATED 400°F (200°C) OVEN FOR 20 TO 25 MINUTES. MAKES 12 TO 15 LARGE MUFFINS.

SOME WAITERS SHOULD VISIT THE ZOO AND
WATCH THE TURTLES ZIP BY!

Eggs Olé! (page 6)

Midnight French Toast (page 17)

Health Nut Muffins (page 24)

Sour Cream Ginger Buns (page 58)

CHEESE AND BACON MUFFINS

TASTY WHEN SERVED WITH SCRAMBLED EGGS.

8	STRIPS BACON	8
1 1/2 CUPS	ALL-PURPOSE FLOUR	375 ML
1/2 CUP	CORNMEAL	125 ML
1 TBSP	BAKING POWDER	15 ML
1/2 TSP	SALT	2 ML
1/2 TSP	CAYENNE PEPPER	2 ML
2 CUPS	SHREDDED SHARP (OLD) CHEDDAR CHEESE	500 ML
1	EGG	1
1 CUP	MILK	250 ML
3 TBSP	BUTTER	45 ML
1/3 CUP	COARSELY SHREDDED CHEDDAR CHEESE	75 ML

COOK AND DRAIN BACON, RESERVING ABOUT 2 TBSP (30 ML) DRIPPINGS. CRUMBLE BACON. COMBINE FLOUR, CORNMEAL, BAKING POWDER, SALT, CAYENNE, CHEESE AND CRUMBLED BACON. MELT BUTTER AND ADD TO RESERVED BACON DRIPPINGS. IN A MEDIUM BOWL, BEAT EGG LIGHTLY AND MIX IN MILK AND BUTTER-BACON MIXTURE. ADD TO FIRST SEVEN INGREDIENTS AND STIR THOROUGHLY. FILL GREASED MUFFIN CUPS THREE-QUARTERS FULL. SPRINKLE 1 TBSP (15 ML) CHEESE ON EACH. BAKE AT 425°F (220°C) FOR 20 MINUTES. MAKES ABOUT 18 MEDIUM MUFFINS.

GOING BANANAS

YOU ARE ABOUT TO CHANGE YOUR ATTITUDE
ABOUT BORING OLD BANANA BREAD. WE ARE
HOOKED ON THIS ONE.

1 1/2 CUPS	GRANULATED SUGAR	375 ML
3	EGGS	3
3/4 CUP	VEGETABLE OIL	175 ML
2 CUPS	ALL-PURPOSE FLOUR	500 ML
2 TBSP	BAKING SODA	10 ML
1/2 TSP	SALT	2 ML
1 TSP	GROUND CINNAMON	5 ML
1 TSP	GROUND ALLSPICE	5 ML
2 CUPS	MASHED BANANAS	500 ML
1/2 CUP	RAISINS	125 ML

SET OVEN AT 350°F (180°C). GREASE AND FLOUR A 10-INCH
(25 CM) BUNDT PAN OR TWO 8- BY 4-INCH (20 BY 10 CM)
LOAF PANS. BEAT SUGAR AND EGGS UNTIL CREAMY. MIX
IN OIL. SIFT FLOUR, BAKING SODA, SALT, CINNAMON AND
ALLSPICE. ADD TO CREAMED MIXTURE. MIX IN BANANAS AND
RAISINS. POUR INTO BUNDT PAN AND BAKE FOR 1 HOUR OR
UNTIL DONE. (TEST WITH A TOOTHPICK; IT SHOULD COME
OUT DRY.) TURN OUT OF PAN WHEN COOL. IT'S SO MOIST
IT DOESN'T EVEN NEED BUTTER. MAKES 1 OR 2 LOAVES.

BY THE TIME WE'VE MADE IT, WE'VE HAD IT.
— MALCOLM FORBES

BEST-EVER BANANA BREAD

DAY-O! HEY, MISTER TALLYMAN, TALLY THIS ONE!

1 CUP	BUTTER	250 ML
2 CUPS	GRANULATED SUGAR	500 ML
2½ CUPS	MASHED RIPE BANANAS (ABOUT 5)	625 ML
4	EGGS, WELL BEATEN	4
2½ CUPS	ALL-PURPOSE FLOUR	625 ML
2 TSP	BAKING SODA	10 ML
1 TSP	SALT	5 ML
1 TSP	GROUND NUTMEG	5 ML

PREHEAT OVEN TO 350°F (180°C). CREAM BUTTER AND SUGAR UNTIL LIGHT AND FLUFFY. ADD BANANAS AND EGGS AND BEAT UNTIL WELL MIXED. MIX DRY INGREDIENTS AND BLEND WITH BANANA MIXTURE, BUT DO NOT OVERMIX. POUR INTO TWO LIGHTLY GREASED LOAF PANS OR A 10-INCH (25 CM) BUNDT PAN. BAKE FOR 55 TO 60 MINUTES; TEST FOR DONENESS (TOOTHPICK INSERTED IN MIDDLE COMES OUT CLEAN) AND COOL ON RACK FOR 10 MINUTES BEFORE REMOVING FROM PANS. FREEZES BEAUTIFULLY. MAKES 2 LOAVES.

TIP: FREEZE OVERRIPE BANANAS IN THEIR SKINS IN A PLASTIC BAG.

THERE ARE THREE TYPES OF PEOPLE: THOSE THAT MAKE IT HAPPEN, THOSE THAT WATCH IT HAPPEN AND THOSE WHO SIT AROUND AND SAY "WHAT THE HECK'S HAPPENING?"

BLUEBERRY BANANA BREAD

1 1/2 CUPS	ALL-PURPOSE FLOUR	375 ML
2/3 CUP	GRANULATED SUGAR	150 ML
1/2 TSP	SALT	2 ML
2 TSP	BAKING POWDER	10 ML
3/4 CUP	ROLLED OATS	175 ML
1/3 CUP	VEGETABLE OIL	75 ML
2	EGGS, SLIGHTLY BEATEN	2
1 CUP	MASHED BANANAS	250 ML
2 TBSP	LEMON JUICE	30 ML
1 TBSP	GRATED LEMON ZEST	15 ML
3/4 CUP	BLUEBERRIES (FRESH OR FROZEN)	175 ML

PREHEAT OVEN TO 350°F (180°C). GREASE A 10-INCH
(25 CM) BUNDT PAN. SIFT FLOUR, SUGAR, SALT AND BAKING
POWDER TOGETHER. ADD OATS, OIL, EGGS, BANANAS,
LEMON JUICE AND ZEST. DO NOT OVERMIX. GENTLY FOLD
IN BLUEBERRIES. POUR INTO PAN AND BAKE FOR 1 HOUR
AT 350°F (180°C). COOL IN PAN AND TURN OUT ONTO WIRE
RACK WHEN COMPLETELY COOL. CHILL. MUCH TASTIER IF
LEFT A FEW HOURS BEFORE CUTTING. MAKES 1 LOAF.

THREE RULES FOR HEALTHY TEETH:
BRUSH AFTER EVERY MEAL, SEE YOUR DENTIST OFTEN
AND MIND YOUR OWN BUSINESS!

PINEAPPLE LOAF

MOIST AND MARVELOUS!

1/4 CUP	BUTTER	60 ML
3/4 CUP	BROWN SUGAR	175 ML
1	EGG	1
1/3 CUP	ORANGE JUICE CONCENTRATE	75 ML
1 TBSP	GRATED ORANGE ZEST	15 ML
2 CUPS	ALL-PURPOSE FLOUR	500 ML
1 TSP	BAKING SODA	5 ML
1/2 TSP	SALT	2 ML
1 CUP	CRUSHED PINEAPPLE WITH JUICE	250 ML
1/2 CUP	CHOPPED PECANS	125 ML

CREAM BUTTER, SUGAR AND EGG. ADD ORANGE JUICE AND ZEST AND MIX WELL. SIFT FLOUR, BAKING SODA AND SALT. ADD TO CREAMED MIXTURE AND THEN STIR IN PINEAPPLE AND PECANS. POUR INTO A GREASED 9- BY 5-INCH (23 BY 13 CM) LOAF PAN. LET STAND WHILE OVEN HEATS TO 350°F (180°C). BAKE FOR 45 MINUTES. MAKES 1 LOAF.

SOME PEOPLE ARE NO GOOD AT COUNTING CALORIES, AND THEY HAVE THE FIGURES TO PROVE IT.

STRAWBERRY BREAD

3 CUPS	ALL-PURPOSE FLOUR	750 ML
I TSP	BAKING SODA	5 ML
I TSP	SALT	5 ML
3 TSP	GROUND CINNAMON	15 ML
2 CUPS	GRANULATED SUGAR	500 ML
I	PACKAGE (15 OZ/424 ML) FROZEN STRAWBERRIES (THAWED)	I
4	EGGS, WELL BEATEN	4
1¼ CUPS	VEGETABLE OIL	300 ML
1¼ CUPS	CHOPPED PECANS	300 ML

PREHEAT OVEN TO 350°F (180°C). MIX DRY INGREDIENTS TOGETHER IN A LARGE BOWL. MAKE A WELL IN CENTER AND ADD STRAWBERRIES AND EGGS. ADD OIL AND PECANS. MIX THOROUGHLY. POUR BATTER INTO TWO GREASED AND FLOURED 8- BY 4-INCH (20 BY 10 CM) LOAF PANS. BAKE AT 350°F (180°C) FOR I HOUR OR UNTIL TOOTHPICK COMES OUT CLEAN WHEN TESTED. MAKES 2 LOAVES.

HAPPINESS IS WHEN YOU SEE YOUR HUSBAND'S OLD GIRLFRIEND AND SHE'S FATTER THAN YOU.

PART II
LUNCH AND DINNER BUFFETS

DIPS AND SPREADS

RAILROAD DIP. 44

SPRINGTIME SPINACH
    DIP. 44

HOT ARTICHOKE DIP. 45

LAYERED CRAB DIP 45

SMOKED OYSTER
SPREAD 46

EASY SALMON PÂTÉ 47

JALAPEÑO PEPPER JELLY
    WITH LUMPS 48

COCKTAIL SPREAD 49

PEPPER RELISH. 50

BREADS

OATMEAL BREAD 51

MAPLE SYRUP GRAHAM
    BREAD. 52

QUICK MOLASSES BROWN
    BREAD. 53

STEAMED BROWN BREAD
    FOR BEANS 54

COUNTRY CORNBREAD. 55

NAAN 56

PITA TOASTS 57

SOUR CREAM GINGER
    BUNS 58

BUTTERMILK BISCUITS. 59

WELSH CAKES. 60

TEA SCONES. 61

APPETIZERS

DRESSED-UP FRENCH
    BREAD. 62

HOW CHEESY DO YOU
    WANT IT!. 63

RAREBIT IN A HOLE. 64

NUTS AND BOLTS. 65

DILLED COCKTAIL
    CRACKERS 66

COCKTAIL CRISPS. 67

CHRISTMAS CHEESE BALLS. . 68

BRANDY-NUT BRIE 69

STUFFED CAMEMBERT
    APPETIZER 70

CHIPPY KNEES BITES 71

SPINACH-STUFFED
    MUSHROOM CAPS 71

HOT MUSHROOM
    TURNOVERS 72

SPANAKOPITA 73

BOMB SHELTER
    CROUSTADES. 74

GUACAMOLE CHERRY
    TOMATO HALVES 75

SMOKED SALMON
    SUPERB. 76

CADILLAC OYSTERS 77

CHEF TONER'S MUSSELS
    CREOLE. 78

CRAB-STUFFED ARTICHOKE
    HEARTS 79

SNOW PEAS WITH CRAB. . . .80

CRAB TARTLETS. 81

SEAFOOD IN WINE. 82

ASPARAGUS CHICKEN
PUFFS. 83

TANGY CHICKEN TIDBITS . .84

"TALK ABOUT EASY"
CHICKEN WINGS. 85

SORTAS. 86

HOT 'N' SPICY WINGS. 87

HAM AND CHEESE PUFFS. . .88

JELLY BALLS 89

SUPER NACHOS. 90

AUNTY LIL'S SIMPLE
ANTIPASTO 91

MEXICANA ANTIPASTO 92

SALADS AND DRESSINGS

KILLER COLESLAW. 93

ARTICHOKE AND ZUCCHINI
SALAD. 94

HOT MUSHROOM SALAD. . . .95

MARINATED ARTICHOKE AND
MUSHROOM SALAD 96

RUSSIAN BEET SALAD. 97

ROMAINE WITH ORANGES
AND PECANS 98

A DIFFERENT SPINACH
SALAD. 99

SPINACH SALAD WITH SOUR
CREAM DRESSING 100

ZUCCHINI SALAD 101

GREEK SALAD 102

ORIENTAL GARDEN TOSS. . 103

COMMITTEE SALAD. 104

PEACHTREE PLAZA SALAD. . 105

ASPARAGUS PASTA SALAD. .106

PASTA VEGETABLE SALAD. . 107

SALMON PASTA SALAD . . . 108

PAPAYA WITH SHRIMP AND
CURRY MAYONNAISE . . . 109

CHICKEN ATLANTA. 110

KOREAN CHICKEN SALAD . . .112

LAYERED CHICKEN SALAD. . .114

FRUIT AND LIME CHICKEN
SALAD. 115

ARIZONA FRUIT SALAD 116

FRESH FRUIT DRESSING. . . .117

MARINATED FRUIT SALAD. . .118

DOCTORED MAYO
DRESSING. 119

THOUSAND ISLAND
DRESSING. 120

PESTO DRESSING. 120

CHART HOUSE BLUE
CHEESE DRESSING 121

SOUPS

GINGERED MELON
SOUP 122

AVOCADO SOUP 123

BROCCOLI SOUP 124

CAULIFLOWER SOUP
WITH BLUE CHEESE. . . . 125

MUSHROOM SOUP 126

MUSHROOM AND LEEK
SOUP 127

FRENCH ONION SOUP
AU GRATIN 128

CREAM OF PARSLEY AND
   BASIL SOUP 129
POTATO SOUP 130
CREAM OF SPINACH SOUP. . .131
FRESH TOMATO BISQUE . . .132
CREAM OF CURRY SOUP. . . .133
EGG DROP SOUP. 133
AVGOLEMONO 134
FISHERMAN'S CHOWDER . . .135
HERB'S SOUP WITH
   SHRIMP. 136
MULLIGATAWNY SOUP 137

FISH AND SEAFOOD

WINE-POACHED HALIBUT. . . 138
O-SOLE-O-MIO 139
TERIYAKI BARBECUED
   SALMON STEAKS 139
POTLATCH SALMON 140
CREAMY DILLED SNAPPER . .141
BAKED FISH MOZZARELLA . .142
MARINATED FISH FILLETS
   WITH BASIL BUTTER 143
LUNCHEON SOUFFLÉ ROLL . .144
MUSSELS AND SCALLOPS
   IN CREAM. 146
SEAFOOD KABOBS. 147
"THE LADIES" SEAFOOD
   CASSEROLE 148

CHICKEN, DUCK AND PHEASANT

CLASSY CHICKEN 149
SAM'S BRANDIED CHICKEN. . 150
CHICKEN PARMESAN. 152
CHICKEN MANDALAY. 153
YUMMY CHICKEN 154
CRISPY SESAME CHICKEN . .155
SWEET AND SPICY
   CASHEW CHICKEN. 156
CHICKEN ARTICHOKE
   CASSEROLE 158
CHICKEN CACCIATORE 159
CHICKEN TETRAZZINI. 160
CHICKEN POT PIE 161
WHIP-LASH CHICKEN. 162
CHICKEN MEXICANA 163
CHICKEN ENCHILADAS 164
CHICKEN ENCHILADA
   CASSEROLE 165
ALMOND ORANGE PHEASANT
   (OR CORNISH HENS) . . . 166
DUCK BREASTS EN
   CASSEROLE 168

BEEF AND VEAL

BEEF EXTRAORDINAIRE
   WITH SAUCE DIANE 169
UNATTENDED ROAST
   BEEF 170
SUPER TENDER FLANK
   STEAK 171
GINGER-FRIED BEEF. 172
SIMPLY SAUERBRATEN 173
BEEF-ON-A-STICK 174
STEAK AND MUSHROOM
   KABOBS 175
SHORTCUT STROGANOFF . .176
FAMILY FAVORITE
   MEATLOAF 177

MAD ABOUT CABBAGE
    ROLLS. 178
CABBAGE ROLL
    CASSEROLE 179
TACO PIE. 180
BURRITOS 181
LIVER STIR-FRY. 182
VEAL SCALOPPINI AND
    MUSHROOMS. 183

PORK AND LAMB
TOMATO CANTONESE
    PORK. 184
HAM BAKED IN BEER. 185
HOLY HAM LOAF WITH
    MARVELOUS MUSTARD
    SAUCE. 186
CASHEW PORK
    TENDERLOIN 187
BARBECUED PORK ROAST. . 188
GREEK RIBS. 189
NOODLE MAKER'S
    CHOP SUEY 190
SPUNKY ORANGE RIBS 191
PORK DUMPLINGS. 192
MARINATED BARBECUED
    LAMB. 194
LEG OF LAMB WITH RED
    CURRANT SAUCE 195
MOUSSAKA 196

PASTA
GOURMET MACARONI AND
    CHEESE 198
FETTUCCINE VERDE 199
SPICY PENNE 200

ASPARAGUS NOODLE BAKE . . 201
PASTA PRIMAVERA 202
PASTA POT 204
PASTA WITH CRAB AND
    BASIL 205
LINGUINE WITH WHITE
    CLAM SAUCE 206
LINGUINE WITH RED CLAM
    SAUCE. 207
SPAGHETTI CARBONARA. . .208
ITALIAN SAUSAGE AND
    PASTA 209
MANICOTTI 210
BROCCOLI LASAGNA AU
    GRATIN. 211
SPINACH LASAGNA. 212
"DEATH TO DIETERS"
    CHICKEN LASAGNA 213
HAM AND MUSHROOM
    LASAGNA 214

SIDE DISHES
BAKED BANANAS IN ORANGE
    AND LEMON JUICE 216
VIVA! VEGGIES. 217
BAKED ASPARAGUS. 218
TISDALE ANNIE'S
    ASPARAGUS PUFF 219
BAKED BEANS 220
SPEEDY BAKED BEANS 221
CALICO BEAN POT. 222
SICILIAN BROCCOLI 223
TOLERABLE BRUSSELS
    SPROUTS. 224
FRIED CABBAGE 225

NIFTY CARROTS 226

CARROTS L'ORANGE 227

CURRIED CAULIFLOWER. . . . 228

CHILES RELLENOS 229

SUDDEN VALLEY GREEN
    BEANS 230

MANDARIN GREEN BEANS . . 231

BOOZY ONIONS 231

CHEESE MARINATED
    ONIONS 232

ONIONS STUFFED WITH
    BROCCOLI 233

PERFECT PARSNIPS 234

COLD DILLED PEAS 235

ÉPINARDS, EH!. 236

SPINACH OR BROCCOLI
    TIMBALES. 237

DILL AND PARMESAN
    TOMATOES 238

TOMATO AND ARTICHOKE
    CASSEROLE 239

TOMATO CHEESE BAKE . . . 240

TOMATOES FLORENTINE . . 241

CHEESE-FRIED ZUCCHINI . . 242

ITALIAN ZUCCHINI 243

SPAGHETTI SQUASH
    PRIMAVERA. 244

CHEESY ACORN SQUASH . . 246

YAMMY APPLES. 247

SWEET POTATOES IN
    ORANGE SAUCE 248

FLUFFY BAKED POTATOES. . 249

BUTTER-BAKED TATERS. . . 250

POTATO SKINS 251

POTATOES RÖSTI. 252

MEXICAN RICE 253

RICE WITH MUSHROOMS
    AND PINE NUTS 254

WILD RICE AND ARTICHOKE
    HEARTS 255

WILD BUFFET RICE! 256

OVEN-BAKED WILD RICE . . 257

WILD RICE CASSEROLE 258

CRANBERRY STUFFING. . . . 259

TERRIFIC TURKEY
    STUFFING 260

SAUCES, CONDIMENTS AND SEASONINGS

GOURMET CRANBERRY
    SAUCE. 261

PLUM SAUCE 261

CUMBERLAND SAUCE 262

SALSA 262

PESTO SAUCE. 263

ALFREDO SAUCE 264

PEANUT SAUCE. 265

MONK'S MUSTARD 266

TARRAGON MUSTARD. 267

PICCALILLI. 268

CORN RELISH 269

ZUCCHINI RELISH 270

GREEN TOMATO
    MARMALADE. 271

MISS SCARLETT'S WINE
    CORDIAL 272

SEASONED FLOUR 273

SALT SUBSTITUTE. 274

RAILROAD DIP

WE WERE RAILROADED INTO THIS ONE AND GUESS WHAT? IT'S GREAT!

4 CUPS	SHREDDED CHEDDAR CHEESE	1 L
1½	MEDIUM ONIONS, CHOPPED	1½
2 CUPS	MAYONNAISE	500 ML
	SODA CRACKERS (SALTED)	

MIX CHEESE, ONIONS AND MAYONNAISE AND BAKE IN A 12-CUP (3 L) GLASS DISH AT 350°F (180°C) UNTIL HOT AND BUBBLING AND PUFFED UP. SERVE WITH SALTED CRACKERS AS IT BLENDS WITH CHEESE FOR *THE* TASTE. MAKES ABOUT 6 CUPS (1.5 L).

SPRINGTIME SPINACH DIP

2 CUPS	MAYONNAISE	500 ML
1	PACKAGE (10 OZ/300 G) FROZEN CHOPPED SPINACH, COOKED AND DRAINED	1
½ CUP	CHOPPED GREEN ONION	125 ML
½ CUP	CHOPPED FRESH PARSLEY	125 ML
1 TSP	SALT	5 ML
½ TSP	BLACK PEPPER	2 ML

COMBINE INGREDIENTS AND MIX WELL. CHILL SEVERAL HOURS OR OVERNIGHT. SERVE AS A SPREAD ON CRACKERS OR WITH ASSORTED VEGETABLES AS A DIP. MAKES 3 CUPS (750 ML).

HOT ARTICHOKE DIP

SERVE WITH CRACKERS.

1	CAN (14 OZ/398 ML) ARTICHOKE HEARTS, DRAINED AND CHOPPED	398 ML
1/2 CUP	FRESHLY GRATED PARMESAN CHEESE	125 ML
1 CUP	MAYONNAISE	250 ML
1	CLOVE GARLIC, MINCED	1
DASH	LEMON JUICE	DASH

MIX ALL INGREDIENTS. BAKE AT 350°F (180°C) FOR 10 MINUTES. IF YOU LOVE IT, SERVES 1! OTHERWISE, SERVES 6.

LAYERED CRAB DIP

LAST-MINUTE COMPANY? NO PROBLEM! SERVE THIS DIP WITH ASSORTED CRACKERS.

8 OZ	CREAM CHEESE, SOFTENED	250 G
1 TBSP	GRATED ONION	15 ML
1 TBSP	WORCESTERSHIRE SAUCE	15 ML
1 1/2 TSP	LEMON JUICE	7 ML
1/2 CUP	CHILI OR COCKTAIL SAUCE	125 ML
1	CAN (6 1/2 OZ/185 G) CRABMEAT	1
2 TBSP	CHOPPED FRESH PARSLEY	30 ML

MIX CHEESE, ONION, WORCESTERSHIRE SAUCE AND LEMON JUICE TOGETHER. SPREAD IN A SHALLOW SERVING DISH. SPREAD CHILI SAUCE OVER TOP. DRAIN AND RINSE CRAB AND SPREAD OVER CHILI SAUCE. SPRINKLE WITH PARSLEY. MAKES ABOUT 2 CUPS (500 ML).

SMOKED OYSTER SPREAD

SERVE WITH ASSORTED CRACKERS.

I	PACKAGE (8 OZ/250 G) CREAM CHEESE, SOFTENED	I
¼ CUP	WHIPPING (35%) CREAM, WHIPPED	60 ML
I TBSP	CHOPPED ONION	15 ML
I TBSP	CHOPPED FRESH PARSLEY	15 ML
I	CAN (4 OZ/105 G) SMOKED OYSTERS, DRAINED AND CHOPPED	I
I TSP	BRANDY	5 ML
¼ TSP	WORCESTERSHIRE SAUCE	I ML
DASH	HOT PEPPER SAUCE	DASH

MIX CREAM CHEESE WITH WHIPPING CREAM UNTIL SMOOTH. ADD THE ONION AND PARSLEY. MIX WELL. FOLD IN THE OYSTERS AND BRANDY. ADD WORCESTERSHIRE SAUCE AND HOT PEPPER SAUCE. MAKES I CUP (250 ML).

LADY TO A HANDSOME MAN:
"YOU LOOK LIKE MY THIRD HUSBAND."
HIM: "HOW MANY HAVE YOU HAD?"
HER: "JUST TWO."

EASY SALMON PÂTÉ

SERVE WITH MELBA TOAST OR ASSORTED CRACKERS.

1	CAN (7 1/2 OZ/213 G) RED SALMON, DRAINED	1
1 TBSP	MINCED ONION	15 ML
1 TBSP	FRESHLY SQUEEZED LEMON JUICE	15 ML
1/4 TSP	GRATED LEMON ZEST	1 ML
2 TBSP	MAYONNAISE	30 ML
1/2 CUP	BUTTER OR MARGARINE, MELTED	125 ML
2 TSP	CHOPPED FRESH DILL (OR 1/4 TSP/1 ML DRIED DILLWEED)	10 ML
	SALT AND BLACK PEPPER TO TASTE	

BLEND ALL INGREDIENTS TO SMOOTH CONSISTENCY. POUR INTO A CROCK OR SERVING BOWL. COVER AND CHILL SEVERAL HOURS OR OVERNIGHT. GARNISH WITH DILL. FREEZES WELL. MAKES 1 1/2 CUPS (375 ML).

YOU MUST REMEMBER THIS, A KISS IS STILL A KISS,
A HAT IS STILL A HAT...

JALAPEÑO PEPPER JELLY
WITH LUMPS

*THIS IS ONE OF OUR CHRISTMAS EXCHANGE
FAVORITES — MEN LOVE IT! SERVE ON CRACKERS
(KAVLI FLATBREAD IS BEST) WITH SOFT CREAM CHEESE.*

3	GREEN BELL PEPPERS, SEEDED AND FINELY CHOPPED	3
6	JALAPEÑO PEPPERS, WITH SEEDS, FINELY CHOPPED (OR TWO 4-OZ/ 114 ML CANS)	6
1 1/2 CUPS	WHITE VINEGAR	375 ML
6 1/2 CUPS	GRANULATED SUGAR	1.63 L
1/2 TO 1 TSP	CAYENNE PEPPER	2 TO 5 ML
2	POUCHES (EACH 3 OZ/85 ML) LIQUID PECTIN	2
4 TO 6 DROPS	GREEN FOOD COLORING	4 TO 6 DROPS

CHOP ALL PEPPERS AND COMBINE THEM WITH VINEGAR,
SUGAR AND CAYENNE PEPPER IN A LARGE POT, COOKING
OVER MEDIUM-HIGH HEAT. STIR FREQUENTLY UNTIL
MIXTURE BEGINS TO BOIL. BOIL FOR 10 MINUTES, STIRRING
CONSTANTLY. ADD PECTIN AND BOIL FOR 1 MINUTE
LONGER, WITHOUT STIRRING. REMOVE FROM HEAT AND
SKIM OFF FOAM. LADLE INTO HOT, STERILIZED JARS,
LEAVING 1/2 INCH (1 CM) HEADSPACE. WIPE RIMS AND SEAL
WITH TWO-PIECE CANNING LIDS. PROCESS IN A BOILING
WATER CANNER FOR 10 MINUTES. CHECK SEALS AND
REFRIGERATE ANY JARS THAT ARE NOT SEALED. MAKES
ABOUT 7 SMALL JARS.

CONTINUED ON NEXT PAGE...

> TIP: IF JELLY DOES NOT SET, RETURN TO POT, BRING TO A BOIL, ADD I POUCH (3 OZ/85 ML) LIQUID PECTIN AND BOIL FOR I MINUTE. THEN PROCESS AGAIN.

ALWAYS WASH YOUR HANDS BEFORE MEALS; THAT WAY, YOU CAN GET A BETTER GRIP ON YOUR FOOD.

— COCKTAIL SPREAD —

GUESTS WILL ASK FOR A SPOON. JIMMY DID! SERVE WITH CRACKERS.

I	PACKAGE (8 OZ/250 G) CREAM CHEESE, SOFTENED	I
1/2 CUP	SOUR CREAM	125 ML
1/4 CUP	MAYONNAISE	60 ML
3	CANS (EACH 4 OZ/114 G) BROKEN SHRIMP, RINSED AND DRAINED (OR 1 1/2 CUPS/375 ML FRESH BABY SHRIMP)	3
I CUP	SEAFOOD COCKTAIL SAUCE	250 ML
2 CUPS	SHREDDED MOZZARELLA CHEESE	500 ML
3	GREEN ONIONS, CHOPPED	3
I	TOMATO, DICED	I
I	GREEN BELL PEPPER, CHOPPED	I

COMBINE CHEESE, SOUR CREAM AND MAYONNAISE. SPREAD IN A 12-INCH (30 CM) DISH OR PIE PLATE. SCATTER SHRIMP OVER CHEESE. LAYER SEAFOOD SAUCE, THEN MOZZARELLA, GREEN ONIONS, TOMATO AND GREEN PEPPER. COVER UNTIL READY TO SERVE. SERVES 12.

PEPPER RELISH

THIS IS A MILD VERSION OF JALAPEÑO PEPPER JELLY. IT TAKES ON THE COLOR OF THE RED PEPPERS AND MAKES AN ATTRACTIVE CHRISTMAS GIFT. SERVE SPREAD ON CREAM CHEESE AND CRACKERS.

6	GREEN BELL PEPPERS	6
6	RED BELL PEPPERS	6
1½ CUPS	VINEGAR	375 ML
5 CUPS	GRANULATED SUGAR	1.25 L
2	POUCHES (EACH 3 OZ/85 ML) LIQUID PECTIN	2

PUT PEPPERS THROUGH GRINDER OR FOOD CHOPPER. DRAIN WELL. PUT CHOPPED PEPPERS IN DUTCH OVEN AND ADD VINEGAR AND SUGAR. MIX WELL. BRING TO ROLLING BOIL AND BOIL HARD FOR 1 MINUTE, STIRRING CONSTANTLY. REMOVE FROM HEAT AND ADD PECTIN. BOIL FOR 5 TO 10 MINUTES. LADLE INTO HOT, STERILIZED JARS, LEAVING ½ INCH (1 CM) HEADSPACE. WIPE RIMS AND SEAL WITH TWO-PIECE CANNING LIDS. PROCESS IN A BOILING WATER CANNER FOR 10 MINUTES. CHECK SEALS AND REFRIGERATE ANY JARS THAT ARE NOT SEALED. MAKES 5 MEDIUM JARS.

ONE FOR THE MONEY, TWO FOR THE SHOW, THREE TO GET READY, FOUR TO GO AND TEN WHEN YOU GET BACK FOR THE BABYSITTER.

OATMEAL BREAD

VERY LIGHT. EXCELLENT TOASTED AND GREAT WITH CHEESE.

1	PACKAGE (1 TBSP/15 G) DRY YEAST	1
1/2 CUP	WARM WATER	125 ML
1 TSP	GRANULATED SUGAR	5 ML
2 CUPS	BOILING WATER	500 ML
1 CUP	OATMEAL	250 ML
1/2 CUP	LIGHT (FANCY) MOLASSES	125 ML
2 TSP	SALT	10 ML
1 TBSP	SHORTENING	15 ML
4 TO 5 CUPS	ALL-PURPOSE FLOUR	1 TO 1.25 L

DISSOLVE YEAST IN WARM WATER. STIR IN SUGAR. LET STAND FOR 10 MINUTES. POUR BOILING WATER OVER OATMEAL AND ADD MOLASSES, SALT AND SHORTENING. LET STAND UNTIL LUKEWARM, THEN ADD YEAST MIXTURE AND BEAT WELL. ADD ENOUGH FLOUR TO MAKE A STIFF MIXTURE WITHOUT BEING TOO STICKY. FORM INTO A LARGE, SOFT BALL, COVER AND LET RISE UNTIL TWICE THE ORIGINAL SIZE. MAKE SURE IT IS PLACED IN A DRY, WARM PLACE.

PUNCH DOWN DOUGH AND DIVIDE INTO TWO GREASED 9- BY 5-INCH (23 BY 13 CM) BREAD PANS. LET RISE AGAIN, COVERED, UNTIL IT DOUBLES ITS SIZE. BAKE AT 350°F (180°C) FOR 40 MINUTES. TEST BREAD AFTER BAKING BY TAPPING THE TOP. IT SHOULD BE BROWN AND SOUND HOLLOW WHEN COOKED. MAKES 2 LOAVES.

MAPLE SYRUP GRAHAM BREAD

YUMMEE! TRY IT TOASTED.

2	EGGS	2
1 1/2 CUPS	BUTTERMILK	375 ML
1/2 CUP	SOUR CREAM	125 ML
1 1/3 CUPS	MAPLE SYRUP	325 ML
1 CUP	ALL-PURPOSE FLOUR	250 ML
2 CUPS	GRAHAM FLOUR	500 ML
2 TSP	BAKING POWDER	10 ML
2 TSP	BAKING SODA	10 ML
1 TSP	SALT	5 ML

COMBINE EGGS, BUTTERMILK, SOUR CREAM AND SYRUP, BEATING UNTIL WELL MIXED. COMBINE DRY INGREDIENTS. GRADUALLY ADD TO EGG MIXTURE, MIXING WELL. POUR INTO TWO 9- BY 5-INCH (23 BY 13 CM) BUTTERED LOAF PANS. BAKE AT 325°F (160°C) FOR 45 MINUTES. MAKES 2 LOAVES.

A HOT LUNCH: A PEANUT BUTTER SANDWICH, STOLEN FROM ANOTHER KID'S LOCKER.

QUICK MOLASSES BROWN BREAD

THIS IS VERY MOIST AND EASY TO MAKE. SERVE WITH SPEEDY BAKED BEANS (PAGE 221). YOU'LL HAVE A HEARTY MEAL IN NO TIME AT ALL. TOOT! TOOT!

I CUP	ALL-PURPOSE FLOUR	250 ML
I¼ TSP	BAKING SODA	6 ML
¾ TSP	SALT	3 ML
¾ CUP	FINE DRY BREAD CRUMBS	175 ML
3 TBSP	SOFT BUTTER	45 ML
I	EGG	I
I CUP	BUTTERMILK	250 ML
½ CUP	LIGHT (FANCY) MOLASSES	125 ML
½ CUP	RAISINS	125 ML

SIFT FLOUR, SODA AND SALT TOGETHER. ADD BREAD CRUMBS AND MIX WELL. CUT IN BUTTER. BEAT EGG AND COMBINE WITH BUTTERMILK, MOLASSES AND RAISINS. ADD TO DRY MIXTURE. STIR JUST UNTIL BLENDED. POUR INTO A WELL-GREASED ANGEL FOOD PAN. BAKE AT 400°F (200°C) FOR ABOUT 30 TO 35 MINUTES. TEST WITH TOOTHPICK. MAKES I LOAF.

STEAMED BROWN BREAD FOR BEANS

SERVE WITH BAKED BEANS (PAGE 220).

I CUP	ALL-PURPOSE FLOUR	250 ML
I TSP	BAKING POWDER	5 ML
I TSP	BAKING SODA	5 ML
I TSP	SALT	5 ML
I CUP	CORNMEAL	250 ML
I CUP	WHOLE WHEAT FLOUR	250 ML
2 CUPS	BUTTERMILK	500 ML
2 TBSP	VEGETABLE OIL	30 ML
I CUP	RAISINS	250 ML
3/4 CUP	LIGHT (FANCY) MOLASSES	175 ML

SIFT FLOUR, BAKING POWDER, BAKING SODA AND SALT. STIR IN CORNMEAL AND WHOLE WHEAT FLOUR. ADD BUTTERMILK, OIL, RAISINS AND MOLASSES. BEAT WELL. GREASE AND FLOUR TWO I-LB (500 G) COFFEE CANS. DIVIDE BATTER INTO CANS AND COVER TIGHTLY WITH FOIL. PLACE IN CANNER OR DUTCH OVEN WITH I INCH (2.5 CM) OF BOILING WATER. COVER POT AND BAKE AT 350°F (180°C) FOR 2 HOURS. ADD WATER IF NEEDED. TEST FOR DONENESS WITH A TOOTHPICK. MAKES 2 LOAVES.

LAUGH AND THE WORLD LAUGHS WITH YOU.
SNORE AND YOU SLEEP ALONE.

COUNTRY CORNBREAD

1 CUP	YELLOW CORNMEAL	250 ML
1/2 CUP	ALL-PURPOSE FLOUR	125 ML
1 TSP	SALT	5 ML
1/2 TSP	BAKING SODA	2 ML
1 TBSP	BAKING POWDER	15 ML
1 CUP	BUTTERMILK	250 ML
1/2 CUP	MILK	125 ML
1	EGG, BEATEN	1
1/2 CUP	COOKING OIL	125 ML

PREHEAT OVEN TO 450°F (230°C). GREASE AN 8-INCH (20 CM) SQUARE PAN OR MUFFIN TIN AND PLACE IN OVEN TO HEAT UNTIL PIPING HOT (ABOUT 3 MINUTES). COMBINE CORNMEAL, FLOUR, SALT, BAKING SODA AND BAKING POWDER. MIX THOROUGHLY. ADD BUTTERMILK, MILK, EGG AND OIL AND STIR WELL. POUR CORNBREAD BATTER INTO HOT PAN OR MUFFIN TIN (FILL TO TOP) AND BAKE FOR ABOUT 20 MINUTES OR UNTIL GOLDEN BROWN. MAKES 1 LOAF OR 12 LARGE MUFFINS.

MY HUSBAND AND I HAVE A MAGICAL RELATIONSHIP. WHENEVER I ASK HIM TO DO SOMETHING, HE DISAPPEARS.

NAAN

*A BREAD BASKET FAVORITE. THIS DOUGH
LENDS ITSELF WELL TO PIZZA.*

3½ TO 4 CUPS	ALL-PURPOSE FLOUR	875 ML TO 1 L
1 TSP	BAKING POWDER	5 ML
1 TSP	GRANULATED SUGAR	5 ML
1½ TSP	SALT	7 ML
1	EGG	1
1 TBSP	PLAIN YOGURT	15 ML
1½ CUPS	WATER	375 ML

MIX DRY INGREDIENTS. MAKE A WELL IN THE CENTRE
AND ADD EGG, YOGURT AND WATER GRADUALLY. MIX UNTIL
A FIRM DOUGH COMES AWAY FROM THE SIDES. KNEAD
DOUGH ON A FLOURED BOARD UNTIL IT'S SOMEWHAT
ELASTIC. PINCH OFF PIECES A LITTLE BIGGER THAN A GOLF
BALL. PLACE IN A BUTTERED PAN, COVER WITH A DAMP
CLOTH AND LET SIT FOR 1 HOUR. (MAY BE REFRIGERATED
FOR SEVERAL DAYS AT THIS POINT.)

TO COOK: PAT AND PULL "DOUGH BALLS" INTO THIN, 4-INCH
(10 CM) DIAMETER CIRCLES. PLACE ON A BAKING SHEET
AND BAKE AT 450°F (230°C) FOR 10 MINUTES UNTIL PUFFY
AND SLIGHTLY BROWN. BUTTER AND SERVE. MAKES 25 TO
30 PIECES.

PITA TOASTS

SERVE WITH YOUR FAVORITE DIPS OR IN
PLACE OF GARLIC TOAST OR ROLLS.

3/4 CUP	BUTTER	175 ML
2 TBSP	FINELY CHOPPED FRESH PARSLEY	30 ML
I TBSP	CHOPPED FRESH CHIVES	15 ML
I TBSP	LEMON JUICE	15 ML
I	LARGE CLOVE GARLIC, MINCED	I
6	PITA ROUNDS	6

PREHEAT OVEN TO 450°F (230°C). CREAM TOGETHER FIRST
FIVE INGREDIENTS, COVER; SET ASIDE FOR AT LEAST
I HOUR. CUT PITA ROUNDS INTO 4 WEDGES AND SEPARATE
LAYERS. SPREAD EACH PIECE WITH SOME OF THE BUTTER
MIXTURE. ARRANGE ON A LARGE BAKING SHEET IN ONE
LAYER. BAKE FOR 5 MINUTES, UNTIL LIGHTLY BROWNED
AND CRISP. MAKES 48 TOASTS.

THE THREE-DAY WEEKEND WAS CREATED BECAUSE IT'S
IMPOSSIBLE TO CRAM ALL THE BAD WEATHER INTO TWO DAYS.

SOUR CREAM GINGER BUNS

JOANNE GOOD, FORMER FOOD EDITOR OF THE CALGARY HERALD, INVENTED THESE — AND WE'RE GLAD SHE DID!

2 CUPS	SIFTED FLOUR	500 ML
2 1/2 TSP	BAKING POWDER	12 ML
1/4 TSP	BAKING SODA	1 ML
3/4 TSP	SALT	3 ML
2 TBSP	GRANULATED SUGAR	30 ML
1/3 CUP	COLD SHORTENING	75 ML
1/2 CUP	FINELY CHOPPED CRYSTALLIZED GINGER	125 ML
2/3 CUP	SOUR CREAM	150 ML
1	EGG, SLIGHTLY BEATEN	1
3 TBSP	BUTTER, MELTED	45 ML

SIFT FIRST FIVE INGREDIENTS TOGETHER. CUT IN SHORTENING UNTIL MIXTURE RESEMBLES COARSE MEAL. ADD GINGER AND MIX. MAKE A WELL IN THE CENTRE AND POUR IN SOUR CREAM AND EGG AND STIR BRISKLY WITH A FORK JUST UNTIL DOUGH HOLDS TOGETHER. KNEAD GENTLY 7 OR 8 TIMES ON LIGHTLY FLOURED SURFACE. ROLL OR PAT TO 1/2-INCH TO 3/4-INCH (1 TO 2 CM) THICKNESS. CUT WITH 2-INCH (5 CM) DIAMETER COOKIE CUTTER. ARRANGE ON UNGREASED COOKIE SHEET. BRUSH WITH MELTED BUTTER. BAKE IN PREHEATED 425°F (220°C) OVEN FOR 12 TO 15 MINUTES OR UNTIL LIGHTLY BROWNED. MAKES 18 BUNS.

BUTTERMILK BISCUITS

A GREAT COMPLEMENT TO ANY MEAL.

2 CUPS	ALL-PURPOSE FLOUR	500 ML
1 TBSP	BAKING POWDER	15 ML
1/2 TSP	BAKING SODA	2 ML
1/2 TSP	SALT	2 ML
1/2 CUP	BUTTER	125 ML
1 CUP	BUTTERMILK	250 ML

MIX FLOUR, BAKING POWDER, BAKING SODA AND SALT TOGETHER. CUT IN BUTTER AND MIX TOGETHER LIGHTLY. ADD BUTTERMILK AND MIX JUST ENOUGH TO BLEND TOGETHER. DO NOT OVERMIX. ROLL OUT DOUGH TO 1/2-INCH (1 CM) THICKNESS. CUT WITH ROUND CUTTER OR GLASS TO MEASURE 2 INCHES (5 CM) DIAMETER. BAKE ON GREASED COOKIE SHEET IN 450°F (230°C) OVEN FOR 15 MINUTES. MAKES 18 BISCUITS.

*OUR LAUNDRY HAS JUST SENT BACK
SOME BUTTONS WITH NO SHIRT ON THEM!*

WELSH CAKES

1 1/2 CUPS	ALL-PURPOSE FLOUR	375 ML
1/2 TSP	SALT	2 ML
1/2 TSP	BAKING POWDER	2 ML
1/2 CUP	GRANULATED SUGAR	125 ML
1 TSP	GROUND NUTMEG	5 ML
1/2 CUP	BUTTER	125 ML
1	EGG	1
2 TBSP	ORANGE JUICE (OR LESS)	30 ML
1/2 CUP	CURRANTS	125 ML
2 TBSP	BUTTER (MORE IF NEEDED)	30 ML

SIFT DRY INGREDIENTS TOGETHER. CUT IN BUTTER UNTIL CRUMBLY. ADD EGG AND MIX. ADD ENOUGH ORANGE JUICE TO BIND DOUGH TOGETHER. ADD CURRANTS AND MIX WELL. ROLL ON A FLOURED SURFACE TO 1/2-INCH (1 CM) THICKNESS AND CUT CAKES WITH A 2-INCH (5 CM) CUTTER. MELT BUTTER IN A FRYING PAN AND COOK CAKES OVER MEDIUM HEAT UNTIL LIGHTLY BROWNED, ABOUT 3 TO 4 MINUTES EACH SIDE. MAKES ABOUT 20 LITTLE CAKES.

TO BE NATURAL IS SUCH A DIFFICULT POSE TO KEEP UP!

TEA SCONES

TRADITIONAL AT HIGH TEA. SERVE WITH
BUTTER AND STRAWBERRY JAM.

3 CUPS	ALL-PURPOSE FLOUR	750 ML
1/2 CUP	GRANULATED SUGAR	125 ML
4 TSP	BAKING POWDER	20 ML
1/2 TSP	SALT	2 ML
1/2 CUP	MARGARINE	125 ML
1 TBSP	ORANGE OR LEMON ZEST	15 ML
1/2 CUP	RAISINS OR CURRANTS	125 ML
2	EGGS	2
	MILK	

MIX FLOUR, SUGAR, BAKING POWDER AND SALT TOGETHER.
CUT IN MARGARINE TO MAKE A CRUMB-LIKE MIXTURE.
STIR IN ORANGE ZEST AND RAISINS. BEAT EGGS IN A
1-CUP (250 ML) MEASURING CUP. FILL UP TO 1-CUP (250 ML)
MEASURE WITH MILK. STIR LIGHTLY INTO DRY MIXTURE, TO
FORM A SOFT DOUGH. ROLL OUT DOUGH TO 1/2-INCH (1 CM)
THICKNESS. CUT IN ROUNDS WITH A CUTTER. PLACE ON
LIGHTLY GREASED COOKIE SHEET. BAKE AT 450°F (230°C)
FOR 15 MINUTES. MAKES ABOUT 12 SCONES.

THERE'S NO FOOL LIKE AN OLD FOOL — YOU CAN'T
BEAT EXPERIENCE!

DRESSED-UP FRENCH BREAD

1	LOAF FRENCH BREAD, UNSLICED	1
1	CAN (14 OZ/398 ML) PITTED RIPE OLIVES, DRAINED AND CHOPPED	1
1 CUP	MARGARINE	250 ML
4	GREEN ONIONS, CHOPPED	4
1/2 TSP	GARLIC SALT	2 ML
1/2 TSP	DRIED OREGANO	2 ML
	GRATED PARMESAN CHEESE	
	PAPRIKA	

CUT LOAF IN HALF LENGTHWISE. LAY FLAT. MIX NEXT FIVE INGREDIENTS AND SPREAD ON LOAF HALVES. COVER WITH CHEESE AND SPRINKLE WITH PAPRIKA. WRAP IN FOIL AND BAKE AT 325°F (160°C) FOR 10 TO 20 MINUTES. MAKES 1 LOAF.

SOME PEOPLE HAVE LOUSY MEMORIES: THEY NEVER FORGET ANYTHING!

HOW CHEESY DO YOU WANT IT!

HOW EASY DO YOU WANT IT?

1	LOAF FROZEN BREAD DOUGH, THAWED UNTIL SLICEABLE (ABOUT 1 HOUR)	1
1/4 CUP	BUTTER	60 ML
1 TO 2 CUPS	SHREDDED CHEDDAR CHEESE (PARMESAN WORKS TOO)	250 TO 500 ML

CUT LOAF INTO 10 TO 12 PIECES. DIP BOTH SIDES IN BUTTER, THEN CHEESE. ARRANGE IN A 10-INCH (25 CM) BUNDT PAN. LET RISE FOR 2 TO 3 HOURS. BAKE FOR 20 MINUTES AT 375°F (190°C). IF MAKING THE NIGHT BEFORE, COVER BUNDT PAN WITH DAMP TEA TOWEL AND REFRIGERATE. BAKE WHEN READY. TO SERVE, PULL APART AND PUT IN A BREAD BASKET. MAKES 10 TO 12 PIECES.

WOMEN DESERVE TO HAVE MORE THAN 12 YEARS
BETWEEN THE AGES OF 28 AND 40.
— JAMES THURBER

RAREBIT IN A HOLE

A CHEESY BEER FONDUE IN
A HOLLOWED-OUT LOAF — UNREAL!

2 1/2 CUPS	SHREDDED CHEDDAR CHEESE	625 ML
1/4 CUP	SOUR CREAM	60 ML
1 TO 2	CLOVES GARLIC, CHOPPED	1 TO 2
2 TSP	WORCESTERSHIRE SAUCE	10 ML
1 TSP	DRY MUSTARD	5 ML
PINCH	CAYENNE PEPPER	PINCH
1/2 TO	BEER	125 TO
3/4 CUP		175 ML
	ROUND LOAF OF RYE, SOURDOUGH OR PUMPERNICKEL BREAD	

COMBINE ALL INGREDIENTS EXCEPT BREAD. SET ASIDE. SLICE TOP OFF LOAF (BEST DONE WHEN SLIGHTLY FROZEN). USING A SHARP KNIFE, SLICE AROUND RIM, LEAVING 1/2-INCH (1 CM) SIDES. PULL OUT BREAD AND CUT INTO 1-INCH (2.5 CM) CUBES. PUT IN PLASTIC BAG UNTIL READY TO SERVE. FILL BREAD WITH CHEESE MIXTURE, WRAP WITH FOIL AND BAKE AT 400°F (200°C) FOR 15 MINUTES OR UNTIL BUBBLY. PLACE ON A PLATTER AND SERVE WITH BREAD CUBES AROUND LOAF. SERVES 8.

ALL THIS SHAKING AND BAKING, THAWING, READY-MIXING, BOILING PLASTIC BAGS, OPENING CANS... I TELL YOU, I'M SICK AND TIRED OF COOKING!

NUTS AND BOLTS

FOR THOSE WHO ARE MECHANICALLY DECLINED.
AND JUST ABOUT ANYONE ELSE!

1 LB	BUTTER	500 G
2 TBSP	WORCESTERSHIRE SAUCE	30 ML
1 TBSP	GARLIC POWDER	15 ML
1 1/2 TSP	ONION SALT	7 ML
1 1/2 TSP	CELERY SALT	7 ML
4 CUPS	CHEERIOS	1 L
4 CUPS	LIFE CEREAL	1 L
4 CUPS	SHREDDIES OR WHEAT CHEX	1 L
2	BOXES (EACH 16 OZ/454 G) PRETZELS	2
2 CUPS	PEANUTS, SALTED (IF YOU INSIST)	500 ML
1	BOX (5 1/2 OZ/150 G) BUGLES	1
1	BOX (8 OZ/250 G) CHEESE NIPS OR CHEESE BITES	1

PREHEAT OVEN TO 250°F (120°C). PLACE BUTTER IN A VERY
LARGE ROASTER. PLACE IN OVEN TO MELT WHILE OVEN
IS PREHEATING. REMOVE ROASTER AND ADD SPICES; STIR.
ADD REMAINING INGREDIENTS, MIXING WELL TO COAT
EVENLY WITH BUTTER MIXTURE. BAKE FOR 1 1/2 HOURS.
STIR AND TURN EVERY 30 MINUTES. MAKES ABOUT
24 CUPS (6 L).

IT'S EASY TO IDENTIFY PEOPLE WHO CAN'T COUNT TO TEN.
THEY'RE IN FRONT OF YOU IN THE MARKET EXPRESS LANE.

DILLED COCKTAIL CRACKERS

*THIS ALL-TIME FAVORITE MAKES A
GREAT HOSTESS GIFT.*

1	BOX (8 OZ/250 G) MINI RITZ ORIGINAL CRACKERS OR OYSTER CRACKERS	1
1	PACKAGE (1 OZ/28 G) RANCH STYLE SALAD DRESSING MIX	1
1 TBSP	DRIED DILLWEED	15 ML
1/2 CUP	VEGETABLE OIL	125 ML
1 TSP	GARLIC POWDER	5 ML

COMBINE ALL INGREDIENTS IN A PLASTIC CONTAINER.
SEAL. SHAKE OFTEN. LET STAND OVERNIGHT OR AT LEAST
6 HOURS. MAKES ABOUT 3 CUPS (750 ML).

*BEHIND EVERY SUCCESSFUL WOMAN
IS AN ENORMOUS PILE OF LAUNDRY!*

COCKTAIL CRISPS

OUR FAVORITE COCKTAIL COOKIE — AND
IT FREEZES WELL.

1 CUP	BUTTER	250 ML
1	PACKAGE (8 OZ/250 G) IMPERIAL CHEESE (SHARP COLD-PACK CHEDDAR CHEESE)	1
PINCH	SALT	PINCH
1/4 TSP	CAYENNE PEPPER OR HOT PEPPER SAUCE	1 ML
1/4 TSP	WORCESTERSHIRE SAUCE	1 ML
1 1/2 CUPS	ALL-PURPOSE FLOUR	375 ML
4 CUPS	RICE KRISPIES	1 L

CREAM BUTTER AND CHEESE TOGETHER. ADD SEASONINGS.
BEAT IN FLOUR THEN ADD RICE KRISPIES. MIX WELL. SHAPE
INTO BALLS. PRESS DOWN WITH A FORK WHICH HAS BEEN
DIPPED IN COLD WATER. BAKE AT 350°F (180°C) FOR 15 TO
20 MINUTES, UNTIL LIGHTLY BROWNED. MAKES ABOUT
4 DOZEN.

WHEN THE GOING GETS TOUGH,
THE TOUGH GO SHOPPING!

CHRISTMAS CHEESE BALLS

A "MUST" AT OUR CHRISTMAS EXCHANGE.

2	PACKAGES (EACH 8 OZ/250 G) PHILADELPHIA CREAM CHEESE	2
2 TBSP	GRATED ONION	30 ML
I LB	INGERSOLL CHEESE	500 G
I	PACKAGE (8 OZ/250 G) IMPERIAL CHEESE	250 G
3 OZ	BLUE CHEESE	90 G
2 TSP	WORCESTERSHIRE SAUCE	IO ML
4 OZ	SHARP (OLD) CHEDDAR CHEESE, SHREDDED	125 G
I CUP	CHOPPED PECANS	250 ML
I CUP	DRIED PARSLEY	250 ML

COMBINE ALL INGREDIENTS, EXCEPT PECANS AND PARSLEY, IN DOUBLE BOILER OR LARGE PAN OVER VERY LOW HEAT. STIR UNTIL WELL BLENDED, THEN COOL. IF MAKING DOUBLE QUANTITIES, COMBINE IN A ROASTING PAN OR DUTCH OVEN, AND HEAT IN SLOW OVEN TO MELT. WHEN COOL, SHAPE INTO BALLS OR LOGS, THEN ROLL IN PECANS AND PARSLEY. TO STORE, WRAP IN PLASTIC AND REFRIGERATE. SERVES 24.

NEVER LEND MONEY TO A FRIEND;
IT RUINS THEIR MEMORY.

BRANDY-NUT BRIE

WHAT COULD BE EASIER?

1/4 CUP	BROWN SUGAR	60 ML
1/4 CUP	PECANS OR CASHEWS, CHOPPED	60 ML
1 TBSP	BRANDY OR WHISKY	15 ML
7 1/2 OZ	ROUND BRIE CHEESE	235 G
	CRACKERS	

GET READY... STIR TOGETHER SUGAR, NUTS AND BRANDY. SCORE THE TOP OF THE CHEESE AND PLACE ON AN OVENPROOF PLATTER. BAKE AT 400°F (200°C) FOR 4 TO 5 MINUTES, UNTIL CHEESE IS SOFTENED. MOUND SUGAR MIXTURE OVER CHEESE AND BAKE FOR 2 TO 3 MINUTES MORE, UNTIL SUGAR IS MELTED. SERVE WARM WITH CRACKERS. SERVES 6.

WHEN YOUR KIDS ARE FIT TO LIVE WITH,
THEY'RE LIVING WITH SOMEONE ELSE.

STUFFED CAMEMBERT APPETIZER

1	8 OZ (250 G) WHOLE CAMEMBERT	1
3 OZ	CREAM CHEESE	90 G
1 1/4 OZ	ROQUEFORT CHEESE, CRUMBLED	35 G
4 OZ	CHEDDAR CHEESE, SHREDDED	125 G
1	CLOVE GARLIC, MINCED	1
1/4 TSP	DRIED BASIL	1 ML
1/4 TSP	DRIED OREGANO	1 ML
1/4 TSP	DRIED ROSEMARY	1 ML
1/4 TSP	DRIED THYME	1 ML
1 TBSP	CHOPPED FRESH PARSLEY	15 ML
2 TBSP	SOFT BUTTER	30 ML
1/4 CUP	CHOPPED GREEN ONION	60 ML

CHILL CAMEMBERT. CAREFULLY SCOOP CHEESE USING A
SHARP KNIFE, LEAVING 1/8-INCH (3 MM) SHELL INTACT.
SAVE CHEESE FOR FILLING. CHILL SHELL. BLEND SOFT
CAMEMBERT AND REMAINING INGREDIENTS AND FILL
SHELL. CHILL FOR AT LEAST 24 HOURS. SERVE AT ROOM
TEMPERATURE WITH CRACKERS OR MELBA TOAST.
SERVES 12.

*MEMORY EXPERT: ANY WOMAN WHO
JUST LEARNED ANOTHER WOMAN'S AGE.*

CHIPPY KNEES BITES

GAME MISCONDUCT IF YOU DON'T TRY THEM!

1	CAN (4 OZ/114 ML) CHOPPED MILD GREEN CHILES	1
4 CUPS	SHREDDED SHARP (OLD) CHEDDAR CHEESE	1 L
6	EGGS	6
1 TBSP	FINELY CHOPPED ONION	15 ML

GREASE AN 8-INCH (20 CM) SQUARE BAKING PAN. SPREAD CHILES EVENLY OVER BOTTOM, SPRINKLE CHEESE OVER CHILES. BEAT EGGS AND ADD ONION. POUR OVER CHEESE. BAKE AT 350°F (180°C) FOR 30 MINUTES (OR UNTIL EGGS ARE FIRM). CUT INTO 1-INCH (2.5 CM) SQUARES. MAKES 64 PIECES.

SPINACH-STUFFED MUSHROOM CAPS

1	PACKAGE (10 OZ/300 G) FROZEN CHOPPED SPINACH	1
1	ENVELOPE DRY ONION SOUP MIX	1
1 CUP	SOUR CREAM	250 ML
1	CLOVE GARLIC, MINCED	1
2 LBS	LARGE MUSHROOMS	1 KG

THAW SPINACH; PRESS OUT LIQUID. MIX WITH ONION SOUP, SOUR CREAM AND GARLIC. REMOVE MUSHROOM STEMS AND DISCARD. GREASE BAKING SHEET. FILL MUSHROOMS AND CHILL. HEAT 12 MINUTES AT 350°F (180°C). MAKES ABOUT 16.

HOT MUSHROOM TURNOVERS

A BIT FUSSY, BUT D-LISH!

DOUGH

1	PACKAGE (8 OZ/250 G) CREAM CHEESE	1
1 1/2 CUPS	ALL-PURPOSE FLOUR	375 ML
1/2 CUP	MARGARINE	125 ML

FILLING

1 LB	MUSHROOMS, MINCED	500 G
1	LARGE ONION, MINCED	1
3 TBSP	MARGARINE	45 ML
1/4 CUP	SOUR CREAM	50 ML
1/4 TSP	DRIED THYME	1 ML
1/2 TSP	SALT	2 ML
1	EGG, BEATEN	1

DOUGH: BLEND ALL INGREDIENTS IN A MIXER, THEN FORM INTO A BALL. REFRIGERATE FOR 1 HOUR.

FILLING: SAUTÉ MUSHROOMS AND ONION IN MARGARINE. WHEN COOKED, ADD SOUR CREAM, THYME AND SALT. ROLL DOUGH OUT TO 1/4-INCH (1 CM) THICKNESS. CUT IN 3-INCH (7.5 CM) CIRCLES. FILL WITH 1 TSP (5 ML) FILLING, DRAINED SLIGHTLY. BRUSH EDGES WITH EGG. FOLD AND SEAL BY PRESSING EDGE WITH A FORK. PIERCE TOP IN 2 OR 3 PLACES. BRUSH TOP WITH EGG. BAKE AT 400°F (200°C) FOR 10 TO 20 MINUTES OR UNTIL LIGHTLY BROWNED. FREEZES WELL. MAKES 24 TURNOVERS.

SPANAKOPITA

A SHORT-CUT ROUTE TO GREEK GOURMET.

2	BUNCHES SPINACH	2
1 1/3 CUPS	FINELY CHOPPED ONIONS	325 ML
1/2 CUP	DICED MUSHROOMS	125 ML
	SALT AND BLACK PEPPER TO TASTE	
2	EGGS, BEATEN	2
8 OZ	FETA CHEESE, CRUMBLED	250 G
1/3 CUP	BREAD CRUMBS	75 ML
1 TSP	DRIED DILLWEED	5 ML
PINCH	GROUND NUTMEG	PINCH
1/2 CUP	BUTTER, MELTED	125 ML
12	SHEETS PHYLLO DOUGH	12

WASH, STEM AND STEAM SPINACH UNTIL WILTED; CHOP. SAUTÉ ONIONS, MUSHROOMS, SALT AND PEPPER UNTIL LIQUID HAS EVAPORATED (ABOUT 5 MINUTES). ADD TO SPINACH. ADD EGGS, CHEESE, BREAD CRUMBS, DILL AND SPICES. FOLLOW PACKAGE INSTRUCTIONS FOR KEEPING PHYLLO MOIST. BRUSH EACH SHEET WITH BUTTER, LAYERING 4 SHEETS ON TOP OF EACH OTHER. PUT FILLING ALONG LENGTH OF TOP LAYER, LEAVING 1-INCH (2.5 CM) MARGIN AT EACH EDGE. SEAL BY FOLDING AND ROLLING UP LIKE A JELLY ROLL. BRUSH TOPS WITH BUTTER AND BAKE AT 425°F (220°C) FOR 20 MINUTES. COOL 10 MINUTES. SLICE AND SERVE. MESSY BUT MARVELOUS! MAY BE REHEATED IN MICROWAVE. MAKES 3 ROLLS.

BOMB SHELTER CROUSTADES

| 24 | SLICES WHITE BREAD, THINLY ROLLED | 24 |
| 2 TBSP | BUTTER | 30 ML |

MUSHROOM FILLING

1/4 CUP	BUTTER	60 ML
3 TBSP	FINELY CHOPPED ONION	45 ML
8 OZ	FINELY CHOPPED MUSHROOMS	250 G
2 TBSP	ALL-PURPOSE FLOUR	30 ML
1 CUP	WHIPPING (35%) CREAM	250 ML
3 TBSP	DRY WHITE WINE	45 ML
1/2 TSP	SALT	2 ML
PINCH	CAYENNE PEPPER	PINCH
1 TBSP	FINELY CHOPPED FRESH PARSLEY	15 ML
1 1/2 TBSP	FINELY CHOPPED GREEN ONION	22 ML
3 TBSP	GRATED PARMESAN CHEESE	45 ML

CROUSTADES: PREHEAT OVEN TO 400°F (200°C). GENEROUSLY BUTTER SMALL TART TINS. CUT A 3-INCH (7.5 CM) ROUND FROM EACH SLICE OF BREAD. CAREFULLY FIT INTO TART TINS. BAKE FOR 10 MINUTES, OR UNTIL RIMS ARE LIGHTLY BROWNED. REMOVE FROM TINS AND COOL. (MAY BE FROZEN AT THIS POINT.)

FILLING: MELT BUTTER IN A FRYING PAN AND SAUTÉ ONION AND MUSHROOMS. STIR AND COOK UNTIL MOISTURE EVAPORATES. SPRINKLE WITH FLOUR. STIR THOROUGHLY AND ADD CREAM, STIRRING UNTIL IT BOILS. ADD WINE, REDUCE HEAT AND SIMMER A FEW MINUTES LONGER. REMOVE FROM HEAT, STIR IN SALT, CAYENNE, PARSLEY

CONTINUED ON NEXT PAGE...

AND GREEN ONION. TRANSFER TO A BOWL. COVER AND REFRIGERATE.

TO SERVE: PREHEAT OVEN TO 350°F (180°C). SPOON MUSHROOM FILLING INTO CROUSTADES; LIGHTLY SPRINKLE WITH PARMESAN AND PLACE ON COOKIE SHEET. HEAT IN OVEN FOR 10 MINUTES, THEN BRIEFLY UNDER THE BROILER. MAKES 24 PIECES.

GUACAMOLE CHERRY TOMATO HALVES

TOMATO LOVERS WILL BE HAPPY TO SEE THESE SAVORY LITTLE APPETIZERS.

1	SMALL BASKET CHERRY TOMATOES	1
1	LARGE RIPE AVOCADO	1
4 TSP	LEMON JUICE	20 ML
1 TBSP	FINELY CHOPPED ONION	15 ML
1	CLOVE GARLIC, MINCED	1
1/2 TSP	SALT	2 ML
6	STRIPS BACON, COOKED AND CRUMBLED	6

REMOVE STEMS FROM TOMATOES; CUT EACH IN HALF CROSSWISE. SCOOP OUT AND DISCARD SEED FILLING. LAY CUT SIDE DOWN ON PAPER TOWELS FOR ABOUT HALF AN HOUR. PREPARE GUACAMOLE FILLING BY PEELING AND REMOVING PIT FROM AVOCADO. IN A SMALL BOWL, MASH THE AVOCADO COARSELY WITH A FORK. STIR IN LEMON JUICE, ONION, GARLIC AND SALT. BLEND WELL. FILL TOMATOES. SPRINKLE WITH BACON. SERVES 8.

SMOKED SALMON SUPERB

SERVE THIS TO 10 OF YOUR CLOSEST FRIENDS.

1 1/2 CUPS	FRESH BABY SHRIMP, COOKED	375 ML
1 TBSP	HORSERADISH	15 ML
2 TSP	CAPERS, WITH SOME JUICE	10 ML
	SALT AND FRESHLY GROUND BLACK PEPPER TO TASTE	
1 CUP	WHIPPING (35%) CREAM, WHIPPED	250 ML
10	STRIPS (EACH 3 X 5 INCHES/ 7 X 13 CM) SMOKED SALMON (PAPER-THIN LOX IS BEST)	10
	LETTUCE LEAVES	

FOLD SHRIMP, HORSERADISH, CAPERS, SALT AND PEPPER INTO WHIPPED CREAM. PLACE 1 TBSP (15 ML) OF MIXTURE ON EACH STRIP OF SALMON AND ROLL UP (NO TOOTHPICKS NEEDED). CUT IN HALF AND ARRANGE ON LETTUCE LEAVES ON A SERVING PLATTER. SERVES 10.

MAN BLAMES FATE FOR OTHER ACCIDENTS, BUT FEELS PERSONALLY RESPONSIBLE WHEN HE MAKES A HOLE-IN-ONE.

CADILLAC OYSTERS

36	FRESH OYSTERS	36
10 OZ	CHAMPAGNE	300 ML
4	SHALLOTS, FINELY CHOPPED	4
PINCH	BLACK PEPPER	PINCH
2 TO 3 TSP	LEMON JUICE	10 TO 15 ML
3	EGG YOLKS, WELL BEATEN	3
1/4 CUP	BUTTER	60 ML

SHUCK AND RINSE OYSTERS AND RETURN TO CLEANED HALF SHELLS. IN A HEAVY SAUCEPAN, SIMMER 8 OZ (250 ML) OF CHAMPAGNE, SHALLOTS AND PEPPER UNTIL CHAMPAGNE ALMOST EVAPORATES. MIX LEMON JUICE, REMAINING 2 OZ (60 ML) CHAMPAGNE AND EGG YOLKS. POUR ON REDUCED MIXTURE AND THICKEN OVER LOW HEAT. ADD BUTTER IN SMALL AMOUNTS AND WHISK UNTIL BLENDED. POUR OVER OYSTERS AND BROIL UNTIL BUBBLY AND BROWN. HOW MANY CAN YOU EAT? MAKES 3 DOZEN.

WHEN A TEENAGER IS WATCHING TV, LISTENING TO HER MP3 PLAYER AND TALKING ON THE PHONE, SHE IS PROBABLY DOING HER HOMEWORK.

CHEF TONER'S MUSSELS CREOLE

4 CUPS	MUSSELS, TRIMMED, SCRAPED AND WASHED	1 L
1/4 CUP	WHITE WINE	60 ML
1 TBSP	SHALLOTS, FINELY CHOPPED (OR 1 TBSP/15 ML GREEN ONIONS, FINELY CHOPPED)	15 ML
1 TBSP	CHOPPED FRESH PARSLEY	15 ML
1/4 TSP	DRIED THYME	1 ML
1/4	BAY LEAF	1/4
2 TBSP	BUTTER	30 ML
1/4 CUP	CHOPPED PEELED TOMATO	60 ML
1 TBSP	FRESHLY SQUEEZED LEMON JUICE	15 ML
1/2 TSP	HOT PEPPER SAUCE	2 ML
1/2 TSP	WORCESTERSHIRE SAUCE	2 ML
1 1/2 TBSP	BUTTER	22 ML
	SALT AND BLACK PEPPER TO TASTE	

SOAK MUSSELS IN VERY COLD WATER. DISCARD ANY THAT ARE STILL OPEN. HEAT A LARGE HEAVY POT. WHEN VERY HOT, ADD MUSSELS AND WHITE WINE, COVER AND STEAM FOR 2 TO 3 MINUTES. ADD NEXT NINE INGREDIENTS AND COOK, COVERED, FOR 2 MINUTES OR UNTIL SHELLS OPEN. REMOVE MUSSELS TO SERVING PLATE AND KEEP WARM. DISCARD ANY MUSSELS THAT DID NOT OPEN. CONTINUE COOKING SAUCE ON HIGH FOR 1 MINUTE. ADD BUTTER. SEASON WITH SALT AND PEPPER. POUR SAUCE OVER MUSSELS AND SERVE IMMEDIATELY. SERVES 8.

CRAB-STUFFED ARTICHOKE HEARTS

3	GREEN ONIONS, FINELY CHOPPED	3
1/4 CUP	BUTTER	60 ML
1	CAN (6 1/2 OZ/185 G) CRABMEAT	1
1/2 CUP	WHITE WINE	125 ML
1	CAN (14 OZ/398 ML) ARTICHOKE HEARTS, DRAINED (6 TO 8 COUNT IS BEST)	1
1 CUP	HOLLANDAISE SAUCE (SUCH AS KNORR'S, OR HOMEMADE)	125 ML

SAUTÉ ONION IN BUTTER UNTIL SOFT. ADD CRAB AND WINE. SIMMER FOR 3 MINUTES AND SET ASIDE. CUT ARTICHOKE HEARTS IN HALF LENGTHWISE AND PLACE IN SHALLOW OVENPROOF CASSEROLE OR INDIVIDUAL SCALLOP SHELLS. TOP WITH CRABMEAT MIXTURE AND COVER WITH HOLLANDAISE SAUCE. PLACE UNDER BROILER UNTIL BUBBLY; WATCH CAREFULLY! MAKES 12 TO 16.

YOU KNOW THAT IT IS TIME TO DIET WHEN YOU NOD ONE CHIN AND TWO OTHERS SECOND THE MOTION.

SNOW PEAS WITH CRAB

30	SNOW PEAS	30
1	CAN (6$\frac{1}{2}$ OZ/185 G) CRABMEAT	1
2 TBSP	MAYONNAISE	30 ML
$\frac{1}{2}$ TSP	DRIED TARRAGON	2 ML
1 TBSP	LEMON JUICE	15 ML
DASH	WORCESTERSHIRE SAUCE	DASH

COVER SNOW PEAS WITH BOILING WATER. LET STAND FOR 1 MINUTE. DRAIN WELL. PLUNGE INTO ICE WATER AND DRAIN AGAIN. REMOVE STEMS AND STRINGS FROM PEA PODS AND CAREFULLY OPEN WITH A TOOTHPICK. COMBINE CRABMEAT WITH REMAINING INGREDIENTS AND FILL PODS WITH THE MIXTURE. CHILL AND SERVE. SERVES 6 TO 8.

THERE'S ONE THING ABOUT BEING BALD — IT'S NEAT!

CRAB TARTLETS

TART SHELLS

36	SLICES VERY THINLY SLICED WHITE BREAD (LOW-CALORIE BREAD IS THE PERFECT SIZE)	36
3 TBSP	BUTTER	45 ML

CRAB FILLING

3 TBSP	BUTTER	45 ML
1/4 CUP	ALL-PURPOSE FLOUR	60 ML
1 1/2 CUPS	MILK	375 ML
1 CUP	SHREDDED CHEDDAR CHEESE	250 ML
1	CAN (6 1/2 OZ/185 G) CRABMEAT	1
1 TBSP	MINCED GREEN ONION	15 ML
1 TSP	GRATED LEMON ZEST	5 ML
1 TBSP	LEMON JUICE	15 ML
2 TBSP	CHOPPED FRESH PARSLEY	30 ML
1 TSP	WORCESTERSHIRE SAUCE	5 ML
1 TSP	PREPARED MUSTARD	5 ML
1/2 TSP	SALT	2 ML
DASH	HOT PEPPER SAUCE	DASH

TART SHELLS: GENEROUSLY BUTTER SMALL MUFFIN TINS. CUT A 3-INCH (7.5 CM) ROUND FROM EACH SLICE OF BREAD. PRESS INTO MUFFIN TINS. BAKE AT 400°F (200°C) FOR 10 MINUTES OR UNTIL GOLDEN.

FILLING: MELT 3 TBSP (45 ML) BUTTER. STIR IN FLOUR; COOK UNTIL BUBBLY. STIR IN MILK; COOK, STIRRING UNTIL THICKENED. STIR IN CHEESE UNTIL MELTED. ADD REMAINING INGREDIENTS. FILL EACH TARTLET WITH MIXTURE. BAKE AT 400°F (200°C) FOR 5 MINUTES OR UNTIL BUBBLY. FREEZES WELL. MAKES 3 DOZEN.

SEAFOOD IN WINE

A LIGHT, ELEGANT APPETIZER SERVED IN A CHAFING DISH.

1 LB	ASSORTED COOKED SEAFOOD: SHRIMP, LOBSTER, SCALLOPS	500 G
1/2 CUP	DRY WHITE WINE	125 ML
1/4 CUP	VEGETABLE OIL	60 ML
2 TSP	MINCED ONION	10 ML
1/4 TSP	CRUMBLED DRIED ROSEMARY	1 ML
2 TBSP	BUTTER	30 ML
1 TBSP	LEMON JUICE	15 ML

COOK SEAFOOD ACCORDING TO PACKAGE DIRECTIONS AND CUT INTO BITE-SIZE PIECES. LEAVE SCALLOPS WHOLE. COMBINE WINE, OIL, ONION AND ROSEMARY AND MARINATE SEAFOOD IN FRIDGE FOR SEVERAL HOURS. DRAIN AND RESERVE LIQUID. PLACE SEAFOOD IN CHAFING DISH. MELT BUTTER; ADD LEMON JUICE AND MARINADE. POUR OVER SEAFOOD. HEAT AND SERVE WARM WITH COCKTAIL PICKS. SERVES 8.

SOME CHILDREN ARE LIKE POLITICIANS;
YOU SEE THEM ONLY WHEN THEY NEED HELP.

ASPARAGUS CHICKEN PUFFS

1	LARGE BONELESS CHICKEN BREAST, COOKED AND CUBED	1
2 TBSP	MAYONNAISE	30 ML
1/2 TO 1 TSP	CURRY POWDER	2 TO 5 ML
	SALT AND BLACK PEPPER TO TASTE	
1	PACKAGE (14 OZ/400 G) PUFF PASTRY	1
1	CAN (12 OZ/341 ML) ASPARAGUS, WELL-DRAINED (OR 12 FRESH SMALL ASPARAGUS, BLANCHED)	1
1	EGG, BEATEN	1
	SESAME SEEDS	

IN A FOOD PROCESSOR, PURÉE CHICKEN, MAYONNAISE, CURRY, SALT AND PEPPER UNTIL SMOOTH. ROLL PASTRY INTO A 14- BY 10-INCH (35 BY 25 CM) RECTANGLE. CUT LENGTHWISE INTO 3 EVEN STRIPS. SPREAD CHICKEN MIXTURE ALONG ONE SIDE OF EACH STRIP OF PASTRY. PLACE ASPARAGUS SPEARS LENGTHWISE BESIDE CHICKEN MIXTURE. BRUSH EDGES OF PASTRY WITH EGG. ROLL PASTRY OVER TO CLOSE COMPLETELY. BRUSH TOP WITH EGG, CUT ROLLS DIAGONALLY INTO 1-INCH (2.5 CM) PIECES AND SPRINKLE WITH SESAME SEEDS. PLACE ON GREASED COOKIE SHEET AND BAKE AT 450°F (230°C) FOR 10 MINUTES. LOWER TEMPERATURE TO 350°F (180°C); BAKE FOR ANOTHER 10 MINUTES OR UNTIL GOLDEN BROWN. MAKES 4 DOZEN.

A CHILD IS A PERSON WHO CAN'T UNDERSTAND WHY SOMEONE WOULD GIVE AWAY A PERFECTLY GOOD CAT.

TANGY CHICKEN TIDBITS

3 TBSP	BUTTER	45 ML
I TBSP	SESAME OIL	15 ML
I TSP	CAYENNE PEPPER	5 ML
1/2 CUP	DIJON MUSTARD	125 ML
1/3 CUP	CIDER VINEGAR	75 ML
2 TBSP	BROWN SUGAR, FIRMLY PACKED	30 ML
3 TBSP	LIQUID HONEY	45 ML
I TBSP	SOY SAUCE	15 ML
2 LBS	CHICKEN BREAST, SKINNED, BONED AND CUT INTO I-INCH (2.5 CM) CUBES	I KG
	CHOPPED FRESH PARSLEY	

MELT THE BUTTER AND OIL IN A PAN, ADD THE REMAINING INGREDIENTS EXCEPT THE CHICKEN AND SIMMER FOR 5 MINUTES. ADD THE CHICKEN AND SAUTÉ UNTIL THE CHICKEN IS BROWNED ON ALL SIDES. SERVE THE CHICKEN WITH THE SAUCE IN A CHAFING DISH WITH TOOTHPICKS. GARNISH WITH PARSLEY. SERVES 12.

SHE'S A LIGHT EATER — AS SOON AS IT'S LIGHT SHE STARTS EATING!

"TALK ABOUT EASY" CHICKEN WINGS

1½ LBS	CHICKEN WINGS	750 G
6	GREEN ONIONS, CHOPPED	6
½ CUP	SOY SAUCE	125 ML
½ CUP	COOKING BURGUNDY	125 ML

CUT CHICKEN WINGS IN HALF AND REMOVE TIPS. PLACE IN OPEN ROASTING PAN. SPRINKLE WITH ONIONS AND POUR SOY AND BURGUNDY OVER ALL. BAKE FOR 30 MINUTES AT 400°F (200°C), THEN REDUCE HEAT TO 300°F (150°C) AND BAKE FOR 45 MINUTES, STIRRING EVERY 15 MINUTES. IF THE SAUCE IS DRYING UP TOO QUICKLY, REDUCE THE FINAL COOKING TIME. GOOD HOT OR COLD. SERVES 6.

MARRIAGE IS LIKE STRONG HORSERADISH;
YOU CAN PRAISE IT AND STILL HAVE TEARS IN YOUR EYES.

SORTAS

SORTA CURRIED, SORTA GLAZED, SORTA SWEET CHICKEN WINGS.

2 TBSP	BUTTER	30 ML
1/2 CUP	LIQUID HONEY	125 ML
1/4 CUP	PREPARED MUSTARD	60 ML
1/2 TO 1 TSP	CURRY POWDER (TO TASTE)	2 TO 5 ML
12	CHICKEN WINGS	12
1/4 CUP	SESAME SEEDS	60 ML

COMBINE BUTTER, HONEY, MUSTARD AND CURRY POWDER AND HEAT UNTIL BLENDED. BAKE CHICKEN WINGS ON COOKIE SHEET AT 400°F (200°C) FOR 15 MINUTES. BASTE WITH SAUCE AND CONTINUE COOKING UNTIL BROWN, ABOUT 20 MINUTES. REMOVE FROM OVEN AND DIP IN SESAME SEEDS. SERVES 4.

THE PERSON WHO IS BORED WHEN HE IS ALONE SHOULD UNDERSTAND THE POSITION OF OTHERS WHEN HE'S AROUND.

HOT 'N' SPICY WINGS

GET OUT THE FINGER BOWLS FOR
EVERYONE'S FAVORITE.

3 LBS	CHICKEN WINGS, CUT IN TWO, TIPS REMOVED	1.5 KG
1/2 CUP	KETCHUP (TRY "HOT" IF YOU'RE NOT CHICKEN)	125 ML
1/4 CUP	WATER	60 ML
1/4 CUP	LIQUID HONEY	60 ML
1/4 CUP	RED WINE VINEGAR	60 ML
2 TBSP	BROWN SUGAR	30 ML
1 TBSP	DIJON MUSTARD	15 ML
1 TBSP	WORCESTERSHIRE SAUCE	15 ML
1 TBSP	SOY SAUCE	15 ML
2 TBSP	HOT PEPPER SAUCE	30 ML
2	CLOVES GARLIC, MINCED	2
2 TBSP	DRIED MINCED ONIONS	30 ML

COVER A BROILER PAN WITH FOIL. POKE HOLES IN FOIL. ARRANGE WINGS IN SINGLE LAYER. PLACE UNDER BROILER UNTIL LIGHTLY BROWNED. IN A SAUCEPAN, COMBINE ALL REMAINING INGREDIENTS AND BRING TO A BOIL; REDUCE HEAT AND SIMMER FOR 5 TO 10 MINUTES. USING TONGS, DIP EACH WING IN HOT SAUCE AND PLACE ON BAKING SHEET; BAKE AT 375°F (190°C) FOR 35 TO 40 MINUTES. BASTE WITH REMAINING SAUCE DURING BAKING. DURING THE LAST FEW MINUTES, TURN ON BROILER AND CRISP WINGS. SERVES 6 TO 8.

HAM AND CHEESE PUFFS

*THEY FREEZE WELL. IF YOU'VE GOT TENNIS ELBOW,
YOU'LL NEED HELP BEATING THESE.*

I CUP	WATER	250 ML
⅓ CUP	BUTTER	75 ML
I CUP	ALL-PURPOSE FLOUR	250 ML
4	EGGS	4
I½ CUPS	SHREDDED SHARP (OLD) CHEDDAR CHEESE	375 ML
I CUP	HAM OR CRISP BACON, FINELY CHOPPED	250 ML
½ TO I TSP	DRY MUSTARD	2 TO 5 ML
I	CAN (4 OZ/II4 ML) CHOPPED JALAPEÑOS, DRAINED (OPTIONAL)	I

COMBINE WATER AND BUTTER IN A HEAVY SAUCEPAN
AND BRING TO A BOIL. REMOVE FROM HEAT AND ADD
FLOUR ALL AT ONCE. BEAT WITH A WOODEN SPOON UNTIL
WELL MIXED. RETURN TO MEDIUM HEAT AND BEAT UNTIL
MIXTURE LEAVES SIDES OF PAN AND FORMS A BALL.
REMOVE FROM HEAT AND BEAT IN EGGS ONE AT A TIME
TO FORM A SMOOTH MIXTURE (BE PATIENT AND BEAT
THOROUGHLY). STIR IN CHEESE, HAM, MUSTARD AND
JALAPEÑOS (IF USING). DROP BY SMALL TEASPOONFULS
ONTO GREASED COOKIE SHEET. BAKE AT 400°F (200°C)
FOR I5 TO 20 MINUTES. REHEAT IF FROZEN IN 350°F (I80°C)
OVEN FOR 5 TO I0 MINUTES. MAKES ABOUT 64 PUFFS.

JOIN THE FUTURE NOW BEFORE IT'S SOLD OUT.

JELLY BALLS

BELIEVE IT OR NOT, THE FLAVOR COMBINATION IN THIS SAUCE IS FANTASTIC. RALLY 'ROUND THE CHAFING DISH!

MEATBALLS

1 LB	LEAN GROUND BEEF	500 G
1	EGG, BEATEN	1
1/2 CUP	FINE BREAD CRUMBS	125 ML
3 TBSP	CHOPPED FRESH PARSLEY	45 ML
1/2 CUP	CHOPPED ONION	125 ML
1 TSP	WORCESTERSHIRE SAUCE	5 ML
	SALT AND BLACK PEPPER TO TASTE	

CHILI GRAPE SAUCE

1	BOTTLE (12 OZ/341 ML) CHILI SAUCE	1
1	JAR (10 OZ/284 ML) GRAPE JELLY	1
1 TSP	LEMON JUICE	5 ML
2 TBSP	BROWN SUGAR	30 ML
1 TBSP	SOY SAUCE	15 ML

MEATBALLS: MIX GROUND BEEF WITH EGG, BREAD CRUMBS, PARSLEY, ONION, WORCESTERSHIRE SAUCE, SALT AND PEPPER. ROLL INTO BALLS 1 INCH (2.5 CM) IN DIAMETER.

SAUCE: HEAT CHILI SAUCE, JELLY, LEMON JUICE, BROWN SUGAR AND SOY SAUCE IN A LARGE POT. BRING TO A BOIL AND ADD UNCOOKED MEATBALLS. SIMMER MEATBALLS IN SAUCE FOR 30 MINUTES. SERVE IN A CHAFING DISH (AVEC TOOTHPICKS!). FREEZES WELL. MAKES ABOUT 50 BALLS.

SUPER NACHOS

*A MEXICAN "MUST" THAT ALWAYS TASTES
LIKE MORE. THE VERY THING FOR LARGE GROUPS.*

1 LB	LEAN GROUND BEEF	500 G
1	MEDIUM TO LARGE ONION, CHOPPED	1
1 TSP	SALT	5 ML
1	CAN (14 OZ/398 ML) REFRIED BEANS	1
1	CAN (4 OZ/114 ML) GREEN CHILES, DRAINED AND CHOPPED	1
8 OZ	SHREDDED MONTEREY JACK OR MILD CHEDDAR CHEESE	250 G
3/4 CUP	TACO SAUCE (TRY HOT)	175 ML
1	MEDIUM AVOCADO, MASHED (OR 6 OZ/170 G PACKAGE FROZEN AVOCADO DIP)	1
1 CUP	SOUR CREAM	250 ML
1/4 CUP	CHOPPED GREEN ONION	60 ML
1 CUP	SLICED PITTED RIPE OLIVES	250 ML
	TOSTADOS ROUND TORTILLA CHIPS	

BROWN BEEF AND ONION, CRUMBLING BEEF INTO FINE PIECES, AND DRAIN. SEASON WITH SALT. SPREAD REFRIED BEANS IN A SHALLOW 12-CUP (3 L) OVENPROOF DISH. SPRINKLE GREEN CHILES OVER BEANS, TOP WITH MEAT MIXTURE, THEN CHEESE. DRIZZLE TACO SAUCE OVER ALL. IF MADE AHEAD, COVER AND CHILL AT THIS POINT.

BAKE AT 400°F (200°C) FOR 20 MINUTES. SPREAD MASHED AVOCADO OVER MIXTURE, THEN SOUR CREAM. GARNISH WITH GREEN ONIONS AND OLIVES. SERVE WITH TORTILLA CHIPS.

CONTINUED ON NEXT PAGE...

TO REHEAT ANY LEFTOVERS, GRATE ENOUGH CHEESE TO MAKE A NEW TOP LAYER AND BAKE UNTIL HEATED THROUGH. SERVES 20, BUT MAY BE CUT IN HALF FOR SMALLER GATHERINGS.

MOST OF US CAN FORGIVE AND FORGET — WE JUST DON'T WANT THE OTHER PERSON TO FORGET WHAT WE FORGAVE!

AUNTY LIL'S SIMPLE ANTIPASTO

1	BOTTLE (12 OZ/341 ML) HOT KETCHUP	1
1	BOTTLE (10 OZ/284 ML) CHILI SAUCE	1
1	JAR (4 OZ/114 ML) PIMENTO OLIVE PIECES	1
1	JAR (12 OZ/341 ML) SWEET GREEN RELISH	1
1	CAN (10 OZ/284 ML) MUSHROOMS, DRAINED	1
2	CANS (EACH $6\frac{1}{2}$ OZ/185 G) CRABMEAT OR SHRIMP, DRAINED	2
1	CAN ($6\frac{1}{2}$ OZ/185 G) SOLID WHITE TUNA, BROKEN	1
	HOT PEPPER SAUCE TO TASTE	

MIX ALL INGREDIENTS IN A LARGE SAUCEPAN. BRING TO A BOIL AND SIMMER FOR 5 MINUTES. POUR INTO AIRTIGHT CONTAINERS AND STORE IN THE REFRIGERATOR FOR UP TO 1 WEEK. MAKES ABOUT 7 CUPS (1.75 L).

MEXICANA ANTIPASTO

BANDITOS STEAL FOR THIS! SERVE WITH
CORN CHIPS OR TACO CHIPS.

8 OZ	CREAM CHEESE	250 G
PINCH	GARLIC POWDER	PINCH
1/2 CUP	SOUR CREAM (FAT-FREE IS FINE)	125 ML
1	LARGE AVOCADO, MASHED	1
1/4 TSP	LEMON JUICE	1 ML
1	TOMATO, FINELY CHOPPED	1
1	CAN (4 OZ/114 ML) GREEN CHILES	1
5	SLICES BACON, COOKED CRISP AND DICED	5
3 TO 4	GREEN ONIONS, CHOPPED	3 TO 4
1/4 CUP	SLICED RIPE OLIVES	60 ML
1/4 CUP	SLICED STUFFED GREEN OLIVES	60 ML
1	BOTTLE (8 OZ/227 ML) TACO SAUCE (HOT)	1
1 CUP	SHREDDED CHEDDAR CHEESE	250 ML

COMBINE CHEESE, GARLIC AND SOUR CREAM AND USE AS
THE FIRST LAYER IN A 9-INCH (23 CM) PIE PLATE. COMBINE
AVOCADO, LEMON JUICE, TOMATO AND GREEN CHILES FOR
THE SECOND LAYER. SPRINKLE ON BACON, GREEN ONION
AND OLIVES. SPREAD TACO SAUCE OVER ALL AND SPRINKLE
WITH CHEESE. REFRIGERATE. SERVES 10 TO 12 (HOPEFULLY).

SHE HAS THE PERSONALITY OF A DIAL TONE.

KILLER COLESLAW

*ANOTHER FOREVER FAVORITE. IF THERE'S ANY
LEFT OVER, SAVE IT — KIDS LOVE IT THE NEXT DAY!*

SALAD

1/2	CABBAGE, CHOPPED	1/2
5	GREEN ONIONS, CHOPPED	5
1/4 CUP	SLIVERED ALMONDS, TOASTED	60 ML
1/4 CUP	SUNFLOWER SEEDS, TOASTED (OR SESAME SEEDS)	60 ML
1	PACKAGE (3 OZ/85 G) JAPANESE NOODLE SOUP MIX (SAVE SEASONING PACKAGE FOR DRESSING)	1

DRESSING

1/4 CUP	RICE (OR WHITE) VINEGAR	60 ML
1/4 CUP	SALAD OIL	60 ML
	SEASONING PACKAGE FROM NOODLES	

COMBINE ALL SALAD INGREDIENTS EXCEPT NOODLES.
BEFORE SERVING, CRUSH NOODLES, COMBINE WITH SALAD
INGREDIENTS AND TOSS WITH DRESSING. SERVES 6.

*CAN YOU IMAGINE THE INCREDIBLE COURAGE IT TOOK
TO FIRST DISCOVER FROGS' LEGS WERE EDIBLE?*

ARTICHOKE AND ZUCCHINI SALAD

YOU MUST TRY THIS SALAD FOR YOUR NEXT SPECIAL OCCASION. THE SECOND TIME AROUND, YOU WON'T EVEN NEED ONE.

3	SMALL ZUCCHINI (ABOUT 6 INCHES/15 CM)	3
1	CAN (14 OZ/398 ML) ARTICHOKE HEARTS, QUARTERED	1
1/2 CUP	OLIVE OR CORN OIL	125 ML
1/4 CUP	RED WINE VINEGAR	60 ML
1 TBSP	FRESHLY SQUEEZED LEMON JUICE	15 ML
2 TBSP	GRATED PARMESAN CHEESE	30 ML
2 TBSP	GRATED ONION	30 ML
3/4 TSP	WORCESTERSHIRE SAUCE	3 ML
1 TSP	SALT	5 ML
3/4 TSP	FRESHLY GROUND BLACK PEPPER	3 ML
3/4 TSP	GRANULATED SUGAR	3 ML
3/4 TSP	DRIED BASIL	3 ML
3/4 TSP	DRIED OREGANO	3 ML
3/4 TSP	DRY MUSTARD	3 ML
1	HEAD ROMAINE LETTUCE	1
2 TO 3 TBSP	CHOPPED FRESH PARSLEY	30 TO 45 ML
1 CUP	SLICED MUSHROOMS	250 ML

LEAVING SKIN ON ZUCCHINI, SLICE THINLY AND PLACE IN BOWL. ADD DRAINED AND QUARTERED ARTICHOKES. COMBINE ALL EXCEPT LAST THREE INGREDIENTS IN A BLENDER FOR 30 SECONDS (OR SHAKE WELL). POUR OVER ARTICHOKES AND ZUCCHINI AND MARINATE AT LEAST 2 HOURS.

CONTINUED ON NEXT PAGE...

TEAR LETTUCE INTO BITE-SIZE PIECES AND PLACE IN SALAD BOWL. ADD PARSLEY AND MUSHROOMS. JUST BEFORE SERVING, ADD ARTICHOKES AND ZUCCHINI WITH MARINADE AND TOSS. DELICIOUS! SERVES 8 TO 10.

SHE SUFFERS IN SILENCE LOUDER THAN ANYONE I KNOW.

HOT MUSHROOM SALAD

A GOURMET BEGINNING.

1/2 CUP	OLIVE OIL	125 ML
1/4 CUP	TARRAGON VINEGAR	60 ML
2 TO 3 TBSP	DIJON MUSTARD	30 TO 45 ML
1	CLOVE GARLIC, MINCED	1
	SALT AND BLACK PEPPER TO TASTE	
1	HEAD BUTTER LETTUCE, TORN INTO BITE-SIZE PIECES	1
4 OZ	MONTEREY JACK CHEESE, SHREDDED	125 G
8 OZ	MUSHROOMS	250 G
2 TBSP	BUTTER	30 ML

SET SALAD PLATES IN FREEZER FOR AT LEAST 1 HOUR. MAKE SALAD DRESSING BY COMBINING OIL, VINEGAR, MUSTARD, GARLIC, SALT AND PEPPER IN A SCREW-TOP JAR. SHAKE WELL. MIX THE TORN LETTUCE, CHEESE AND DRESSING IN A BOWL. PLACE ON COLD SALAD PLATES. IMMEDIATELY SAUTÉ THE MUSHROOMS UNTIL VERY HOT AND SPOON OVER SALAD SO THE HOT MUSHROOMS MELT CHEESE. SERVE FAST TO 4.

MARINATED ARTICHOKE AND MUSHROOM SALAD

MARINADE

1/2 CUP	TARRAGON VINEGAR	125 ML
2 TBSP	WATER	30 ML
1 TBSP	GRANULATED SUGAR	15 ML
1 1/2 TSP	SALT	7 ML
PINCH	BLACK PEPPER	PINCH
1	CLOVE GARLIC, MINCED	1
1/2 CUP	SALAD OIL	125 ML

SALAD

1	CAN (14 OZ/398 ML) ARTICHOKE HEARTS, DRAINED	398 ML
1 CUP	SLICED MUSHROOMS	250 ML
1	MEDIUM RED ONION, SLICED IN RINGS	1
1	HEAD ROMAINE LETTUCE, TORN INTO BITE-SIZE PIECES	1
1/2 CUP	CHOPPED FRESH PARSLEY	125 ML
	PAPRIKA	

COMBINE MARINADE INGREDIENTS AND MIX THOROUGHLY. TOSS ARTICHOKES, MUSHROOMS AND ONIONS WITH MARINADE. COVER AND REFRIGERATE AT LEAST 2 HOURS, STIRRING OCCASIONALLY. SERVE ON LETTUCE, USING MARINADE AS THE DRESSING. SPRINKLE WITH PARSLEY AND PAPRIKA. SERVES 6.

Christmas Cheese Balls (page 68) and
Guacamole Cherry Tomato Halves (page 75)

Killer Coleslaw (page 93)

Arizona Fruit Salad (page 116)

French Onion Soup au Gratin (page 128)

RUSSIAN BEET SALAD

GREAT FOR A BUFFET — WHY NOT RUSH INTO IT?

1	CAN (16 OZ/500 ML) BEETS, SLICED	1
1	PACKAGE (3 OZ/85 G) LEMON JELL-O	1
1/4 CUP	GRANULATED SUGAR	60 ML
1/4 CUP	VINEGAR	60 ML
1 TBSP	PREPARED HORSERADISH	15 ML
2 TSP	LEMON JUICE	10 ML
4 OZ	CREAM CHEESE	125 G
	MILK OR CREAM	
1 TBSP	MAYONNAISE	15 ML

DRAIN BEETS, RESERVING LIQUID, AND SLICE INTO
SHOESTRINGS. ADD ENOUGH WATER TO BEET JUICE
TO MAKE 1 1/2 CUPS (375 ML). BRING LIQUID TO A BOIL.
ADD JELL-O AND STIR UNTIL JELL-O IS DISSOLVED. COOL
AND ADD SUGAR, VINEGAR, HORSERADISH AND LEMON
JUICE. ADD BEETS AND POUR INTO A 9-INCH (23 CM)
SQUARE GLASS DISH AND REFRIGERATE UNTIL SALAD IS
COMPLETELY SET. MIX CREAM CHEESE AND MAYONNAISE
ADDING ENOUGH MILK UNTIL IT IS THE CONSISTENCY
OF ICING. SPREAD OVER TOP OF SALAD AND REFRIGERATE
UNTIL SERVING TIME. SERVES 8.

A DIAMOND IS A CHUNK OF COAL
THAT MADE GOOD UNDER PRESSURE!

ROMAINE WITH ORANGES AND PECANS

A REAL FAVORITE!

2	HEADS ROMAINE LETTUCE (WASH AND TEAR INTO BITE-SIZE PIECES)	2
I CUP	PECAN HALVES, TOASTED	250 ML
2	ORANGES, PEELED AND SLICED	2

DRESSING

1/4 CUP	VINEGAR	60 ML
1/2 CUP	VEGETABLE OIL	125 ML
1/4 CUP	GRANULATED SUGAR	60 ML
I TSP	SALT	5 ML
1/2	SMALL RED ONION, CHOPPED	1/2
I TSP	DRY MUSTARD	5 ML
2 TBSP	WATER	30 ML

PLACE LETTUCE, PECANS AND ORANGES IN SALAD BOWL. COMBINE DRESSING INGREDIENTS IN BLENDER. BLEND UNTIL WELL MIXED. MAKE AHEAD AND REFRIGERATE UNTIL READY TO TOSS SALAD. USE EXTRA DRESSING AS A DIP FOR FRESH FRUIT! SERVES 6 TO 8.

A HORSE, DIVIDED AGAINST ITSELF, CANNOT STAND.

A DIFFERENT SPINACH SALAD

THE DRESSING REALLY HAS ADDED ZIP!

1		PACKAGE (10 OZ/300 G) FRESH SPINACH	1
1		HEAD BUTTER LETTUCE	1
1 CUP		BEAN SPROUTS	250 ML
1		CAN (8 OZ/227 ML) WATER CHESTNUTS, DRAINED AND SLICED	1
3/4 CUP		BACON, COOKED AND CRUMBLED	175 ML
1		RED BELL PEPPER, CHOPPED	1

DRESSING

1/2 CUP	SALAD OIL	125 ML
1/4 CUP	GRANULATED SUGAR	60 ML
1/4 CUP	KETCHUP	60 ML
2 TBSP	RED WINE VINEGAR	30 ML
1/2 TSP	WORCESTERSHIRE SAUCE	2 ML
1/2	RED ONION, FINELY CHOPPED	1/2
1/4 TSP	DRY MUSTARD	1 ML
1/2 TSP	SALT	2 ML
1/4 TO 1/2 TSP	CAYENNE PEPPER	1 TO 2 ML

COMBINE DRESSING INGREDIENTS AND BLEND UNTIL SMOOTH. SET IN FRIDGE FOR AT LEAST 1 HOUR. WASH SPINACH AND LETTUCE, DRAIN AND DRY. PLACE GREENS IN A LARGE BOWL AND ADD REMAINING INGREDIENTS. ADD DRESSING JUST BEFORE SERVING. SERVES 12.

SPINACH SALAD WITH SOUR CREAM DRESSING

A PLEASANT VARIATION.

½ CUP	MAYONNAISE	125 ML
½ CUP	SOUR CREAM	125 ML
2 TBSP	CHOPPED GREEN ONION	30 ML
2 TBSP	CHOPPED FRESH PARSLEY	30 ML
I TBSP	VINEGAR	15 ML
2 TBSP	LEMON JUICE	30 ML
I TO 2	CLOVES GARLIC, MINCED	I TO 2
	FRESH SPINACH (ENOUGH FOR 4 TO 6 AFTER IT HAS BEEN WASHED AND TORN INTO BITE-SIZE PIECES)	
I CUP	SLICED MUSHROOMS	250 ML

IN BLENDER, COMBINE MAYONNAISE, SOUR CREAM, ONION, PARSLEY, VINEGAR, LEMON JUICE AND GARLIC. TOSS SPINACH AND MUSHROOMS WITH THE DRESSING AND SERVE. SERVES 4 TO 6.

THE ONLY WAY TO GET RID OF FACIAL WRINKLES IS TO IRON YOUR FACE.

ZUCCHINI SALAD

GREAT FIRST COURSE OR USE DRESSING AS A DIP!

I CUP	MAYONNAISE	250 ML
1/2 CUP	SOUR CREAM	125 ML
1/2 CUP	CHOPPED FRESH PARSLEY	125 ML
3	GREEN ONIONS, CHOPPED	3
3 TBSP	WHITE WINE VINEGAR	45 ML
1/2 TSP	DRIED TARRAGON	2 ML
I TSP	WORCESTERSHIRE SAUCE	5 ML
1/2 TSP	DRY MUSTARD	2 ML
1/4 TSP	FRESHLY GROUND BLACK PEPPER	I ML
2	CLOVES GARLIC	2
I TBSP	FRESHLY SQUEEZED LEMON JUICE	15 ML
2 TBSP	CHOPPED FRESH CHIVES	30 ML
8	MEDIUM ZUCCHINI, THINLY SLICED ON DIAGONAL	8
	CHERRY TOMATOES FOR GARNISH	

PLACE ALL INGREDIENTS EXCEPT ZUCCHINI AND CHERRY TOMATOES IN A BLENDER OR FOOD PROCESSOR AND BLEND THOROUGHLY. TOSS ZUCCHINI WITH DRESSING. MOUND ON CRISP LETTUCE LEAVES AND GARNISH WITH CHERRY TOMATOES. SERVES 6.

NEVER INSULT AN ALLIGATOR UNTIL YOU'VE CROSSED THE RIVER.

GREEK SALAD

ANY GREEK WHO BRINGS THIS IS BEARING A GIFT!
AS A VARIATION, SERVE IN A PITA POCKET.

SALAD

1	HEAD ROMAINE LETTUCE, TORN	1
1	LARGE TOMATO, CUT IN WEDGES	1
1	GREEN BELL PEPPER, CUT INTO STRIPS	1
1	SMALL RED ONION, SLICED AND SEPARATED INTO RINGS	1
1	MEDIUM CUCUMBER, SEEDED AND CHOPPED	1
1/4 CUP	GREEK OLIVES (KALAMATA)	60 ML
1/2 CUP	CRUMBLED FETA CHEESE	125 ML

DRESSING

6 TBSP	OLIVE OIL	90 ML
2 TBSP	FRESHLY SQUEEZED LEMON JUICE	30 ML
1 TSP	DRIED OREGANO	5 ML
	SALT AND COARSELY GROUND BLACK PEPPER TO TASTE	

COMBINE ALL SALAD INGREDIENTS, EXCEPT FETA CHEESE, IN A LARGE SALAD BOWL. BEAT DRESSING INGREDIENTS UNTIL WELL BLENDED. POUR OVER SALAD, TOSS WELL AND SPRINKLE ON FETA CHEESE. SERVES 8.

SHE CALLS HER CAR "FLATTERY"
BECAUSE IT GETS HER NOWHERE.

ORIENTAL GARDEN TOSS

6 OZ	FRESH PEA PODS (OR TWO 8-OZ/250 G PACKAGES FROZEN PEA PODS, THAWED)	175 G
4 CUPS	SLICED CHINESE CABBAGE	1 L
4 CUPS	TORN LEAF LETTUCE	1 L
1 CUP	BEAN SPROUTS	250 ML
2 TBSP	CHOPPED PIMENTO	30 ML

DRESSING

1/2 CUP	SALAD OIL	125 ML
1/3 CUP	VINEGAR	75 ML
2 TBSP	GRANULATED SUGAR	30 ML
1 TBSP	SOY SAUCE	15 ML
1/2 TSP	FINELY CHOPPED GINGERROOT	2 ML

TRIM ENDS FROM FRESH PEA PODS. COOK PEA PODS IN 2 CUPS (500 ML) BOILING SALTED WATER FOR 1 MINUTE. DRAIN WELL. IN A SCREW-TOP JAR, COMBINE OIL, VINEGAR, SUGAR, SOY SAUCE AND GINGER. SHAKE VIGOROUSLY. POUR DRESSING OVER PEA PODS. MARINATE 1 TO 2 HOURS. TOSS PEA PODS AND MARINADE WITH CABBAGE, LETTUCE, BEAN SPROUTS AND PIMENTO. SERVES 6 TO 8.

COTTAGE: WHERE YOU'RE BOTHERED ALL SUMMER LONG BY PESTS — MOSQUITOES, ANTS, UNCLES, COUSINS...

COMMITTEE SALAD

WE ALL WORKED ON IT AND WE ALL LOVE IT.

DRESSING

1/2 CUP	VEGETABLE OIL	125 ML
3 TBSP	RED WINE VINEGAR	45 ML
1 TBSP	LEMON JUICE	15 ML
2 TSP	GRANULATED SUGAR	10 ML
1/2 TSP	SALT	2 ML
1/2 TSP	DRY MUSTARD	2 ML
1	CLOVE GARLIC, MINCED	1

SALAD

2 TBSP	BUTTER	30 ML
1/2 CUP	SUNFLOWER SEEDS, SHELLED	125 ML
1/2 CUP	SLIVERED ALMONDS	125 ML
1	HEAD LEAF LETTUCE	1
2	GREEN ONIONS, FINELY CHOPPED	2
1	CAN (10 OZ/284 ML) MANDARIN ORANGES, DRAINED	1
1	RIPE AVOCADO, PEELED AND SLICED	1

COMBINE ALL DRESSING INGREDIENTS IN A JAR; SHAKE TO BLEND. MELT BUTTER IN A FRYING PAN AND SAUTÉ SUNFLOWER SEEDS AND ALMONDS UNTIL GOLDEN BROWN. PREPARE REMAINING INGREDIENTS. ADD COOLED SEEDS AND ALMONDS. TOSS WITH DRESSING JUST BEFORE SERVING. SERVES 6.

PEACHTREE PLAZA SALAD

1 CUP	PECAN HALVES	250 ML
1	LARGE HEAD RED LETTUCE	1
8 OZ	THICK-SLICED BACON, SLICED INTO 1-INCH (2.5 CM) PIECES	250 G
1/3 CUP	BACON FAT	75 ML
1 TBSP	BROWN SUGAR	15 ML
1/3 CUP	CIDER VINEGAR	75 ML
	SALT AND FRESHLY GROUND BLACK PEPPER TO TASTE	

PLACE PECANS IN A SHALLOW ROASTING PAN AND BAKE FOR 15 TO 20 MINUTES AT 325°F (160°C). WASH GREENS AND TEAR INTO BITE-SIZE PIECES. COOK BACON UNTIL CRISP, REMOVE FROM PAN AND DRAIN. POUR OFF ALL BUT 1/3 CUP (75 ML) OF BACON FAT; ADD BROWN SUGAR. STIR TO DISSOLVE, ADD VINEGAR AND STIR UNTIL MIXTURE BUBBLES. PLACE THE LETTUCE IN SALAD BOWL, ADD PECANS AND TOSS. ADD BACON PIECES. ADD HOT DRESSING WHEN READY TO SERVE. SPRINKLE SALT AND PEPPER TO TASTE. TOSS AND SERVE. SERVES 8.

TGIF: THANK GOODNESS I'M FABULOUS.

ASPARAGUS PASTA SALAD

*A TASTY AND ATTRACTIVE LUNCHEON,
SPRINGTIME PICNIC OR BUFFET DISH!*

DRESSING

1	CLOVE GARLIC, MINCED	1
2	ANCHOVY FILLETS, RINSED	2
2 TSP	DIJON MUSTARD	10 ML
1/2 TSP	SALT	2 ML
1/2 TSP	BLACK PEPPER	2 ML
1/2 TSP	WORCESTERSHIRE SAUCE	2 ML
1	EGG YOLK	1
2 TBSP	FRESHLY SQUEEZED LEMON JUICE	30 ML
1 TBSP	WHITE WINE VINEGAR	15 ML
1/2 CUP	OLIVE OIL	125 ML
1/4 CUP	GRATED PARMESAN CHEESE	60 ML

SALAD

2 CUPS	SMALL PASTA SHELLS, COOKED, DRAINED AND COOLED	500 ML
1 LB	ASPARAGUS, CUT INTO 2-INCH (5 CM) PIECES, COOKED TENDER-CRISP AND COOLED	500 G
1	MEDIUM RED BELL PEPPER, CHOPPED	1
1 CUP	SLICED MUSHROOMS	250 ML
1 CUP	SLICED GREEN ONION	250 ML
1/4 CUP	CHOPPED FRESH PARSLEY	60 ML
2 TBSP	CHOPPED FRESH BASIL	30 ML
2 TBSP	SLIVERED ALMONDS	30 ML

PLACE ALL DRESSING INGREDIENTS IN BLENDER AND BLEND
WELL. ASSEMBLE SALAD INGREDIENTS IN A LARGE BOWL,
TOSS WITH DRESSING AND REFRIGERATE FOR AT LEAST
1 HOUR BEFORE SERVING. SERVES 6.

PASTA VEGETABLE SALAD

A MAIN DISH SALAD FOR PICNIC OR PATIO. TRAVELS
WELL! SUBSTITUTE ITALIAN DRESSING, IF DESIRED.

1 CUP	THINLY SLICED CARROTS	250 ML
2 CUPS	SLICED CELERY	500 ML
2 CUPS	CAULIFLOWER FLORETS	500 ML
2 CUPS	BROCCOLI FLORETS	500 ML
2 CUPS	SLICED MUSHROOMS	500 ML
2 TBSP	CHOPPED FRESH PARSLEY	30 ML
1 1/3 CUPS	PESTO DRESSING (PAGE 120)	500 ML
6 OZ	SHELL PASTA	175 G
	SALT AND BLACK PEPPER TO TASTE	

PREPARE VEGETABLES. PLACE IN A LARGE BOWL AND POUR
PESTO DRESSING OVER TOP, COVER AND REFRIGERATE.
COOK PASTA UNTIL AL DENTE AND DRAIN. TOSS WITH
VEGETABLES, ADDING SALT AND PEPPER TO TASTE.
SERVES 8 TO 10.

POVERTY: A STATE OF MIND BROUGHT ON
BY A NEIGHBOR'S NEW CAR.

SALMON PASTA SALAD

3/4 TO 1 LB	SALMON FILLETS	375 TO 500 G
1/8 TSP	SALT	0.5 ML
1 TBSP	LEMON JUICE	15 ML
1	PACKAGE (8 OZ/250 G) SPIRAL OR SHELL-SHAPED PASTA, COOKED AND DRAINED	1
	ROMAINE LETTUCE LEAVES	
	CUCUMBER SLICES	
	FRESH DILL SPRIGS	

CUCUMBER DRESSING

1	ENGLISH CUCUMBER	1
3/4 CUP	SOUR CREAM	175 ML
1/4 CUP	MAYONNAISE	60 ML
2 TBSP	CHOPPED FRESH DILL	30 ML
1 TBSP	WHITE VINEGAR	15 ML
2 TBSP	CHOPPED GREEN ONIONS	30 ML
	SALT AND BLACK PEPPER TO TASTE	

PLACE SALMON FILLETS, SKIN SIDE DOWN, IN A SMALL
BAKING PAN. SPRINKLE WITH SALT AND LEMON JUICE
AND COVER WITH BUTTERED WAX PAPER, BUTTERED
SIDE DOWN. BAKE IN PREHEATED 350°F (180°C) OVEN FOR
12 TO 15 MINUTES OR UNTIL SALMON FLAKES EASILY. COOL
AND REFRIGERATE, COVERED, UNTIL WELL CHILLED, ABOUT
2 HOURS.

DRESSING: GRATE CUCUMBER, PLACE IN SIEVE AND
LET DRAIN AT ROOM TEMPERATURE FOR AT LEAST
30 MINUTES. COMBINE SOUR CREAM, MAYONNAISE,

CONTINUED ON NEXT PAGE...

VINEGAR, DILL, GREEN ONION, SALT AND PEPPER IN A
SMALL BOWL. ADD THE GRATED CUCUMBER.

TO SERVE: PUT PASTA IN BOWL AND TOSS WITH
DRESSING. BREAK SALMON INTO PIECES AND GENTLY FOLD
INTO SALAD. ARRANGE ON LETTUCE LEAVES AND GARNISH
WITH CUCUMBER SLICES AND DILL SPRIGS. SERVES 8.

PAPAYA WITH SHRIMP
AND CURRY MAYONNAISE

*THIS MAKES AN ELEGANT STARTER FOR A SPECIAL
DINNER OR CAN BE USED AS A LUNCHEON SALAD.*

DRESSING

1 CUP	MAYONNAISE	250 ML
1/4 TSP	GROUND GINGER	1 ML
1/2 TO 1 TSP	CURRY POWDER	2 TO 5 ML
1 TBSP	LIME JUICE	15 ML
1 TSP	LIQUID HONEY	5 ML

SALAD

2	RIPE PAPAYAS	2
1	HEAD BUTTER LETTUCE	1
1 1/2 LBS	COOKED SHRIMP	750 ML

DRESSING: COMBINE ALL INGREDIENTS AND WHISK UNTIL
SMOOTH. CHILL.

SALAD: PEEL AND SLICE PAPAYA AND ARRANGE ON LETTUCE
WITH SHRIMP. TOP WITH CURRY MAYONNAISE. SERVES 6.

CHICKEN ATLANTA

WE WERE GIFTED WITH THIS RECIPE WHILE
ON A PROMOTIONAL TRIP TO ATLANTA.
MINT JULEPS, ANYONE?

ORANGE SOUFFLÉ

2	ENVELOPES (EACH $\frac{1}{4}$ OZ/7 G) UNFLAVORED GELATIN POWDER (ABOUT 2 TBSP/30 ML)	2
2 CUPS	GRANULATED SUGAR	500 ML
PINCH	SALT	PINCH
4	EGG YOLKS	4
$2\frac{1}{2}$ CUPS	ORANGE JUICE, DIVIDED	625 ML
$1\frac{1}{2}$ TSP	GRATED ORANGE ZEST	7 ML
1 TSP	GRATED LEMON ZEST	5 ML
3 TBSP	LEMON JUICE	45 ML
1 CUP	HALVED ORANGE SECTIONS	250 ML
2 CUPS	WHIPPING (35%) CREAM, WHIPPED	500 ML

CHICKEN SALAD

1 CUP	MAYONNAISE	250 ML
DASH	WHITE VINEGAR	DASH
$\frac{1}{2}$ CUP	WHIPPING (35%) CREAM, WHIPPED	125 ML
	SALT AND BLACK PEPPER TO TASTE	
3 CUPS	DICED COOKED CHICKEN BREAST OR TURKEY	750 ML
$\frac{1}{2}$ CUP	DICED CELERY	125 ML
$\frac{1}{2}$ CUP	SLIVERED ALMONDS, TOASTED	125 ML

SOUFFLÉ: MIX GELATIN, SUGAR AND SALT IN A SAUCEPAN.
BEAT TOGETHER EGG YOLKS AND 1 CUP (250 ML) OF
ORANGE JUICE. STIR INTO GELATIN MIXTURE; COOK OVER

CONTINUED ON NEXT PAGE...

MEDIUM HEAT, STIRRING CONSTANTLY, UNTIL MIXTURE COMES TO A BOIL. REMOVE FROM HEAT AND STIR IN ORANGE AND LEMON ZEST AND REMAINING JUICES. CHILL, STIRRING OCCASIONALLY, UNTIL MIXTURE MOUNDS WHEN DROPPED FROM A SPOON. STIR IN ORANGE SECTIONS. FOLD IN WHIPPED CREAM AND POUR INTO A 2-QUART (2 L) RING MOLD. COVER AND CHILL OVERNIGHT.

SALAD: COMBINE MAYONNAISE AND VINEGAR. FOLD IN WHIPPED CREAM, SALT AND PEPPER. ADD CHICKEN AND CELERY. REFRIGERATE UNTIL READY TO ASSEMBLE.

TO SERVE: UNMOLD SOUFFLÉ ONTO A GLASS PLATE AND MOUND CHICKEN IN CENTER. GARNISH WITH ALMONDS. SERVES 8.

VACATION: WHAT YOU TAKE WHEN YOU CAN NO LONGER TAKE WHAT YOU'VE BEEN TAKING ALL ALONG!

KOREAN CHICKEN SALAD

A PERFECT SUMMER MEAL. THE ONLY THING THAT'S
DIFFICULT IS FINDING THE KOREAN CHICKENS!

3 LBS	BONELESS SKINLESS CHICKEN BREASTS	1.5 KG

MARINADE

1/4 CUP	SOY SAUCE	60 ML
2 TBSP	VEGETABLE OIL	30 ML
2 TBSP	SHERRY OR WHITE WINE	30 ML
1/2 TSP	GROUND GINGER	2 ML
1/2 TSP	GROUND CINNAMON	2 ML
2	CLOVES GARLIC, FINELY CHOPPED	2

SALAD VEGGIES

2 CUPS	SHREDDED ICEBERG LETTUCE	500 ML
1 CUP	THINLY SLICED CUCUMBER	250 ML
1 CUP	THINLY SLICED CARROTS	250 ML
2/3 CUP	CHOPPED GREEN ONION	150 ML
1 CUP	BEAN SPROUTS	250 ML
3/4 CUP	SLIVERED ALMONDS, TOASTED AND SALTED	175 ML
2 TBSP	SESAME SEEDS, TOASTED	30 ML

DRESSING

1/2 TSP	DRY MUSTARD	2 ML
1/2 TSP	SALT	2 ML
1/2 TSP	HOT PEPPER SAUCE	2 ML
1 TBSP	SOY SAUCE	15 ML
1/4 CUP	CORN OIL	60 ML
1/4 CUP	SESAME OIL	60 ML
4 TSP	LEMON JUICE	20 ML

CONTINUED ON NEXT PAGE...

CUT CHICKEN BREASTS IN HALF. COMBINE MARINADE INGREDIENTS. THOROUGHLY COAT CHICKEN IN MARINADE. PLACE IN SHALLOW ROASTING PAN. POUR REMAINDER OF MARINADE OVER TOP AND COOK, UNCOVERED, AT 400°F (200°C) FOR 40 MINUTES, TURNING AT HALF TIME. (IF YOUR TEAM IS LOSING, HAVE ANOTHER BEER!) COOL COOKED CHICKEN AND CUT IN THIN STRIPS. PREPARE SALAD VEGGIES AND PLACE IN A LARGE BOWL. WHISK TOGETHER ALL DRESSING INGREDIENTS. JUST BEFORE SERVING, TOSS THE CHICKEN AND VEGGIES WITH DRESSING, ALMONDS AND SESAME SEEDS. ENJOY! SERVES 6.

MOSQUITO: THE ORIGINAL SKIN DIVER!

LAYERED CHICKEN SALAD

A REAL WINNER! PREPARE THIS SALAD THE
NIGHT BEFORE AND SERVE FOR LUNCH.

SALAD

4 TO 5 CUPS	SHREDDED ICEBERG LETTUCE	1 TO 1.25 L
4 OZ	BEAN SPROUTS	125 G
1	CAN (8 OZ/227 G) WATER CHESTNUTS, SLICED	1
1	MEDIUM CUCUMBER, THINLY SLICED	1
1/2 CUP	THINLY SLICED GREEN ONIONS	125 ML
2 CUPS	SNOW PEAS (FROZEN IS FINE)	250 ML
4 CUPS	COOKED CHICKEN, CUT INTO STRIPS	1 L

DRESSING

2 CUPS	MAYONNAISE	500 ML
2 TSP	CURRY POWDER	10 ML
1/2 TSP	GROUND GINGER	2 ML
1 TBSP	GRANULATED SUGAR	15 ML
12	CHERRY TOMATOES, HALVED	12

SPREAD LETTUCE EVENLY IN A 4-QUART (4 L) GLASS
BOWL. TOP WITH ONE LAYER EACH OF SPROUTS, WATER
CHESTNUTS, CUCUMBER, ONIONS, PEAS AND CHICKEN
(MAKE SURE PEAS ARE DRY). STIR TOGETHER MAYONNAISE,
CURRY, GINGER AND SUGAR. SPREAD EVENLY OVER THE
SALAD. DECORATE WITH HALVED CHERRY TOMATOES.
COVER AND REFRIGERATE UNTIL READY TO SERVE (YOU
MAY WANT TO MAKE EXTRA MAYONNAISE MIXTURE TO
SERVE ON THE SIDE). SERVES 8 TO 10 DELIGHTED GUESTS.

FRUIT AND LIME CHICKEN SALAD

PERFECT FOR LUNCH — THE LADIES WILL LOVE IT!

3 TBSP	GRANULATED SUGAR	45 ML
1/4 CUP	VINEGAR	60 ML
2 TBSP	LIME JUICE	30 ML
1/4 TSP	DRY MUSTARD	1 ML
PINCH	SALT	PINCH
1/2 TSP	POPPY SEEDS	2 ML
1/2 CUP	SALAD OIL	125 ML
3 CUPS	CUBED COOKED CHICKEN	750 ML
1	HONEYDEW MELON	1
1	CANTALOUPE	1
1	HEAD LEAF LETTUCE	1
1 CUP	STRAWBERRIES, GREEN GRAPES OR CANTALOUPE BALLS (WHICHEVER YOU LIKE)	250 ML
1/2 CUP	PECAN HALVES, TOASTED	125 ML
1/2 CUP	BLUEBERRIES	125 ML

COMBINE SUGAR, VINEGAR, LIME JUICE, MUSTARD, SALT AND POPPY SEEDS IN A BLENDER. WHIRL TO MIX, THEN GRADUALLY ADD OIL IN A THIN STREAM. COVER AND BLEND 2 MINUTES UNTIL DRESSING IS SLIGHTLY THICKENED. RESERVE 1/3 CUP (75 ML) AND POUR REMAINING DRESSING OVER CHICKEN. CHILL. TO SERVE, LINE 4 TO 6 SALAD PLATES WITH LETTUCE AND ARRANGE HONEYDEW AND CANTALOUPE WEDGES AROUND EDGE. SPOON CHICKEN INTO CENTER. TOSS STRAWBERRIES, PECANS AND BLUEBERRIES IN RESERVED DRESSING; SPOON OVER. SERVES 4 TO 6.

ARIZONA FRUIT SALAD

GREAT WITH MEXICAN FARE. DELICIOUS WITH OUR
CHICKEN ENCHILADA CASSEROLE (PAGE 165).

SALAD

1	AVOCADO	1
2 TBSP	LIME JUICE	30 ML
1	PAPAYA	1
2	ORANGES	2
1	GRAPEFRUIT	1
1	SMALL RED ONION	1
1/2	POMEGRANATE (OPTIONAL)	1/2

DRESSING

2 TBSP	ORANGE JUICE	30 ML
2 TBSP	LIME JUICE	30 ML
2 TSP	LIQUID HONEY	10 ML
1/4 TSP	HOT PEPPER FLAKES	1 ML
1/2 CUP	VEGETABLE OIL	125 ML

1	HEAD ROMAINE LETTUCE	1

SALAD: PEEL AND SLICE AVOCADO. SPRINKLE WITH 1 TBSP
(15 ML) LIME JUICE. PEEL, SEED AND SLICE PAPAYA THINLY.
SPRINKLE WITH REMAINING LIME JUICE. PEEL ORANGES
AND GRAPEFRUIT. CUT FRUIT INTO SEGMENTS. SLICE RED
ONION. IN A LARGE BOWL, COMBINE AVOCADO, PAPAYA,
ORANGE AND GRAPEFRUIT SEGMENTS AND ONION. SET
ASIDE. IF USING POMEGRANATE, SCOOP OUT SEEDS AND
SET ASIDE.

CONTINUED ON NEXT PAGE...

DRESSING: WHISK TOGETHER ORANGE JUICE, LIME JUICE, HONEY, PEPPER FLAKES AND OIL.

TO SERVE: POUR DRESSING OVER FRUIT AND TOSS WELL. SPOON ONTO LETTUCE-LINED PLATTER. SPRINKLE POMEGRANATE SEEDS OVER ALL. SERVES 6 TO 8.

I'M MAKING MY FAVORITE THING FOR DINNER — RESERVATIONS.

— FRESH FRUIT DRESSING —

LOW-CAL — TASTES GREAT RIGHT OUT OF THE JAR!

2/3 CUP	PLAIN YOGURT	150 ML
1/4 CUP	VEGETABLE OIL	60 ML
2 TBSP	FROZEN ORANGE JUICE CONCENTRATE	30 ML
2 TBSP	LIQUID HONEY	30 ML
1/2 TSP	GRATED ORANGE ZEST	2 ML

COMBINE ALL INGREDIENTS AND MIX WELL. REFRIGERATE OVERNIGHT IN A SEALED CONTAINER. MAKES ABOUT 1 1/4 CUPS (300 ML).

MARINATED FRUIT SALAD

SERVE IN A SCOOPED-OUT PINEAPPLE
OR YOUR PRETTIEST GLASS BOWL.

I CUP	PINEAPPLE CHUNKS	250 ML
I CUP	HONEYDEW MELON CHUNKS	250 ML
I CUP	CANTALOUPE CHUNKS	250 ML
I CUP	GRAPES	250 ML
I CUP	PLUM PIECES	250 ML
2 TBSP	GRAND MARNIER	30 ML
I TBSP	AMARETTO	15 ML
DASH	LEMON JUICE	DASH

PREPARE FRUIT PIECES. SPRINKLE FRUIT WITH THE
LIQUEURS AND LEMON JUICE. MARINATE FOR 2 HOURS.
SERVE WITH FRUIT SAUCE. SERVES 6.

FRUIT SAUCE

2	EGG YOLKS	2
1/4 CUP	BROWN SUGAR	60 ML
1/4 CUP	GRAND MARNIER	60 ML
I CUP	WHIPPING (35%) CREAM	250 ML

BEAT EGG YOLKS, SUGAR AND LIQUEUR UNTIL LIGHT. WHIP
CREAM UNTIL STIFF AND FOLD INTO EGG MIXTURE. CHILL
FOR A COUPLE OF HOURS BEFORE SERVING. SERVES 6.

NOTE: THIS RECIPE CONTAINS RAW EGG YOLKS. IF THE
FOOD SAFETY OF RAW EGGS IS A CONCERN FOR YOU,
SUBSTITUTE PASTEURIZED EGG YOLKS OR 1/4 CUP (60 ML)
PASTEURIZED LIQUID WHOLE EGGS.

DOCTORED MAYO DRESSING

A FOOD PROCESSOR MAKES THIS IN A JIFFY.

1 1/4 CUPS	MAYONNAISE (NOT MIRACLE WHIP)	300 ML
1/2 CUP	VEGETABLE OIL	125 ML
1/4 CUP	LIQUID HONEY	60 ML
1/4 CUP	PREPARED MUSTARD	60 ML
3 TBSP	FRESHLY SQUEEZED LEMON JUICE	45 ML
2	GREEN ONIONS, CHOPPED	2
1 TBSP	CHOPPED FRESH PARSLEY	15 ML
1 TSP	CELERY SEEDS	5 ML
1/4 TSP	DRY MUSTARD	1 ML
1/4 TSP	CURRY POWDER	1 ML

THOROUGHLY BLEND ALL INGREDIENTS AND CHILL.

MAKES 2 CUPS (500 ML).

*MORE MONEY IS NOW SPENT AMUSING CHILDREN
THAN WAS SPENT ON THE EDUCATION OF THEIR PARENTS.*

THOUSAND ISLAND DRESSING

ALSO GREAT ON HAMBURGERS AND REUBEN SANDWICHES.

1 CUP	MAYONNAISE	250 ML
1 TBSP	VINEGAR	15 ML
1/4 CUP	CHILI SAUCE	60 ML
1 TSP	MINCED ONION	5 ML
2 TBSP	FINELY CHOPPED GREEN BELL PEPPER	30 ML
2 TBSP	FINELY CHOPPED STUFFED OLIVES	30 ML
1	EGG, HARD-BOILED, COARSELY CHOPPED	1

PLACE ALL INGREDIENTS IN BLENDER; MIX WELL. CHILL. WILL KEEP IN REFRIGERATOR FOR UP TO 1 WEEK. MAKES ABOUT 1 1/2 CUPS (375 ML).

PESTO DRESSING

6 TBSP	PESTO SAUCE (PAGE 263)	90 ML
1/3 CUP	WHITE WINE VINEGAR	75 ML
2/3 CUP	OLIVE OIL	150 ML

BLEND INGREDIENTS TOGETHER. MAKES ABOUT 1 1/3 CUPS (325 ML).

CHART HOUSE BLUE CHEESE DRESSING

GET OUT YOUR STOP WATCH!

3/4 CUP	SOUR CREAM	175 ML
1/2 TSP	DRY MUSTARD	2 ML
1/2 TSP	BLACK PEPPER	2 ML
1/2 TSP	SALT	2 ML
PINCH	GARLIC POWDER	PINCH
1 TSP	WORCESTERSHIRE SAUCE	5 ML
1 1/3 CUPS	MAYONNAISE	325 ML
4 OZ	DANISH BLUE CHEESE, CRUMBLED	125 G

BLEND FIRST SIX INGREDIENTS FOR 2 MINUTES AT LOW SPEED. ADD MAYONNAISE AND BLEND FOR 30 SECONDS AT LOW SPEED, THEN 2 MINUTES AT MEDIUM SPEED. ADD CHEESE AND BLEND AT LOW SPEED FOR 3 TO 4 MINUTES. COVER AND REFRIGERATE FOR 24 HOURS. MAKES 2 1/2 CUPS (625 ML).

GINGERED MELON SOUP

SIMPLE SUMMER SOUP!

8 CUPS	CHOPPED RIPE HONEYDEW MELON	2 L
1 1/2 TSP	FINELY GRATED GINGERROOT (OR MORE, IF DESIRED)	7 ML
	JUICE OF 1 LEMON	
1 TSP	FRUIT-FRESH (ASCORBIC ACID)	5 ML
1 1/2 CUPS	FROZEN APPLE JUICE CONCENTRATE	375 ML
	MINT LEAVES FOR GARNISH, IF AVAILABLE	

PLACE ALL INGREDIENTS, EXCEPT MINT LEAVES, IN BLENDER. BLEND AND CHILL THOROUGHLY. SERVES 8.

SHE DRIVES A VEHICLE THAT COSTS $1000 A MILE — A SHOPPING CART.

AVOCADO SOUP

A RICH, ELEGANT STARTER!

2	LARGE AVOCADOS, PEELED AND HALVED	2
I CUP	WHIPPING (35%) CREAM	250 ML
½ CUP	MILK	125 ML
I	CAN (10 OZ/284 ML) CHICKEN BROTH	I
I TO 2 TSP	LIME JUICE	5 TO 10 ML
I TSP	MAGGI SEASONING	5 ML
I TSP	WHITE PEPPER	5 ML
	SALT TO TASTE	
	SOUR CREAM OR CRISP BACON, CRUMBLED	
	CHOPPED FRESH CHIVES	

PLACE AVOCADO IN BLENDER. ADD WHIPPING CREAM, MILK, BROTH, LIME JUICE, MAGGI SEASONING, PEPPER AND SALT. BLEND UNTIL SMOOTH. CHILL. WHEN READY TO SERVE, ADD A SPOONFUL OF SOUR CREAM OR BACON AND GARNISH WITH CHIVES. SERVE CHILLED. SERVES 4 TO 6.

YOU HAVE TWO CHOICES FOR DINNER: TAKE IT OR LEAVE IT!

BROCCOLI SOUP

OKAY, IT'S THE MIDDLE OF WINTER AND YOU HAVE NOTHING PLANNED FOR DINNER. TRY THIS!

6 CUPS	CHOPPED BROCCOLI FLORETS	1.5 L
1/4 CUP	FINELY CHOPPED ONION	60 ML
2 CUPS	CHICKEN BROTH	500 ML
2 TBSP	BUTTER	30 ML
I TBSP	ALL-PURPOSE FLOUR	15 ML
I TSP	SALT	5 ML
	BLACK PEPPER TO TASTE	
PINCH	GROUND MACE	PINCH
2 CUPS	HALF-AND-HALF CREAM	500 ML
2 CUPS	SHREDDED CHEDDAR CHEESE (OPTIONAL)	500 ML

IN A LARGE SAUCEPAN, COMBINE BROCCOLI WITH ONION AND BROTH. BRING TO A BOIL, REDUCE HEAT AND SIMMER FOR 10 MINUTES. BLEND FOR A SMOOTH CONSISTENCY. IN A LARGE SAUCEPAN, MELT BUTTER; ADD FLOUR, SALT, PEPPER AND MACE. SLOWLY ADD CREAM AND STIR UNTIL SMOOTH. ADD BROCCOLI AND CHEESE (IF USING), AND WARM UNTIL CHEESE IS MELTED. SERVES 4 TO 6.

WHEN CHOOSING BETWEEN TWO EVILS, ALWAYS TRY THE ONE YOU'VE NEVER TRIED BEFORE.

CAULIFLOWER SOUP
WITH BLUE CHEESE

2	PACKAGES (EACH 10 OZ/300 G) CHOPPED FROZEN CAULIFLOWER (OR 4 CUPS/1 L FRESH)	2
1/4 CUP	FINELY CHOPPED ONION	60 ML
2 CUPS	CHICKEN BROTH	500 ML
2 OZ	BLUE CHEESE	60 G
2 TBSP	BUTTER	30 ML
1 TBSP	ALL-PURPOSE FLOUR	15 ML
1 TSP	SALT	5 ML
	BLACK PEPPER TO TASTE	
PINCH	GROUND MACE OR NUTMEG	PINCH
2 CUPS	HALF-AND-HALF CREAM	500 ML

THAW CAULIFLOWER AND COMBINE WITH ONION AND BROTH. BRING TO A BOIL, REDUCE HEAT AND SIMMER FOR 10 MINUTES. ADD CHEESE AND BLEND TO A SMOOTH CONSISTENCY. IN A LARGE SAUCEPAN, MELT BUTTER; ADD FLOUR, SALT, PEPPER AND MACE. SLOWLY ADD CREAM AND STIR UNTIL SMOOTH. ADD CAULIFLOWER MIXTURE. HEAT BEFORE SERVING. SERVES 6.

THE PERSON WHO COINED "OUT OF SIGHT, OUT OF MIND" HAD NO CHILDREN OF DATING AGE OUT ON SATURDAY NIGHT!

MUSHROOM SOUP

1 LB	MUSHROOMS	500 G
	JUICE OF $1/2$ LEMON	
1 TBSP	BUTTER	15 ML
2 TBSP	MINCED SHALLOTS OR GREEN ONIONS	30 ML
$1/2$	BAY LEAF	$1/2$
$1/4$ TSP	DRIED THYME	1 ML
2 CUPS	WHIPPING (35%) CREAM	500 ML
$1 1/2$ CUPS	CHICKEN STOCK	375 ML
1 TSP	SALT	5 ML
$1 1/2$ TSP	BLACK PEPPER	7 ML
1 TSP	CORNSTARCH	5 ML
1 TBSP	WATER	15 ML
1 TBSP	CHOPPED FRESH PARSLEY	15 ML

FINELY CHOP MUSHROOMS, THEN COMBINE WITH LEMON JUICE. MELT BUTTER IN A LARGE SKILLET, ADD SHALLOTS AND SAUTÉ. ADD MUSHROOMS, BAY LEAF AND THYME AND COOK, STIRRING FREQUENTLY, UNTIL LIQUID COMPLETELY EVAPORATES. BLEND IN CREAM, CHICKEN STOCK, SALT AND PEPPER AND BRING TO A BOIL. REDUCE HEAT. DISSOLVE CORNSTARCH IN WATER, ADD TO SOUP AND SIMMER FOR 20 MINUTES. LADLE INTO HEATED BOWLS AND SPRINKLE WITH PARSLEY. SERVES 6.

IF YOU CAN'T SAY ANYTHING NICE ABOUT SOMEONE,
YOU'RE PROBABLY A LOT OF FUN TO TALK TO.

MUSHROOM AND LEEK SOUP

A WINTER TREAT FOR YOUR DINNER GUESTS — OR YOUR FAMILY!

2	LEEKS	2
2 TBSP	BUTTER	30 ML
8 OZ	MUSHROOMS, FINELY CHOPPED	250 G
1/4 CUP	ALL-PURPOSE FLOUR	60 ML
1/2 TSP	SALT	2 ML
2 PINCHES	CAYENNE PEPPER	2 PINCHES
I CUP	CHICKEN BROTH	250 ML
3 TO 4 CUPS	MILK	750 ML TO I L
2 TBSP	SHERRY (OR I TBSP/I5 ML LEMON JUICE)	30 ML
6	LEMON SLICES	6
	CHOPPED FRESH PARSLEY	

WASH AND FINELY CHOP WHITE PART OF LEEKS. IN A HEAVY SAUCEPAN OVER MEDIUM HEAT, MELT BUTTER AND SAUTÉ LEEKS UNTIL TENDER BUT NOT BROWN. REMOVE FROM PAN AND SET ASIDE. IN REMAINING BUTTER, SAUTÉ CHOPPED MUSHROOMS TILL SOFT, ABOUT 5 MINUTES. (DON'T WORRY ABOUT EXTRA JUICE.) BLEND IN FLOUR, SALT AND CAYENNE PEPPER. ADD LEEKS. GRADUALLY STIR IN CHICKEN BROTH, MILK AND SHERRY (OR LEMON JUICE). COOK UNTIL THICKENED AND MIXTURE COMES TO A BOIL. SIMMER FOR IO MINUTES. SERVE WITH THIN SLICES OF LEMON AND A SPRINKLE OF PARSLEY. *MAKES 6 SMALL SERVINGS.*

FRENCH ONION SOUP AU GRATIN

*THIS IS THE BEST! SERVE WITH A
SALAD AND GARLIC BREAD.*

4	LARGE ONIONS, THINLY SLICED	4
1/4 CUP	BUTTER	60 ML
4	CANS (EACH 10 OZ/284 ML) BEEF BROTH	4
1/2 CUP	DRY SHERRY	125 ML
2 TSP	WORCESTERSHIRE SAUCE	10 ML
PINCH	BLACK PEPPER	PINCH
6	SLICES FRENCH BREAD, EACH 1/2 INCH (1 CM) THICK, TOASTED	6
3/4 CUP	GRATED PARMESAN CHEESE	175 ML
1 TO 2 CUPS	SHREDDED MOZZARELLA CHEESE	250 TO 500 ML

IN A LARGE SAUCEPAN, COOK ONIONS IN BUTTER UNTIL TENDER BUT NOT BROWN. ADD BEEF BROTH, SHERRY, WORCESTERSHIRE SAUCE AND PEPPER AND BRING TO A BOIL. POUR INTO INDIVIDUAL OVENPROOF BOWLS. FLOAT A SLICE OF TOASTED FRENCH BREAD IN EACH. SPRINKLE WITH PARMESAN AND TOP WITH MOZZARELLA. PLACE UNDER BROILER AND HEAT UNTIL CHEESE BUBBLES. SCRUMPTIOUS! SERVES 6.

CREAM OF PARSLEY AND BASIL SOUP

A LIGHT, REFRESHING STARTER.

3 TBSP	BUTTER	45 ML
1 1/2 CUPS	CHOPPED FRESH PARSLEY	375 ML
1/2 CUP	FRESH BASIL, STEMS REMOVED	125 ML
2 CUPS	CHICKEN STOCK	500 ML
3	MEDIUM POTATOES, PEELED AND CUT INTO CHUNKS	3
3 CUPS	LIGHT CREAM	750 ML
	SALT, PEPPER AND NUTMEG TO TASTE	
	BASIL LEAVES	

HEAT BUTTER IN A LARGE SAUCEPAN OVER LOW HEAT. ADD PARSLEY AND BASIL. SIMMER FOR 5 MINUTES; ADD STOCK AND POTATOES, COVER AND SIMMER FOR 20 MINUTES. COOL SLIGHTLY, ADD CREAM AND BLEND UNTIL SMOOTH. ADD SEASONINGS. SERVE HOT. GARNISH EACH SERVING WITH A BASIL LEAF. SERVES 4 TO 6.

SMILE! IT'S THE SECOND BEST THING YOU CAN DO WITH YOUR LIPS.

POTATO SOUP

THE SOUR CREAM MAKES THE DIFFERENCE.

4	LARGE POTATOES, PEELED AND DICED	4
1/2 CUP	DICED CELERY	125 ML
1/2 CUP	FINELY CHOPPED ONION	125 ML
1 1/2 CUPS	WATER	375 ML
4	CHICKEN BOUILLON CUBES	4
1/2 TSP	SALT	2 ML
2 CUPS	MILK	500 ML
2 CUPS	SOUR CREAM	500 ML
1 TBSP	ALL-PURPOSE FLOUR	15 ML
	CHOPPED FRESH PARSLEY OR GREEN ONIONS	

PUT POTATOES, CELERY, ONION, WATER, BOUILLON CUBES AND SALT IN A LARGE POT. COVER AND COOK UNTIL VEGETABLES ARE TENDER, ABOUT 20 MINUTES. REMOVE FROM STOVE AND MIX WITH ELECTRIC MIXER UNTIL MIXTURE IS A SMOOTH PASTE. ADD 1 CUP (250 ML) MILK AND HEAT. IN A MEDIUM BOWL, BLEND SOUR CREAM WITH FLOUR. STIR IN 1 CUP (250 ML) MILK. VERY SLOWLY, POUR ONE-THIRD OF THE HEATED MIXTURE INTO SOUR CREAM. POUR THIS MIXTURE SLOWLY INTO THE REMAINDER OF SOUP MIXTURE. HEAT AND STIR UNTIL THICKENED. SERVES 6.

CREAM OF SPINACH SOUP

POPEYE NEVER HAD IT SO GOOD,
EVEN WITHOUT OLIVE OYL!

2 CUPS	CHICKEN BROTH	500 ML
1	BAG (10 OZ/300 G) BABY SPINACH	1
3/4 CUP	WHIPPING (35%) CREAM	175 ML
	SALT AND BLACK PEPPER TO TASTE	
2	SLICES BACON, COOKED CRISP AND CRUMBLED (OPTIONAL)	2

SIMMER CHICKEN BROTH AND SPINACH UNTIL SPINACH IS WILTED. PURÉE MIXTURE IN BLENDER OR FOOD PROCESSOR. RETURN TO SAUCEPAN AND STIR IN CREAM AND SALT AND PEPPER. ADD BACON (IF USING). SIMMER ABOUT 5 MINUTES OR UNTIL PIPING HOT. SERVES 4.

TO ERR IS HUMAN, BUT TO BLAME IT ON SOMEONE ELSE IS HUMANER.

FRESH TOMATO BISQUE

3 LBS	RIPE TOMATOES	1.5 KG
1/3 CUP	BUTTER	75 ML
2 CUPS	DRY BREAD CRUMBS	500 ML
1 1/2 TSP	SALT	7 ML
	BLACK PEPPER	
3	CLOVES GARLIC, MINCED	3
6 CUPS	WATER	1.5 L
1 1/2 CUPS	CREAM	375 ML
2	EGG YOLKS, BEATEN	2

PURÉE TOMATOES (SEEDS AND SKINS INCLUDED). STRAIN
THROUGH SIEVE. HEAT BUTTER; ADD TOMATOES AND
SIMMER FOR 5 MINUTES. ADD CRUMBS, SALT, PEPPER,
GARLIC AND WATER; BRING TO A BOIL. BEAT CREAM
INTO EGG YOLKS. ADD TO TOMATO PURÉE, STIRRING
CONSTANTLY. HEAT TO SERVING TEMPERATURE. DO NOT
BOIL. SERVES 8.

THERE ARE ONLY TWO THINGS A CHILD WILL SHARE WILLINGLY:
COMMUNICABLE DISEASES AND HIS MOTHER'S AGE.
— DR. BENJAMIN SPOCK

CREAM OF CURRY SOUP

1/3 CUP	BUTTER	75 ML
1	LARGE ONION, FINELY CHOPPED	1
2 TO 3 TBSP	ALL-PURPOSE FLOUR	30 TO 45 ML
2 TSP	CURRY POWDER	10 ML
3 CUPS	CHICKEN BROTH (CANNED)	750 ML
3 CUPS	CEREAL CREAM (OR MILK)	750 ML
1/4 CUP	SHERRY	60 ML
1/2 CUP	FLAKED ALMONDS, TOASTED	125 ML

MELT BUTTER AND SAUTÉ ONION UNTIL LIMP. ADD FLOUR AND CURRY. STIR UNTIL BUBBLY. ADD CHICKEN BROTH AND BRING TO A BOIL. REDUCE HEAT AND STIR IN CREAM. ADD SHERRY, SPRINKLE WITH ALMONDS. DELICIOUS! SERVES 6.

EGG DROP SOUP

3	CANS (EACH 10 OZ/284 ML) CHICKEN BROTH	3
1	EGG, SLIGHTLY BEATEN	1
2 TBSP	CHOPPED FRESH PARSLEY	30 ML

HEAT BROTH JUST TO BOILING. BLEND IN BEATEN EGG VERY SLOWLY, STIRRING CONSTANTLY, JUST UNTIL EGG COOKS AND SEPARATES INTO STRINGS. REMOVE FROM HEAT AND COOL SLIGHTLY. LADLE INTO BOWLS AND SPRINKLE LIGHTLY WITH PARSLEY. SERVES 6.

AVGOLEMONO

WELL, THE GREEKS CAN SAY IT!
(THEY ALSO SAY, "IT'S GOOD")

6 CUPS	CHICKEN OR TURKEY BROTH	1.5 L
1/4 CUP	LONG GRAIN RICE	60 ML
1 TSP	SALT	5 ML
3	EGGS	3
1/4 CUP	FRESHLY SQUEEZED LEMON JUICE	60 ML
1	LEMON, THINLY SLICED	1

COMBINE BROTH, RICE AND SALT IN A LARGE POT AND BRING TO A BOIL. COVER AND SIMMER UNTIL RICE IS TENDER (ABOUT 25 MINUTES). COOL ONLY SLIGHTLY. BEAT THE EGGS IN A BOWL UNTIL THICK, THEN BEAT IN LEMON JUICE. CAREFULLY STIR 2 CUPS (500 ML) BROTH INTO EGG MIXTURE AND BEAT WELL. RETURN TO SOUP POT AND BEAT UNTIL SLIGHTLY THICKENED. COOL AND REFRIGERATE. SOUP WILL THICKEN AS IT BECOMES WELL CHILLED. STIR BEFORE SERVING. GARNISH WITH LEMON SLICES. SERVES 6.

THE THREE WISE MEN: TAX ACCOUNTANT, LAWYER AND GOLF PRO.

FISHERMAN'S CHOWDER

DON'T TELL YOUR GUESTS HOW EASY IT IS TO MAKE THIS DELICIOUS SOUP. THEY'LL NEVER BELIEVE IT!

2	CANS (EACH 10 OZ/284 ML) CREAM OF CELERY SOUP (REDUCED SODIUM)	2
2	CANS (EACH 10 OZ/284 ML) CREAM OF MUSHROOM SOUP (REDUCED SODIUM)	2
1	CAN (10 OZ/284 ML) CREAM OF ASPARAGUS SOUP (REDUCED SODIUM)	1
3 CUPS	MILK	750 ML
2	CANS (EACH 4 OZ/114 G) SMALL SHRIMP	2
2	CANS (EACH 6 1/2 OZ/185 G) CRABMEAT OR LOBSTER	2
1 TSP	PIMENTO	5 ML
1/2 CUP	CHOPPED CELERY	125 ML
1/2 CUP	CHOPPED ONION	125 ML
1/2 CUP	CHOPPED GREEN ONION	125 ML

HEAT ALL INGREDIENTS TOGETHER VERY SLOWLY. DO NOT LET MIXTURE BOIL. SERVES 10 TO 12.

TIP: USE REDUCED-SODIUM SOUP WHENEVER POSSIBLE.

IF MY HOME IS MY CASTLE, WHERE ARE MY SERVANTS?

HERB'S SOUP WITH SHRIMP

HIS FRIENDS LIKE IT TOO!

2 TBSP	BUTTER	30 ML
1/2 CUP	FINELY CHOPPED GREEN ONION	125 ML
1/4 CUP	FINELY CHOPPED GREEN BELL PEPPER	60 ML
3/4 CUP	FINELY CHOPPED MUSHROOMS	175 ML
1 TBSP	LEMON JUICE	15 ML
1/2 TSP	DRIED BASIL	2 ML
1/2 TSP	DRIED SAVORY	2 ML
PINCH	DRIED TARRAGON	PINCH
	SALT AND BLACK PEPPER TO TASTE	
3 CUPS	CHICKEN STOCK	750 ML
1	CAN (4 OZ/114 G) SHRIMP, DRAINED	1
2	TOMATOES, PEELED, SEEDED AND CHOPPED	2
	CHOPPED FRESH PARSLEY	

HEAT BUTTER AND ADD ONIONS, GREEN PEPPER AND MUSHROOMS. COOK GENTLY, STIRRING, FOR 3 MINUTES. ADD LEMON JUICE AND HERBS. STIR IN CHICKEN STOCK AND BOIL. ADD SHRIMP AND SIMMER FOR 5 MINUTES. PUT A FEW PIECES OF TOMATO IN BOTTOM OF SOUP CUPS. LADLE IN SOUP AND SPRINKLE WITH PARSLEY. SERVES 6.

NOTHING SUCCEEDS LIKE INHERITANCE.

MULLIGATAWNY SOUP

*A BRITISH-INDIAN SOUP POPULAR WITH
THE RANKS — GUNGA DIN LOVED IT!*

2 TBSP	BUTTER	30 ML
3	STALKS CELERY, SLICED	3
1	LARGE POTATO, PEELED AND DICED	1
2	LARGE ONIONS, FINELY CHOPPED	2
4	CLOVES GARLIC, FINELY CHOPPED	4
2	CARROTS, DICED	2
4 TSP	CURRY POWDER	20 ML
1/4 TSP	GROUND CLOVES	1 ML
1/2 TSP	GROUND GINGER	2 ML
2 TSP	CAYENNE PEPPER	10 ML
1 TO 2 TSP	SALT	5 TO 10 ML
2 TSP	BLACK PEPPER	10 ML
8 CUPS	CHICKEN OR TURKEY BROTH	2 L
3 CUPS	DICED COOKED CHICKEN OR TURKEY	750 ML
3 CUPS	COOKED RICE	750 ML
2	GRANNY SMITH APPLES, PEELED AND GRATED	2
2 TBSP	LEMON JUICE	30 ML
1 CUP	PLAIN YOGURT	250 ML

IN A LARGE POT, MELT BUTTER AND SAUTÉ CELERY,
POTATO, ONION, GARLIC, CARROT AND SEASONINGS FOR
5 MINUTES. ADD BROTH AND SIMMER FOR 20 MINUTES.
ADD CHICKEN/TURKEY, RICE, APPLES AND LEMON JUICE.
BEFORE SERVING, ADD YOGURT AND HEAT TO NEAR
BOILING. SERVES 8 TO 10.

WINE-POACHED HALIBUT

SERVE WITH GREEN BEANS, RICE AND DILL
AND PARMESAN TOMATOES (PAGE 238) AND,
OF COURSE, THE REST OF THE WINE.

3	HALIBUT STEAKS (EACH ABOUT 1 LB/500 G), CUT IN HALF	3
1/2 CUP	DRY WHITE WINE	125 ML
3 TBSP	LEMON JUICE	45 ML
1/4 CUP	MARGARINE OR BUTTER	60 ML
1/2 CUP	THINLY SLICED GREEN ONION	125 ML
	SALT AND BLACK PEPPER TO TASTE	

ARRANGE STEAK HALVES SIDE BY SIDE IN A GREASED
13- BY 9-INCH (33 BY 23 CM) BAKING DISH. POUR WINE AND
LEMON JUICE OVER FISH AND COVER DISH TIGHTLY WITH
FOIL. BAKE AT 375°F (190°C) FOR 15 MINUTES. REMOVE
FISH TO PLATTER AND KEEP WARM. POUR JUICE FROM
FISH INTO SMALL SAUCEPAN, ADD BUTTER AND ONIONS,
BRING TO A BOIL AND REDUCE LIQUID TO 2/3 CUP (150 ML).
SEASON WITH SALT AND PEPPER. SPOON OVER FISH.
SERVES 6.

IF A MAN SPEAKS IN THE FOREST WHEN NO WOMAN
IS LISTENING, IS HE STILL WRONG?

O-SOLE-O-MIO

SERVE WITH RICE AND A GREEN VEGETABLE.

4	SOLE FILLETS	4
4 TSP	BUTTER	20 ML
1/4 CUP	FROZEN ORANGE JUICE CONCENTRATE	60 ML
4	GREEN ONIONS, CHOPPED	4
	SALT AND BLACK PEPPER	

PREHEAT OVEN TO 450°F (230°C). USING FOUR 10-INCH (25 CM) PIECES OF FOIL, PLACE 1 FILLET IN CENTER OF EACH. PLACE 1 TSP (5 ML) BUTTER, 1 TBSP (15 ML) ORANGE CONCENTRATE AND CHOPPED GREEN ONION ON EACH FILLET. SEASON WITH SALT AND PEPPER. WRAP AND SEAL. PLACE ON BAKING SHEET; BAKE FOR 15 MINUTES. SERVES 4.

TERIYAKI BARBECUED SALMON STEAKS

4 TO 6	SALMON STEAKS	4 TO 6
1 CUP	SOY SAUCE	250 ML
2 TBSP	BROWN SUGAR	30 ML
1 TBSP	DRY MUSTARD	15 ML

MIX SOY SAUCE, BROWN SUGAR AND MUSTARD TOGETHER. MARINATE SALMON IN MIXTURE FOR AT LEAST 1 HOUR BEFORE COOKING. BARBECUE (OR BROIL) FOR 4 TO 5 MINUTES EACH SIDE, DEPENDING ON THICKNESS OF STEAKS. IN A SMALL SAUCEPAN, BRING MARINADE TO A FULL ROLLING BOIL OVER HIGH HEAT AND BOIL FOR AT LEAST 1 MINUTE. BRUSH MARINADE ON STEAKS AS THEY COOK. SERVES 4 TO 6.

POTLATCH SALMON

A WONDERFUL WAY TO BARBECUE A WHOLE SALMON. THE BOTTOM LINE: DEE-LISHUS!

I	WHOLE SALMON	I
2 TBSP	BUTTER, SOFTENED	30 ML
	JUICE OF I LEMON	
2 TSP	DRY MUSTARD	IO ML
2/3 TO I CUP	BROWN SUGAR	I50 TO 250 ML

TO BUTTERFLY SALMON: REMOVE HEAD, TAIL AND FINS. RUN SHARP KNIFE DOWN BACKBONE UNTIL SALMON OPENS FLAT. PLACE SKIN-SIDE DOWN ON A GREASED SHEET OF FOIL. SPREAD BUTTER OVER FISH. SPRINKLE LIBERALLY WITH LEMON JUICE AND MUSTARD. COVER WITH 1/4 TO 1/2 INCH (0.5 TO I CM) BROWN SUGAR.

TO COOK: PLACE SALMON ON BARBECUE, LOWER LID AND COOK OVER LOW HEAT FOR 20 TO 30 MINUTES. SALMON IS COOKED WHEN FLESH FLAKES. DON'T OVERCOOK! NOW IS THE TIME TO REMOVE THE BONES. LIFT BACKBONE AT ONE END AND GENTLY REMOVE IN ONE PIECE. SERVES 6 TO 8.

TODAY, A GIRL'S GOT TO STAY ON HER TOES TO AVOID THE HEELS!

CREAMY DILLED SNAPPER

SERVE WITH RICE, SPINACH SALAD AND BREAD STICKS.

2 LBS	RED SNAPPER (FRESH IS BEST)	1 KG
	SALT AND BLACK PEPPER TO TASTE	
1 CUP	SOUR CREAM OR PLAIN YOGURT	250 ML
1/2 CUP	MAYONNAISE	125 ML
1/4 CUP	LEMON JUICE	60 ML
1/4 CUP	ALL-PURPOSE FLOUR	60 ML
1/2 TSP	DRIED DILLWEED (1 TSP/5 ML IF FRESH)	2 ML
	PAPRIKA	

CUT FISH INTO SERVING-SIZE PIECES AND ARRANGE IN SINGLE LAYER IN A 13- BY 9-INCH (33 BY 23 CM) BAKING DISH. SPRINKLE LIGHTLY WITH SALT AND PEPPER. IN A BOWL, COMBINE THE NEXT FIVE INGREDIENTS; STIR UNTIL SMOOTH AND WELL BLENDED. SPREAD OVER FISH. COVER AND BAKE AT 400°F (200°C) FOR 20 TO 25 MINUTES OR UNTIL FLESH IS OPAQUE AND FLAKES. SPRINKLE WITH PAPRIKA. SERVES 6.

I'M STUBBORN ONLY WHEN I DON'T GET MY WAY.

BAKED FISH MOZZARELLA

*THIS IS SO GOOD! SERVE IMMEDIATELY WITH RICE,
ASPARAGUS AND CRUNCHY CARROT STICKS.*

2 LBS	THICK FLOUNDER OR SOLE FILLETS (FRESH IS BEST)	1 KG
1 CUP	SHREDDED MOZZARELLA CHEESE	250 ML
1	LARGE TOMATO, THINLY SLICED	1
1/2 TO 1 TSP	DRIED OREGANO	2 TO 5 ML
	SALT, FRESHLY GROUND BLACK PEPPER AND GARLIC SALT TO TASTE	

PREHEAT OVEN TO 375°F (190°C). BUTTER A 13- BY 9-INCH
(33 BY 23 CM) BAKING DISH. RINSE FILLETS AND PAT
DRY. ARRANGE FISH IN SINGLE LAYER IN DISH. SPRINKLE
WITH CHEESE AND TOP WITH TOMATO SLICES. SPRINKLE
SEASONINGS OVER ALL. BAKE FOR 15 MINUTES OR UNTIL
OPAQUE AND FISH FLAKES. SERVES 5 TO 6 (OR SERVE AT
5 TO 6).

*WHEN SOMEONE SAYS, "NOW THAT'S A GOOD QUESTION,"
YOU CAN BET THAT THE QUESTION WILL BE
BETTER THAN THE ANSWER.*

MARINATED FISH FILLETS WITH BASIL BUTTER

THE FISH IS MOIST, THE CALORIES ARE MINIMAL AND THE TASTE IS TERRIFIC! USE FRESH FISH AND FRESH HERBS IF AVAILABLE.

2 TBSP	LIME JUICE	30 ML
2 TBSP	VEGETABLE OIL	30 ML
4	FISH FILLETS	500 G
1 TBSP	LEMON JUICE	15 ML
1 TBSP	BUTTER, MELTED	15 ML
1 TBSP	CHOPPED FRESH BASIL, DILL OR TARRAGON (OR $1/2$ TSP/2 ML DRIED)	15 ML
	SALT AND BLACK PEPPER TO TASTE	

WHISK TOGETHER LIME JUICE AND OIL. MARINATE FISH IN MIXTURE FOR 1 HOUR BEFORE COOKING. REMOVE FILLETS FROM MIXTURE AND ARRANGE IN A SINGLE LAYER IN A MICROWAVABLE OR CONVENTIONAL OVEN BAKING DISH. IN A SMALL DISH, MIX LEMON JUICE, BUTTER AND BASIL. DRIZZLE OVER FISH. SPRINKLE WITH SALT AND PEPPER. BAKE UNCOVERED AT 450°F (230°C) FOR 8 TO 10 MINUTES OR UNTIL FISH IS OPAQUE. SERVES 4.

FOR MICROWAVE: COVER WITH PLASTIC WRAP; TURN BACK ONE CORNER TO VENT STEAM. MICROWAVE ON HIGH FOR $3 1/2$ TO 4 MINUTES.

LUNCHEON SOUFFLÉ ROLL

SOUFFLÉ

1/4 CUP	BUTTER	60 ML
1/2 CUP	ALL-PURPOSE FLOUR	125 ML
2 CUPS	MILK	500 ML
1/2 TSP	SALT	2 ML
DASH	HOT PEPPER SAUCE	DASH
2 TSP	CHOPPED GREEN ONIONS	10 ML
4	EGGS, SEPARATED	4
1/4 TSP	CREAM OF TARTAR	1 ML

CRABMEAT FILLING

4	GREEN ONIONS, CHOPPED	4
2 TBSP	BUTTER	30 ML
2	CANS (EACH 6 1/2 OZ/185 G) CRABMEAT, DRAINED	2
1	PACKAGE (8 OZ/250 G) CREAM CHEESE	1
1/3 CUP	CREAM	75 ML
2 TBSP	CHOPPED FRESH PARSLEY	30 ML
DASH	HOT PEPPER SAUCE	DASH
	SALT AND BLACK PEPPER TO TASTE	

SOUFFLÉ: PREHEAT OVEN TO 350°F (180°C). GREASE A RIMMED COOKIE SHEET, LINE IT WITH WAX PAPER, THEN GREASE AGAIN AND LIGHTLY FLOUR. MELT BUTTER AND STIR IN FLOUR. COOK FOR 2 OR 3 MINUTES. SLOWLY ADD MILK, STIRRING CONSTANTLY, AND COOK OVER LOW HEAT UNTIL SMOOTH. ADD SALT, HOT PEPPER SAUCE AND ONIONS, SIMMERING FOR 2 MINUTES. REMOVE FROM HEAT. BEAT EGG YOLKS AND GRADUALLY ADD TO SAUCE. SET ASIDE.

CONTINUED ON NEXT PAGE...

IN A BOWL, BEAT EGG WHITES WITH CREAM OF TARTAR UNTIL STIFF. FOLD ONE-QUARTER OF THE EGG WHITES INTO THE YOLK MIXTURE, THEN GENTLY FOLD THE YOLK MIXTURE INTO THE REMAINING EGG WHITES. POUR ONTO THE COOKIE SHEET AND BAKE UNTIL PUFFED AND BROWN, ABOUT 45 MINUTES. IMMEDIATELY LOOSEN SOUFFLÉ FROM EDGES OF PAN AND INVERT ON PAPER TOWEL.

FILLING: COOK ONIONS IN BUTTER UNTIL SOFT. ADD THE REMAINING INGREDIENTS AND COOK UNTIL WELL BLENDED.

TO ASSEMBLE: SPREAD CRABMEAT FILLING OVER SOUFFLÉ AND ROLL UP FROM NARROW END. CUT IN THICK SLICES TO SERVE. SERVES 6 TO 8.

VARIATION: USE A 10-OZ (300 ML) PACKAGE OF DRAINED CHOPPED FROZEN SPINACH INSTEAD OF CRABMEAT.

WHEN YOU CROSS A GORILLA AND A MINK YOU GET A BEAUTIFUL COAT, BUT THE SLEEVES ARE TOO LONG!

MUSSELS AND SCALLOPS IN CREAM

*SERVE WITH LOTS OF CRUSTY BREAD
FOR DUNKING IN THE SAUCE.*

2½ LBS	MUSSELS (FRESH)	1.25 KG
1	LARGE ONION, CHOPPED	1
¼ CUP	BUTTER	60 ML
3	CLOVES GARLIC, MINCED	3
	JUICE OF ½ LEMON	
1½ CUPS	DRY WHITE WINE	375 ML
1½ LBS	SCALLOPS	750 G
2 CUPS	WHIPPING (35%) CREAM	500 ML
½ CUP	CHOPPED FRESH PARSLEY	125 ML
	FRESHLY GROUND BLACK PEPPER	

WASH MUSSELS IN COLD WATER, REMOVE BEARDS (ONE SHOULD ALWAYS SHAVE FOR COMPANY) AND DISCARD ANY THAT ARE NOT TIGHTLY CLOSED. IN A LARGE, HEAVY SAUCEPAN, SAUTÉ ONION IN BUTTER UNTIL TRANSPARENT. ADD GARLIC, LEMON JUICE AND WINE; BRING TO A BOIL. ADD MUSSELS, COVER, REDUCE HEAT AND STEAM FOR 2 TO 3 MINUTES. SHELLS WILL OPEN. DISCARD ANY MUSSELS THAT DO NOT OPEN. ADD SCALLOPS, COVER AND COOK FOR 2 TO 3 MINUTES LONGER. REMOVE FROM HEAT AND GRADUALLY ADD CREAM, STIRRING UNTIL WELL BLENDED. SIMMER ON MEDIUM HEAT BEFORE SERVING. LADLE INTO SHALLOW SOUP BOWLS. GARNISH WITH PARSLEY AND PEPPER. SERVES 6.

SEAFOOD KABOBS

*NO FUSS GOURMET. SERVE WITH SALAD —
LOW-CAL AND DELICIOUS!*

8 OZ	SCALLOPS	250 G
12 OZ	RAW SHRIMP (TAILS ON)	375 G
1	CANTALOUPE MELON (30 BALLS)	1
1	HONEYDEW MELON (30 BALLS)	1
1/4 CUP	LEMON JUICE	60 ML
2 TBSP	BUTTER, MELTED	30 ML
1/4 CUP	BRIE CHEESE (REMOVE SKIN)	60 ML
1/4 CUP	LIGHT CREAM	60 ML

ON SIX 8-INCH (20 CM) SKEWERS, ALTERNATE SEAFOOD AND MELON BALLS. MIX LEMON JUICE AND BUTTER. BROIL KABOBS 10 MINUTES, TURNING AND BRUSHING OCCASIONALLY WITH LEMON JUICE MIXTURE. (SEAFOOD SHOULD BE OPAQUE.) IN A SMALL SAUCEPAN, MELT CHEESE AND GRADUALLY WHISK IN CREAM. DRIZZLE THE CHEESE MIXTURE OVER KABOBS. BROIL UNTIL GOLDEN BROWN. SERVE OVER RICE. SERVES 6.

NOTE: 2 LBS (1 KG) OF FIRM FISH SUCH AS MONKFISH, SHARK OR SWORDFISH IS A TASTY ALTERNATIVE TO THE SCALLOPS AND SHRIMP.

WHAT YOU SEIZE IS WHAT YOU GET!

"THE LADIES" SEAFOOD CASSEROLE

ASSEMBLE EARLY IN THE MORNING AND YOU'RE FREE TO ORGANIZE YOURSELF WITH LAST-MINUTE DETAILS. FRESH SEAFOOD IS BEST. DELICIOUS SERVED OVER RICE WITH A GREEN SALAD AND WARM ROLLS.

1/3 CUP	BUTTER	75 ML
1/3 CUP	ALL-PURPOSE FLOUR	75 ML
2 TSP	PREPARED MUSTARD	10 ML
1 TBSP	GRATED ONION	15 ML
1 TBSP	WORCESTERSHIRE SAUCE	15 ML
1/2 TSP	PAPRIKA	2 ML
1/2 TSP	SALT	2 ML
1/4 TSP	HOT PEPPER SAUCE	1 ML
3 CUPS	MILK	750 ML
6 OZ	GRUYÈRE CHEESE, CUBED	175 G
2 CUPS	MEDIUM SHRIMP	500 ML
2 CUPS	CRABMEAT	500 ML
1/2 CUP	SLICED RIPE OLIVES	125 ML
1 TBSP	LEMON JUICE	15 ML

IN A LARGE SAUCEPAN, MELT BUTTER OVER LOW HEAT. BLEND IN FLOUR, MUSTARD, ONION, WORCESTERSHIRE, PAPRIKA, SALT AND HOT PEPPER SAUCE. GRADUALLY ADD MILK, STIRRING CONSTANTLY UNTIL THICKENED. ADD CHEESE AND STIR UNTIL MELTED. REMOVE FROM HEAT AND BLEND IN SEAFOOD AND OLIVES. POUR INTO A LARGE CASSEROLE AND BRUSH WITH LEMON JUICE. COVER AND REFRIGERATE FOR UP TO 8 HOURS. BAKE AT 350°F (180°C) FOR 30 MINUTES OR UNTIL BUBBLY. SERVES 6.

CLASSY CHICKEN

THIS IS REALLY EASY AND YOUR COMPANY WILL LOVE IT.

3	BONELESS SKINLESS CHICKEN BREASTS	3
1/4 TSP	BLACK PEPPER	1 ML
3 TBSP	VEGETABLE OIL	45 ML
1	PACKAGE (10 OZ/300 G) FROZEN ASPARAGUS OR BROCCOLI (FRESH IS EVEN BETTER)	1
1	CAN (10 OZ/284 ML) CREAM OF CHICKEN SOUP (REDUCED SODIUM)	284 ML
1/2 CUP	MAYONNAISE	125 ML
1 TSP	CURRY POWDER	5 ML
1 TSP	LEMON JUICE	5 ML
1/2 CUP	SHREDDED CHEDDAR CHEESE	125 ML

CUT CHICKEN INTO BITE-SIZE PIECES AND SPRINKLE WITH PEPPER. SAUTÉ IN OIL OVER MEDIUM HEAT UNTIL OPAQUE, ABOUT 6 MINUTES. DRAIN. COOK ASPARAGUS OR BROCCOLI UNTIL TENDER-CRISP; DRAIN AND ARRANGE IN BOTTOM OF BUTTERED CASSEROLE. PLACE CHICKEN ON TOP. MIX TOGETHER SOUP, MAYONNAISE, CURRY AND LEMON JUICE AND POUR OVER CHICKEN. SPRINKLE WITH CHEDDAR CHEESE AND BAKE, UNCOVERED, AT 350°F (180°C) FOR 30 TO 35 MINUTES. SERVES 6.

SOME COME TO THE "FOUNTAIN OF KNOWLEDGE" TO DRINK... I PREFER TO JUST GARGLE.

SAM'S BRANDIED CHICKEN

REALLY RICH AND DEFINITELY PARTY TIME!
SERVE WITH NOODLES OR RICE.

1	EGG, BEATEN	1
1/4 CUP	MILK	60 ML
4	BONELESS SKINLESS CHICKEN BREASTS, HALVED AND POUNDED INTO CUTLETS	4
2 CUPS	FINE BREAD CRUMBS	500 ML
1/4 TSP	POULTRY SEASONING	1 ML
1/4 TSP	SEASONED PEPPER	1 ML
1/4 TSP	SEASONED SALT	1 ML
3	CLOVES GARLIC, SMASHED	3
1/4 CUP	BUTTER	60 ML
1/4 CUP	OLIVE OIL	60 ML
6 TO 8	CHICKEN LIVERS, CHOPPED (OR 3 TO 4 SLICES COOKED HAM, DICED)	6 TO 8
1	CLOVE GARLIC, MINCED	1
1	MEDIUM ONION, CHOPPED	1
1 TBSP	BUTTER	15 ML
1 TBSP	OLIVE OIL	15 ML
1 LB	MUSHROOMS, SLICED	500 G
1/4 TO 1/3 CUP	BRANDY	60 TO 75 ML
2 TBSP	LIQUID BEEF OXO CONCENTRATE	30 ML
1 CUP	WHIPPING (35%) CREAM	250 ML

COMBINE EGG AND MILK AND DIP CUTLETS IN MIXTURE.
MIX BREAD CRUMBS WITH POULTRY SEASONING,
SEASONED PEPPER AND SALT. ROLL CUTLETS IN CRUMBS.
SAUTÉ SMASHED GARLIC IN BUTTER AND OLIVE OIL.

CONTINUED ON NEXT PAGE...

DISCARD GARLIC AND SAUTÉ CUTLETS UNTIL GOLDEN (ABOUT 4 MINUTES PER SIDE). KEEP WARM IN OVEN.

QUICKLY SAUTÉ CHICKEN LIVERS (OR HAM), MINCED GARLIC AND ONION IN BUTTER AND OIL. SET ASIDE. SAUTÉ MUSHROOMS AND ADD TO CHICKEN LIVER MIXTURE. KEEP WARM.

TRANSFER CUTLETS BACK TO A LARGE SKILLET OVER MEDIUM HEAT. POUR BRANDY OVER CHICKEN AND IGNITE. AFTER FLAMES DIE DOWN, ADD OXO AND CREAM, REDUCE HEAT AND COOK UNTIL SAUCE THICKENS. TRANSFER TO A 10-CUP (2.5 L) CASSEROLE DISH. TOP WITH ONION, MUSHROOM AND LIVER MIXTURE. SERVES 4 TO 6.

PEDIATRICIANS ARE DOCTORS OF LITTLE PATIENTS.

CHICKEN PARMESAN

GEPPETTO'S FAVORITE.

I CUP	BREAD CRUMBS	250 ML
3 TBSP	GRATED PARMESAN CHEESE	45 ML
2	BONELESS SKINLESS CHICKEN BREASTS, HALVED	2
3	EGGS, BEATEN	3
I	CAN (14 OZ/398 ML) TOMATO SAUCE	I
1/2 CUP	SHREDDED MOZZARELLA CHEESE	125 ML
1/4 CUP	GRATED PARMESAN CHEESE	60 ML

MIX BREAD CRUMBS AND 3 TBSP (45 ML) PARMESAN CHEESE TOGETHER. DIP CHICKEN PIECES IN EGGS, THEN IN CRUMB MIXTURE. FRY UNTIL GOLDEN BROWN. PUT PIECES IN BAKING DISH AND SPREAD TOMATO SAUCE OVER ALL. SPRINKLE WITH MOZZARELLA AND PARMESAN CHEESES. BAKE AT 350°F (180°C) FOR I HOUR. SERVES 4.

THE SECRET TO SUCCESS IS SINCERITY.
ONCE YOU CAN FAKE THAT, YOU'VE GOT IT MADE.

CHICKEN MANDALAY

3	BONELESS SKINLESS CHICKEN BREASTS	3
1/4 CUP	ALL-PURPOSE FLOUR	60 ML
5 TBSP	VEGETABLE OIL	75 ML
2 TSP	POWDERED CHICKEN BOUILLON	10 ML
2 TBSP	CORNSTARCH	30 ML
1 TBSP	BROWN SUGAR	15 ML
2 TO 3 TSP	CURRY POWDER	10 TO 15 ML
1/2 TSP	SALT	2 ML
2 TBSP	LEMON JUICE	30 ML
2 TBSP	SOY SAUCE	30 ML
1	MEDIUM ONION, CHOPPED	1
1	CAN (8 OZ/227 ML) WATER CHESTNUTS, DRAINED	1
1	CAN (10 OZ/284 ML) APRICOTS, WITH JUICE	1

CUT CHICKEN INTO LARGE PIECES, SHAKE IN FLOUR AND
BROWN IN OIL. SET IN A 10-CUP (2.5 L) CASSEROLE DISH.

DISSOLVE CHICKEN BOUILLON IN 1/2 CUP (125 ML) WATER.
DISSOLVE CORNSTARCH IN 1/4 CUP (60 ML) WATER. IN
A BOWL, COMBINE BOUILLON MIXTURE, CORNSTARCH
MIXTURE AND REMAINING INGREDIENTS. POUR OVER
CHICKEN, COVER AND BAKE AT 350°F (180°C) FOR 1 HOUR.
SERVES 6.

YUMMY CHICKEN

THE NAME SAYS IT ALL!

1/4 CUP	ALL-PURPOSE FLOUR	60 ML
2 TSP	SALT	10 ML
1/4 TSP	BLACK PEPPER	1 ML
PINCH	DRIED THYME	PINCH
1/4 CUP	MELTED BUTTER	60 ML
3 TO 4 LBS	CUT-UP CHICKEN	1.5 TO 2 KG
	BUTTER	
4	GREEN ONIONS, CHOPPED	4
1/2 CUP	SLICED MUSHROOMS	125 ML
2 TBSP	LEMON JUICE	30 ML
1 TSP	GRANULATED SUGAR	5 ML
1 TSP	SALT	5 ML
1/3 CUP	APPLE JUICE	75 ML

MIX FLOUR, SALT, PEPPER AND THYME IN A PLASTIC BAG. SHAKE CHICKEN IN FLOUR MIXTURE TO COAT WELL. MELT BUTTER IN A LARGE FRYING PAN AND BROWN CHICKEN. REMOVE CHICKEN TO A CASSEROLE. ADD GREEN ONIONS AND MUSHROOMS TO FRYING PAN. COVER AND SIMMER FOR 3 MINUTES. ADD TO CASSEROLE. COMBINE LEMON JUICE, SUGAR, SALT AND APPLE JUICE. POUR OVER CHICKEN AND BAKE AT 325°F (160°C) FOR 1 HOUR. SERVES 6.

NO ONE EVER DIED FROM SLEEPING IN AN UNMADE BED.
— ERMA BOMBECK

CRISPY SESAME CHICKEN

FORGET SHAKE 'N' BAKE — TRY THIS!

3 LBS	CUT UP CHICKEN	1.5 KG
	MAYONNAISE	
1 CUP	CORN FLAKES OR HONEY NUT CORN FLAKES, CRUSHED	250 ML
2 TBSP	SESAME SEEDS	30 ML
	SALT AND BLACK PEPPER TO TASTE	

COAT CHICKEN WITH MAYONNAISE. MIX CORN FLAKES, SESAME SEEDS, SALT AND PEPPER TOGETHER IN A SHALLOW DISH. ROLL CHICKEN IN MIXTURE UNTIL PIECES ARE WELL COATED. PLACE IN OVENPROOF DISH AND BAKE AT 350°F (180°C) FOR 1 TO 1½ HOURS. SERVES 6.

*A VERBAL CONTRACT ISN'T WORTH
THE PAPER IT'S WRITTEN ON.*

SWEET AND SPICY
CASHEW CHICKEN

*A DELICIOUS AND COLORFUL STIR-FRY. SERVE
OVER RICE ON A LARGE PLATTER OR TAKE
THE WOK RIGHT TO THE TABLE.*

<u>SAUCE</u>

1/2 CUP	KETCHUP	125 ML
4 TSP	SOY SAUCE	20 ML
1/2 TSP	SALT	2 ML
2 TBSP	WORCESTERSHIRE SAUCE	30 ML
3 TBSP	GRANULATED SUGAR	45 ML
1 1/2 TSP	SESAME OIL	7 ML
1/4 TSP	CAYENNE PEPPER	1 ML
1/2 CUP	CHICKEN BROTH	125 ML

<u>THE REST</u>

2 TBSP	CORNSTARCH	30 ML
1/2 TSP	GRANULATED SUGAR	2 ML
1/4 TSP	SALT	1 ML
3	BONELESS SKINLESS CHICKEN BREASTS, CUT INTO CUBES	3
1/4 CUP	VEGETABLE OIL	60 ML
2 TO 3 TBSP	MINCED GINGERROOT	30 TO 45 ML
1 TBSP	MINCED GARLIC	15 ML
1	SMALL ONION, CHOPPED	1
2	RED BELL PEPPERS, CUT IN STRIPS	2
2	CARROTS, THINLY SLICED ON DIAGONAL	2
2 CUPS	SNOW PEAS	500 ML
1 1/2 CUPS	CASHEWS	375 ML
	SPRINKLING OF SESAME SEEDS, TOASTED	

CONTINUED ON NEXT PAGE...

ARE YOU READY? COMBINE SAUCE INGREDIENTS AND SET ASIDE. IN A BOWL, COMBINE CORNSTARCH, SUGAR AND SALT. ADD CHICKEN AND TOSS. HEAT A WOK OR FRYING PAN TO HIGHEST HEAT. ADD OIL. HEAT TO HOT, NOT SMOKING. ADD CHICKEN, GINGER, GARLIC AND ONION. STIR UNTIL CHICKEN IS OPAQUE (ABOUT 1 MINUTE). ADD PEPPERS AND CARROTS. STIR 2 TO 3 MINUTES. ADD PEAS AND SAUCE. COOK UNTIL SAUCE COMES TO A BOIL. ADD CASHEWS AND SPRINKLE WITH SESAME SEEDS. SERVE IMMEDIATELY. SERVES 6.

HE WHO HESITATES IS INTERRUPTED.

CHICKEN ARTICHOKE CASSEROLE

I CUP	BUTTER OR MARGARINE	250 ML
$\frac{1}{2}$ CUP	ALL-PURPOSE FLOUR	125 ML
$3\frac{1}{2}$ CUPS	MILK	875 ML
$\frac{1}{4}$ TSP	CAYENNE PEPPER	I ML
I	CLOVE GARLIC, MINCED	I
4 OZ	SHARP (OLD) CHEDDAR CHEESE, SHREDDED	125 G
I	CAN (IO OZ/284 ML) BUTTON MUSHROOMS	I
I	WHOLE CHICKEN (4 TO 5 LBS/ 2 TO 2.5 KG), COOKED, SKINNED AND DEBONED	I
2	CANS (EACH I4 OZ/398 ML) ARTICHOKE HEARTS, HALVED	2
I CUP	BREAD CRUMBS OR RICE KRISPIES	250 ML
2 TBSP	MELTED BUTTER	30 ML

MELT BUTTER OR MARGARINE AND STIR IN FLOUR, MAKING A ROUX. ADD MILK AND STIR UNTIL THICK AND SMOOTH. ADD CAYENNE, GARLIC AND CHEESE. STIR UNTIL CHEESE MELTS AND MIXTURE BUBBLES. ADD MUSHROOMS. SLICE OR CUBE CHICKEN INTO BITE-SIZE PIECES AND ARRANGE IN 13- BY 9-INCH (33 BY 23 CM) CASSEROLE. TOP WITH ARTICHOKES AND SAUCE. MIX CRUMBS (OR RICE KRISPIES) AND BUTTER AND SPRINKLE OVER ALL. BAKE AT 350°F (180°C) FOR 30 MINUTES. SERVES 8.

CHICKEN CACCIATORE

SERVE OVER SPAGHETTI OR WITH RICE.

3	WHOLE CHICKEN BREASTS, SKINNED, BONED AND CUT INTO PIECES	3
	ALL-PURPOSE FLOUR	
	VEGETABLE OIL	
1	CAN (28 OZ/796 ML) TOMATOES	1
1/2 CUP	WHITE WINE	125 ML
2 TBSP	MINCED ONION	30 ML
1/8 TSP	GARLIC POWDER	0.5 ML
1/8 TSP	GROUND ALLSPICE	0.5 ML
1/4 TSP	BLACK PEPPER	1 ML
1 TSP	ITALIAN SEASONING	5 ML
1/4 TSP	PAPRIKA	1 ML
1 TSP	DRIED OREGANO	5 ML
2 TSP	SEASONED SALT	10 ML

DREDGE CHICKEN IN FLOUR AND FRY IN OIL AT HIGH HEAT UNTIL GOLDEN (ABOUT 3 MINUTES). DRAIN OFF OIL. ADD REMAINING INGREDIENTS TO CHICKEN AND SIMMER FOR 45 MINUTES. SERVES 6.

LEAD ME NOT INTO TEMPTATION — I CAN FIND IT BY MYSELF.

CHICKEN TETRAZZINI

8 OZ	NOODLES	250 G
I CUP	SLICED MUSHROOMS	250 ML
2 TBSP	BUTTER	30 ML
2 TBSP	ALL-PURPOSE FLOUR	30 ML
2 CUPS	CHICKEN BROTH	500 ML
	SALT AND BLACK PEPPER TO TASTE	
I TSP	DRIED BASIL	5 ML
I CUP	WHIPPING (35%) CREAM, HEATED	250 ML
1/3 CUP	SHERRY	75 ML
3 CUPS	SHREDDED COOKED CHICKEN	750 ML
1/2 CUP	BLANCHED, SLIVERED ALMONDS	125 ML
1/2 CUP	FRESH BREAD CRUMBS	125 ML
2 TBSP	BUTTER, MELTED	30 ML
1/2 CUP	GRATED PARMESAN CHEESE	125 ML

PREHEAT OVEN TO 325°F (160°C). BUTTER AN 8-CUP (2 L) OVAL CASSEROLE DISH. COOK NOODLES ACCORDING TO PACKAGE DIRECTIONS UNTIL JUST TENDER. DRAIN THOROUGHLY. SAUTÉ MUSHROOMS IN BUTTER. BLEND IN FLOUR. SLOWLY ADD CHICKEN BROTH AND COOK UNTIL SMOOTH. SEASON WITH SALT, PEPPER AND BASIL. REMOVE FROM HEAT AND GRADUALLY BLEND IN HOT CREAM AND SHERRY. COMBINE COOKED NOODLES AND HALF THE SAUCE. BLEND REST OF SAUCE WITH CHICKEN AND ALMONDS. PLACE NOODLE MIXTURE IN CASSEROLE AND TOP WITH CHICKEN MIXTURE. COMBINE BREAD CRUMBS AND MELTED BUTTER AND SPRINKLE OVER ALL. TOP WITH PARMESAN CHEESE. BAKE FOR 30 MINUTES OR UNTIL BUBBLING HOT AND BROWNED ON TOP. SERVES 6.

Mulligatawny Soup (page 137)

Seafood Kabobs (page 147)

Sweet and Spicy Cashew Chicken (page 156)

Ginger-Fried Beef (page 172)

CHICKEN POT PIE

THANKS FOR THE MEMORIES!

1/4 CUP	BUTTER	60 ML
1/4 CUP	ALL-PURPOSE FLOUR	60 ML
	SALT AND BLACK PEPPER TO TASTE	
2 TBSP	FINELY CHOPPED ONION	30 ML
3 CUPS	CHICKEN BROTH	750 ML
2	CARROTS, CHOPPED IN SMALL PIECES	2
2	CELERY STALKS, CHOPPED IN SMALL PIECES	2
2	POTATOES, CUBED IN SMALL PIECES	2
3 CUPS	SLICED MUSHROOMS	750 ML
2 TBSP	BUTTER	30 ML
1/2 CUP	PEAS	125 ML
3 CUPS	DICED COOKED CHICKEN	750 ML
	PASTRY TO COVER CASSEROLE, OR FROZEN PUFF PASTRY DOUGH	

MELT BUTTER IN A LARGE SAUCEPAN OVER MEDIUM HEAT. BLEND IN FLOUR, SALT, PEPPER AND ONION. GRADUALLY STIR IN CHICKEN BROTH. COOK, STIRRING CONSTANTLY, UNTIL SMOOTH AND THICKENED. ADD CARROTS, CELERY AND POTATOES. COOK UNTIL FORK TENDER. IN A SMALL FRYING PAN, COOK THE MUSHROOMS IN BUTTER. ADD MUSHROOMS, PEAS AND CHICKEN TO VEGETABLE MIXTURE. MIX WELL AND POUR INTO A 12-CUP (3 L) CASSEROLE DISH. COVER WITH ROLLED PASTRY AND SLASH (WATCH IT!) TO ALLOW STEAM TO ESCAPE. BAKE IN PREHEATED 400°F (200°C) OVEN FOR ABOUT 45 MINUTES OR UNTIL PASTRY IS GOLDEN. IF PASTRY BECOMES TOO BROWN, COVER LOOSELY WITH FOIL. SERVES 6.

WHIP-LASH CHICKEN

HOT AND SPICY — OOH-DA-LOLLY! SERVE WITH RICE.

1	LARGE ONION, THINLY SLICED AND SEPARATED INTO RINGS	1
1	GREEN BELL PEPPER, CUT INTO THIN STRIPS	1
1 CUP	SLICED MUSHROOMS	250 ML
2 TBSP	WATER	30 ML
2 TSP	DRIED OREGANO	10 ML
2 TSP	HOT PEPPER FLAKES	10 ML
1 TSP	GARLIC SALT	5 ML
$\frac{1}{2}$ TSP	HOT PEPPER SAUCE	2 ML
1	CAN (14 OZ/398 ML) TOMATOES, WITH JUICE	1
$\frac{2}{3}$ CUP	PEANUT BUTTER	150 ML
2 TSP	INSTANT CHICKEN BOUILLON	10 ML
3	BONELESS SKINLESS CHICKEN BREASTS, CUT INTO BITE-SIZE PIECES	3

IN A LARGE SAUCEPAN, COMBINE ONION, GREEN PEPPER, MUSHROOMS, WATER, OREGANO, HOT PEPPER FLAKES, GARLIC SALT AND HOT PEPPER SAUCE. COOK OVER MEDIUM HEAT, STIRRING FREQUENTLY UNTIL VEGGIES ARE TENDER-CRISP. IN A BLENDER OR FOOD PROCESSOR, COMBINE TOMATOES WITH JUICE, PEANUT BUTTER AND BOUILLON. PROCESS TILL SMOOTH. PLACE UNCOOKED CHICKEN IN A LARGE CASSEROLE. TOP WITH VEGGIE MIXTURE. POUR TOMATO MIXTURE OVER ALL. COVER AND BAKE AT 350°F (180°C) FOR 50 MINUTES. SERVES 8.

CHICKEN MEXICANA

CHA, CHA, CHA!

3 TBSP	OLIVE OIL	45 ML
4 LBS	BONELESS SKINLESS CHICKEN BREASTS, CUT INTO BITE-SIZE PIECES	2 KG
2 TBSP	BUTTER	30 ML
1	MEDIUM ONION, FINELY CHOPPED	1
1	GREEN BELL PEPPER, SEEDED AND CHOPPED	1
2	CLOVES GARLIC, MINCED	2
1	CAN (28 OZ/796 ML) TOMATOES	1
2	CANS (EACH 10 OZ/284 ML) BUTTON MUSHROOMS	2
1/4 CUP	CHOPPED FRESH PARSLEY	60 ML
1 TSP	GRANULATED SUGAR	5 ML
1 TSP	BLACK PEPPER	5 ML
1 TSP	CHILI POWDER	5 ML
1/2 TSP	DRIED OREGANO	2 ML
2 CUPS	CHICKEN BROTH	500 ML
1 TBSP	CORNSTARCH	15 ML
1/4 CUP	COLD WATER	60 ML

HEAT OIL IN A LARGE SKILLET AND SAUTÉ CHICKEN IN BATCHES, THEN REMOVE TO A LARGE BAKING DISH. MELT BUTTER IN SKILLET AND SAUTÉ ONION, GREEN PEPPER AND GARLIC. COMBINE TOMATOES, MUSHROOMS, PARSLEY, SUGAR, PEPPER, CHILI POWDER AND OREGANO, THEN ADD TO SAUTÉED MIXTURE. ADD BROTH. MIX CORNSTARCH WITH WATER AND ADD TO SAUCE MIXTURE. COOK FOR 1 MINUTE. POUR SAUCE OVER CHICKEN. COVER AND BAKE AT 325°F (160°C) FOR 1 HOUR. SERVES 10 TO 12.

CHICKEN ENCHILADAS

1/2 CUP	CHOPPED ONION	125 ML
2 TBSP	SALAD OIL	30 ML
2 CUPS	CHOPPED COOKED CHICKEN	500 ML
1	CAN (7 OZ/198 ML) GREEN CHILI SAUCE	1
1 CUP	SOUR CREAM	250 ML
1/4 TSP	SALT	1 ML
1 CUP	LIGHT CREAM	250 ML
1 CUP	CHICKEN STOCK	250 ML
	SALAD OIL	
15	SOFT CORN TORTILLAS	15
1 1/2 CUPS	SHREDDED CHEDDAR CHEESE	375 ML

SAUTÉ ONION IN OIL UNTIL TENDER. REMOVE FROM HEAT AND ADD CHICKEN, CHILI SAUCE, SOUR CREAM AND SALT. IN A SHALLOW DISH, COMBINE CREAM AND CHICKEN STOCK. IN A SKILLET, HEAT SALAD OIL AND DIP TORTILLAS IN HOT OIL FOR A FEW SECONDS ON EACH SIDE. DRAIN ON PAPER TOWELS AND THEN DIP INTO CREAM MIXTURE. REMOVE. SPREAD CHICKEN MIXTURE ON EACH TORTILLA, ROLL UP AND PLACE SEAM SIDE DOWN IN A SHALLOW, GREASED BAKING DISH. POUR REMAINING CREAM MIXTURE EVENLY OVER TORTILLAS AND TOP WITH CHEESE. BAKE AT 350°F (180°C) FOR 30 MINUTES. SERVE HOT. SERVES 6 TO 8.

CUISINE: ANY FOOD YOU CAN'T PRONOUNCE.

CHICKEN ENCHILADA CASSEROLE

THIS IS A MUST!

6	SMALL CORN TORTILLAS (OR 3 LARGE FLOUR TORTILLAS)	6
1	LARGE ONION, FINELY CHOPPED	1
2 TBSP	VEGETABLE OIL	30 ML
1	CAN (4 OZ/114 ML) GREEN CHILES, SEEDED AND FINELY CHOPPED	1
1	CAN (10 OZ/284 ML) CREAM OF MUSHROOM SOUP (REDUCED SODIUM)	1
2 CUPS	SHREDDED CHEDDAR CHEESE	500 ML
2 CUPS	SHREDDED MOZZARELLA CHEESE	500 ML
1 CUP	SALSA	250 ML
3 TO 4 CUPS	COOKED CHICKEN, CUT INTO LARGE BITE-SIZE PIECES	750 ML TO 1 L

CUT EACH TORTILLA INTO 6 PIECES. SAUTÉ ONION IN OIL. ADD CHILES, SOUP AND HALF THE CHEESES. COOK SLOWLY UNTIL CHEESE MELTS. LINE A BUTTERED 6-CUP (1.5 L) CASSEROLE DISH WITH HALF THE TORTILLA PIECES. COVER WITH $\frac{1}{2}$ CUP (125 ML) SALSA. LAYER WITH HALF THE CHICKEN, THEN HALF THE CHEESE SAUCE. REPEAT LAYERS. TOP WITH THE REMAINING CHEESES. BAKE AT 325°F (160°C) FOR 50 TO 60 MINUTES. LET STAND (OR SIT, IF YOU PREFER!) FOR 10 MINUTES. SERVES 6.

A MAN IN LOVE IS INCOMPLETE UNTIL HE'S MARRIED. THEN HE'S FINISHED!

ALMOND ORANGE PHEASANT (OR CORNISH HENS)

1	WILD PHEASANT (OR 2 CORNISH HENS)	1

MARINADE

1/2 TSP	DRIED TARRAGON	2 ML
1/2 TSP	POULTRY SEASONING	2 ML
1/2 TSP	BLACK PEPPER	2 ML
1 TSP	GROUND GINGER	5 ML
2 TSP	SALT	10 ML
2 TSP	GRATED ORANGE ZEST	10 ML
3 TBSP	VEGETABLE OIL	45 ML
2 TBSP	LIQUID HONEY	30 ML
1/4 CUP	CHOPPED GREEN ONION	60 ML
1/4 CUP	FINELY CHOPPED CELERY	60 ML
1/4 CUP	VINEGAR	60 ML
2 TBSP	LIME JUICE	30 ML
1 CUP	DRY WHITE WINE (ADD AN EXTRA GLASS FOR THE COOK)	250 ML
1	CAN (10 OZ/284 ML) MANDARIN ORANGE SEGMENTS (RESERVE JUICE)	1
1 CUP	JUICE FROM CANNED ORANGES (ADD ENOUGH WATER TO MAKE 1 CUP/250 ML)	250 ML

DRESSING

1/3 CUP	WILD OR WHITE RICE	75 ML
	STRAINED FRUIT AND VEGETABLE MIXTURE	
1/4 CUP	ALMONDS, SLIVERED AND TOASTED	60 ML

GARNISH

1	CAN (10 OZ/284 ML) MANDARIN ORANGE SEGMENTS	1
	CHOPPED FRESH PARSLEY	

CONTINUED ON NEXT PAGE...

COMBINE MARINADE INGREDIENTS IN A MEDIUM BOWL (NOT METAL). PLACE PHEASANT OR 2 CORNISH GAME HENS IN MARINADE, COVER AND REFRIGERATE OVERNIGHT. COOK RICE. REMOVE BIRD(S) FROM MARINADE. STRAIN MARINADE INTO SMALL BOWL, RESERVING FRUIT AND VEGETABLES FOR DRESSING.

COMBINE RICE, FRUIT, VEGETABLES AND ALMONDS. STUFF BIRD(S), SKEWER CAVITY CLOSED AND TIE LEGS TOGETHER. PLACE IN A SMALL ROASTING PAN, POUR RESERVED MARINADE OVER BIRD(S), COVER AND ROAST AT 375°F (190°C) FOR 1 HOUR OR UNTIL LEGS ARE TENDER. REMOVE COVER, BASTE AND INCREASE TEMPERATURE TO 400°F (200°C). COOK FOR 5 MORE MINUTES OR UNTIL GOLDEN. PLACE BIRD(S) ON PLATTER. ADD 2 TBSP (30 ML) CORNSTARCH DISSOLVED IN $1/4$ CUP (60 ML) OF COLD WATER TO REMAINING JUICES AND COOK UNTIL THICKENED. GARNISH WITH PARSLEY AND MANDARIN ORANGE SLICES. MAKE "SOCKS" FOR THE PHEASANT (OR HENS) OUT OF A BROWN PAPER BAG (THEY'RE OVERDRESSED IN WHITE!). YOU'VE DONE IT AGAIN, YOU CLEVER GOURMET! SERVES 2 — YOU DIDN'T WANT COMPANY ANYWAY.

THE TROUBLE WITH THE RAT RACE IS THAT EVEN IF YOU WIN, YOU'RE STILL A RAT.

DUCK BREASTS EN CASSEROLE

A PLEASANT CHANGE FROM THE
TRADITIONAL ROAST DUCK.

6	LARGE DUCK BREASTS	6
1/4 CUP	ALL-PURPOSE FLOUR	60 ML
1 1/2 TSP	SALT	7 ML
2 TSP	PAPRIKA	10 ML
1/4 CUP	BUTTER, MELTED	60 ML
1	CAN (10 OZ/284 ML) WHOLE MUSHROOMS, DRAINED (RESERVE LIQUID)	1
2	BEEF BOUILLON CUBES	2
1	CAN (14 OZ/398 ML) TOMATO SAUCE	1
1/2 CUP	CHOPPED GREEN BELL PEPPER	125 ML
1/4 CUP	CHOPPED CELERY	60 ML
1/4 CUP	CHOPPED ONION	60 ML
	DRY RED WINE (MAYBE)	

CUT EACH BREAST INTO 8 PIECES. SHAKE IN A BAG WITH
FLOUR, SALT AND PAPRIKA. USE ALL THE FLOUR MIXTURE
OR SAUCE WILL BE THIN. BROWN BREASTS IN BUTTER.
PLACE IN CASSEROLE. DISSOLVE BOUILLON CUBES IN
2 CUPS (500 ML) HOT WATER PLUS MUSHROOM LIQUID.
POUR OVER DUCK. ADD SCRAPINGS FROM BROWNING PAN.
BAKE AT 300°F (150°C) FOR 1 HOUR. BLEND TOMATO SAUCE,
GREEN PEPPER, CELERY, ONIONS AND MUSHROOMS. ADD
TO THE CASSEROLE AND STIR WELL. BAKE ANOTHER HOUR
OR MORE, STIRRING OCCASIONALLY. ADD MORE LIQUID IF
NECESSARY — HERE IT COMES — DRY RED WINE IS BEST.
SERVES 6.

BEEF EXTRAORDINAIRE WITH SAUCE DIANE

WHEN THE BOSS COMES TO DINNER...

4 LBS	BEEF TENDERLOIN	2 KG
12 OZ	MUSHROOMS, SLICED	375 G
1 1/2 CUPS	SLICED GREEN ONIONS	375 ML
1/2 CUP	BUTTER, MELTED	125 ML
2 TSP	DRY MUSTARD	10 ML
1 TBSP	LEMON JUICE	15 ML
1 TBSP	WORCESTERSHIRE SAUCE	15 ML
1 TSP	SALT	5 ML

PREHEAT OVEN TO 500°F (260°C). PLACE TENDERLOIN ON RACK IN PAN AND ROAST FOR 30 MINUTES. ADD 1/4 CUP (60 ML) WATER TO PAN TO STOP ANY SMOKING. USE A MEAT THERMOMETER; 30 MINUTES WILL COOK BEEF TO MEDIUM-RARE STAGE. WHILE MEAT IS COOKING, SAUTÉ THE MUSHROOMS AND GREEN ONIONS IN THE MELTED BUTTER WITH MUSTARD FOR 5 MINUTES. ADD REMAINING INGREDIENTS AND COOK AN ADDITIONAL 5 MINUTES. KEEP WARM. PLACE MEAT ON PLATTER. SERVE WITH SAUCE. SERVES 8.

NOTE: SERVE WITH TOMATOES FLORENTINE (PAGE 241). DID YOU GET THE RAISE?

I MAY RISE, BUT I REFUSE TO SHINE!

UNATTENDED ROAST BEEF

PARTY TIME! YOU NEVER NEED TO WORRY AGAIN
ABOUT OVER- OR UNDERCOOKING YOUR ROAST!

8 TO	ROLLED RIB ROAST OF BEEF,	4 TO
14 LBS	BONES REMOVED	7 KG
	SALT, PEPPER AND GARLIC POWDER	

REMOVE BEEF FROM REFRIGERATOR 1 HOUR BEFORE
COOKING. PREHEAT OVEN TO 500°F (260°C). SPRINKLE
ROAST LIBERALLY WITH SALT, PEPPER AND GARLIC POWDER.
PLACE ON A RACK IN A WARM ROASTING PAN. ROAST FOR
20 MINUTES AT 500°F (260°C), THEN TURN OVEN DOWN
TO LOWEST SETTING. LEAVE FOR 8 HOURS — AND DON'T
PEEK! TAPE OVEN DOOR SO YOU WON'T FORGET. BEFORE
SERVING, TURN OVEN TO 350°F (180°C) FOR 20 MINUTES.
GUARANTEED TO MELT IN YOUR MOUTH AND LIQUIDATE
YOUR BANK ACCOUNT. SERVES 30 TO 50.

IF AT FIRST YOU DO SUCCEED,
TRY TO HIDE YOUR ASTONISHMENT.

SUPER TENDER FLANK STEAK

*THIS TENDER, TASTY STEAK MAY BE SERVED HOT
ON FRENCH BREAD AND COLD THE NEXT DAY
FOR SANDWICHES.*

1	FLANK STEAK	1
1/3 CUP	VEGETABLE OIL	75 ML
1/3 CUP	RED WINE VINEGAR	75 ML
1/3 CUP	DARK SOY SAUCE	75 ML

SLASH EDGES OF STEAK SO THEY DON'T CURL UP UNDER
BROILER. COMBINE OIL, VINEGAR AND SOY SAUCE IN A
13- BY 9-INCH (33 BY 23 CM) GLASS CASSEROLE OR A LARGE
SEALABLE PLASTIC BAG. PUT IN STEAK, TURN OVER AND
MARINATE, COVERED, IN THE REFRIGERATOR OVERNIGHT,
TURNING ONCE OR TWICE BEFORE YOU GO TO BED.

TO COOK: REMOVE FROM MARINADE. PLACE ON BROILER
RACK CLOSE TO HEAT AND BROIL 4 MINUTES ON EACH
SIDE (BARBECUED IS EVEN BETTER; MEAT MUST BE PINK
ON INSIDE). PLACE ON CUTTING BOARD AND SLICE THINLY
ON THE DIAGONAL FROM NARROW END OF STEAK. BE
SURE TO SAVE PAN DRIPPINGS AND JUICE FOR BEEF DIP.
SERVES 4 TO 6.

*IF EVERYTHING IS COMING YOUR WAY,
YOU'RE IN THE WRONG LANE!*

GINGER-FRIED BEEF

SERVE WITH STEAMED RICE, OF COURSE.

1 LB	FLANK OR SIRLOIN STEAK	500 G
2	EGGS, BEATEN	2
3/4 CUP	CORNSTARCH	175 ML
1/2 CUP	WATER	125 ML
	VEGETABLE OIL	
2/3 CUP	SHREDDED CARROTS	150 ML
2 TBSP	CHOPPED GREEN ONIONS	30 ML
1/4 CUP	FINELY CHOPPED GINGERROOT	60 ML
4	CLOVES GARLIC, CHOPPED	4
3 TBSP	SOY SAUCE	45 ML
2 TBSP	WINE, RED OR WHITE	30 ML
2 TBSP	WHITE VINEGAR	30 ML
1 TBSP	SESAME OIL	15 ML
1/2 CUP	GRANULATED SUGAR	125 ML
PINCH	HOT PEPPER FLAKES	PINCH

SLICE PARTIALLY FROZEN STEAK ACROSS THE GRAIN
INTO NARROW STRIPS. MIX BEEF AND EGGS. DISSOLVE
CORNSTARCH IN WATER AND MIX WITH BEEF-EGG MIXTURE.
POUR 1 INCH (2.5 CM) OF OIL INTO WOK; HEAT TO BOILING
HOT BUT NOT SMOKING. ADD BEEF TO OIL, ONE-QUARTER
AT A TIME. SEPARATE WITH A FORK (OR CHOPSTICKS IF
YOU'RE TALENTED) AND COOK, STIRRING FREQUENTLY
UNTIL CRISPY. REMOVE, DRAIN AND SET ASIDE. (THIS MUCH
CAN BE DONE IN ADVANCE.) PUT 1 TBSP (15 ML) OIL IN
WOK. ADD CARROTS, ONION, GINGER AND GARLIC AND STIR
BRIEFLY OVER HIGH HEAT. ADD REMAINING INGREDIENTS
AND BRING TO A BOIL. ADD BEEF; MIX WELL. SERVES 4.

SIMPLY SAUERBRATEN

TENDER BEEF AND GREAT GRAVY!

1½ LBS	ROUND STEAK	750 G
2 TBSP	VEGETABLE OIL	30 ML
1	ENVELOPE (1 OZ/30 G) BROWN GRAVY MIX	1
2 CUPS	WATER	500 ML
4½ TSP	DRIED MINCED ONION	22 ML
1 TBSP	BROWN SUGAR	15 ML
2 TBSP	RED WINE VINEGAR	30 ML
1 TSP	WORCESTERSHIRE SAUCE	5 ML
¼ TSP	GROUND GINGER	1 ML
½ TSP	SALT	2 ML
	FRESHLY GROUND BLACK PEPPER TO TASTE	
1	BAY LEAF	1
	HOT BUTTERED NOODLES	

TRIM STEAK AND CUT INTO 1-INCH (2.5 CM) CUBES. BROWN IN HOT OIL. REMOVE FROM SKILLET WITH SLOTTED SPOON AND PLACE IN 6-CUP (1.5 L) CASSEROLE DISH. ADD GRAVY MIX AND WATER TO SKILLET AND BRING TO A BOIL, STIRRING CONSTANTLY. STIR IN ONION, SUGAR, VINEGAR, WORCESTERSHIRE SAUCE, GINGER, SALT, PEPPER AND BAY LEAF. POUR OVER MEAT. COVER AND BAKE AT 325°F (160°C) FOR 1½ HOURS. REMOVE BAY LEAF AND SERVE SAUERBRATEN PIPING HOT OVER NOODLES. SPRINKLE WITH PARSLEY. SERVES 6.

BEEF-ON-A-STICK

2 TO 3 LBS	ROUND OR SIRLOIN STEAK	1 TO 1.5 KG
1/2 CUP	VEGETABLE OIL	125 ML
1/2 CUP	SOY SAUCE	125 ML
1/2 CUP	GRANULATED SUGAR	125 ML

SLICE STEAK INTO 1/4-INCH (0.5 CM) STRIPS. IT IS EASIER TO DO THIS WHILE MEAT IS SLIGHTLY FROZEN. MARINATE IN OIL, SOY SAUCE AND SUGAR MIXTURE, COVERED IN THE REFRIGERATOR, FOR 2 TO 3 HOURS. TURN MEAT TO COAT WELL DURING THIS TIME. THREAD MEAT ON WOODEN SKEWERS. BARBECUE OR BROIL FOR ABOUT 5 MINUTES. SERVES 6 TO 8.

SERVING COFFEE ON AN AIRCRAFT CAUSES TURBULENCE!

STEAK AND MUSHROOM KABOBS

BARBECUE OR BROIL. MARVELOUS MARINADE!

1/3 CUP	RED WINE	75 ML
1/2 CUP	VEGETABLE OIL	125 ML
2 TO 3	CLOVES GARLIC, MINCED (OR 1/2 TSP/2 ML GARLIC POWDER)	2 TO 3
1/2 TSP	DRIED MARJORAM	2 ML
1/2 TSP	DRIED ROSEMARY	2 ML
1/2 TSP	DRIED BASIL	2 ML
1/2 TSP	DRIED OREGANO	2 ML
1 1/2 TSP	SALT	7 ML
2 TBSP	KETCHUP	30 ML
1 TBSP	VINEGAR	15 ML
1 TSP	WORCESTERSHIRE SAUCE	5 ML
3 LBS	SIRLOIN STEAK, CUT INTO 2-INCH (5 CM) CUBES	1.5 KG
2 CUPS	LARGE MUSHROOMS	500 ML

IN A LARGE, NON-METAL BOWL, COMBINE ALL INGREDIENTS, ADDING STEAK AND MUSHROOMS LAST. STIR TO COAT ALL. COVER TIGHTLY AND LET STAND FOR AT LEAST 3 HOURS OR OVERNIGHT IN REFRIGERATOR. TURN ONCE OR TWICE. DRAIN.

PLACE MEAT AND MUSHROOMS IN SERVING DISHES AND LET YOUR GUESTS MAKE THEIR OWN KABOBS. IF DESIRED FOR VARIETY, A SEPARATE PLATTER CAN BE ARRANGED WITH CHUNKS OF GREEN PEPPER, PINEAPPLE, ONION AND WHOLE CHERRY TOMATOES. BARBECUE OR BROIL UNTIL MEAT IS COOKED TO DESIRED DONENESS. SERVES 6 TO 8.

SHORTCUT STROGANOFF

THIS HAS TO BE GOOD — IT'S GOT WINE IN IT!

2 LBS	STEWING BEEF	1 KG
	ALL-PURPOSE FLOUR	
	SALT, PEPPER AND GARLIC POWDER TO TASTE	
2 TBSP	VEGETABLE OIL	30 ML
1	CAN (10 OZ/284 ML) CREAM OF MUSHROOM SOUP (REDUCED SODIUM)	1
1/2 CUP	DRY WHITE WINE	125 ML
1	MEDIUM ONION, CHOPPED	1
1	CAN (10 OZ/284 ML) SLICED MUSHROOMS	1

DREDGE BEEF IN SEASONED FLOUR AND BROWN IN OIL. MIX SOUP, WINE, ONION AND MUSHROOMS IN A CASSEROLE. ADD BROWNED BEEF. COVER WITH A TIGHT-FITTING LID AND BAKE AT 300°F (150°C) FOR 3 TO 4 HOURS. SERVE OVER RICE OR NOODLES. CAESAR SALAD IS GREAT WITH THIS DINNER. SERVES 4 TO 6.

IF AT FIRST YOU DON'T SUCCEED, LOWER YOUR STANDARDS.

FAMILY FAVORITE MEATLOAF

WE ARE AMAZED AT HOW OFTEN WE ARE ASKED FOR GOOD OLD MEATLOAF. HERE'S OUR FAVORITE. SERVE WITH BAKED POTATOES AND A GREEN VEGETABLE.

I LB	LEAN GROUND BEEF	500 G
I	MEDIUM ONION, CHOPPED	I
1/2 CUP	MILK	125 ML
I	EGG, BEATEN	I
8	CRUSHED SODA CRACKERS	8
	SALT AND BLACK PEPPER TO TASTE	

SAUCE

1/4 CUP	KETCHUP	60 ML
1/4 CUP	WATER	60 ML
I TSP	DRY MUSTARD	5 ML
1/2 CUP	BROWN SUGAR	125 ML

COMBINE GROUND BEEF, ONION, MILK, EGG, CRACKERS, SALT AND PEPPER AND MIX WELL. PLACE IN A LARGE LOAF PAN AND MAKE A GROOVE DOWN THE CENTER OF LOAF. IN A BOWL, COMBINE KETCHUP, WATER, MUSTARD AND BROWN SUGAR. POUR OVER MEAT AND BAKE AT 350°F (180°C) FOR I HOUR; DRAIN. SERVES 4 TO 6.

MAD ABOUT CABBAGE ROLLS

THE WINE IN THE INGREDIENTS LIST ISN'T FOR THE CABBAGE ROLLS, IT'S FOR THE COOK — YOU'LL NEED IT!

2 CUPS	LONG-GRAIN RICE, UNCOOKED	500 ML
2 LBS	LEAN GROUND BEEF	1 KG
1 LB	GROUND PORK	500 G
1	LARGE ONION, CHOPPED	1
1 TSP	SALT	5 ML
1 TSP	BLACK PEPPER	5 ML
	GARLIC POWDER TO TASTE	
2	LARGE GREEN CABBAGES	2
2	CANS (EACH 48 OZ/1.36 L) TOMATO JUICE OR TOMATOES	2
2	LARGE GLASSES WINE	750 ML

COOK RICE ACCORDING TO PACKAGE DIRECTIONS UNTIL FAIRLY DRY. MIX GROUND BEEF, PORK AND ONION TOGETHER. ADD SALT, PEPPER AND GARLIC POWDER TO THE COOKED RICE, MIX WELL AND ADD TO MEAT MIXTURE. CUT OUT CORE FROM CABBAGES AND BOIL WHOLE IN RAPIDLY BOILING WATER. BOIL UNTIL JUST TENDER AND OUTER LEAVES START TO FALL. DRAIN AND PEEL OFF LEAVES, THEN DRY ON PAPER TOWELS. CUT OUT THICK, CORE-LIKE STEM FROM LEAVES. PLACE 1 TO 2 TBSP (15 TO 30 ML) OF MEAT AND RICE MIXTURE ON CABBAGE LEAF AND ROLL TIGHTLY. LINE THE BOTTOM OF CASSEROLE DISHES WITH ANY DISCARDED LEAVES OR CORES.

PLACE CABBAGE ROLLS CLOSE TOGETHER IN CASSEROLE DISHES, SEAM SIDE DOWN, AND POUR TOMATO JUICE

CONTINUED ON NEXT PAGE...

OVER TOP. COVER AND BAKE AT 325°F (160°C) FOR 2 HOURS. FREEZE THE EXTRAS AFTER COOKING. WHEN THAWED, REHEAT IN 325°F (160°C) OVEN UNTIL HOT. YOU MAY WANT TO ADD MORE TOMATO JUICE. MAKES ABOUT 40 ROLLS.

PEOPLE WHO NEVER PLAY GOLF LIE ABOUT OTHER THINGS.

CABBAGE ROLL CASSEROLE

A FAST ALTERNATIVE FOR CABBAGE ROLLS!

1½ LBS	GROUND BEEF	750 G
2	MEDIUM ONIONS, CHOPPED	2
1	CLOVE GARLIC, MINCED	1
1 TSP	SALT	5 ML
¼ TSP	BLACK PEPPER	1 ML
1	CAN (14 OZ/398 ML) TOMATO SAUCE	1
1	CAN (14 OZ/398 ML) WATER	1
½ CUP	UNCOOKED LONG-GRAIN RICE	125 ML
4 CUPS	SHREDDED CABBAGE	1 L
	SOUR CREAM	

BROWN BEEF WITH ONIONS. ADD GARLIC, SALT, PEPPER, TOMATO SAUCE AND WATER. BRING TO A BOIL AND STIR IN RICE. COVER AND SIMMER FOR 20 MINUTES. PLACE HALF THE CABBAGE IN A GREASED BAKING DISH; COVER WITH HALF THE RICE MIXTURE. REPEAT LAYERS. COVER AND BAKE IN 350°F (180°C) OVEN FOR 1 HOUR. SERVE WITH SOUR CREAM. MAY BE REFRIGERATED BEFORE BAKING. SERVES 6.

TACO PIE

I LB	GROUND BEEF	500 G
1/2 CUP	CHOPPED ONION	125 ML
I	PACKAGE (1 1/4 OZ/33 G) TACO SEASONING	I
I	CAN (4 OZ/114 ML) GREEN CHILES, CHOPPED	I
1 1/4 CUPS	MILK	300 ML
3/4 CUP	BISCUIT MIX	175 ML
3	EGGS	3
2	TOMATOES, SLICED	2
I CUP	SHREDDED MOZZARELLA OR CHEDDAR CHEESE	250 ML
	SALSA	
	SHREDDED LETTUCE, SOUR CREAM, AVOCADOS OR OLIVES	

BROWN BEEF AND ONION. DRAIN. STIR IN TACO SEASONING. SPREAD ON BOTTOM OF 10-INCH (25 CM) PIE PLATE. SPRINKLE WITH CHILES. IN BLENDER, BEAT MILK, BISCUIT MIX AND EGGS UNTIL SMOOTH. POUR OVER MEAT MIXTURE. BAKE FOR 25 MINUTES AT 400°F (200°C). TOP WITH TOMATO SLICES. SPRINKLE WITH CHEESE. BAKE FOR 5 MINUTES MORE OR UNTIL CHEESE MELTS. CUT IN WEDGES AND SERVE WITH SALSA AND TOPPINGS. SERVES 6.

MEN SHOULD COME WITH DIRECTIONS.

BURRITOS

*GREAT FOR HUNGRY KIDS! NUKE 'EM
WHEN YOU NEED 'EM.*

2 LBS	LEAN GROUND BEEF	1 KG
1	MEDIUM ONION, CHOPPED	1
2 TBSP	TACO SEASONING	30 ML
1/4 TSP	BLACK PEPPER	1 ML
1/4 TSP	DRIED OREGANO	1 ML
2 TBSP	CHOPPED FRESH PARSLEY	30 ML
1 CUP	SOUR CREAM (FAT-FREE IS FINE)	250 ML
2 LBS	MONTEREY JACK CHEESE, SHREDDED	1 KG
1 CUP	MEDIUM TACO SAUCE	250 ML
20	FLOUR TORTILLA SHELLS	20

IN A LARGE FRYING PAN, BROWN GROUND BEEF AND
ONIONS. ADD TACO SEASONING, PEPPER, OREGANO,
PARSLEY AND SOUR CREAM. ADD HALF THE CHEESE AND
HALF THE TACO SAUCE, MIXING WELL. PLACE 2 TBSP
(30 ML) OR MORE OF BEEF MIXTURE ON EACH TORTILLA
SHELL AND ROLL UP. PLACE SEAM SIDE DOWN IN 13- BY
9-INCH (33 BY 23 CM) CASSEROLE. TOP WITH REMAINING
CHEESE AND TACO SAUCE. BAKE AT 350°F (180°C) FOR
15 MINUTES, OR UNTIL CHEESE MELTS AND IS HEATED
THROUGH. IF YOU WANT TO MAKE INDIVIDUAL BURRITOS,
USE ALL THE CHEESE AND TACO SAUCE, THEN WRAP EACH
BURRITO IN PLASTIC AND FREEZE. MAKES 20 BURRITOS.

LIVER STIR-FRY

A SURE-FIRE STIR-FRYER.

1 LB	CALF'S LIVER	500 G
1 TSP	CORNSTARCH	5 ML
1	CLOVE GARLIC, MINCED	1
1 TBSP	BRANDY (OPTIONAL)	15 ML
2 TBSP	VEGETABLE OIL	30 ML
1	MEDIUM ONION, THINLY SLICED	1
2 CUPS	MUSHROOMS, THINLY SLICED	500 ML
4	GREEN ONIONS, SLICED	4
1 TBSP	SOY SAUCE	15 ML

SLICE LIVER INTO THIN STRIPS. MIX WITH CORNSTARCH, GARLIC AND BRANDY (IF USING). BROWN QUICKLY IN HOT OIL. ADD ONIONS AND MUSHROOMS. STIR-FRY UNTIL LIMP (NOT YOU, THE FOOD). ADD GREEN ONIONS AND SOY SAUCE. COOK AND STIR FOR 2 TO 3 MINUTES. SERVES 4.

A WOMAN'S PLACE IS IN THE MALL!

VEAL SCALOPPINI AND MUSHROOMS

SERVE WITH BUTTERED NOODLES AND ARTICHOKE AND ZUCCHINI SALAD (PAGE 94).

1 1/2 LBS	VEAL SCALOPPINI	750 G
1/4 CUP	ALL-PURPOSE FLOUR	60 ML
1/2 TSP	SALT	2 ML
1/4 CUP	BUTTER	60 ML
1	CLOVE GARLIC, MINCED	1
3 CUPS	SLICED MUSHROOMS	750 ML
3 TBSP	LEMON JUICE	45 ML
1/4 CUP	CHICKEN BROTH	60 ML
1/4 CUP	DRY WHITE WINE (VERMOUTH IS FINE)	60 ML

CUT VEAL INTO SERVING-SIZE PIECES. MIX FLOUR AND SALT TOGETHER IN A BAG AND SHAKE WITH VEAL TO COAT. SAUTÉ IN BUTTER. REMOVE MEAT AND SET ASIDE. SAUTÉ GARLIC AND MUSHROOMS; ADD LEMON JUICE, CHICKEN BROTH AND WINE. ADD VEAL, COVER AND SIMMER OVER MEDIUM HEAT FOR 20 MINUTES. SERVES 4 TO 6.

THE ONLY PROBLEM WITH BUYING A BOOK ON AMNESIA IS THAT YOU ARE LIKELY TO FORGET WHERE YOU PUT IT!

TOMATO CANTONESE PORK

SERVE THIS TO YOUR FAMILY WITH RICE AND STIR-FRIED
BROCCOLI OR ASPARAGUS (PORK IN MUSHROOM SOUP
DOES GET TEDIOUS!)

12	BONELESS PORK CHOPS, FAT REMOVED	12
1/4 CUP	MILK	60 ML
1/4 CUP	FINE BREAD CRUMBS	60 ML
1/4 CUP	ALL-PURPOSE FLOUR	60 ML
	SALT AND BLACK PEPPER TO TASTE	
1/4 CUP	VEGETABLE OIL	60 ML

SAUCE

1	MEDIUM ONION	1
1 TBSP	VEGETABLE OIL	15 ML
1 TBSP	CORNSTARCH	15 ML
1/4 CUP	COLD WATER	60 ML
1	CAN (14 OZ/398 ML) TOMATOES, QUARTERED, WITH JUICE	1
2 TBSP	KETCHUP	30 ML
1 TBSP	HP SAUCE	15 ML
1 TO 2 TBSP	LIQUID HONEY OR BROWN SUGAR	15 TO 30 ML

DIP CHOPS INTO MILK, THEN INTO MIXTURE OF BREAD
CRUMBS, FLOUR, SALT AND PEPPER. FRY IN OIL OVER
MEDIUM HEAT UNTIL CHOPS ARE BROWNED. DRAIN AND
SET IN SHALLOW CASSEROLE.

SAUCE: CUT ONION IN HALF LENGTHWISE AND SLICE
FINELY TO FORM HALF RINGS. BROWN IN OIL. COMBINE
CORNSTARCH AND COLD WATER. ADD TOMATOES,

CONTINUED ON NEXT PAGE...

CORNSTARCH MIXTURE AND REMAINING INGREDIENTS TO
ONIONS AND BRING TO A BOIL. POUR OVER PORK, COVER
AND BAKE AT 300°F (150°C) FOR 30 MINUTES. SERVES 6.

HAM BAKED IN BEER

*SERVE WITH YAMMY APPLES (PAGE 247). YOUR
FAMILY WILL WONDER WHERE THE COMPANY IS!*

5 LB	HAM, BONE-IN	2.5 KG
I	CAN (12 OZ/341 ML) GINGER ALE	I
	WHOLE CLOVES	
I CUP	LIGHT (FANCY) MOLASSES	250 ML
2 TSP	DRY MUSTARD	10 ML
I TSP	BLACK PEPPER	5 ML
I CUP	BEER	250 ML

PREHEAT OVEN TO 325°F (160°C). USING A SHARP KNIFE,
REMOVE SKIN FROM HAM. SCORE FAT DIAGONALLY IN
DIAMOND DESIGN. SOAK HAM IN GINGER ALE FOR AT LEAST
2 HOURS TO REMOVE EXCESS SALT. DRAIN. STUD TOP
OF HAM WITH CLOVES. PLACE HAM IN MIDDLE OF A LARGE
PIECE OF FOIL IN A SHALLOW ROASTING PAN.

COMBINE MOLASSES, MUSTARD, PEPPER AND BEER.
POUR MARINADE OVER HAM, THEN COVER COMPLETELY
WITH FOIL SO JUICES DON'T ESCAPE. BAKE FOR
20 MINUTES PER POUND (500 G). SERVES 10 TO 12.

HOLY HAM LOAF WITH MARVELOUS MUSTARD SAUCE

THIS IS THE DINNER WE ALWAYS LOOK FORWARD TO WHEN VISITING GRANDMA!

1/3 CUP	BROWN SUGAR	75 ML
1	CAN (14 OZ/398 ML) CRUSHED PINEAPPLE, WELL DRAINED	398 ML
1 LB	LEAN GROUND HAM (LEAN COTTAGE ROLL)	500 G
1 LB	LEAN GROUND PORK	500 G
1 CUP	BREAD CRUMBS	250 ML
1/4 TSP	BLACK PEPPER	1 ML
2	EGGS, BEATEN	2
1 CUP	MILK	250 ML

MUSTARD SAUCE

1 CUP	BROWN SUGAR	250 ML
2 TBSP	DRY MUSTARD	30 ML
2/3 CUP	VINEGAR	150 ML
2	EGGS, WELL BEATEN	2

LINE A LOAF PAN WITH FOIL. MIX BROWN SUGAR AND PINEAPPLE TOGETHER AND POUR INTO PAN. COMBINE HAM, PORK, BREAD CRUMBS, PEPPER, EGGS AND MILK. PRESS DOWN ON PINEAPPLE. BAKE AT 375°F (190°C) FOR 1 1/4 HOURS.

WHILE LOAF IS BAKING, COMBINE INGREDIENTS FOR SAUCE. COOK SLOWLY UNTIL THICKENED. INVERT HAM LOAF ONTO PLATTER AND SERVE WITH MUSTARD SAUCE. FREEZES WELL. SERVES 6.

CASHEW PORK TENDERLOIN

SHORTCUT GOURMET. YOU SHOULD ALSO TRY THIS
RECIPE USING BONELESS SKINLESS CHICKEN BREASTS.

2 LBS	PORK TENDERLOIN	1 KG
1/4 CUP	ALL-PURPOSE FLOUR, SEASONED WITH SALT AND PEPPER	60 ML
1/4 CUP	BUTTER OR MARGARINE, DIVIDED	60 ML
3 CUPS	SLICED MUSHROOMS	750 ML
2	CANS (EACH 10 OZ/284 ML) MUSHROOM SOUP (REDUCED SODIUM)	2
	JUICE OF 1 LEMON	
1/2 CUP	WHITE WINE	125 ML
1/2 TSP	DRIED THYME	2 ML
1/2 TSP	FRESHLY GROUND BLACK PEPPER	2 ML
1 CUP	COARSELY CHOPPED CASHEWS	250 ML

CUT PORK ACROSS THE GRAIN INTO 1-INCH (2.5 CM) THICK
MEDALLIONS AND POUND SLIGHTLY WITH A MALLET. YOU
HAVE JUST FRENCHED THE PORK, YOU GOURMET COOK, YOU.

PREHEAT OVEN TO 325°F (160°C). IN A PLASTIC BAG,
SHAKE SEASONED FLOUR WITH PIECES OF PORK TO
LIGHTLY COAT. IN A LARGE FRYING PAN, HEAT 2 TBSP
(30 ML) OF THE BUTTER AND LIGHTLY BROWN THE
MEDALLIONS. REMOVE TO AN OVENPROOF BAKING DISH.
ADD REMAINING BUTTER TO PAN AND SAUTÉ MUSHROOMS
UNTIL GOLDEN. ADD MUSHROOM SOUP, LEMON JUICE,
WINE, THYME AND PEPPER AND BLEND CAREFULLY; POUR
OVER PORK. BAKE FOR 30 MINUTES, ADDING CASHEWS
JUST BEFORE SERVING. SERVES 6.

NOTE: MAKES LOTS OF GRAVY - SERVE WITH TINY
ROASTED POTATOES OR BROAD NOODLES.

BARBECUED PORK ROAST

A BACKYARD BONANZA!

4 TO 5 LB	BONED AND ROLLED LOIN PORK ROAST	2 TO 2.5 KG
I	CLOVE GARLIC	I
2 TSP	FENNEL SEEDS	IO ML
2 TSP	DILL SEEDS	IO ML
2 TBSP	BROWN SUGAR	30 ML
I TSP	DRIED THYME	5 ML
I TSP	SEASONING SALT	5 ML
I TSP	BLACK PEPPER	5 ML
1½ CUPS	FINELY CHOPPED FRESH PARSLEY	375 ML
I	CAN (I4 OZ/398 ML) APRICOT HALVES	I
2 TBSP	SOY SAUCE	30 ML
2 TBSP	VEGETABLE OIL	30 ML

UNTIE ROAST; OPEN OUT FLAT WITH FAT SIDE DOWN. CUT TWO OR THREE LENGTHWISE SLASHES ½ INCH (I CM) DEEP ALONG THE THICKEST PART. COMBINE GARLIC, FENNEL, DILL, SUGAR, THYME, SALT AND PEPPER. RUB MIXTURE INTO PORK SURFACE AND INTO SLASHES. COVER INSIDE OF ROAST WITH PARSLEY. ROLL INTO ORIGINAL SHAPE AND TIE SECURELY.

BUILD A MEDIUM FIRE IN BARBECUE OR SET ELECTRIC OR GAS BARBECUE TO MEDIUM. INSERT SPIT OF ROTISSERIE LENGTHWISE THROUGH CENTER OF ROAST. BALANCE AND SECURE FIRMLY WITH PRONGS. INSERT MEAT THERMOMETER IN CENTER OF MEAT, NOT TOUCHING SPIT OR FAT. PLACE SPIT WITH ROAST 8 TO IO INCHES (20 TO

CONTINUED ON NEXT PAGE...

25 CM) FROM HEAT. PLACE FOIL DRIP PAN UNDER ROAST.
COOK FOR 30 TO 35 MINUTES PER POUND (500 G) OR
UNTIL THERMOMETER READS 170°F (77°C).

DRAIN SYRUP FROM APRICOTS INTO BOWL, RESERVE
APRICOTS. BLEND SOY SAUCE AND OIL INTO SYRUP. BASTE
ROAST FREQUENTLY WITH APRICOT SYRUP MIXTURE
DURING LAST HALF-HOUR OF ROASTING. LET ROAST REST
FOR 15 MINUTES BEFORE CARVING. SERVE WITH APRICOT
HALVES. SERVES 10 TO 12.

GREEK RIBS

*DON'T ASK! JUST MAKE THEM. SERVE WITH RICE
AND ROMAINE WITH ORANGES AND PECANS (PAGE 98).
YOUR COMPANY WILL BE THRILLED.*

PORK BACK RIBS
FRESHLY SQUEEZED LEMON JUICE
SEASONING SALT
GARLIC SALT
DRIED TARRAGON OR OREGANO

REMOVE SKIN FROM UNDERSIDE OF RIBS. PLACE ON
BROILER PAN AND BROIL ON BOTH SIDES TO REMOVE
EXCESS FAT. SQUEEZE LEMON JUICE LIBERALLY OVER RIBS
AND THEN SPRINKLE THE SEASONINGS TO YOUR HEART'S
CONTENT. BAKE AT 350°F (180°C) FOR 30 TO 40 MINUTES.
SERVES AS MANY AS YOU WANT IT TO.

— NOODLE MAKER'S CHOP SUEY —

ANOTHER GREAT WAY TO CELEBRATE THE FRESH ASPARAGUS SEASON! FROM THE NOODLE MAKER'S RESTAURANT IN VANCOUVER.

12 OZ	PORK TENDERLOIN OR ANY OTHER TENDER CUT OF PORK, SLICED $\frac{1}{8}$ INCH (3 MM) THICK ACROSS THE GRAIN (EASIEST TO DO IF FROZEN AND THAWED TO CRYSTAL STAGE)	375 G
3 TO 4	SLICES PEELED GINGERROOT	3 TO 4
1 TBSP	VEGETABLE OIL	15 ML
$1\frac{1}{2}$ LBS	ASPARAGUS, CUT INTO 2-INCH (5 CM) LENGTHS DISCARDING BOTTOM 2 INCHES (5 CM) OF STEM	750 G
1	SMALL ONION, CUT IN HALF LENGTHWISE AND FINELY SLICED TO FORM $\frac{1}{2}$-INCH (1 CM) RINGS	1
2 TSP	RYE, SCOTCH OR GIN	10 ML
$\frac{1}{2}$ CUP	WATER	125 ML
8 OZ	SMALL WHOLE MUSHROOMS (OR CANNED BUTTONS)	250 G
1 TSP	SALT	5 ML
PINCH	BLACK PEPPER	PINCH
1 TSP	SOY SAUCE	5 ML
$\frac{1}{4}$ CUP	COLD WATER	60 ML
2 TSP	CORNSTARCH	10 ML
$\frac{1}{4}$ TSP	VEGETABLE OIL	1 ML

STIR-FRY PORK AND GINGER IN OIL OVER HIGH HEAT. ADD ASPARAGUS AND ONIONS AND STIR-FRY UNTIL ONIONS START TO TURN COLOR. ADD RYE, THEN WATER. ADD MUSHROOMS, SALT AND PEPPER. COVER FOR 3 MINUTES.

CONTINUED ON NEXT PAGE...

(ASPARAGUS SHOULD STILL BE CRISP.) ADD SOY SAUCE. MIX COLD WATER AND CORNSTARCH TOGETHER. ADD SLOWLY TO VEGETABLES, STIRRING CONSTANTLY UNTIL GRAVY THICKENS. ADD 1/4 TSP (1 ML) OIL AND STIR. THIS WILL GIVE THE GRAVY A GLAZED APPEARANCE. SERVE IMMEDIATELY WITH RICE. SERVES 6.

THERE MUST BE MORE TO LIFE THAN HAVING EVERYTHING.
— MAURICE SENDAK

SPUNKY ORANGE RIBS

4 LBS	PORK BACK RIBS	2 KG
2/3 CUP	FROZEN ORANGE JUICE CONCENTRATE (THAWED)	150 ML
1 1/2 TSP	WORCESTERSHIRE SAUCE	7ML
1/2 TSP	GARLIC SALT	2 ML
PINCH	BLACK PEPPER	PINCH

PLACE RIBS, MEATY SIDE DOWN, IN SHALLOW ROASTING PAN. ROAST AT 450°F (230°C) FOR 15 MINUTES. DRAIN OFF FAT. TURN RIBS OVER AND ROAST ANOTHER 15 MINUTES. DRAIN AGAIN. COMBINE JUICE, WORCESTERSHIRE SAUCE, GARLIC AND PEPPER. BRUSH ON RIBS. REDUCE OVEN TO 350°F (180°C). ROAST, COVERED, FOR 1 1/2 HOURS OR UNTIL TENDER. BASTE WITH SAUCE OCCASIONALLY. SERVES 4 TO 6.

PORK DUMPLINGS

TAKE AN AFTERNOON AND MAKE A BUNCH AND
FREEZE. THESE ARE A CHINESE APPETIZER.

2 LBS	LEAN GROUND PORK	1 KG
1/2 CUP	FINELY CHOPPED MUSHROOMS	125 ML
1/3 CUP	FINELY CHOPPED GREEN ONIONS	75 ML
1/4 CUP	FINELY CHOPPED CELERY	60 ML
1/4 TSP	GROUND GINGER	1 ML
2 TBSP	CORNSTARCH	30 ML
3 TBSP	SOY SAUCE	45 ML
1	EGG, SEPARATED	1
2 TBSP	WATER	30 ML
1	PACKAGE WONTON WRAPPERS (SIZES VARY)	1
2 TBSP	SALAD OIL	30 ML
1/2 CUP	WATER OR CHICKEN BROTH	125 ML

CONDIMENTS

SOY SAUCE

VINEGAR WITH GRATED GINGERROOT

HOT MUSTARD

IN A BOWL, COMBINE PORK, MUSHROOMS, GREEN ONIONS,
CELERY AND GINGER. IN A SMALL BOWL, MIX CORNSTARCH
WITH SOY SAUCE. ADD EGG WHITE AND THEN COMBINE
WITH THE PORK MIXTURE, BLENDING THOROUGHLY. FORM
MIXTURE INTO 1-INCH (2.5 CM) BALLS.

TO MAKE DUMPLINGS: COMBINE EGG YOLK AND WATER.
ONE AT A TIME, PLACE A MEATBALL ON THE CENTER OF
WONTON WRAPPER AND BRUSH EDGE OF HALF OF WRAPPER

CONTINUED ON NEXT PAGE...

WITH THE YOLK MIXTURE. FOLD WRAPPER OVER INTO A TRIANGLE OR HALF MOON SHAPE AND PRESS EDGES TO SEAL, TRYING TO REMOVE ALL AIR, THEN FOLD OVER ALL POINTS, SEALING AGAIN WITH MORE YOLK MIXTURE, TO FORM A NEAT PACKAGE. PLACE ON A COOKIE SHEET, NOT TOUCHING. KEEP COVERED WITH PLASTIC WRAP AT ALL TIMES. THESE MAY BE FROZEN AT THIS POINT, THEN REMOVED TO FREEZER CONTAINERS.

TO COOK: HEAT SALAD OIL IN A SKILLET OVER HIGH HEAT. PLACE DUMPLINGS, EITHER FROZEN OR THAWED, IN PAN. COOK FOR 2 TO 3 MINUTES, UNTIL BOTTOMS ARE LIGHTLY BROWNED. REDUCE HEAT TO LOW AND ADD WATER OR BROTH. COVER AND SIMMER FOR 12 TO 15 MINUTES OR UNTIL LIQUID EVAPORATES. UNCOVER, INCREASE HEAT TO MEDIUM-HIGH AND COOK FOR 5 MINUTES LONGER, TURNING ONCE, UNTIL BROWNED. SERVE ON PLATTER WITH CONDIMENTS. MAKES ABOUT 36.

FOOLS RUSH IN — AND GET THE BEST SEATS.

MARINATED BARBECUED LAMB

USE THIS MARINADE ON LAMB CHOPS OR A BUTTERFLIED
LEG OF LAMB (ONLY YOUR BUTCHER KNOWS FOR SURE).

GARLIC AND HERB MARINADE

1 CUP	DRY RED WINE	250 ML
1/2 CUP	OLIVE OIL	125 ML
2 TO 3	CLOVES GARLIC, MINCED	2 TO 3
1 TSP	DRIED OREGANO	5 ML
1 TSP	DRIED THYME	5 ML
1 TSP	DRIED PARSLEY	5 ML
	SALT AND BLACK PEPPER TO TASTE	
	JUICE OF 1 LEMON	
	BONED LEG OF LAMB	

MIX ALL MARINADE INGREDIENTS TOGETHER. POUR
OVER LAMB, COVER AND MARINATE FOR 24 HOURS IN
REFRIGERATOR. TURN OCCASIONALLY.

PREHEAT BARBECUE TO HIGH. SEAR LAMB OVER HIGH
HEAT FOR 5 MINUTES ON EACH SIDE. MEANWHILE, IN A
SAUCEPAN, BRING MARINADE TO A FULL ROLLING BOIL OVER
HIGH HEAT FOR AT LEAST 1 MINUTE. REDUCE BARBECUE TO
MEDIUM HEAT AND FINISH COOKING LAMB UNTIL DESIRED
DONENESS, BASTING FREQUENTLY WITH MARINADE. LAMB
CAN BE SLIGHTLY PINK. SERVES 8 TO 12.

WHEN I TOLD HIM IT WOULD BE NICE TO HAVE BREAKFAST
IN BED, HE TOLD ME TO SLEEP IN THE KITCHEN!

LEG OF LAMB WITH RED CURRANT SAUCE

1	LEG OF LAMB (4 TO 5 LBS/2 TO 2.5 KG)	1
1 TBSP	GIN	15 ML
2 TSP	SALT	10 ML
1/2 TSP	DRY MUSTARD	2 ML
1/4 TSP	BLACK PEPPER	1 ML

RED CURRANT SAUCE

1/2 CUP	RED CURRANT JELLY	125 ML
1 CUP	WATER	250 ML
1/4 TSP	SALT	1 ML
1/4 CUP	GIN	60 ML
3 TBSP	ALL-PURPOSE FLOUR	45 ML
1/4 CUP	WATER	60 ML

PLACE LAMB ON A RACK IN ROASTING PAN, FAT SIDE UP. COMBINE GIN, SALT, MUSTARD AND PEPPER TO MAKE A PASTE; SPREAD OVER LAMB. ROAST AT 350°F (180°C) FOR 2 1/2 HOURS OR UNTIL MEAT THERMOMETER READS 180°F (90°C). SET ON A PLATTER AND COVER WITH FOIL.

SAUCE: REMOVE EXCESS FAT FROM ROASTING PAN. BLEND JELLY INTO PAN JUICES. ADD WATER AND HEAT OVER MEDIUM-LOW HEAT UNTIL JELLY MELTS. STIR IN SALT AND GIN. BLEND FLOUR IN WATER AND STIR INTO SAUCE. STIR UNTIL SAUCE BOILS AND THICKENS. POUR INTO GRAVY BOAT AND SERVE WITH LAMB. SERVES 8 TO 12.

MOUSSAKA

| 2 | EGGPLANTS OR MEDIUM ZUCCHINI | 2 |
| 1/2 TSP | SALT | 2 ML |

MEAT SAUCE

2 LBS	GROUND LAMB OR LEAN BEEF	1 KG
1 TBSP	BUTTER	15 ML
	SALT AND BLACK PEPPER TO TASTE	
2	MEDIUM ONIONS, CHOPPED	2
2	CLOVES GARLIC, MINCED	2
1/4 TSP	GROUND CINNAMON	1 ML
1/4 TSP	GROUND NUTMEG	1 ML
2 TBSP	CHOPPED FRESH PARSLEY	30 ML
8 OZ	TOMATO SAUCE	250 G
1/2 CUP	RED WINE	125 ML

BÉCHAMEL SAUCE

1/4 CUP	BUTTER	60 ML
1/4 CUP	ALL-PURPOSE FLOUR	60 ML
1 CUP	MILK	250 ML
1 CUP	WHIPPING (35%) CREAM	250 ML
3	EGG YOLKS, BEATEN	3
	SALT AND BLACK PEPPER TO TASTE	
2 TBSP	OLIVE OIL	30 ML
1 LB	MONTEREY JACK CHEESE, SHREDDED	500 G

CUT EGGPLANT INTO 1/4-INCH (0.5 CM) SLICES, SPRINKLE WITH SALT AND SET ASIDE.

MEAT SAUCE: SAUTÉ GROUND MEAT IN BUTTER WITH SALT AND PEPPER, ONIONS, GARLIC, CINNAMON, NUTMEG,

CONTINUED ON NEXT PAGE...

PARSLEY AND TOMATO SAUCE. ADD WINE AND SIMMER FOR 20 MINUTES, STIRRING OCCASIONALLY.

BÉCHAMEL SAUCE: MELT BUTTER AND STIR IN FLOUR. GRADUALLY ADD MILK AND CREAM, STIRRING CONSTANTLY UNTIL MIXTURE THICKENS. ADD EGG YOLKS IN A SLOW STREAM, AWAY FROM HEAT AND STIRRING CONSTANTLY. RETURN TO HEAT AND SIMMER FOR 2 TO 3 MINUTES LONGER. REMOVE FROM HEAT AND SEASON WITH SALT AND PEPPER.

WIPE EGGPLANT DRY AND QUICKLY BROWN IN OLIVE OIL. SET ON PAPER TOWEL TO DRAIN. IN GREASED 13- BY 9-INCH (33 BY 23 CM) PAN, PLACE A LAYER OF EGGPLANT, THEN COVER WITH MEAT SAUCE, SPRINKLE WITH ONE-THIRD OF THE CHEESE, COVER WITH REMAINING EGGPLANT, SPRINKLE WITH ONE-THIRD OF THE CHEESE, COVER WITH BÉCHAMEL SAUCE AND TOP WITH REMAINING CHEESE. BAKE AT 350°F (180°C) FOR 1 HOUR. SERVES 6 TO 8.

DIET: THE TRIUMPH OF MIND OVER PLATTER.

GOURMET MACARONI AND CHEESE

COMFORT FOOD.

2½ CUPS	MACARONI	625 ML
¼ CUP	BUTTER	60 ML
¼ CUP	ALL-PURPOSE FLOUR	60 ML
2 CUPS	MILK	500 ML
1 TSP	SALT	5 ML
1 TSP	GRANULATED SUGAR	5 ML
8 OZ	PROCESSED CHEESE, CUBED (VELVEETA)	250 G
⅔ CUP	SOUR CREAM (FAT-FREE IS FINE)	150 ML
1⅓ CUPS	COTTAGE CHEESE	325 ML
2 CUPS	SHREDDED SHARP (OLD) CHEDDAR CHEESE	500 ML
1½ CUPS	SOFT BREAD CRUMBS	375 ML
2 TBSP	BUTTER	30 ML
	PAPRIKA	

COOK AND DRAIN MACARONI AND PLACE IN A GREASED 10-CUP (2.5 L) CASSEROLE DISH. MELT BUTTER OVER MEDIUM HEAT; STIR IN FLOUR; MIX WELL. ADD MILK AND COOK OVER MEDIUM HEAT, STIRRING CONSTANTLY UNTIL SAUCE THICKENS. ADD SALT, SUGAR AND CHEESE. MIX WELL. MIX SOUR CREAM AND COTTAGE CHEESE INTO SAUCE. POUR OVER MACARONI. MIX WELL. SPRINKLE CHEDDAR CHEESE AND CRUMBS OVER TOP. DOT WITH BUTTER AND SPRINKLE WITH PAPRIKA. MAY BE FROZEN AT THIS POINT. BAKE AT 350°F (180°C) FOR 45 TO 50 MINUTES. SERVES 6.

WHEN YOU'RE OVER THE HILL, YOU PICK UP SPEED!

FETTUCCINE VERDE

8 OZ	GREEN FETTUCCINE NOODLES	250 G
6 TBSP	BUTTER	90 ML
I CUP	FINELY SLICED GREEN ONIONS	250 ML
2	CLOVES GARLIC, MINCED	2
I CUP	WHIPPING (35%) CREAM	250 ML
1/2 CUP	FRESHLY GRATED PARMESAN CHEESE	125 ML
PINCH	GROUND NUTMEG	PINCH
	SALT AND BLACK PEPPER TO TASTE	
	PARMESAN CHEESE	

COOK NOODLES ACCORDING TO PACKAGE DIRECTIONS.
DRAIN WELL. MELT BUTTER IN FRYING PAN. ADD ONIONS
AND GARLIC; COOK, STIRRING, FOR 2 MINUTES. ADD CREAM
AND COOK UNTIL BUBBLING. ADD HOT NOODLES TO PAN;
STIR GENTLY WITH TWO FORKS. ADD PARMESAN CHEESE
AND STIR UNTIL THE NOODLES ARE WELL COATED.
ADD NUTMEG, SALT AND PEPPER, STIR AND SERVE
IMMEDIATELY. SERVE WITH PARMESAN CHEESE AT THE
TABLE. SERVES 4 TO 6.

I'D GIVE MY RIGHT ARM TO BE AMBIDEXTROUS!

SPICY PENNE

EASY AND GOOD!

2 TBSP	OLIVE OIL	30 ML
4	CLOVES GARLIC, MINCED	4
1/2 TSP	HOT PEPPER FLAKES	2 ML
1	CAN (28 OZ/796 ML) CRUSHED ITALIAN TOMATOES	1
1 TSP	SALT	5 ML
1/2 TSP	FRESHLY GROUND BLACK PEPPER	2 ML
1/4 CUP	CHOPPED FRESH PARSLEY, DIVIDED	60 ML
1 LB	PENNE NOODLES	500 G
1/2 CUP	FRESHLY GRATED PARMESAN CHEESE	125 ML

IN A LARGE HEAVY FRYING PAN, HEAT OIL. ADD GARLIC AND PEPPER FLAKES. DO NOT BROWN. STIR IN TOMATOES, SALT AND PEPPER. COOK FOR 10 TO 15 MINUTES, OR UNTIL THICKENED. STIR IN HALF THE PARSLEY. SET ASIDE. IN A LARGE POT OF BOILING, SALTED WATER, COOK PENNE FOR 10 TO 15 MINUTES. DRAIN WELL. REHEAT SAUCE AND POUR OVER PENNE. SPRINKLE WITH PARMESAN AND REMAINING PARSLEY. TOSS WELL. SERVE IN INDIVIDUAL PASTA BOWLS. SERVES 6.

I'M NOT YOUNG ENOUGH TO KNOW EVERYTHING.

ASPARAGUS NOODLE BAKE

MIKEY LOVES IT! TRUST US... IT IS GOOD!

1	CAN (10 OZ/284 ML) MUSHROOM, CELERY OR ASPARAGUS SOUP (REDUCED SODIUM)	1
1 CUP	WATER	250 ML
3 CUPS	CRISP CHOW MEIN NOODLES	750 ML
2	CANS (EACH 10 OZ/284 ML) ASPARAGUS TIPS, DRAINED (OR FRESH ASPARAGUS TIPS)	2
2 CUPS	SHREDDED CHEDDAR CHEESE	500 ML

COMBINE SOUP AND WATER UNTIL SMOOTH. SPOON SMALL AMOUNT INTO BOTTOM OF A 6-CUP (1.5 L) CASSEROLE DISH. ADD HALF THE NOODLES, HALF THE ASPARAGUS, HALF THE REMAINING SOUP AND HALF THE CHEESE. REPEAT THE LAYERS. BAKE AT 350°F (180°C) FOR 30 MINUTES. SERVES 4 TO 6.

IF THE SHOE FITS, IT'S UGLY!

PASTA PRIMAVERA

*RAID THE GARDEN AND GET OUT THE VINO —
IT'S ITALIAN TONIGHT!*

1	BUNCH BROCCOLI, FLORETS ONLY	1
1	BUNCH ASPARAGUS, TRIMMED	1
1	SMALL ZUCCHINI, SLICED	1
1 CUP	GREEN BEANS, CUT	250 ML
1/2 CUP	PEAS	125 ML
2 TBSP	BUTTER	30 ML
1 CUP	THINLY SLICED MUSHROOMS	250 ML
1	BUNCH GREEN ONIONS, CHOPPED	1
2	CLOVES GARLIC, MINCED	2
2 CUPS	CHERRY TOMATOES, CUT IN HALVES	500 ML
1/4 CUP	CHOPPED FRESH PARSLEY	60 ML
2 TBSP	CHOPPED FRESH BASIL (OR 1 TSP/ 5 ML DRIED)	30 ML
1/2 TSP	HOT PEPPER FLAKES	2 ML
1/4 CUP	BUTTER	60 ML
2 TBSP	CHICKEN BROTH	30 ML
3/4 CUP	WHIPPING (35%) CREAM	175 ML
2/3 CUP	GRATED PARMESAN CHEESE	150 ML
	SALT AND FRESHLY GROUND BLACK PEPPER TO TASTE	
	TOASTED PINE NUTS (OPTIONAL)	
1 LB	VERMICELLI, COOKED AL DENTE	500 G

COOK FIRST FIVE VEGETABLES IN BOILING WATER UNTIL TENDER-CRISP. RINSE IMMEDIATELY IN COLD WATER UNTIL CHILLED. DRAIN WELL. (HOT TIP FROM MAMA LEONE: "YOU KEEP THE VEGETABLES CRISP.")

CONTINUED ON NEXT PAGE...

IN A MEDIUM SKILLET, SAUTÉ MUSHROOMS, ONIONS AND GARLIC IN 2 TBSP (30 ML) OF BUTTER FOR 2 TO 3 MINUTES. ADD TOMATOES AND COOK FOR 1 MINUTE MORE, STIRRING GENTLY. ADD TO THE VEGETABLES ALONG WITH PARSLEY, BASIL AND HOT PEPPER FLAKES. IN A LARGE POT, MELT 1/4 CUP (60 ML) BUTTER. ADD CHICKEN BROTH, CREAM, CHEESE AND SALT AND PEPPER. STIR WITH A WHISK UNTIL SMOOTH BUT DO NOT BOIL. ADD VEGETABLES AND HEAT THROUGH. CHECK SEASONING. SERVE IMMEDIATELY ON COOKED PASTA. SPRINKLE WITH TOASTED PINE NUTS, IF DESIRED. SERVES 6.

A VIRGIN FOREST IS A PLACE WHERE THE HAND OF MAN HAS NEVER SET FOOT.

PASTA POT

PASS DA WINE!

2 LBS	GROUND BEEF	1 KG
2	MEDIUM ONIONS, CHOPPED	2
1 TO 2	CLOVES GARLIC, CHOPPED	1 TO 2
2 TBSP	VEGETABLE OIL	30 ML
2 CUPS	SPAGHETTI SAUCE	500 ML
1	CAN (19 OZ/540 ML) STEWED TOMATOES	1
1 TO 2 TSP	SALT	5 TO 10 ML
PINCH	GRANULATED SUGAR	PINCH
1/2 TSP	DRIED BASIL	2 ML
1/2 TSP	DRIED OREGANO	2 ML
1	CAN (10 OZ/284 ML) MUSHROOMS, WITH LIQUID	1
2 CUPS	MEDIUM-SIZE SHELL PASTA	500 ML
3 CUPS	SOUR CREAM	750 ML
8 OZ	GOUDA CHEESE, SHREDDED	250 G
8 OZ	MOZZARELLA CHEESE, SHREDDED	250 G

BROWN MEAT, ONIONS AND GARLIC IN OIL. ADD NEXT SEVEN INGREDIENTS AND SIMMER ABOUT 20 MINUTES. MEANWHILE, COOK SHELL PASTA. DRAIN AND RINSE. POUR HALF THE SHELLS INTO A GREASED 16-CUP (4 L) CASSEROLE DISH. COVER WITH HALF THE MEAT SAUCE AND THEN COVER WITH HALF THE SOUR CREAM. TOP WITH GOUDA CHEESE. REPEAT AND TOP WITH MOZZARELLA CHEESE. COVER AND BAKE AT 350°F (180°C) FOR 40 TO 50 MINUTES. UNCOVER AND COOK FOR 10 MINUTES MORE TO BROWN CHEESE. SERVES 8 TO 10.

PASTA WITH CRAB AND BASIL

WE'VE TRIED THIS WITH FRESH CRAB AND MOCK CRAB.
BOTH WERE GREAT, BUT THE LATTER IS
FAR MORE REASONABLE.

4 OZ	BUTTER	125 G
2 TBSP	CHOPPED SHALLOTS	30 ML
2 TBSP	CHOPPED FRESH BASIL (OR I TSP/ 5 ML DRIED)	30 ML
2 TBSP	CHOPPED FRESH PARSLEY	30 ML
3	CANS (EACH 14 OZ/398 ML) CHOPPED TOMATOES, DRAINED	3
1/2 CUP	DRY WHITE WINE	125 ML
1 1/2 LBS	CRABMEAT OR MOCK CRAB	750 G
1 LB	VERMICELLI OR ANY FINE PASTA, COOKED AL DENTE AND DRAINED	500 G
	FRESHLY GRATED PARMESAN CHEESE	

IN A LARGE SKILLET, MELT BUTTER AND SAUTÉ SHALLOTS,
BASIL AND PARSLEY FOR 2 TO 3 MINUTES. STIR IN
TOMATOES AND HEAT TO BOILING. COOK UNTIL REDUCED
BY HALF. ADD WINE AND SIMMER FOR 5 MINUTES. ADD CRAB
AND SIMMER FOR 2 TO 3 MINUTES. SERVE OVER PASTA.
SPRINKLE WITH PARMESAN. SERVES 6.

ONE WAY TO SAVE FACE IS TO KEEP THE LOWER HALF SHUT.

LINGUINE WITH WHITE CLAM SAUCE

THIS IS A SMOOTH WHITE CLAM SAUCE —
THE ULTIMATE!

1	CLOVE GARLIC, MASHED	1
1	MEDIUM ONION, FINELY CHOPPED	1
2 TSP	OLIVE OIL	10 ML
1/2 CUP	DRY WHITE WINE	125 ML
2 CUPS	CHICKEN BROTH	500 ML
2	CANS (EACH 5 OZ/142 G) BABY CLAMS, RESERVE LIQUID	2
1	CAN (4 OZ/114 G) SHRIMP, DRAINED (OPTIONAL)	1
1	CAN (4 OZ/114 G) CRABMEAT, DRAINED (OPTIONAL)	1
PINCH	FRESHLY GROUND BLACK PEPPER	PINCH
3 DASHES	HOT PEPPER SAUCE	3 DASHES
1 TSP	DRIED OREGANO	5 ML
8 OZ	LIGHT CREAM CHEESE, CUT INTO SMALL PIECES	250 G
1 LB	LINGUINE NOODLES	500 G
	GRATED PARMESAN CHEESE	
	CHOPPED FRESH PARSLEY	

IN A 4-QUART (4 L) SAUCEPAN, SAUTÉ GARLIC AND ONION IN OIL UNTIL SOFT. DO NOT BROWN. ADD WINE, CHICKEN BROTH AND CLAM LIQUID. ADD BLACK PEPPER, HOT PEPPER SAUCE AND OREGANO. SIMMER FOR 15 MINUTES. ADD CREAM CHEESE; STIR INTO SAUCE UNTIL WELL BLENDED. ADD CLAMS AND, IF DESIRED, OTHER SEAFOOD. COOK LINGUINE ACCORDING TO PACKAGE DIRECTIONS. DRAIN WELL AND ADD TO SAUCE. LET PASTA REST IN SAUCE FOR

CONTINUED ON NEXT PAGE...

5 MINUTES TO ABSORB FLAVORS. SERVE IN A PASTA BOWL AND SPRINKLE WITH PARMESAN AND PARSLEY. SERVE IMMEDIATELY. SERVES 6.

LINGUINE WITH RED CLAM SAUCE

1	MEDIUM ONION, CHOPPED	1
3 TO 4	CLOVES GARLIC, MINCED	3 TO 4
3	STALKS CELERY, SLICED	3
3 TBSP	OLIVE OIL	45 ML
1	CAN (28 OZ/796 ML) ITALIAN TOMATOES	1
1 TSP	SALT	5 ML
2	CANS (EACH 6½ OZ/185 G) BABY CLAMS, WITH LIQUID	2
1	BAY LEAF	1
1 TSP	DRIED OREGANO	5 ML
8	SLICES BACON, COOKED AND CRUMBLED	8
	COARSELY GROUND BLACK PEPPER TO TASTE	
	LINGUINE FOR 4 PEOPLE	

IN A MEDIUM FRYING PAN, SAUTÉ ONION, GARLIC AND CELERY IN OIL UNTIL LIGHTLY GOLDEN. ADD NEXT SEVEN INGREDIENTS AND SIMMER, COVERED, FOR 1 HOUR OR MORE. JUST BEFORE SERVING, COOK LINGUINE. DRAIN WELL. MIX WITH HALF THE CLAM SAUCE AND TOSS. SERVE IN BOWLS AND PASS THE REMAINING SAUCE. SERVES 4.

SPAGHETTI CARBONARA

1 TSP	MINCED GARLIC	5 ML
8	THIN SLICES PROSCIUTTO, CHOPPED (BACON OR HAM MAY BE USED)	8
2 TBSP	OLIVE OIL	30 ML
5	EGG YOLKS	5
1 LB	SPAGHETTI	500 G
1/2 CUP	CREAM	125 ML
1/2 CUP	PARMESAN CHEESE	125 ML
	FRESHLY GROUND BLACK PEPPER TO TASTE	

SAUTÉ GARLIC AND HAM IN OLIVE OIL. BEAT YOLKS. COOK SPAGHETTI; DRAIN AND RETURN TO POT TO KEEP WARM. ADD HAM MIXTURE AND YOLKS TO SPAGHETTI AND TOSS THOROUGHLY. ADD CREAM AND PARMESAN. COMBINE WELL AND HEAT THROUGH. SERVE IMMEDIATELY AND PASS THE PEPPER MILL! SERVES 6.

THERE'S ONE GOOD THING ABOUT A DENTIST APPOINTMENT. YOU DON'T HAVE TO GET WEIGHED FIRST.

ITALIAN SAUSAGE AND PASTA

MY BAMBINO'S FAVORITE!

1 LB	HOT ITALIAN SAUSAGE	500 G
1 LB	BEEF AND PORK SAUSAGE	500 G
1/4 CUP	VINEGAR	60 ML
4 CUPS	WATER	1 L
1	CAN (28 OZ/796 ML) TOMATOES, MASHED	1
1	CAN (14 OZ/398 ML) TOMATO SAUCE	1
3/4 CUP	WATER	175 ML
1 1/2 TSP	SALT	7 ML
1	CLOVE GARLIC	1
2 TSP	DRIED OREGANO	10 ML
1 TSP	DRIED BASIL	5 ML
1 TSP	DRIED THYME	5 ML
1/2 TSP	DRIED SAGE	2 ML
1 1/2 TSP	GRANULATED SUGAR	7 ML
1/2 TSP	WORCESTERSHIRE SAUCE	2 ML
	SPAGHETTI (WHATEVER YOU THINK YOU NEED)	

PLACE SAUSAGES IN A LARGE FRYING PAN, ADDING VINEGAR AND WATER TO COVER. BOIL UNTIL THREE-QUARTERS REDUCED. DRAIN. RETURN SAUSAGE TO PAN AND LIGHTLY BROWN. REMOVE FROM PAN AND DRAIN ALL GREASE. CUT UP SAUSAGE. COMBINE ALL INGREDIENTS EXCEPT PASTA IN PAN. BRING TO A BOIL AND SIMMER FOR 1 HOUR OR MORE. SERVE OVER COOKED SPAGHETTI. SERVES 6.

MANICOTTI

SERVE WITH A TOSSED GREEN SALAD
AND DRY RED WINE.

10	MANICOTTI SHELLS	10
1 TBSP	VEGETABLE OIL	15 ML
1 1/2 LBS	LEAN GROUND BEEF	750 G
	GARLIC TO TASTE	
1/2 CUP	MILK	125 ML
2	SLICES WHITE BREAD, CRUMBLED	2
2 1/2 CUPS	SHREDDED MOZZARELLA CHEESE, DIVIDED	625 ML
1	EGG, BEATEN	1
1/4 CUP	CHOPPED FRESH PARSLEY	60 ML
	SALT AND BLACK PEPPER TO TASTE	
1	CAN (14 OZ/398 ML) MARINARA SAUCE OR SEASONED TOMATO SAUCE	1
1/2 CUP	GRATED PARMESAN CHEESE	125 ML

COOK MANICOTTI SHELLS ACCORDING TO PACKAGE
DIRECTIONS IN BOILING SALTED WATER, ADDING OIL TO
PREVENT SHELLS FROM STICKING. BROWN MEAT AND
GARLIC. MIX MILK AND BREAD CRUMBS AND ALLOW TO
SOAK FOR 2 MINUTES. SET ASIDE. ADD 2 CUPS (500 ML) OF
THE MOZZARELLA, BEATEN EGG, PARSLEY, SALT, PEPPER
AND MILK AND BREAD CRUMB MIXTURE TO BROWNED
MEAT. MIX WELL.

FILL COOKED SHELLS WITH MEAT MIXTURE USING
A SMALL SPOON. PLACE HALF OF MARINARA SAUCE IN
BOTTOM OF A GREASED 13- BY 9-INCH (33 BY 23 CM)
BAKING DISH. ARRANGE FILLED SHELLS IN DISH; POUR

CONTINUED ON NEXT PAGE...

OVER REMAINING SAUCE. SPRINKLE WITH PARMESAN AND REMAINING MOZZARELLA. BAKE, COVERED, AT 350°F (180°C) FOR 40 MINUTES. UNCOVER AND BAKE FOR 10 MINUTES MORE. SERVES 4 TO 6.

A FOOL AND YOUR MONEY ARE SOON PARTNERS!

BROCCOLI LASAGNA AU GRATIN

5 CUPS	BROCCOLI FLORETS	1.25 L
1	JAR (24 OZ/682 ML) SPICY SPAGHETTI SAUCE	1
8	LASAGNA NOODLES, COOKED	8
2 CUPS	RICOTTA CHEESE	500 ML
2	EGGS, SLIGHTLY BEATEN	2
2 CUPS	SHREDDED MOZZARELLA CHEESE	500 ML
1/2 CUP	GRATED PARMESAN CHEESE	125 ML

PARBOIL BROCCOLI FOR 1 MINUTE. SPREAD A THIN LAYER OF SPAGHETTI SAUCE IN A 13- BY 9-INCH (33 BY 23 CM) BAKING DISH. COVER WITH 4 LASAGNA NOODLES. MIX TOGETHER BROCCOLI, RICOTTA CHEESE AND EGGS. SPREAD HALF THE MIXTURE OVER NOODLES. TOP WITH HALF THE REMAINING SPAGHETTI SAUCE, HALF THE MOZZARELLA AND HALF THE PARMESAN. REPEAT LAYERS. BAKE AT 350°F (180°C) FOR 30 TO 35 MINUTES. SERVES 8 TO 10.

SPINACH LASAGNA

8	LASAGNA NOODLES	8
1/2 CUP	CHOPPED ONION	125 ML
2 TO 4	CLOVES GARLIC, MINCED	2 TO 4
3 TBSP	BUTTER	45 ML
2 TBSP	CORNSTARCH	30 ML
2 TBSP	CHOPPED FRESH PARSLEY	30 ML
I TSP	DRIED BASIL	5 ML
1/8 TSP	GROUND NUTMEG	0.5 ML
2 CUPS	MILK	500 ML
I	PACKAGE (IO OZ/300 G) FROZEN CHOPPED SPINACH, THAWED AND DRAINED	I
1/2 CUP	SLICED RIPE OLIVES	125 ML
2 CUPS	RICOTTA OR COTTAGE CHEESE	500 ML
I	EGG, BEATEN	I
I CUP	SHREDDED MOZZARELLA CHEESE	250 ML
1/2 CUP	GRATED PARMESAN CHEESE	125 ML

COOK LASAGNA NOODLES UNTIL TENDER; DRAIN AND RINSE IN COLD WATER. IN A MEDIUM SAUCEPAN, SAUTÉ ONION AND GARLIC IN BUTTER. STIR IN CORNSTARCH, PARSLEY, BASIL, NUTMEG AND MILK. COOK UNTIL THICKENED. ADD SPINACH AND OLIVES. SET ASIDE. IN A MEDIUM BOWL, MIX RICOTTA CHEESE, EGG, MOZZARELLA CHEESE AND 1/4 CUP (60 ML) PARMESAN CHEESE. SET ASIDE. ARRANGE 4 LASAGNA NOODLES IN BOTTOM OF A 13- BY 9-INCH (33 BY 23 CM) PAN. TOP WITH HALF THE SPINACH MIXTURE, THEN HALF THE CHEESE MIXTURE. REPEAT LAYERS. SPRINKLE WITH REMAINING PARMESAN CHEESE. BAKE AT 350°F (180°C) FOR 45 MINUTES. SERVES 8 TO 12.

"DEATH TO DIETERS" CHICKEN LASAGNA

3 CUPS	SLICED MUSHROOMS	750 ML
2 CUPS	CHOPPED ONION	500 ML
3 CUPS	HOLLANDAISE SAUCE (SUCH AS KNORR'S, OR HOMEMADE)	750 ML
8	LASAGNA NOODLES, COOKED	8
2 LBS	CHICKEN OR TURKEY BREAST, COOKED AND THINLY SLICED	1 KG
	SALT AND BLACK PEPPER TO TASTE	
1 TSP	DRIED BASIL	5 ML
1 TSP	DRIED OREGANO	5 ML
3 CUPS	SHREDDED MOZZARELLA CHEESE	750 ML
1 CUP	GRATED PARMESAN CHEESE	250 ML
1 LB	ASPARAGUS, COOKED TENDER-CRISP	500 G

SPRAY A NONSTICK FRYING PAN WITH COOKING SPRAY. SAUTÉ MUSHROOMS AND ONIONS UNTIL SOFT. SPREAD A SMALL AMOUNT OF HOLLANDAISE ON THE BOTTOM OF A 13- BY 9-INCH (33 BY 23 CM) PAN. PLACE A LAYER OF NOODLES ON TOP, THEN COVER WITH HALF THE CHICKEN AND SPRINKLE WITH SALT AND PEPPER TO TASTE. TOP WITH HALF THE MUSHROOM AND ONION MIXTURE, THEN HALF THE REMAINING HOLLANDAISE AND SPRINKLE WITH HALF THE BASIL AND OREGANO. TOP THIS WITH HALF THE MOZZARELLA AND PARMESAN CHEESES. PLACE ALL OF THE ASPARAGUS NEATLY IN A LAYER OVER CHEESE. REPEAT THE LAYERS, ENDING WITH THE CHEESES. BAKE, UNCOVERED, AT 350°F (180°C) FOR 35 MINUTES OR UNTIL HOT AND BUBBLY. LET STAND FOR 10 MINUTES BEFORE CUTTING. SERVE A SALAD WITH A TART DRESSING TO OFFSET THE RICHNESS. SERVES 10 TO 12.

HAM AND MUSHROOM LASAGNA

<u>BÉCHAMEL SAUCE</u>

1/4 CUP	BUTTER	60 ML
3 TBSP	ALL-PURPOSE FLOUR	45 ML
2 CUPS	MILK, HEATED	500 ML
	SALT AND BLACK PEPPER TO TASTE	

<u>LASAGNA</u>

1/2 CUP	MINCED ONION	125 ML
1/4 CUP	VEGETABLE OIL	60 ML
2	MEDIUM TOMATOES, PEELED, SEEDED AND CHOPPED	2
3 TBSP	CHOPPED FRESH PARSLEY	45 ML
3 CUPS	SLICED MUSHROOMS	750 ML
	SALT AND BLACK PEPPER TO TASTE	
12	LASAGNA NOODLES	12
2 CUPS	BÉCHAMEL SAUCE	500 ML
1 1/2 LBS	HAM, CUT INTO THIN STRIPS	750 G
2/3 CUP	GRATED PARMESAN CHEESE	150 ML
1/4 CUP	BUTTER	60 ML

BÉCHAMEL SAUCE: MELT BUTTER IN A SAUCEPAN. ADD THE FLOUR AND STIR UNTIL SMOOTH, 3 OR 4 MINUTES. SLOWLY ADD THE MILK, STIRRING CONSTANTLY. SEASON WITH SALT AND PEPPER. CONTINUE COOKING OVER LOW HEAT UNTIL THICKENED. COVER AND SET ASIDE.

LASAGNA: SAUTÉ ONION IN OIL. ADD TOMATOES AND PARSLEY. COOK OVER MODERATE HEAT UNTIL LIQUID HAS EVAPORATED. ADD THE MUSHROOMS, SALT AND PEPPER; MIX WELL, SET ASIDE. PREHEAT OVEN TO 350°F (180°C).

CONTINUED ON NEXT PAGE...

COOK NOODLES ACCORDING TO PACKAGE DIRECTIONS. DRAIN. BUTTER A 13- BY 9-INCH (33 BY 23 CM) DISH. PLACE A LAYER OF NOODLES IN THE BOTTOM OF THE DISH, FOLLOWED BY A LAYER OF HALF THE MUSHROOM MIXTURE. NEXT, DRIZZLE $\frac{1}{2}$ CUP (125 ML) BÉCHAMEL SAUCE AND THEN ADD A LAYER OF HAM AND SPRINKLE WITH PARMESAN CHEESE. REPEAT THE LAYERS AND TOP WITH A LAYER OF NOODLES. POUR THE REMAINING 1 CUP (250 ML) BÉCHAMEL SAUCE ON TOP AND DOT WITH BUTTER. BAKE, UNCOVERED, FOR 25 TO 30 MINUTES OR UNTIL HOT AND BUBBLY. SERVES 6 TO 8.

NOTE: IF FROZEN, PREPARE 1 CUP (250 ML) BÉCHAMEL SAUCE AND POUR OVER LASAGNA BEFORE HEATING.

TO GET MAXIMUM ATTENTION, IT'S HARD TO BEAT A GOOD, BIG MISTAKE!

BAKED BANANAS IN ORANGE AND LEMON JUICE

SERVE WITH CHICKEN, HAM OR ANY CURRIED DISH.
ALSO A GREAT DESSERT SERVED OVER ICE CREAM.

3	BANANAS, PEELED (NOT FULLY RIPE)	3
2	MEDIUM ORANGES, PEELED	2
1/3 CUP	GRANULATED SUGAR	75 ML
1/4 CUP	BUTTER, MELTED	60 ML
2 TBSP	ORANGE JUICE	30 ML
2 TBSP	LEMON JUICE	30 ML

PEEL AND CUT BANANAS LENGTHWISE. PLACE IN SHALLOW BAKING DISH. ARRANGE ORANGE SECTIONS OVER BANANAS AND SPRINKLE WITH SUGAR. COMBINE MELTED BUTTER AND JUICES AND POUR OVER FRUIT. BAKE AT 450°F (230°C) FOR 15 MINUTES. SERVES 6.

LIFE IS LIKE CHESS: ALL THE MISTAKES
ARE THERE, WAITING TO BE MADE.

VIVA! VEGGIES

YUMMY FARE FOR COMPANY.

1	BUNCH BROCCOLI		1
2 TBSP	BUTTER		30 ML
8 OZ	MUSHROOMS, SLICED		250 G
1/2 CUP	MAYONNAISE		125 ML
1/2 CUP	SOUR CREAM		125 ML
1/2 CUP	GRATED PARMESAN CHEESE		125 ML
1	CAN (14 OZ/398 ML) ARTICHOKES, DRAINED AND CUT INTO BITE-SIZE PIECES		1
	SALT AND BLACK PEPPER TO TASTE		
3	TOMATOES, SLICED		3
1/4 CUP	BUTTER, MELTED		60 ML
1/2 CUP	BREAD CRUMBS		125 ML

PRECOOK BROCCOLI UNTIL TENDER-CRISP. SAUTÉ MUSHROOMS IN 2 TBSP (30 ML) BUTTER. GREASE A 13- BY 9-INCH (33 BY 23 CM) DISH. BLEND MAYONNAISE, SOUR CREAM AND PARMESAN. MIX VEGETABLES IN SAUCE AND PLACE IN DISH. COVER WITH TOMATO SLICES. SEASON WITH SALT AND PEPPER. MIX MELTED BUTTER WITH BREAD CRUMBS AND SPRINKLE OVER TOMATOES. BAKE AT 325°F (160°C) FOR 20 MINUTES. SERVES 10 TO 12.

THE QUICKEST WAY TO LEARN HOW TO DO IT YOURSELF IS TO CRITICIZE THE WAY YOUR SPOUSE IS DOING IT!

BAKED ASPARAGUS

*SURPRISE! YOU CAN COOK ASPARAGUS
IN THE OVEN WITH THE ROAST!*

1 TO 1½ LBS	ASPARAGUS	500 TO 750 G
3 TBSP	BUTTER OR MARGARINE	45 ML
	SALT AND BLACK PEPPER TO TASTE	
2 TBSP	LEMON JUICE	30 ML

PREHEAT OVEN TO 350°F (180°C). RINSE AND TRIM
ASPARAGUS; DO NOT PEEL. PLACE ASPARAGUS IN A
SHALLOW DISH IN ONE OR TWO LAYERS. DOT WITH
BUTTER AND SPRINKLE WITH SALT AND PEPPER AND
LEMON JUICE. COVER TIGHTLY WITH FOIL AND BAKE FOR
15 MINUTES OR UNTIL TENDER-CRISP. SERVES 6 TO 8.

*BEHOLD THE TURTLE: HE MAKES PROGRESS
ONLY WHEN HE STICKS HIS NECK OUT!*

TISDALE ANNIE'S ASPARAGUS PUFF

10 OZ	GOUDA OR EDAM CHEESE	300 G
1 LB	ASPARAGUS (CANNED OR FROZEN MAY BE USED)	500 G
4	EGGS	4
1/2 TSP	SALT	2 ML
1/4 TSP	BLACK PEPPER	1 ML
1 CUP	CRACKER CRUMBS	250 ML
1	PIMENTO (OPTIONAL)	1
1 CUP	MILK	250 ML
1/4 CUP	MELTED BUTTER	60 ML

CUT CHEESE IN 1/2-INCH (1 CM) CUBES AND ASPARAGUS IN 1/2-INCH (1 CM) PIECES. BEAT EGGS WELL. ADD SALT, PEPPER, CRUMBS, PIMENTO (IF USING), MILK, ASPARAGUS AND CHEESE. POUR INTO 6-CUP (1.5 L) CASSEROLE DISH. POUR MELTED BUTTER OVER TOP. BAKE AT 350°F (180°C) FOR 40 MINUTES. MAY BE PREPARED AHEAD OF SERVING TIME, BUT DO NOT POUR BUTTER OVER UNTIL READY TO BAKE. SERVE IMMEDIATELY OR YOUR "PUFF" WILL LOSE ITS "POOF." SERVES 6.

SHOW ME A NERVOUS CAT AND I'LL SHOW YOU
A LITTER BOX FILLED WITH QUICKSAND.

BAKED BEANS

RIGHT OFF THE RANGE! SERVE WITH MAPLE SYRUP GRAHAM BREAD (PAGE 52) OR STEAMED BROWN BREAD (PAGE 54).

1 LB	WHITE BEANS	500 G
1	MEDIUM ONION, SLICED	1
1 1/2 TSP	SALT	7 ML
2 TSP	CIDER VINEGAR	10 ML
1 TSP	PREPARED MUSTARD (ADD MORE FOR ZIP)	5 ML
1 TBSP	BROWN SUGAR	15 ML
1/4 CUP	MOLASSES	60 ML
1/2 CUP	KETCHUP	125 ML
1/4 TSP	BLACK PEPPER	1 ML
4 OZ	SALT PORK OR BACON, SLICED	125 G

SOAK BEANS OVERNIGHT IN ENOUGH COLD WATER TO COVER THEM. PICK OUT ANY DISCOLORED BEANS. DRAIN, SAVING THE SOAKING WATER AS PART OF COOKING WATER (IT'S FULL OF VITAMINS AND MINERALS!). USING THIS, PLUS ENOUGH COLD WATER TO MAKE 5 CUPS (1.25 L), COOK BEANS ON STOVE IN A LARGE POT, COVERED, UNTIL BOILING. REDUCE HEAT AND SIMMER FOR 30 MINUTES. DRAIN, RESERVING LIQUID.

PLACE ONION SLICES IN THE BOTTOM OF A BEAN POT OR AN 8-CUP (2 L) CASSEROLE DISH. MIX SPICES AND SEASONINGS AND POUR OVER ONIONS. ADD BEANS, HOT LIQUID AND ENOUGH HOT WATER TO COVER. ARRANGE PORK SLICES ON TOP. COVER AND BAKE AT 250°F (120°C)

CONTINUED ON NEXT PAGE...

FOR 4 HOURS. REMOVE 1 CUP (250 ML) OF BEANS, MASH AND CAREFULLY STIR BACK INTO REMAINING BEANS. COVER AND CONTINUE TO BAKE FOR 3 HOURS. CHECK TO MAKE SURE BEANS ARE ALWAYS JUST COVERED WITH LIQUID. ADD MORE WATER WHEN NECESSARY. SERVES 6 TO 8.

NEVER LET A GIFT HORSE IN THE HOUSE!

SPEEDY BAKED BEANS

SERVE WITH QUICK MOLASSES BROWN BREAD (PAGE 53).

1	CAN (28 OZ/796 ML) PORK AND BEANS IN TOMATO SAUCE	1
1/4 CUP	BROWN SUGAR, PACKED	60 ML
1/4 CUP	KETCHUP	60 ML
3 TBSP	FROZEN ORANGE JUICE CONCENTRATE	45 ML
1 TBSP	DRIED MINCED ONION	15 ML
1 TBSP	WORCESTERSHIRE SAUCE	15 ML
	SALT AND BLACK PEPPER TO TASTE	
1 TSP	DRY MUSTARD	5 ML

PLACE ALL INGREDIENTS IN AN 8-CUP (2 L) CASSEROLE DISH. MIX WELL. BAKE AT 350°F (180°C) FOR 35 TO 40 MINUTES; OR HEAT THOROUGHLY ON STOVETOP OR IN MICROWAVE. SERVES 4.

CALICO BEAN POT

THE WORLD'S BEST BEAN CASSEROLE!

8	SLICES BACON	8
I CUP	CHOPPED ONION	250 ML
I	CAN (14 OZ/398 ML) GREEN BEANS, DRAINED	I
I	CAN (14 OZ/398 ML) LIMA BEANS, DRAINED	I
I	CAN (14 OZ/398 ML) PORK AND BEANS	I
I	CAN (14 OZ/398 ML) KIDNEY BEANS, DRAINED	I
3/4 CUP	BROWN SUGAR, FIRMLY PACKED	175 ML
1/2 CUP	VINEGAR	125 ML
1/2 TSP	GARLIC SALT	2 ML
1/2 TSP	DRY MUSTARD	2 ML
	BLACK PEPPER TO TASTE	

CUT BACON INTO SMALL PIECES AND COOK UNTIL CRISP. COOK ONION UNTIL SOFT. ADD REMAINING INGREDIENTS IN A 10-CUP (2.5 L) CASSEROLE DISH. BAKE AT 350°F (180°C) FOR I HOUR, UNCOVERED. PERFECT WITH HAMBURGERS OR BARBECUED BEEF. SERVES 12.

CAT HAIR ADHERES TO EVERYTHING BUT THE CAT.

SICILIAN BROCCOLI

A VEGETABLE YOU DARE NOT REFUSE!

1	BUNCH BROCCOLI	1
1/4 CUP	BUTTER	60 ML
2	CLOVES GARLIC, MINCED	2
1/4 TO 1/2 CUP	SLICED RIPE OLIVES	50 TO 125 ML
	FRESHLY GRATED PARMESAN CHEESE	

COOK BROCCOLI UNTIL TENDER-CRISP. MELT BUTTER AND SAUTÉ GARLIC. ADD OLIVES AND COOK FOR 2 MINUTES. POUR OVER BROCCOLI AND SPRINKLE WITH PARMESAN. SERVES 4.

PROBABLY NOTHING IN THE WORLD AROUSES MORE FALSE HOPES THAN THE FIRST FOUR HOURS OF A DIET.

TOLERABLE BRUSSELS SPROUTS

IF YOU HAVE TO HAVE THEM, TRY THESE —
THEY'RE DELICIOUS!

4 CUPS	BRUSSELS SPROUTS (ABOUT 2 LBS/1 KG)	1 L
1/2 CUP	CHOPPED ONION	125 ML
2 TBSP	BUTTER	30 ML
1 TBSP	ALL-PURPOSE FLOUR	15 ML
1 TBSP	PACKED BROWN SUGAR	15 ML
1/2 TSP	SALT	2 ML
1/2 TSP	DRY MUSTARD	2 ML
1/2 CUP	MILK	125 ML
1 CUP	FAT-FREE SOUR CREAM	250 ML
1 TBSP	CHOPPED FRESH PARSLEY	15 ML

- WASH AND TRIM SPROUTS; COOK UNTIL TENDER. SAUTÉ
ONION IN BUTTER UNTIL TRANSLUCENT. STIR IN FLOUR,
SUGAR, SALT AND MUSTARD. ADD MILK AND COOK SLOWLY
UNTIL THICKENED. BLEND IN SOUR CREAM. ADD SPROUTS
AND HEAT THROUGH. SPRINKLE WITH PARSLEY BEFORE
SERVING. SERVES 6.

NOSTALGIA ISN'T WHAT IT USED TO BE —
IT'S A THING OF THE PAST.

Greek Ribs (page 189)

Pasta Primavera (page 202)

Pasta with Crab and Basil (page 205)

Perfect Parsnips (page 234)

FRIED CABBAGE

SERVE WITH PEROGIES, SAUSAGE OR HAM.

1	MEDIUM HEAD OF CABBAGE, SLICED	1
1	SPANISH ONION, SLICED	1
10	STRIPS OF BACON	10

FRY BACON UNTIL CRISP, REMOVE FROM FRYING PAN AND CRUMBLE. TO REMAINING DRIPPINGS, ADD ONION AND FRY UNTIL LIMP, THEN ADD CABBAGE GRADUALLY AND COOK UNTIL SOFT, STIRRING FREQUENTLY. BEFORE SERVING, ADD CRUMBLED BACON. SERVES 6 TO 8.

*PEOPLE WHO LIVE IN STONE HOUSES
SHOULDN'T THROW GLASSES.*

KAMIKAZE KARROTS

LOVED THE TITLE, BUT THE RECIPE BOMBED!

NIFTY CARROTS

EVEN GOOD FOR YOUR HEARING!

5 TO 6	LARGE CARROTS, PEELED, SLICED AND COOKED UNTIL TENDER-CRISP (RESERVE COOKING WATER)	5 TO 6
1/4 CUP	RESERVED CARROT WATER	60 ML
1/4 CUP	MAYONNAISE	60 ML
1/4 CUP	SOUR CREAM (FAT-FREE IS FINE)	60 ML
2 TBSP	FINELY CHOPPED ONION	30 ML
1 TBSP	HORSERADISH	15 ML
	SALT AND BLACK PEPPER TO TASTE	
1 TBSP	BUTTER, MELTED	15 ML
1/2 CUP	BREAD CRUMBS	125 ML

PLACE COOKED CARROTS IN A SHALLOW CASSEROLE. COMBINE CARROT WATER, MAYONNAISE, SOUR CREAM, ONION, HORSERADISH, SALT AND PEPPER AND POUR OVER CARROTS. COMBINE BUTTER AND BREAD CRUMBS AND SPRINKLE OVER TOP. BAKE AT 375°F (190°C) FOR 30 MINUTES. SERVES 6.

EARLY TO BED, EARLY TO RISE, MAKES A MAN HEALTHY, WEALTHY AND THE FATHER OF A LARGE FAMILY!

CARROTS L'ORANGE

POUR LES RABBITS AVEC LES YEUX RUINED.

10	MEDIUM CARROTS DIAGONALLY CUT INTO 1-INCH (2.5 CM) SLICES	10
2 TBSP	BROWN SUGAR	30 ML
2 TSP	CORNSTARCH	10 ML
1/2 TSP	GROUND GINGER	2 ML
1/4 TSP	SALT	1 ML
1/2 CUP	ORANGE JUICE	125 ML
1/4 CUP	BUTTER	60 ML

COOK CARROTS IN BOILING SALTED WATER UNTIL TENDER-CRISP. IN A SEPARATE POT, COMBINE SUGAR, CORNSTARCH, GINGER AND SALT. ADD ORANGE JUICE AND COOK, STIRRING CONSTANTLY UNTIL THICKENED, BOILING FOR 1 MINUTE. STIR IN BUTTER AND REMOVE FROM HEAT. POUR OVER HOT, DRAINED CARROTS, TOSSING GENTLY TO COAT EVENLY. THIS MAY BE MADE AHEAD AND CHILLED; REHEAT JUST BEFORE SERVING TIME. SERVES 8.

IF YOUR OUTGO EXCEEDS YOUR INCOME,
THEN YOUR UPKEEP WILL BE YOUR DOWNFALL.

CURRIED CAULIFLOWER

MAKE AHEAD AND FREEZE.

4 CUPS	CAULIFLOWER (1 HEAD)	1 L
1 TBSP	MILK	15 ML
1	CAN (10 OZ/284 ML) CREAM OF CHICKEN SOUP (REDUCED SODIUM)	1
1/4 CUP	MAYONNAISE	60 ML
1/2 CUP	SHREDDED CHEDDAR CHEESE	125 ML
1 TSP	CURRY POWDER	5 ML
2 TBSP	BUTTER, MELTED	30 ML
1 CUP	CRACKER CRUMBS	250 ML

COOK CAULIFLOWER UNTIL TENDER-CRISP AND SET IN A LARGE CASSEROLE DISH. COMBINE MILK, CHICKEN SOUP, MAYONNAISE, CHEESE AND CURRY POWDER AND POUR OVER CAULIFLOWER. MIX MELTED BUTTER AND CRACKER CRUMBS AND SPRINKLE OVER ALL. BAKE AT 350°F (180°C) FOR 30 MINUTES. SERVES 6.

THERE'S NOTHING WRONG WITH TEENAGERS THAT REASONING WON'T AGGRAVATE!

CHILES RELLENOS

2	CANS (EACH 10 OZ/284 ML) GREEN CHILE PEPPERS	2
8 OZ	SWISS CHEESE, SHREDDED	250 G
3	EGGS	3
3 TBSP	ALL-PURPOSE FLOUR	45 ML
1/4 TSP	SALT	1 ML
3 TBSP	ONIONS	45 ML
1	CLOVE GARLIC	1
1 TBSP	BUTTER	15 ML
1	CAN (28 OZ/796 ML) TOMATO SAUCE	1
1/4 TSP	SALT	1 ML
1/4 TSP	DRIED OREGANO	1 ML

SPLIT CHILES AND REMOVE SEEDS. STUFF WITH CHEESE AND ARRANGE IN A 13- BY 9-INCH (33 BY 23 CM) BAKING DISH. SEPARATE EGGS. BEAT WHITES UNTIL STIFF. BEAT YOLKS; ADD FLOUR AND SALT, BEATING UNTIL THICK AND CREAMY. FOLD IN EGG WHITES AND SPREAD OVER CHILES.

TOMATO SAUCE: SAUTÉ ONIONS AND GARLIC IN BUTTER. ADD TOMATO SAUCE, SALT AND OREGANO. POUR SAUCE OVER CHILES. BAKE AT 375°F (190°C) FOR 30 MINUTES. SERVE IMMEDIATELY. SERVES 8 TO 10.

"THE MEEK SHALL INHERIT THE EARTH"... IF THAT'S OKAY WITH THE REST OF YOU.

SUDDEN VALLEY GREEN BEANS

ANOTHER EASY MAKE-AHEAD FOR YOUR
NEXT FAMILY "BUN-FIGHT."

1	PACKAGE (10 OZ/300 G) FROZEN FRENCH-STYLE GREEN BEANS	1
1	CAN (10 OZ/284 ML) SLICED MUSHROOMS, DRAINED	1
1	CAN (10 OZ/284 ML) MUSHROOM SOUP (REDUCED SODIUM)	1
1/3 CUP	CREAM (MILK WILL DO)	75 ML
1/4 TSP	GARLIC SALT	1 ML
PINCH	BLACK PEPPER	PINCH
1/2 CUP	BUTTERED CROUTONS	125 ML
1/3 CUP	PARMESAN CHEESE	75 ML

COOK FROZEN BEANS UNTIL TENDER-CRISP. DRAIN.
BUTTER A 4-CUP (1 L) CASSEROLE DISH AND LAYER BEANS
AND MUSHROOMS. MIX SOUP WITH CREAM; ADD GARLIC
SALT AND PEPPER. POUR OVER BEANS AND MUSHROOMS.
COVER WITH CROUTONS AND SPRINKLE WITH CHEESE.
PREPARE AHEAD OF TIME AND REFRIGERATE COVERED. BAKE
UNCOVERED AT 300°F (150°C) FOR 1 HOUR. SERVES 6.

PEOPLE WITH BAD COUGHS NEVER GO TO DOCTORS —
THEY GO TO MOVIES.

MANDARIN GREEN BEANS

2	PACKAGES (EACH 10 OZ/300 G) FROZEN GREEN BEANS (FRENCH-STYLE)	2
1	CAN (10 OZ/284 ML) MANDARIN ORANGES, DRAINED	1
3 TBSP	BUTTER	45 ML
	SALT AND BLACK PEPPER TO TASTE	
1/2 CUP	TOASTED SLIVERED ALMONDS	125 ML

COOK BEANS ACCORDING TO PACKAGE DIRECTIONS. DRAIN. ADD ORANGES, BUTTER, SALT AND PEPPER. TOSS LIGHTLY AND TURN INTO CASSEROLE DISH; SPRINKLE ALMONDS ON TOP. SERVES 8 TO 10.

BOOZY ONIONS

6	SMALL TO MEDIUM ONIONS, CUT IN 1/2-INCH (1 CM) SLICES	6
1/3 CUP	DRY WHITE WINE	75 ML
PINCH	SALT	PINCH
3 TBSP	CORN SYRUP	45 ML
1 OR 2	WHOLE CLOVES	1 OR 2
1 TBSP	ALL-PURPOSE FLOUR	15 ML
1 TBSP	BUTTER, MELTED	15 ML

PLACE ONION SLICES IN SAUCEPAN ALONG WITH WINE, SALT, CORN SYRUP AND CLOVES. SIMMER UNTIL TENDER (20 MINUTES). BLEND FLOUR AND BUTTER TOGETHER AND STIR INTO ONIONS TO THICKEN. (REMOVE CLOVES BEFORE SERVING.) EXCELLENT WITH ANY MEAT. SERVES 6.

CHEESE MARINATED ONIONS

A REAL ZINGER WITH ROAST BEEF OR HAMBURGERS.

3 OZ	BLUE CHEESE, CRUMBLED	90 G
1/4 CUP	SALAD OIL	60 ML
2 TBSP	LEMON JUICE	30 ML
2 TSP	GRANULATED SUGAR	10 ML
	SALT AND BLACK PEPPER TO TASTE	
2	LARGE ONIONS, THINLY SLICED AND SEPARATED INTO RINGS	2

MIX FIRST FIVE INGREDIENTS AND POUR OVER ONION RINGS. COVER AND CHILL SEVERAL HOURS. SERVES 6.

TO SLOW DOWN TRAFFIC, LET THE POST OFFICE HANDLE IT.

ONIONS STUFFED WITH BROCCOLI

EVER SEE A "FULL" ONION? WELL, HERE'S THREE OF THEM. DON'T EXPECT A DATE FOR TWO OR THREE DAYS!

3	MEDIUM SPANISH ONIONS, PEELED	3
I LB	BROCCOLI	500 G
½ CUP	GRATED PARMESAN CHEESE	125 ML
⅓ CUP	MAYONNAISE	75 ML
2 TSP	LEMON JUICE	10 ML

PREHEAT OVEN TO 375°F (190°C). CUT THE ONIONS IN HALF CROSSWISE. GENTLY PARBOIL IN SALTED WATER FOR 10 TO 12 MINUTES. DRAIN. REMOVE CENTERS, LEAVING ¾-INCH (2 CM) WALLS. CHOP CENTER PORTIONS TO EQUAL I CUP (250 ML). COOK BROCCOLI TOPS UNTIL TENDER-CRISP; CHOP. COMBINE WITH CHOPPED ONION, CHEESE, MAYONNAISE AND LEMON JUICE. MOUND BROCCOLI MIXTURE IN THE ONION HALVES. BAKE, UNCOVERED, IN A BUTTERED, SHALLOW CASSEROLE FOR 20 MINUTES. SERVES 6.

DON'T YOU WISH THAT ALL THOSE PEOPLE TRYING TO FIND THEMSELVES WOULD JUST GET LOST!

PERFECT PARSNIPS

IF YOU ARE A DEVOTEE, THESE ARE PRESENTABLE,
PALATABLE AND POSITIVELY A SNAP.

3	PARSNIPS, PEELED AND SLICED IN MATCHSTICKS	3
I	CARROT, PEELED AND SLICED IN MATCHSTICKS	I
I	STALK CELERY, SLICED IN MATCHSTICKS	I
3 TBSP	BUTTER	45 ML
I TBSP	FRESHLY SQUEEZED LEMON JUICE	15 ML
I TBSP	CHOPPED FRESH DILL (OR I TSP/5 ML DRIED DILLWEED)	15 ML

MELT BUTTER IN A FRYING PAN AND STIR-FRY PARSNIPS, CARROTS AND CELERY OVER MEDIUM-HIGH HEAT FOR 3 TO 4 MINUTES, UNTIL TENDER-CRISP. REMOVE TO A SERVING DISH AND SPRINKLE WITH LEMON JUICE AND DILL. SERVES 4.

THERE'S NO SENSE IN ADVERTISING YOUR TROUBLES —
THERE'S NO MARKET FOR THEM.

COLD DILLED PEAS

*A WARM WEATHER WINNER YOU CAN PREPARE
IN TEN MINUTES.*

2 CUPS	FRESH OR FROZEN TINY PEAS	500 ML
I CUP	SOUR CREAM	250 ML
I TSP	DRIED DILLWEED	5 ML
I TSP	CHOPPED FRESH CHIVES	5 ML
	SALT AND BLACK PEPPER TO TASTE	
½ TO I TSP	CURRY POWDER	2 TO 5 ML
2 TSP	FRESHLY SQUEEZED LEMON JUICE	10 ML

COOK AND DRAIN PEAS. MIX REMAINING INGREDIENTS
TOGETHER AND CAREFULLY FOLD IN PEAS. CHILL AND
GARNISH WITH ADDITIONAL DILL OR CHIVES. SERVES 4.

*SURE, THE COST OF LIVING IS HIGH,
BUT CONSIDER THE ALTERNATIVE!*

ÉPINARDS, EH!

5	MEDIUM CARROTS, PEELED AND SLICED	5
I	MEDIUM ONION, SLICED	I
1½ TBSP	BUTTER	22 ML
1½ TBSP	ALL-PURPOSE FLOUR	22 ML
¾ CUP	MILK	175 ML
½ CUP	VELVEETA CHEESE, CUBED	125 ML
½ CUP	SHREDDED CHEDDAR CHEESE	125 ML
I	PACKAGE (10 OZ/300 G) FROZEN LEAF SPINACH, THAWED AND DRAINED	I
¼ TSP	SALT	I ML
¼ TSP	BLACK PEPPER	I ML

COOK CARROTS AND ONION IN A SMALL AMOUNT OF WATER UNTIL TENDER-CRISP, ABOUT 8 MINUTES. DRAIN. IN A SAUCEPAN, MELT BUTTER AND BLEND IN FLOUR GRADUALLY. STIR IN MILK AND ADD CHEESES. COOK AND STIR UNTIL THICK. PLACE HALF THE SPINACH IN A 4-CUP (I L) CASSEROLE DISH. COVER WITH HALF THE CARROTS AND ONION. COVER WITH THE CHEESE SAUCE. REPEAT VEGETABLES. BAKE, COVERED, AT 350°F (180°C) FOR 15 TO 20 MINUTES. SERVES 6.

TOO MUCH OF A GOOD THING IS WONDERFUL!

SPINACH OR BROCCOLI TIMBALES

A SPECIAL COMPANY VEGETABLE. LOOKS ATTRACTIVE ON A PLATTER SERVED WITH DILL AND PARMESAN TOMATOES (PAGE 238).

2	PACKAGES (EACH 10 OZ/300 G) FROZEN SPINACH OR BROCCOLI	2
1/2 CUP	CHOPPED GREEN ONIONS	125 ML
3 TBSP	BUTTER	45 ML
4	EGGS, BEATEN	4
1 1/2 CUPS	HALF-AND-HALF CREAM	375 ML
3/4 CUP	DRY BREAD CRUMBS	175 ML
1/2 CUP	GRATED PARMESAN CHEESE	125 ML
1/2 TSP	SALT	2 ML
1/4 TSP	BLACK PEPPER	1 ML
1/8 TSP	GROUND NUTMEG	0.5 ML

GREASE 16 LARGE MUFFIN TINS. COOK SPINACH OR BROCCOLI. DRAIN WELL (SPIN SPINACH IN SALAD SPINNER). CHOP. SAUTÉ ONIONS IN BUTTER UNTIL SOFT; COMBINE WITH REMAINING INGREDIENTS. FILL MUFFIN TINS AND BAKE FOR 20 TO 25 MINUTES AT 350°F (180°C) OR UNTIL A TOOTHPICK COMES OUT CLEAN. UNMOLD AND TURN RIGHT SIDE UP. THESE LITTLE MARVELS WILL EVEN SUFFER THE INDIGNITY OF REHEATING. SERVES 8.

DILL AND PARMESAN TOMATOES

*QUICK AND DELICIOUS — VITAMINS AND COLOR
FOR YOUR COMPANY!*

3	MEDIUM TOMATOES	3
2 TBSP	BUTTER	30 ML
1/2 CUP	BREAD CRUMBS	125 ML
1 TBSP	CHOPPED FRESH DILL	15 ML
	(OR 1/2 TSP/2 ML DRIED DILLWEED)	
	SALT AND BLACK PEPPER TO TASTE	
1/2 CUP	GRATED PARMESAN CHEESE	125 ML

CUT EACH TOMATO INTO 4 SLICES AND PLACE ON A
COOKIE SHEET. MELT BUTTER; ADD BREAD CRUMBS, DILL,
SALT, PEPPER AND CHEESE. STIR TOGETHER AND SPOON
CRUMB MIXTURE ONTO TOMATO SLICES. PLACE IN COLD
OVEN UNDER BROILER (NOT TOO CLOSE) AND TURN ON
BROILER. BROIL UNTIL CRUST TURNS GOLDEN, ABOUT
5 MINUTES. SERVES 6.

AT FIRST I WAS HESITANT, BUT NOW I'M NOT SO SURE.

TOMATO AND ARTICHOKE CASSEROLE

EXOTIC BUT EASY.

1	LARGE ONION, CHOPPED	1
5 TBSP	BUTTER	75 ML
3 CUPS	FRESH BREAD CRUMBS	750 ML
1/2 TSP	GRANULATED SUGAR	2 ML
1 TSP	SALT	5 ML
1 TSP	BLACK PEPPER	5 ML
1 TSP	DRIED THYME	5 ML
1 TSP	DRIED BASIL	5 ML
1	CAN (14 OZ/398 ML) ARTICHOKE HEARTS (CUT IN QUARTERS)	1
4	MEDIUM TOMATOES, THICKLY SLICED	4
2 TBSP	BUTTER, MELTED	30 ML

FRY ONION IN BUTTER UNTIL TRANSPARENT. MIX IN BREAD CRUMBS, SUGAR, SALT, PEPPER, THYME AND BASIL. REMOVE FROM HEAT. GREASE A 4-CUP (1 L) CASSEROLE DISH AND FILL WITH ALTERNATE LAYERS OF ARTICHOKES, TOMATOES AND ONION-BREAD CRUMB MIXTURE, ENDING WITH BREAD CRUMBS. DRIZZLE BUTTER OVER TOP. BAKE AT 375°F (190°C) FOR 45 MINUTES. SERVES 6.

PEOPLE WHO PREDICT EARTHQUAKES ARE FAULT FINDERS!

TOMATO CHEESE BAKE

FAST AND TASTY.

4	LARGE TOMATOES, SLICED	4
	SALT AND BLACK PEPPER TO TASTE	
1/2 CUP	MAYONNAISE	125 ML
6	GREEN ONIONS, CHOPPED	6
1 CUP	SHREDDED CHEDDAR CHEESE	250 ML
1 CUP	SHREDDED MOZZARELLA CHEESE	250 ML

IN A SHALLOW BAKING DISH, ARRANGE SLICED TOMATOES. SPRINKLE WITH SALT AND PEPPER. SPREAD MAYONNAISE OVER TOMATOES AND TOP WITH CHOPPED GREEN ONIONS. COVER WITH THE TWO CHEESES. BAKE AT 350°F (180°C) FOR 25 MINUTES. SERVES 6.

THE ONLY PEOPLE WHO HEAR BOTH SIDES OF AN ARGUMENT ARE THE NEIGHBORS.

TOMATOES FLORENTINE

WONDERFUL WITH BEEF EXTRAORDINAIRE (PAGE 169).

6	FAIRLY FIRM TOMATOES (NOT A CHORUS LINE!)	6
1	PACKAGE (10 OZ/300 G) FROZEN CHOPPED SPINACH	1
1 TBSP	MINCED ONION	15 ML
1	CLOVE GARLIC, MINCED	1
1 TSP	DRIED OREGANO	5 ML
PINCH	GROUND NUTMEG	PINCH
1 CUP	SHREDDED CHEDDAR CHEESE	250 ML
	FRESHLY GRATED PARMESAN CHEESE	

SLICE OFF TOP OF TOMATOES AND SCOOP OUT PULP. CHOP AND DRAIN THE PULP. THAW SPINACH AND DRAIN WELL. COMBINE SPINACH, PULP, ONION, SPICES AND CHEDDAR. FILL TOMATOES AND TOP WITH PARMESAN. BAKE AT 350°F (180°C) FOR 20 TO 30 MINUTES. SERVES 6.

NEVER CHOOSE A FIRST MATE WHO TAKES THE WIND OUT OF YOUR SAILS.

CHEESE-FRIED ZUCCHINI

MAY ALSO BE SERVED AS AN APPETIZER.

1/4 CUP	DRIED BREAD CRUMBS	60 ML
2 TBSP	GRATED PARMESAN CHEESE	30 ML
2 TBSP	ALL-PURPOSE FLOUR	30 ML
1 TSP	SALT (GARLIC SALT OR ONION SALT IF PREFERRED)	5 ML
2	MEDIUM ZUCCHINI, SLICED LENGTHWISE IN STICKS	2
1	EGG, BEATEN	1
2 TO 4 TBSP	OLIVE OIL	30 TO 60 ML

COMBINE BREAD CRUMBS, CHEESE, FLOUR AND SALT IN A PLASTIC BAG. DIP ZUCCHINI IN EGG, THEN SHAKE IN PLASTIC BAG. USING A LARGE SKILLET, HEAT OIL AND FRY ZUCCHINI UNTIL GOLDEN BROWN AND CRISPY, TURNING OCCASIONALLY. DRAIN ON PAPER TOWEL. SERVE IMMEDIATELY. SERVES 4.

VEGETABLES: THINGS THAT WOULD BE GOOD TO EAT IF YOU WEREN'T SUPPOSED TO.

ITALIAN ZUCCHINI

8	MEDIUM ZUCCHINI	8
3	MEDIUM ONIONS	3
1	CLOVE GARLIC, CHOPPED	1
1/2 CUP	VEGETABLE OIL	125 ML
1	CAN (28 OZ/796 ML) TOMATOES	1
	SALT AND BLACK PEPPER TO TASTE	
2 TSP	DRIED OREGANO	10 ML
1 TBSP	WINE VINEGAR	15 ML
3 TBSP	PARMESAN CHEESE	45 ML

SLICE ZUCCHINI AND ARRANGE IN A 12-CUP (3 L) CASSEROLE DISH. SAUTÉ ONIONS AND GARLIC IN OIL UNTIL LIGHTLY BROWN AND TENDER. ADD TOMATOES, SALT, PEPPER, OREGANO AND VINEGAR. HEAT TO BOILING, THEN SIMMER FOR 2 MINUTES. POUR TOMATO-ONION MIXTURE OVER ZUCCHINI. TOP WITH CHEESE. BAKE AT 400°F (200°C) FOR 30 MINUTES OR UNTIL TENDER. SERVES 8 TO 10.

BIG TOE: A DEVICE FOR LOCATING
SHARP OBJECTS IN THE DARK.

SPAGHETTI SQUASH PRIMAVERA

*A WONDERFUL VEGETARIAN DINNER OR,
IF YOU'RE NOT INTO THAT, SERVE WITH BEEF,
BOOZE AND A GOOD STOGIE!*

1	MEDIUM SPAGHETTI SQUASH	1
1/3 CUP	BUTTER	75 ML
2	MEDIUM ONIONS, FINELY CHOPPED	2
8 OZ	MUSHROOMS, SLICED	250 G
1	CLOVE GARLIC, MINCED	1
1 1/2 CUPS	BROCCOLI FLORETS	375 ML
1 CUP	PEAS	250 ML
1	MEDIUM ZUCCHINI, SLICED	1
4	CARROTS, CUT DIAGONALLY	4
1 CUP	MILK OR HALF-AND-HALF CREAM	250 ML
1/2 CUP	CHICKEN BROTH	125 ML
1/4 CUP	CHOPPED FRESH BASIL (OR 1 TBSP/15 ML DRIED)	60 ML
1	RED BELL PEPPER, SLICED	1
6	GREEN ONIONS, CHOPPED	6
12	SMALL CHERRY TOMATOES	12
1 1/2 CUPS	GRATED PARMESAN CHEESE	375 ML

CUT SQUASH IN HALF LENGTHWISE AND REMOVE SEEDS.
PLACE CUT SIDE DOWN IN A BAKING DISH, ADD 1 INCH
(2.5 CM) OF WATER AND BAKE AT 375°F (190°C) FOR 1 HOUR.
(OR MICROWAVE USING THE SAME METHOD, COVERED,
ON HIGH UNTIL A SKEWER CAN PENETRATE THE SKIN,
ABOUT 20 MINUTES.) MELT BUTTER IN A LARGE FRYING
PAN AND SAUTÉ ONIONS, MUSHROOMS AND GARLIC UNTIL
SOFT. ADD BROCCOLI, PEAS, ZUCCHINI AND CARROTS. STIR.

CONTINUED ON NEXT PAGE...

ADD MILK, CHICKEN BROTH AND BASIL. BOIL BRISKLY TO REDUCE SAUCE A LITTLE, ABOUT 2 MINUTES. ADD RED PEPPER, GREEN ONIONS, CHERRY TOMATOES AND CHEESE. HEAT THOROUGHLY. USING A FORK, SCRAPE STRANDS OF SQUASH INTO A LARGE, HEATED, SHALLOW CASSEROLE. TOP IMMEDIATELY WITH HOT VEGETABLE MIXTURE. SERVE WITH EXTRA PARMESAN CHEESE. SERVES 8 TO 10.

A BABYSITTER: A TEENAGER WHO COMES TO YOUR HOME TO ACT LIKE AN ADULT SO YOU CAN GO OUT AND ACT LIKE A TEENAGER.

CHEESY ACORN SQUASH

SCORE ONE FOR SQUASH! SERVE WITH CORNISH HENS OR ROAST CHICKEN, RICE AND A GREEN SALAD.

3	MEDIUM ACORN SQUASH	3
1 CUP	DICED CELERY	250 ML
1 CUP	FINELY CHOPPED ONION	250 ML
1/4 CUP	BUTTER	60 ML
1 CUP	SLICED MUSHROOMS	250 ML
1/2 TSP	SALT	2 ML
PINCH	BLACK PEPPER	PINCH
2 TBSP	CHOPPED FRESH PARSLEY	30 ML
1 CUP	SHREDDED CHEDDAR CHEESE	250 ML

CUT SQUASH IN HALF AND PLACE, CUT SIDE DOWN, IN ROASTING PAN. BAKE SQUASH AT 350°F (180°C) FOR 1 HOUR OR UNTIL ALMOST TENDER. SAUTÉ CELERY AND ONION IN BUTTER UNTIL TRANSPARENT; ADD MUSHROOMS AND COOK FOR 2 TO 3 MINUTES LONGER. ADD SALT, PEPPER AND PARSLEY. TURN SQUASH CUT SIDE UP AND DISTRIBUTE CELERY MIXTURE EVENLY IN SQUASH. COVER ROASTING PAN AND CONTINUE TO BAKE FOR 15 MINUTES. UNCOVER AND SPRINKLE CHEESE OVER MIXTURE. COOK FOR ABOUT 5 MINUTES OR UNTIL CHEESE MELTS AND IS BUBBLY. SERVES 6.

I HATE INTOLERANT PEOPLE!

YAMMY APPLES

*THIS IS A HIT WITH CHILDREN.
IF THEY LIKE IT, EVERYONE WILL!*

2	CANS (EACH 19 OZ/540 ML) YAMS, SLICED INTO THIN CHUNKS	2
4	JUICY RED APPLES, PEELED AND SLICED	4
3 TBSP	LEMON JUICE	45 ML
3 TBSP	BROWN SUGAR	45 ML
1½ TSP	GROUND CINNAMON	7 ML
3 TBSP	BUTTER	45 ML
	MINIATURE MARSHMALLOWS (OPTIONAL)	

THIS RECIPE IS MADE IN LAYERS; START WITH A BUTTERED 10-CUP (2.5 L) CASSEROLE DISH AND MAKE A 1-INCH (2.5 CM) LAYER OF SLICED YAMS. COVER COMPLETELY WITH 2 OF THE SLICED APPLES. SPRINKLE WITH HALF THE LEMON JUICE, HALF THE BROWN SUGAR AND HALF THE CINNAMON, THEN DAB WITH HALF THE BUTTER. REPEAT THE LAYERS. BAKE AT 350°F (180°C) FOR 30 MINUTES. IF DESIRED, 10 MINUTES BEFORE COOKING TIME HAS EXPIRED, COVER WITH A LAYER OF MINIATURE MARSHMALLOWS AND BAKE UNTIL THEY TURN GOLDEN BROWN. SERVES 8.

*GIVE SOME PEOPLE AN INCH
AND THEY THINK THEY'RE RULERS.*

SWEET POTATOES IN ORANGE SAUCE

FOR NON-BELIEVERS!

4 LBS	SWEET POTATOES	2 KG
1¼ CUPS	GRANULATED SUGAR	300 ML
2 TBSP	CORNSTARCH	30 ML
1 TSP	SALT	5 ML
2 CUPS	ORANGE JUICE	500 ML
¼ CUP	BUTTER	60 ML
1½ TSP	GRATED ORANGE ZEST	7 ML
1	ORANGE, THINLY SLICED	1

PEEL POTATOES AND CUT INTO ½-INCH (1 CM) SLICES. OVERLAPPING SLICES, ARRANGE IN ROWS IN A SHALLOW 12-CUP (3 L) BAKING DISH. SET ASIDE. IN A SMALL PAN, COMBINE SUGAR, CORNSTARCH AND SALT. STIR IN ORANGE JUICE UNTIL WELL BLENDED. BRING MIXTURE TO A BOIL AND COOK, STIRRING CONSTANTLY UNTIL THICK AND CLEAR, ABOUT 1 MINUTE. REMOVE FROM HEAT AND ADD BUTTER AND ORANGE ZEST. POUR OVER SWEET POTATOES. AT THIS POINT YOU MAY COVER AND SET ASIDE UNTIL READY TO BAKE. BAKE AT 400°F (200°C) FOR 45 TO 50 MINUTES. UNCOVER AND BASTE THOROUGHLY WITH SAUCE. BAKE UNCOVERED 15 TO 20 MINUTES MORE OR UNTIL TENDER AND WELL GLAZED. ARRANGE ORANGE SLICES OVER TOP TO SERVE. SERVES 10 TO 12.

PICK A WINNER. ANYONE CAN PICK A LOSER.

FLUFFY BAKED POTATOES

6	BAKING POTATOES	6
2 TBSP	BUTTER	30 ML
1/2 CUP	HOT MILK	125 ML
1 TSP	SALT	5 ML
1/4 TSP	BLACK PEPPER	1 ML
1 TSP	BAKING POWDER	5 ML
PINCH	GROUND NUTMEG	PINCH
2	EGG YOLKS (PLACE IN SEPARATE BOWLS)	2
2	EGG WHITES	2
1/2 CUP	FINELY SHREDDED SWISS CHEESE	125 ML
2 TBSP	GRATED ONION (OPTIONAL)	30 ML
1 TBSP	WATER	15 ML

PREHEAT OVEN TO 425°F (220°C). PRICK AND BAKE POTATOES FOR 1 HOUR. CUT THIN SLICE FROM TOP HALF OF EACH POTATO AND DISCARD. SCOOP POTATO PULP INTO BOWL WITH TEASPOON, BEING CAREFUL NOT TO BREAK SKIN. MASH PULP WELL (USE BEATER). ADD BUTTER, MILK, SALT, PEPPER, BAKING POWDER, NUTMEG AND 1 EGG YOLK AND ONION (IF USING). WHIP UNTIL FLUFFY. BEAT EGG WHITES UNTIL STIFF AND FOLD INTO MIXTURE. MIX IN CHEESE AND PILE BACK INTO POTATO SKINS. BEAT REMAINING EGG YOLK WITH WATER. BRUSH OVER EACH POTATO. SET IN PAN AND BAKE FOR 15 MINUTES AT 400°F (200°C). SERVES 6.

BUTTER-BAKED TATERS

¼ CUP	BUTTER	60 ML
3 TBSP	FINELY CHOPPED GREEN ONIONS	45 ML
3	LARGE POTATOES, PEELED	3
	SALT AND BLACK PEPPER TO TASTE	
2 TBSP	GRATED PARMESAN CHEESE	30 ML

PREHEAT OVEN TO 500°F (260°C). MELT BUTTER IN A FRYING PAN, ADD ONION AND SAUTÉ UNTIL TENDER. HALVE POTATOES LENGTHWISE, THEN SLICE CROSSWISE INTO ⅛-INCH (3 MM) THICK SLICES. IMMEDIATELY LINE UP IN BUTTERED 13- BY 9-INCH (33 BY 23 CM) BAKING PAN WITH SLICES OVERLAPPING. POUR BUTTER MIXTURE OVER POTATOES. SEASON WITH SALT AND PEPPER. BAKE FOR 20 MINUTES. REMOVE FROM OVEN AND SPRINKLE WITH PARMESAN CHEESE. BAKE AN ADDITIONAL 5 TO 7 MINUTES OR UNTIL CHEESE IS SLIGHTLY BROWNED AND MELTED. SERVES 4.

VARIATION: SOME LIKE 'EM HOT! COMBINE 1 CUP (250 ML) SHREDDED CHEDDAR CHEESE, 1 CUP (250 ML) CRUSHED CORN FLAKES CEREAL AND 1 TSP (5 ML) CAYENNE PEPPER. SPRINKLE OVER BUTTERED POTATOES AND BAKE AT 400°F (200°C) FOR 30 MINUTES, OMITTING THE PARMESAN CHEESE.

POTATO SKINS

A DELI DELIGHT.

POTATOES
BACON, COOKED AND CRUMBLED
CHEDDAR CHEESE, SHREDDED
MELTED BUTTER
SOUR CREAM

SCRUB AND PRICK POTATOES. RUB WITH OIL. BAKE FOR
1 HOUR AT 400°F (200°C) OR UNTIL COOKED. COOL. SLICE
LENGTHWISE IN HALF, THEN SLICE IN HALF AGAIN. SCOOP
OUT MOST OF THE POTATO, LEAVING $1/8$ INCH (3 MM)
IN SKIN. BRUSH POTATO INSIDE AND OUT WITH BUTTER
AND PLACE ON COOKIE SHEET. BAKE AT 500°F (260°C)
FOR 12 MINUTES OR UNTIL CRISP. REMOVE AND SPRINKLE
GENEROUSLY WITH CHEDDAR CHEESE AND BACON. RETURN
TO OVEN UNTIL CHEESE MELTS. GREEN ONIONS AND/
OR HAM CAN ALSO BE ADDED FOR A CHANGE. SERVE WITH
SOUR CREAM. SERVES AS MANY AS YOU LIKE.

*YOU KNOW CHILDREN ARE GROWING UP WHEN THEY
START ASKING QUESTIONS THAT HAVE ANSWERS.*

POTATOES RÖSTI

GREAT WITH STEAK, ROAST BEEF OR LAMB.

POTATOES, SCRUBBED, UNPEELED
BUTTER
VEGETABLE OIL
SEASONING SALT

PREPARE POTATOES USING A MELON BALLER (ALLOW 8 TO 10 BALLS PER PERSON). PREHEAT OVEN TO 350°F (180°C). ADD BUTTER AND OIL TO ROASTING PAN AND HEAT FOR 10 MINUTES; ADD POTATOES AND BAKE FOR 45 MINUTES, STIRRING OFTEN. DRAIN ON PAPER TOWEL. SPRINKLE WITH SALT. THESE MAY ALSO BE COOKED IN A FRYING PAN.

ANOTHER WAY: USE SMALL NEW POTATOES. PLACE EACH ON A WOODEN SPOON AND SLICE, BUT NOT ALL THE WAY THROUGH. TOSS WITH MELTED BUTTER AND OIL. SPRINKLE WITH SEASONING SALT. BAKE AT 350°F (180°C) FOR 30 MINUTES, STIRRING OFTEN. THEY WILL FAN OUT WHILE COOKING — VERY CLEVER! SERVES AS MANY AS YOU NEED IT TO.

MEXICAN RICE

2 TBSP	VEGETABLE OIL	30 ML
1 CUP	UNCOOKED RICE	250 ML
1	CAN (14 OZ/398 ML) STEWED TOMATOES	1
1	SMALL ONION, MINCED	1
1/4 CUP	CHOPPED GREEN BELL PEPPER	60 ML
2 TSP	SALT	10 ML
1 TSP	CHILI POWDER	5 ML
2 CUPS	WATER	500 ML

IN A LARGE SKILLET, HEAT OIL AND ADD RICE. SAUTÉ, STIRRING, FOR 5 MINUTES OR UNTIL EVENLY BROWNED. ADD ALL INGREDIENTS AND MIX WELL. COVER WITH A LID AND SIMMER UNTIL RICE IS TENDER, ABOUT 30 MINUTES. REMOVE LID AND ALLOW TO DRY OUT. SERVES 6.

A SPILLED DRINK FLOWS IN THE DIRECTION OF THE MOST EXPENSIVE DRESS!

RICE WITH MUSHROOMS AND PINE NUTS

1 CUP	BOILING WATER	250 ML
1/3 CUP	RAISINS	75 ML
6 TBSP	BUTTER, DIVIDED	90 ML
1 TBSP	OLIVE OIL	15 ML
1/2	ONION, CHOPPED	1/2
1 CUP	LONG-GRAIN RICE, UNCOOKED	250 ML
2	CHICKEN BOUILLON CUBES	2
2 CUPS	BOILING WATER	500 ML
1 CUP	SLICED MUSHROOMS	250 ML
1/4 CUP	PINE NUTS	60 ML
	SALT AND BLACK PEPPER TO TASTE	

PREHEAT OVEN TO 375°F (190°C). POUR 1 CUP (250 ML) BOILING WATER OVER RAISINS. SET ASIDE. MELT 3 TBSP (45 ML) BUTTER IN OVENPROOF BAKING DISH, ADD OIL AND SAUTÉ ONION UNTIL SOFT. ADD UNCOOKED RICE AND STIR 2 TO 3 MINUTES. DISSOLVE CUBES IN THE LAST 2 CUPS (500 ML) BOILING WATER AND POUR OVER THE RICE. COVER, PLACE IN OVEN AND BAKE FOR 15 TO 20 MINUTES OR UNTIL LIQUID IS ABSORBED. SAUTÉ MUSHROOMS AND PINE NUTS IN 3 TBSP (45 ML) BUTTER FOR 5 MINUTES. DRAIN RAISINS. ADD MUSHROOMS, RAISINS, PINE NUTS AND SALT AND PEPPER TO COOKED RICE. TOSS WITH A FORK. SERVES 6.

WILD RICE AND ARTICHOKE HEARTS

1 CUP	UNCOOKED WILD RICE	250 ML
1	CAN (10 OZ/284 ML) CONSOMMÉ	1
1 3/4 CUPS	WATER	425 ML
1/2 TSP	SALT	2 ML
3 TBSP	BUTTER	45 ML
1/3 CUP	CHOPPED ONION	75 ML
2	CLOVES GARLIC, MINCED	2
2	JARS (EACH 6 OZ/170 ML) MARINATED ARTICHOKE HEARTS	2
1 TBSP	CHOPPED FRESH PARSLEY	15 ML
1/4 TSP	DRIED OREGANO	1 ML

WASH AND DRAIN WILD RICE. PLACE RICE, CONSOMMÉ, WATER AND SALT IN SAUCEPAN. HEAT TO BOILING; REDUCE HEAT AND SIMMER, COVERED, UNTIL TENDER, ABOUT 45 MINUTES.

IN A LARGE FRYING PAN, MELT BUTTER AND SAUTÉ ONION AND GARLIC UNTIL SOFT. DRAIN AND CUT ARTICHOKES INTO QUARTERS. ADD TO FRYING PAN WITH COOKED RICE, PARSLEY AND OREGANO. STIR UNTIL HEATED THROUGH. SERVES 4 TO 6.

SHE DOESN'T USE THE TIMER ANYMORE — SHE USES THE SMOKE ALARM!

WILD BUFFET RICE!

MAKES LOTS AND IS PERFECT WITH ANY MEAT.

I CUP	WILD RICE	250 ML
I	CAN (IO OZ/284 ML) REDUCED-SODIUM CHICKEN BROTH	I
I	CAN (IO OZ/284 ML) WATER	I
IO	PORK SAUSAGES, BROWNED, DRAINED AND CUT INTO SMALL PIECES	IO
8 OZ	MUSHROOMS, SLICED	250 G
I	LARGE ONION, FINELY CHOPPED	I
2 TBSP	ALL-PURPOSE FLOUR	30 ML
I CUP	WHIPPING (35%) CREAM	250 ML
I TSP	SALT	5 ML
1/4 TSP	DRIED OREGANO	I ML
1/4 TSP	DRIED SAGE	I ML
1/4 TSP	DRIED MARJORAM	I ML
1/4 TSP	DRIED THYME	I ML
1/2 CUP	BLANCHED ALMONDS, SLIVERED	125 ML

WASH WILD RICE AND COMBINE WITH BROTH AND WATER IN A LARGE, COVERED POT. BRING TO A BOIL AND REDUCE HEAT TO A SLOW BOIL FOR I HOUR OR UNTIL RICE BEGINS TO OPEN AND IS SOFT. SO FAR, SO GOOD. NOW, SAUTÉ ONION AND MUSHROOMS IN SKILLET AFTER SAUSAGE IS COOKED. ADD SAUSAGE AND ONION MIXTURE TO RICE. IN SAME SKILLET, ON MEDIUM HEAT, COMBINE FLOUR AND CREAM, STIRRING CONSTANTLY TO MAKE A CREAMY SAUCE, ADDING MORE CREAM OR WATER IF NECESSARY. BRING MIXTURE TO A BOIL FOR 3 MINUTES. ADD SEASONINGS. POUR RICE MIXTURE, SAUCE AND ALMONDS INTO LARGE CASSEROLE. MIX WELL AND BAKE AT 350°F (180°C) FOR 30 MINUTES. SERVES IO TO I2.

OVEN-BAKED WILD RICE

FABULOUS FLAVOR. MAKE IT IN THE MORNING
AND BAKE IT WITH THE BEEF.

1 1/2 CUPS	WILD RICE	375 ML
1/2 CUP	BUTTER	125 ML
1/2	CAN (8 OZ/227 ML) WATER CHESTNUTS	1/2
2 CUPS	SLICED MUSHROOMS	500 ML
3	CANS (EACH 10 OZ/284 ML) CONSOMMÉ, UNDILUTED	3

SOAK RICE OVERNIGHT IN A GENEROUS AMOUNT OF
WATER. DRAIN. MELT BUTTER IN AN 8-CUP (2 L) CASSEROLE
DISH. ADD RICE, WATER CHESTNUTS AND MUSHROOMS
AND STIR. POUR IN CONSOMMÉ. COVER AND REFRIGERATE
UNTIL READY TO BAKE. BAKE AT 350°F (180°C) FOR 2 TO
2 1/2 HOURS. GREAT WITH BEEF. SERVES 8.

PUT YOUR TROUBLES IN A POCKET WITH A HOLE IN IT.

WILD RICE CASSEROLE

VOTED "MOST POPULAR DISH TO BE SEEN AT A FOWL DINNER." SEVEN OLD BIRDS CAN'T BE WRONG!

2/3 CUP	WILD RICE	150 ML
2 CUPS	CONSOMMÉ	500 ML
1/4 CUP	BUTTER	60 ML
1/4 CUP	SLICED ONION	60 ML
1/2 CUP	DICED CELERY	125 ML
1/2 CUP	SLICED MUSHROOMS	125 ML
2 TBSP	TOASTED SLIVERED ALMONDS	30 ML

WASH AND DRAIN RICE. SIMMER RICE AND CONSOMMÉ, COVERED, FOR 40 MINUTES OR UNTIL TENDER. SAUTÉ ONION, CELERY AND MUSHROOMS IN BUTTER UNTIL TENDER. DRAIN RICE AND ADD SAUTÉED VEGETABLES. SPRINKLE WITH ALMONDS JUST BEFORE SERVING. SERVES 4 TO 6.

THE TROUBLE WITH OPPORTUNITY IS IT ALWAYS LOOKS BIGGER GOING THAN COMING.

CRANBERRY STUFFING

*GREAT IN THE CENTER OF A CROWN ROAST OF PORK —
OR IN THE MIDDLE OF YOUR TURKEY!*

1/4 CUP	BUTTER	60 ML
1	MEDIUM ONION, CHOPPED	1
1/2 CUP	CHOPPED CELERY	125 ML
4 CUPS	BREAD CRUMBS	1 L
1 TSP	SALT	5 ML
1/2 TSP	POULTRY SEASONING	2 ML
1/8 TSP	BLACK PEPPER	0.5 ML
1 CUP	CRANBERRIES, FRESH OR FROZEN AND THAWED	250 ML
2 CUPS	APPLES, PEELED, SLICED AND SPRINKLED WITH LEMON	500 ML

MELT BUTTER IN FRYING PAN; ADD ONIONS AND CELERY
AND SAUTÉ. COMBINE NEXT FOUR INGREDIENTS. ADD TO
ONION MIXTURE. STIR IN CRANBERRIES AND APPLES. STUFF!
SERVES 8.

*IT'S ALWAYS GOOD TO LEND A SYMPATHETIC EAR,
BUT SOMETIMES IT'S HARD TO GET IT BACK!*

TERRIFIC TURKEY STUFFING

FINALLY SOMETHING THAT'S GOOD FOR YOUR CAVITIES!

3 CUPS	COOKED WILD RICE	750 ML
2 CUPS	FRESH BREAD CRUMBS	500 ML
I LB	BULK PORK SAUSAGE	500 G
2	STALKS CELERY, FINELY CHOPPED	2
I	MEDIUM ONION, FINELY CHOPPED	I
	SALT AND BLACK PEPPER TO TASTE	
I TO 2 TSP	DRIED SAGE	5 TO IO ML
1/2 CUP	DRIED CRANBERRIES	125 ML

PLACE COOKED RICE AND BREAD CRUMBS IN A LARGE BOWL. FRY SAUSAGE, CELERY AND ONION UNTIL SAUSAGE IS BROWN. DRAIN AND ADD TO RICE MIXTURE. ADD SEASONINGS AND DRIED CRANBERRIES AND TOSS. MIXTURE SHOULD BE MOIST BUT NOT STICKY. ADD MORE BREAD CRUMBS IF NECESSARY. SPOON, BUT DON'T PACK, INTO NECK CAVITY AND BREAST CAVITY OF TURKEY. BE SURE TO REMOVE STUFFING FROM BIRD IMMEDIATELY AFTER REMOVING TURKEY FROM OVEN. KEEP WARM IN A SMALL CASSEROLE. SERVES IO TO I2.

IT'S NOT AS EASY AS PEOPLE THINK TO GET A PARKING TICKET. FIRST, YOU HAVE TO FIND SOMEWHERE TO PARK!

GOURMET CRANBERRY SAUCE

3 CUPS	FRESH OR FROZEN CRANBERRIES	750 ML
1	ORANGE, CUT IN QUARTERS	1
1 CUP	BERRY SUGAR	250 ML
1/4 CUP	GRAND MARNIER	60 ML

CHOP CRANBERRIES AND ORANGE IN BLENDER OR FOOD PROCESSOR. ADD BERRY SUGAR AND GRAND MARNIER. *FINI!* SERVES 12.

PLUM SAUCE

THIS IS A VERSATILE, DELICIOUS SAUCE.
SERVE WITH PORK OR FOWL.

1	JAR (12 OZ/341 ML) PLUM JAM	1
2 TBSP	VINEGAR	30 ML
1 TBSP	BROWN SUGAR	15 ML
1 TBSP	FINELY CHOPPED ONION	15 ML
1 TSP	SEEDED AND FINELY CHOPPED DRIED RED CHILE PEPPER OR HOT PEPPER FLAKES	5 ML
1	CLOVE GARLIC, MINCED	1
1/2 TSP	GROUND GINGER	2 ML

IN A SMALL SAUCEPAN, COMBINE PLUM JAM, VINEGAR, BROWN SUGAR, ONION, RED CHILE PEPPER, GARLIC AND GINGER. BRING MIXTURE TO BOILING, STIRRING CONSTANTLY. REMOVE FROM HEAT AND COOL SLIGHTLY. REFRIGERATE, COVERED, OVERNIGHT. MAKES 1 1/4 CUPS (300 ML).

CUMBERLAND SAUCE

SERVED HOT OR COLD, THIS IS A TREAT WITH FOWL!

1 TSP	GRATED ORANGE ZEST	5 ML
3/4 CUP	ORANGE JUICE	175 ML
1/2 CUP	RED CURRANT JELLY	125 ML
2 TBSP	CLARET OR PORT WINE	30 ML
1 TBSP	LEMON JUICE	15 ML
4 TSP	CORNSTARCH	20 ML
1/4 TSP	GROUND GINGER	1 ML

COMBINE ALL INGREDIENTS IN A SMALL SAUCEPAN AND BRING TO A BOIL, STIRRING CONSTANTLY. REDUCE HEAT AND COOK FOR 2 MINUTES LONGER. MAKES 1 1/2 CUPS (375 ML).

SALSA

TRY THIS ON ANY MEAT, FISH OR EGG DISH.
OUR FAVORITE IS MONTEREY JACK CHEESE MELTED ON FLOUR TORTILLA HALVES AND TOPPED WITH SALSA. ROLL THEM UP AND ATTACK!

2	LARGE RIPE TOMATOES, DICED	2
1	MEDIUM ONION, CHOPPED	1
1 TO 2	CLOVES GARLIC, MINCED	1 TO 2
6 TO 10	SMALL GREEN CHILES (OR 2 TO 4 JALAPEÑO PEPPERS; FRESH IS BEST)	6 TO 10

CHOP VEGETABLES, REMOVING SEEDS FROM CHILES. COMBINE ALL INGREDIENTS AND CHILL FOR 2 HOURS BEFORE SERVING. MAKES ABOUT 3 CUPS (750 ML).

PESTO SAUCE

THIS SAUCE CAN BE STORED IN A JAR IN YOUR
REFRIGERATOR FOR SEVERAL WEEKS. IT IS GOOD IN
AND ON SOUP, SALAD, PASTA OR FRENCH BREAD!

4	CLOVES GARLIC, MINCED	4
2 CUPS	FRESH BASIL LEAVES (OR $1/2$ CUP/125 ML DRIED)	500 ML
$1/2$ CUP	FRESHLY GRATED PARMESAN CHEESE	125 ML
$1/4$ CUP	PINE NUTS (OPTIONAL)	60 ML
$1/2$ CUP	OLIVE OIL	125 ML

COMBINE GARLIC, BASIL, CHEESE AND NUTS (IF USING) IN
A BLENDER AND PURÉE. WITH MACHINE RUNNING SLOWLY,
ADD OIL THROUGH FEED TUBE IN A SLOW, STEADY
STREAM UNTIL MIXTURE IS THE CONSISTENCY OF THICK
MAYONNAISE. MAKES ABOUT $1 1/2$ CUPS (375 ML).

NOTE: IF YOU USE THE PINE NUTS, MAKE SURE THEY ARE
FRESH.

A HOST DOESN'T MIND HIS GUEST'S SHORTCOMINGS
NEARLY AS MUCH AS THEIR LONG-STAYINGS.

ALFREDO SAUCE

BASIC AND A BREEZE TO MAKE. SERVE WITH ANY PASTA.
OUR FAVORITE IS FETTUCCINE OR TORTELLINI.

1/3 CUP	BUTTER	75 ML
1 1/2 CUPS	WHIPPING (35%) CREAM	375 ML
3 TO 4 CUPS	COOKED PASTA	750 ML TO 1 L
1 CUP	FRESHLY GRATED PARMESAN CHEESE	250 ML
1/4 CUP	MILK	60 ML
1 TSP	SALT	5 ML
1/2 TSP	BLACK PEPPER	2 ML
PINCH	GROUND NUTMEG	PINCH

IN A LARGE FRYING PAN, MELT BUTTER OVER HIGH HEAT UNTIL IT TURNS LIGHT BROWN. ADD 1/2 CUP (125 ML) OF CREAM AND BOIL, STIRRING CONSTANTLY, UNTIL MIXTURE BECOMES SHINY AND LARGE BUBBLES FORM. SET ASIDE IF MAKING AHEAD.

COOK PASTA ACCORDING TO PACKAGE DIRECTIONS. OVER MEDIUM HEAT, ADD PASTA TO SAUCE, MIXING WITH 2 FORKS TO COAT WELL. ADD PARMESAN CHEESE, REMAINING CREAM AND MILK, A LITTLE OF EACH AT A TIME UNTIL ALL ARE COMBINED. SEASON WITH SALT, PEPPER AND NUTMEG, ADDING MORE OF EACH IF DESIRED. SERVES 4 TO 6.

PEANUT SAUCE

TRY THIS WITH PORK ROAST, MEAT FONDUE OR SATAY.

1	MEDIUM ONION, FINELY CHOPPED	1
1/2 TSP	MINCED GARLIC	2 ML
1/2 TSP	HOT PEPPER FLAKES	2 ML
6 TBSP	SOY SAUCE	90 ML
1/4 CUP	SHERRY	60 ML
1/4 TSP	GROUND GINGER	1 ML
3/4 CUP	SMOOTH PEANUT BUTTER	175 ML
1/2 CUP	CHICKEN STOCK	125 ML
1 CUP	COCONUT MILK	250 ML

SAUTÉ ONION, GARLIC AND HOT PEPPER FLAKES. ADD ALL OTHER INGREDIENTS EXCEPT COCONUT MILK. BRING TO A BOIL, THEN SIMMER FOR 30 MINUTES. STRAIN MIXTURE, COOL, DRAIN EXCESS OIL AND ADD COCONUT MILK. REHEAT TO SERVE. MAKES 3 CUPS (750 ML).

SOME OF US TREAT OUR BODIES AS IF
WE HAD A SPARE IN THE TRUNK.

MONK'S MUSTARD

AMEN!

1 CUP	WHOLE BLACK MUSTARD SEEDS	250 ML
3/4 CUP	WHITE WINE VINEGAR	175 ML
1/4 CUP	SHERRY	60 ML
2 CUPS	DRY MUSTARD, LOOSELY PACKED	500 ML
3/4 CUP	FIRMLY PACKED BROWN SUGAR	175 ML
1/2 TSP	SALT	2 ML

COMBINE MUSTARD SEEDS, VINEGAR AND SHERRY IN A MEDIUM BOWL AND LET STAND FOR 2 TO 3 HOURS. TRANSFER MIXTURE TO PROCESSOR AND BLEND UNTIL ALMOST SMOOTH. ADD DRY MUSTARD, BROWN SUGAR AND SALT; BLEND WELL. PLACE IN TOP OF DOUBLE BOILER OVER SIMMERING WATER AND COOK FOR 7 MINUTES, STIRRING CONSTANTLY. DO NOT OVERCOOK. LET COOL. TRANSFER TO JARS WITH TIGHT-FITTING LIDS AND REFRIGERATE FOR UP TO 3 WEEKS. IF TOO STIFF, ADD EQUAL PORTIONS OF WATER AND OIL. MAKES 3 CUPS (750 ML).

YOU KNOW IT'S GOING TO BE A BAD DAY WHEN YOUR TWIN BROTHER FORGETS YOUR BIRTHDAY.

TARRAGON MUSTARD

PERFECT WITH SHELLFISH.

2 CUPS	DRY MUSTARD, LOOSELY PACKED	500 ML
I CUP	GRANULATED SUGAR	250 ML
3/4 CUP	TARRAGON VINEGAR	175 ML
2 TBSP	CRUMBLED DRIED TARRAGON	30 ML
I TSP	SALT	5 ML
1/2 CUP	OLIVE OIL	125 ML

COMBINE ALL INGREDIENTS EXCEPT OLIVE OIL IN BLENDER AND MIX UNTIL SMOOTH AND CREAMY. WITH MACHINE RUNNING SLOWLY, ADD OLIVE OIL IN SLOW, STEADY STREAM AND BLEND UNTIL MIXTURE IS LIKE MAYONNAISE. POUR INTO JARS WITH TIGHT-FITTING LIDS AND REFRIGERATE FOR UP TO 3 WEEKS. IF TOO STIFF, ADD EQUAL PORTIONS OF WATER AND OIL. MAKES 4 CUPS (I L).

"I DON'T BELIEVE IN HOROSCOPES... BUT, OF COURSE, THAT'S TYPICAL FOR A TAURUS."

PICCALILLI

PICK THIS ONE — IT'S EASIER THAN TRYING TO PICK
ANYTHING ELSE... A ROSE, A MAN, A DRESS...

10 TO 12	MEDIUM GREEN TOMATOES	10 TO 12
6	MEDIUM GREEN BELL PEPPERS	6
6	MEDIUM RED BELL PEPPERS	6
4	MEDIUM ONIONS	4
6 CUPS	VINEGAR	1.5 L
3 1/2 CUPS	GRANULATED SUGAR	875 ML
1/4 CUP	MUSTARD SEEDS	60 ML
1/4 CUP	SALT	60 ML
1 TBSP	CELERY SEEDS	15 ML
2 TSP	GROUND ALLSPICE	10 ML
1 TSP	GROUND CINNAMON	5 ML

GRIND OR FINELY CHOP ALL VEGETABLES AND PLACE IN A
LARGE DUTCH OVEN. ADD 4 CUPS (1 L) VINEGAR AND BRING
TO A FULL BOIL OVER HIGH HEAT. REDUCE HEAT AND
SIMMER FOR 30 MINUTES, STIRRING OCCASIONALLY. DRAIN
AND RETURN TO POT. ADD 2 CUPS (500 ML) VINEGAR AND
REMAINING INGREDIENTS AND BRING MIXTURE TO A BOIL
OVER HIGH HEAT. SIMMER FOR 3 MINUTES. LADLE INTO HOT,
STERILIZED JARS, LEAVING 1/2 INCH (1 CM) HEADSPACE. WIPE
RIMS AND SEAL WITH TWO-PIECE CANNING LIDS. PROCESS
IN A BOILING WATER CANNER FOR 15 MINUTES. CHECK SEALS
AND REFRIGERATE ANY JARS THAT ARE NOT SEALED.
MAKES ABOUT 6 PINT (500 ML) JARS.

CORN RELISH

6 CUPS	CORN KERNELS (FROZEN)	1.5 L
3	MEDIUM ONIONS, FINELY CHOPPED	3
1	RED BELL PEPPER, FINELY CHOPPED	1
1	GREEN BELL PEPPER, FINELY CHOPPED	1
1/2 CUP	FINELY CHOPPED CELERY	125 ML
2 CUPS	CIDER VINEGAR	500 ML
1 CUP	GRANULATED SUGAR	250 ML
2 TBSP	PICKLING SALT	30 ML
2 TBSP	DRY MUSTARD	30 ML
1/2 TSP	CELERY SEEDS	2 ML
1/4 TSP	TURMERIC	1 ML
1/4 TSP	BLACK PEPPER	1 ML

COMBINE ALL INGREDIENTS IN A LARGE DUTCH OVEN.
BRING TO A BOIL; REDUCE HEAT AND SIMMER, UNCOVERED,
FOR 30 MINUTES. STIR OCCASIONALLY. LADLE INTO HOT,
STERILIZED JARS, LEAVING 1/2 INCH (1 CM) HEADSPACE.
WIPE RIMS AND SEAL WITH TWO-PIECE CANNING LIDS.
PROCESS IN A BOILING WATER CANNER FOR 10 MINUTES.
CHECK SEALS AND REFRIGERATE ANY JARS THAT ARE NOT
SEALED. MAKES ABOUT EIGHT 8-OZ (250 ML) JARS.

A DOG'S LIFE WOULDN'T BE TOO BAD... ALL A DOG HAS TO
WORRY ABOUT IS THE TOILET SEAT FALLING ON ITS HEAD!

ZUCCHINI RELISH

SERVE WITH ROAST BEEF OR, IN AN ECONOMIC CRISIS, TRY IT ON A CRACKER.

16 CUPS	FINELY CHOPPED ZUCCHINI	4 L
4 TO 5	LARGE ONIONS, FINELY CHOPPED	4 TO 5
1	GREEN BELL PEPPER, FINELY CHOPPED	1
1/2 CUP	PICKLING SALT	125 ML
1 1/2 CUPS	GRANULATED SUGAR	375 ML
1 1/2 CUPS	BROWN SUGAR	375 ML
3 CUPS	VINEGAR	750 ML
1/2 CUP	WATER	125 ML
2 TBSP	TURMERIC	30 ML
2 TBSP	CELERY SEEDS	30 ML

PLACE ZUCCHINI, ONIONS AND PEPPER IN A LARGE BOWL. SPRINKLE WITH PICKLING SALT AND COVER WITH ICE WATER. LET STAND FOR 1 HOUR. DRAIN AND RINSE WELL UNDER COLD RUNNING WATER. DRAIN THOROUGHLY.

IN A LARGE POT, BOIL SUGARS, VINEGAR, WATER, TURMERIC AND CELERY SEEDS FOR 3 MINUTES. ADD VEGETABLE MIXTURE, BRING TO A BOIL, THEN SIMMER FOR 10 TO 15 MINUTES. LADLE INTO HOT, STERILIZED JARS, LEAVING 1/2 INCH (1 CM) HEADSPACE. WIPE RIMS AND SEAL WITH TWO-PIECE CANNING LIDS. PROCESS IN A BOILING WATER CANNER FOR 15 MINUTES. CHECK SEALS AND REFRIGERATE ANY JARS THAT ARE NOT SEALED. MAKES ABOUT 10 PINT (500 ML) JARS.

GREEN TOMATO MARMALADE

15 TO 20	GREEN TOMATOES (ABOUT 4 LBS/2KG)	15 TO 20
8 CUPS	GRANULATED SUGAR	2 KG
3	LEMONS	3
2 CUPS	WALNUTS, CHOPPED	500 G

WASH TOMATOES AND CHOP FINELY. ADD SUGAR AND LET STAND OVERNIGHT. CUT THE LEMONS, RIND AND ALL, INTO 5 PIECES AND REMOVE SEEDS. PUT TOMATOES AND SUGAR INTO A LARGE PRESERVING KETTLE AND HEAT TO BOILING. ADD LEMON. REDUCE HEAT AND SIMMER FOR 45 TO 50 MINUTES OR UNTIL THICK; ADD WALNUTS 5 MINUTES BEFORE REMOVING FROM HEAT. LADLE INTO HOT, STERILIZED JARS, LEAVING $1/2$ INCH (1 CM) HEADSPACE. WIPE RIMS AND SEAL WITH TWO-PIECE CANNING LIDS. PROCESS IN A BOILING WATER CANNER FOR 10 MINUTES. CHECK SEALS AND REFRIGERATE ANY JARS THAT ARE NOT SEALED. MAKES TEN 8-OZ (250 ML) JARS.

IT'S NOT A SIN TO BE RICH — IT'S A MIRACLE!

MISS SCARLETT'S WINE CORDIAL

AN UNUSUAL LAYERED JELLY — PERFECT FOR
CHRISTMAS GIFTING. SERVE WITH GAME OR FOWL.

6 CUPS	GRANULATED SUGAR	1.5 L
4 CUPS	DRY WHITE WINE (DOMESTIC WILL DO)	1 L
2	POUCHES (EACH 3 OZ/85 ML) LIQUID PECTIN	2
1/4 CUP	ORANGE LIQUEUR	60 ML
1/4 CUP	CRÈME DE CASSIS	60 ML
1/4 CUP	GREEN CRÈME DE MENTHE	60 ML

BRING SUGAR AND WINE TO A SLOW BOIL IN A LARGE POT,
STIRRING CONSTANTLY. ADD PECTIN AND BRING BACK TO
BOILING; BOIL HARD FOR 1 MINUTE. REMOVE FROM HEAT
AND SKIM FOAM FROM TOP. POUR INTO 3 SMALL BOWLS,
ABOUT 2 1/2 CUPS (625 ML) EACH. ADD ORANGE LIQUEUR TO
ONE BOWL, CRÈME DE CASSIS TO SECOND BOWL WITH
A FEW DROPS OF RED FOOD COLORING, AND CRÈME DE
MENTHE TO THE THIRD BOWL. POUR ONE COLOR INTO
BOTTOM THIRD OF HOT, STERILIZED JARS AND LET COOL
FOR 20 MINUTES — BE PATIENT. CAREFULLY ADD SECOND
LAYER AND LET SET, THEN FILL WITH THIRD LAYER,
LEAVING 1/2 INCH (1 CM) HEADSPACE. WIPE RIMS AND SEAL
WITH TWO-PIECE CANNING LIDS. PROCESS IN A BOILING
WATER CANNER FOR 10 MINUTES. CHECK SEALS AND
REFRIGERATE ANY JARS THAT ARE NOT SEALED. MAKES
ABOUT SIX 8-OZ (250 ML) JARS.

NOTE: YOU MAY HAVE TO REHEAT SECOND AND THIRD
LAYER MIXTURES SLIGHTLY IN ORDER TO POUR PROPERLY.

SEASONED FLOUR

A FLAVORFUL COMPLEMENT TO ANY MEAT THAT
REQUIRES "FLOURING." STORE IN A PLASTIC CONTAINER
ET VOILA! YOU'RE ORGANIZED!

2 CUPS	ALL-PURPOSE FLOUR	500 ML
I TBSP	SALT	15 ML
I TSP	CELERY SALT	5 ML
I TBSP	BLACK PEPPER	15 ML
2 TBSP	DRY MUSTARD	30 ML
$\frac{1}{4}$ CUP	PAPRIKA	60 ML
2 TSP	GARLIC SALT	10 ML
I TSP	GROUND GINGER	5 ML
$\frac{1}{2}$ TSP	DRIED THYME	2 ML
$\frac{1}{2}$ TSP	DRIED BASIL	2 ML
$\frac{1}{2}$ TSP	DRIED OREGANO	2 ML

COMBINE ALL INGREDIENTS. MAKES ABOUT $2\frac{1}{2}$ CUPS
(625 ML).

ONCE I THOUGHT I MADE A MISTAKE, BUT I WAS WRONG.

SALT SUBSTITUTE

*IF YOU CAN'T HAVE SALT, THIS ADDS FLAVOR
TO YOUR LIFE!*

I TBSP	DRY MUSTARD	15 ML
I TBSP	GARLIC POWDER	15 ML
I TBSP	ONION POWDER	15 ML
I TBSP	PAPRIKA	15 ML
I 1/2 TSP	BLACK OR CAYENNE PEPPER	7 ML
I TSP	DRIED BASIL	5 ML
I TSP	DRIED THYME	5 ML

COMBINE INGREDIENTS WELL AND PLACE IN A SHAKER JAR. MAKES ABOUT 1/3 CUP (75 ML).

SIGN ON THE BUMPER OF AN ELABORATE MOTOR HOME: "WE'RE SPENDING OUR CHILDREN'S INHERITANCE."

PART III
GOODIES

COOKIES, SQUARES AND CANDIES

AFTER ANGEL FOOD
    COOKIES. 277

CHEWY KIDS' COOKIES. . . . 278

B.L.'S COOKIES 279

WAFER PUFFS 280

GINGER SNAPS 281

PEPPERNUTS. 282

ZUCCHINI COOKIES. 283

PEANUT BUTTER
    COOKIES. 284

PECAN CRISPS 285

POPPY SEED COOKIES 286

FATAL ATTRACTIONS. 287

GLAZED CINNAMON BARS. . 288

COCONUT BARS 289

BUTTER TART SLICE. 290

BROWN BAGGER'S
    SPECIAL 291

SCOTCH SQUARES 292

CHOCOLATE CHIP SLAB
    COOKIES. 293

ROCKY MOUNTAIN
    SQUARES 293

CHEWY CHOCOLATE
    PEANUT BARS 294

PEANUT BUTTER
    BROWNIES 295

MATRIMONIAL BARS. 296

SHORTCUT ALMOND
    ROCA. 297

ALMOND FLORENTINES. . . 298

MICROWAVE PEANUT
    BRITTLE 299

BOURBON BALLS. 300

CHOCOLATE PEANUT
    BUTTER BALLS. 301

CAKES

PUMPKIN CHEESECAKE . . . 302

POPPY SEED CAKE 303

POPPY SEED CHIFFON
    CAKE. 304

APPLE KUCHEN 305

HAZELNUT TORTE 306

BANANA GINGER LOAF . . . 308

EASY PEACH TORTE. 310

COCONUT WHIP CAKE. 311

MOCHA WHIPPED CREAM
    CAKE. 312

DARK CHOCOLATE
    CAKE. 313

CRATER CAKE 314

CHOCOLATE ZUCCHINI
    CAKE. 315

CHOCOLATE MOUSSE
    CAKE. 316

CHOCOLATE RASPBERRY
    TORTE 318

CHOCOLATE CHIFFON
    CAKE. 320

BLACK BOTTOM
    CUPCAKES 321

PIES AND TARTS

FAIL-PROOF PASTRY 322

SHOO-FLY PIE 323

FLAPPER PIE 324

IRISH COFFEE CREAM
    PIE 326

SPIKED APPLE BETTY 328

FRENCH LEMON PIE 329

PEACHES AND CREAM
    PIE 330

RHUBARB CRISP WITH
    BOURBON SAUCE 331

RHUBARB MERINGUE PIE . . . 332

PALACE PIE 333

PUMPKIN CHIFFON PIE 334

PUMPKIN PECAN PIE 335

CHOCOLATE PECAN PIE . . . 336

CHOCOLATE MOUSSE PIE . . 337

FUDGE PIE WITH CUSTARD
    SAUCE 338

PECAN CRUST ICE CREAM
    PIE WITH CARAMEL
    SAUCE 340

TIN ROOF PIE 341

SHORTBREAD TARTS WITH
    CHEESE 'N' FRUIT OR
    LEMON FILLING 342

PECAN CUPS 344

JUST DESSERTS

CHERRY BERRIES ON
    A CLOUD 345

GRAND SLAM FINALE 346

RHUBARB CREAM
    DESSERT 347

RHUBARB DELIGHT 348

TIRAMISU 349

FRUIT POOF 350

FROSTY PEACH
    DESSERT 352

PAVLOVA 353

TOFFEE MERINGUE 354

GRAND MARNIER CRÈME . . 355

CRÈME CARAMEL 356

STELLA BY STARLIGHT 357

CHOCOLATE SABAYON 358

LEMON SORBET 359

FROZEN LEMON MOUSSE
    WITH RASPBERRY
    SAUCE 360

FRUIT DIP 362

HOT FUDGE SAUCE 363

BEVERAGES

FROTHY ORANGE
    SLUSHY 364

A REAL SMOOTHIE 364

GRADUATION PUNCH 365

MARGARITAS MUCHO
    GRANDE 366

FUZZY NAVELS 366

LONG ISLAND ICED TEA . . 367

SANGRIA À LA MOE 368

GLØGG 369

TERRY'S PUNCH 370

MIDSUMMER MADNESS . . . 370

HOT BUTTERED RUM 371

AFTER ANGEL FOOD COOKIES

*THE VERY THING FOR LEFTOVER EGG YOLKS,
THESE SOFT AND CHEWY DELIGHTS ARE ALSO
KNOWN AS AFTER MERINGUE COOKIES.*

2/3 CUP	BUTTER	150 ML
1/2 CUP	BROWN SUGAR	125 ML
1/2 CUP	GRANULATED SUGAR	125 ML
1/2 TSP	VANILLA EXTRACT	2 ML
5	EGG YOLKS	5
1 1/2 CUPS	ALL-PURPOSE FLOUR	375 ML
1/2 TSP	BAKING SODA	2 ML
1 TSP	BAKING POWDER	5 ML
1/4 TSP	SALT	1 ML
1/2 TSP	GROUND CINNAMON	2 ML
1/2 CUP	CHOPPED WALNUTS	125 ML
1/2 CUP	CHOPPED DATES	125 ML
1/2 CUP	RAISINS	125 ML

CREAM BUTTER AND SUGARS. ADD VANILLA AND EGG
YOLKS. MIX FLOUR, BAKING SODA, BAKING POWDER, SALT
AND CINNAMON. ADD TO CREAMED MIXTURE AND MIX
UNTIL SMOOTH. ADD WALNUTS, DATES AND RAISINS AND
BLEND WELL. PLACE MEDIUM SPOONFULS OF DOUGH ON
A GREASED COOKIE SHEET. BAKE AT 350°F (180°C) FOR
10 MINUTES. MAKES 4 DOZEN COOKIES.

ONE GOOD TURN USUALLY TAKES OFF THE COVERS.

CHEWY KIDS' COOKIES

NOT ONLY DO THEY LOVE TO EAT THEM,
THEY LOVE TO MAKE THEM.

1 CUP	BUTTER	250 ML
1 1/2 CUPS	GRANULATED SUGAR	375 ML
1	EGG	1
1 TSP	VANILLA OR ALMOND EXTRACT	5 ML
2 CUPS	ALL-PURPOSE FLOUR	500 ML
2 TSP	BAKING SODA	10 ML
1/2 TSP	SALT	2 ML
2 CUPS	RAISINS (OR CURRANTS FOR VARIETY)	500 ML
1 1/4 CUPS	OATMEAL	300 ML

CREAM TOGETHER BUTTER AND SUGAR. BEAT IN EGG
AND ADD VANILLA. SIFT TOGETHER FLOUR, BAKING SODA
AND SALT. COMBINE DRY INGREDIENTS WITH CREAMED
MIXTURE. ADD RAISINS AND OATMEAL. MIXTURE WILL
BE VERY CRUMBLY BUT DON'T DESPAIR. PAT FIRMLY IN
1/4-INCH (0.5 CM) LAYER ONTO TWO GREASED COOKIE
SHEETS (THERE WILL BE LOTS OF ROOM FOR THE DOUGH
TO EXPAND). BAKE FOR 12 MINUTES AT 350°F (180°C). ALLOW
TO COOL FOR 2 MINUTES, THEN CUT INTO STRIPS WITH
A SHARP KNIFE. ALLOW TO COOL BEFORE REMOVING FROM
COOKIE SHEET. (THE ONLY WAY TO MANAGE THIS IS TO
KEEP THE KIDS OUT OF THE KITCHEN.) MAKES ABOUT
4 DOZEN COOKIES.

B.L.'S COOKIES

GUESS WHAT? YOU'RE ABOUT TO MAKE DAD'S COOKIES!

1 CUP	BUTTER OR MARGARINE	250 ML
1 CUP	GRANULATED SUGAR	250 ML
1/2 CUP	BROWN SUGAR	125 ML
1	EGG	1
1 TSP	VANILLA EXTRACT	5 ML
1 1/2 CUPS	ROLLED OATS	375 ML
1 1/2 CUPS	ALL-PURPOSE FLOUR	375 ML
1 CUP	COCONUT	250 ML
1 TSP	BAKING SODA	5 ML
1 TSP	BAKING POWDER	5 ML
2 TBSP	LIGHT (FANCY) MOLASSES	30 ML
1 1/2 TSP	GROUND CINNAMON	7 ML
1 TSP	GROUND ALLSPICE	5 ML
1 TSP	GROUND NUTMEG	5 ML

CREAM TOGETHER BUTTER AND SUGARS. ADD EGG AND
VANILLA. STIR IN REMAINING INGREDIENTS. MIX WELL. ROLL
INTO SMALL BALLS AND PLACE ON COOKIE SHEET. DO NOT
PRESS DOWN. BAKE AT 350°F (180°C) FOR 10 TO 12 MINUTES.
MAKES 4 DOZEN COOKIES.

SKINNY COOKS CAN'T BE TRUSTED.

WAFER PUFFS

*THESE LITTLE SANDWICH COOKIES MELT IN
YOUR MOUTH AND PUFF UP YOUR CHEEKS!*

1 CUP	BUTTER	250 ML
2 CUPS	ALL-PURPOSE FLOUR	500 ML
1/2 CUP	WHIPPING (35%) CREAM	125 ML
	GRANULATED SUGAR	

FILLING

1/4 CUP	BUTTER	60 ML
1/2 TSP	VANILLA EXTRACT	2 ML
1	EGG YOLK	1
1 1/2 TO 2 CUPS	ICING (CONFECTIONER'S) SUGAR	375 TO 500 ML

IN A MEDIUM BOWL, CUT BUTTER INTO FLOUR TO FORM
A CRUMBLY MIXTURE. ADD CREAM AND MIX LIGHTLY. ROLL
OUT DOUGH TO 1/4 INCH (0.5 CM) AND CUT OUT IN 1-INCH
(2.5 CM) CIRCLES. PRICK WITH A FORK AND SUGAR BOTH
SIDES. PLACE ON UNGREASED COOKIE SHEETS AND BAKE
AT 375°F (190°C) FOR 7 TO 9 MINUTES.

FILLING: BEAT BUTTER, VANILLA AND EGG YOLK TOGETHER.
ADD ENOUGH SUGAR TO MAKE A VERY CREAMY BUT FAIRLY
STIFF ICING. SPREAD FILLING BETWEEN 2 COOKIES TO
MAKE SANDWICHES. MAKES ABOUT 2 DOZEN COOKIES.

NOTE: THIS RECIPE CONTAINS A RAW EGG YOLK. IF THE
FOOD SAFETY OF RAW EGGS IS A CONCERN FOR YOU,
SUBSTITUTE A PASTEURIZED EGG YOLK OR 2 TBSP (30 ML)
PASTEURIZED LIQUID WHOLE EGGS.

GINGER SNAPS

ALSO PERFECT FOR GINGERBREAD MEN.

3/4 CUP	BUTTER OR MARGARINE	175 ML
I CUP	GRANULATED SUGAR	250 ML
1/4 CUP	LIGHT (FANCY) MOLASSES	60 ML
I	EGG, BEATEN	I
2 CUPS	ALL-PURPOSE FLOUR	500 ML
1/4 TSP	SALT	I ML
2 TSP	BAKING SODA	10 ML
I TO 2 TSP	GROUND CINNAMON	5 TO 10 ML
I TO 2 TSP	GROUND CLOVES	5 TO 10 ML
I TO 2 TSP	GROUND GINGER	5 TO 10 ML
	GRANULATED SUGAR	

CREAM TOGETHER BUTTER AND SUGAR. ADD MOLASSES AND EGG. BEAT TOGETHER. COMBINE FLOUR, SALT, BAKING SODA AND SPICES. ADD TO CREAMED MIXTURE AND MIX WELL. ROLL INTO BALLS, THEN IN SUGAR. PRESS FLAT WITH A FORK. BAKE AT 375°F (190°C) FOR 15 MINUTES. MAKES ABOUT 4 DOZEN COOKIES.

THE FIRST SIGN OF MATURITY IS THE DISCOVERY
THAT THE VOLUME KNOB ALSO TURNS LEFT.

PEPPERNUTS

FOR THE HOLIDAY SEASON!

1/3 CUP	LIGHT (FANCY) MOLASSES	75 ML
1/3 CUP	BUTTER	75 ML
1	EGG, BEATEN	1
2 CUPS	ALL-PURPOSE FLOUR	500 ML
1/3 CUP	GRANULATED SUGAR	75 ML
1/2 TSP	BAKING SODA	2 ML
1 TSP	GROUND CINNAMON	5 ML
1 TSP	GROUND GINGER	5 ML
1/4 TSP	GROUND NUTMEG	1 ML
1/4 TSP	GROUND CLOVES	1 ML
PINCH	SALT	PINCH
PINCH	BLACK PEPPER	PINCH
	FRUIT SUGAR, TO COAT	

HEAT MOLASSES WITH BUTTER, STIRRING UNTIL BUTTER MELTS. COOL TO ROOM TEMPERATURE. STIR IN BEATEN EGG. THOROUGHLY MIX DRY INGREDIENTS. ADD DRY MIXTURE TO MOLASSES AND BUTTER GRADUALLY. BLEND THOROUGHLY. SHAPE INTO SMALL BALLS. BAKE AT 375°F (190°C) FOR 10 TO 12 MINUTES. ROLL IN FRUIT SUGAR WHILE WARM. STORE IN A TIGHTLY COVERED TIN TO KEEP THEM SEMISOFT. MAKES ABOUT 3 DOZEN COOKIES.

ZUCCHINI COOKIES

THE GARDEN TURNED TO CALORIES!

3/4 CUP	BUTTER	175 ML
1 1/2 CUPS	GRANULATED SUGAR	375 ML
1	EGG, BEATEN	1
1 TSP	VANILLA EXTRACT	5 ML
1 1/2 CUPS	GRATED ZUCCHINI	375 ML
2 1/2 CUPS	ALL-PURPOSE FLOUR	625 ML
2 TSP	BAKING POWDER	10 ML
1/2 TSP	SALT	2 ML
1 TSP	GROUND CINNAMON	5 ML
1 CUP	ALMONDS OR OTHER NUTS, CHOPPED	250 ML
1 CUP	CHOCOLATE CHIPS	250 ML

CREAM BUTTER AND SUGAR. ADD EGG AND VANILLA, THEN ZUCCHINI. ADD DRY INGREDIENTS, SPICES AND NUTS AND STIR IN CHOCOLATE CHIPS. DROP BY THE TEASPOONFUL ON A GREASED COOKIE SHEET. BAKE AT 350°F (180°C) FOR 10 TO 12 MINUTES. MAKES ABOUT 6 DOZEN COOKIES.

BROKEN COOKIES DON'T HAVE CALORIES!

PEANUT BUTTER COOKIES

YOU ASKED FOR IT! YOU GOT IT!

1/3 CUP	BUTTER	75 ML
1/2 CUP	BROWN SUGAR	125 ML
1/2 CUP	GRANULATED SUGAR	125 ML
1/2 CUP	PEANUT BUTTER	125 ML
1	EGG, LIGHTLY BEATEN	1
1 CUP	ALL-PURPOSE FLOUR	250 ML
1 TSP	BAKING SODA	5 ML
1/2 TSP	SALT	2 ML
	GRANULATED SUGAR FOR COATING	

CREAM TOGETHER BUTTER AND SUGARS. ADD PEANUT BUTTER AND MIX WELL. ADD EGG AND THEN THE DRY INGREDIENTS. ROLL INTO BALLS AND THEN IN SUGAR. PLACE ON GREASED COOKIE SHEET. PRESS FLAT WITH A FORK. BAKE AT 350°F (180°C) FOR 10 MINUTES. MAKES 3 DOZEN COOKIES.

IT'S A SMALL WORLD, BUT I WOULDN'T WANT TO PAINT IT!

PECAN CRISPS

DELIGHTFUL!

I CUP	BUTTER	250 ML
2 TSP	VANILLA EXTRACT	10 ML
I CUP	ICING SUGAR	250 ML
I CUP	ALL-PURPOSE FLOUR	250 ML
I	PACKAGE (3 OZ/85 G) PECANS, CHOPPED	I

COMBINE BUTTER, VANILLA AND ICING SUGAR AND BEAT UNTIL SMOOTH AND LIGHT. BEAT IN FLOUR AND ADD NUTS. SPREAD BATTER ON A 15- BY 10-INCH (38 BY 25 CM) BAKING SHEET. BAKE AT 350°F (180°C) FOR 18 MINUTES. SPRINKLE EVENLY WITH ICING SUGAR. CUT INTO SMALL PIECES WHILE WARM. MAKES ABOUT 3 DOZEN COOKIES.

THE VELOCITY OF THE WIND IS DIRECTLY PROPORTIONAL TO THE PRICE OF THE HAIRDO!

POPPY SEED COOKIES

LIGHT, FLUFFY AND VERY DELICATE.

I CUP	BUTTER	250 ML
1/2 CUP	GRANULATED SUGAR	125 ML
2	EGG YOLKS	2
2 CUPS	ALL-PURPOSE FLOUR	500 ML
1/4 TSP	SALT	I ML
3 TBSP	POPPY SEEDS	45 ML
I TSP	VANILLA EXTRACT	5 ML
	GRANULATED SUGAR	

PREHEAT OVEN TO 375°F (190°C). GREASE A BAKING SHEET. CREAM BUTTER, SUGAR AND EGG YOLKS. ADD FLOUR, SALT, POPPY SEEDS AND VANILLA. MIX WELL. CHILL DOUGH I HOUR. FORM DOUGH INTO TEASPOON-SIZED BALLS. PLACE ON COOKIE SHEET AND DIP THE BOTTOM OF A JUICE GLASS INTO SUGAR AND PRESS BALLS FLAT. BAKE FOR 8 TO 10 MINUTES. MAKES 4 DOZEN COOKIES.

ALWAYS YIELD TO TEMPTATION... IT MIGHT NOT PASS YOUR WAY AGAIN.

FATAL ATTRACTIONS

A CAKE-LIKE COOKIE THAT'S IRRESISTIBLE!

4	SQUARES UNSWEETENED CHOCOLATE	4
1/2 CUP	BUTTER	125 ML
2 CUPS	GRANULATED SUGAR	500 ML
2 TSP	VANILLA EXTRACT	10 ML
4	EGGS	4
2 CUPS	ALL-PURPOSE FLOUR	500 ML
2 TSP	BAKING POWDER	10 ML
1 CUP	CHOCOLATE CHIPS	250 ML
1/2 CUP	ICING SUGAR	125 ML

MELT CHOCOLATE SQUARES AND BUTTER, BUT DO
NOT BOIL. STIR IN SUGAR AND ALLOW TO COOL. SPOON
MIXTURE INTO A BOWL, ADD VANILLA AND BEAT WELL.
ADD EGGS, ONE AT A TIME, BEATING WELL AFTER EACH
ADDITION. COMBINE FLOUR AND BAKING POWDER; ADD TO
CREAMED MIXTURE. BEAT WELL. FOLD IN CHOCOLATE CHIPS.
REFRIGERATE FOR 1 HOUR. ROLL DOUGH INTO 1-INCH (2.5 CM)
BALLS AND ROLL IN ICING SUGAR UNTIL COATED. BAKE
ON GREASED SHEETS AT 350°F (180°C) 10 TO 12 MINUTES.
MAKES ABOUT 5 DOZEN COOKIES.

NEVER OWN ANYTHING THAT EATS WHILE YOU SLEEP.

GLAZED CINNAMON BARS

THE "LUNCH BUNCH" WILL APPRECIATE THIS.

I CUP	BUTTER	250 ML
I CUP	BROWN SUGAR	250 ML
I	EGG, SEPARATED	I
PINCH	SALT	PINCH
1 3/4 CUPS	ALL-PURPOSE FLOUR	425 ML
3 TO 4 TSP	GROUND CINNAMON	15 TO 20 ML
1/2 CUP	ICING (CONFECTIONER'S) SUGAR	125 ML
I CUP	NUTS, CHOPPED	250 ML

COMBINE BUTTER, SUGAR, EGG YOLK AND SALT, BEATING UNTIL CREAMY. STIR IN FLOUR AND CINNAMON, MIXING WELL. SPREAD ON A GREASED 15- BY 10-INCH (38 BY 25 CM) COOKIE SHEET. (BATTER WILL BE THICK AND REQUIRES SOME PATIENCE TO SPREAD.) BEAT EGG WHITE UNTIL FOAMY; STIR IN ICING SUGAR. BRUSH SUGAR MIXTURE OVER THE BATTER AND SPRINKLE WITH NUTS. BAKE AT 350°F (180°C) FOR 30 TO 35 MINUTES. CUT INTO SQUARES WHILE HOT. REMOVE BARS FROM PAN TO COOL. MAKES 24 SQUARES.

MY WIFE HAD AN ACCIDENT; SHE NOW OWNS A MERCEDES-BENT.

Spaghetti Squash Primavera (page 244)

Matrimonial Bars (page 296) and Butter Tart Slice (page 290)

Microwave Peanut Brittle (page 299)

Pumpkin Cheesecake (page 302)

COCONUT BARS

I CUP	BUTTER	250 ML
2 TBSP	CORN SYRUP	30 ML
I CUP	BROWN SUGAR	250 ML
2 TSP	VANILLA EXTRACT	IO ML
3 1/2 CUPS	OATMEAL	875 ML
1/2 TSP	BAKING POWDER	2 ML
1/2 TSP	SALT	2 ML
2/3 CUP	SHREDDED COCONUT	I50 ML

IN A LARGE SAUCEPAN, MELT BUTTER, CORN SYRUP AND BROWN SUGAR. ADD VANILLA, OATMEAL, BAKING POWDER, SALT AND COCONUT. MIX WELL AND PAT ONTO GREASED COOKIE SHEET. A FORK DIPPED IN COLD WATER HELPS TO SPREAD MIXTURE EVENLY. MIXTURE SHOULD BE ABOUT 1/4 INCH (0.5 CM) THICK. BAKE AT 325°F (I60°C) FOR I5 TO 20 MINUTES. CUT INTO SQUARES WHILE WARM. MAKES ABOUT 3 DOZEN BARS.

YOU CAN HAVE IT BOTH WAYS AS LONG AS YOU'RE WILLING TO SETTLE FOR HALVES.

BUTTER TART SLICE

A SLICE OF LIFE — ALL TARTS SHOULD TASTE SO GOOD!

CRUST

1 CUP	BUTTER	250 ML
2 CUPS	ALL-PURPOSE FLOUR	500 ML
1/4 CUP	GRANULATED SUGAR	60 ML
PINCH	SALT	PINCH

BUTTER TART FILLING

1/4 CUP	BUTTER	60 ML
3	EGGS, BEATEN	3
2 CUPS	BROWN SUGAR	500 ML
1 TBSP	BAKING POWDER	15 ML
PINCH	SALT	PINCH
3/4 CUP	COCONUT	175 ML
1 TSP	VANILLA EXTRACT	5 ML
1 CUP	RAISINS	250 ML
1 TBSP	ALL-PURPOSE FLOUR	15 ML
1 CUP	CHOPPED PECANS (OPTIONAL)	250 ML

CRUST: CUT BUTTER INTO DRY INGREDIENTS WITH PASTRY BLENDER UNTIL CRUMBLY. PRESS INTO AN UNGREASED 13- BY 9-INCH (33 BY 23 CM) PAN.

FILLING: MELT BUTTER; ADD EGGS AND REMAINING INGREDIENTS. MIX AND POUR OVER CRUST. BAKE AT 350°F (180°C) FOR 35 MINUTES. CUT WHEN COOL. MAKES 3 DOZEN SQUARES.

BROWN BAGGER'S SPECIAL

3 1/2 CUPS	OATMEAL	875 ML
1 CUP	RAISINS	250 ML
1 CUP	CHOPPED WALNUTS OR PECANS	250 ML
1 CUP	COCONUT	250 ML
2/3 CUP	MELTED BUTTER	150 ML
1/2 CUP	BROWN SUGAR	125 ML
1/3 CUP	LIQUID HONEY OR CORN SYRUP	75 ML
1	EGG, BEATEN	1
1/2 TSP	VANILLA EXTRACT	2 ML
1/2 TSP	SALT	2 ML

TOAST OATMEAL ON A FLAT PAN IN 350°F (180°C) OVEN FOR 20 MINUTES. MIX ALL INGREDIENTS, ADDING OATMEAL LAST. SPREAD MIXTURE ON A COOKIE SHEET AND BAKE AT 350°F (180°C) FOR 20 MINUTES. COOL SLIGHTLY AND CUT INTO SQUARES. MAKES 3 DOZEN SQUARES.

A FLIRT IS A GIRL WHO BELIEVES IN EVERY MAN FOR HERSELF.

SCOTCH SQUARES

1 CUP	BUTTER, MELTED	250 ML
1 CUP	BROWN SUGAR	250 ML
1 TSP	VANILLA EXTRACT	5 ML
1 CUP	ALL-PURPOSE FLOUR	250 ML
2 CUPS	OATMEAL	500 ML
1½ TSP	BAKING SODA	7 ML
1 CUP	CHOPPED WALNUTS	250 ML
1 CUP	CHOCOLATE CHIPS OR SMARTIES (OPTIONAL)	250 ML

MIX BUTTER, BROWN SUGAR AND VANILLA, THEN ADD TO DRY INGREDIENTS. MIX WELL AND SPREAD IN A GREASED 15- BY 10-INCH (38 BY 25 CM) RIMMED BAKING SHEET. BAKE AT 350°F (180°C) FOR 25 MINUTES. CUT WITH A SHARP KNIFE WHILE STILL WARM. FOR VARIETY, ADD CHOCOLATE CHIPS OR SMARTIES. MAKES 4 DOZEN SQUARES.

THERE ARE MANY THINGS THAT MONEY CAN'T BUY, INCLUDING WHAT IT USED TO.

CHOCOLATE CHIP SLAB COOKIES

1 CUP	BUTTER	250 ML
1 CUP	BROWN SUGAR	250 ML
1 TSP	VANILLA EXTRACT	5 ML
2 CUPS	ALL-PURPOSE FLOUR	500 ML
1 CUP	CHOCOLATE CHIPS	250 ML

CREAM BUTTER AND SUGAR TOGETHER, BEATING THOROUGHLY (THE SECRET!). ADD VANILLA AND FLOUR. MIX WELL. STIR IN CHOCOLATE CHIPS. PAT MIXTURE ONTO A GREASED 15- BY 10-INCH (38 BY 25 CM) COOKIE SHEET THAT HAS SIDES. BAKE AT 350°F (180°C) FOR 25 MINUTES. CUT INTO SQUARES WHILE WARM. MAKES 4 DOZEN SQUARES.

ROCKY MOUNTAIN SQUARES

THEY'RE WICKED!

1	PACKAGE (16 OZ/500 G) CHOCOLATE CHIPS	1
1 CUP	BUTTER	250 ML
2 CUPS	ICING SUGAR	500 ML
2	EGGS, BEATEN	2
4 CUPS	MINIATURE MARSHMALLOWS	1 L
	GRAHAM WAFERS	

MIX FIRST FOUR INGREDIENTS TOGETHER AND MELT AT LOW HEAT. LET COOL SLIGHTLY AND ADD MARSHMALLOWS. LINE A 13- BY 9-INCH (33 BY 23 CM) PAN WITH GRAHAM WAFERS. SPREAD MIXTURE OVER WAFERS AND SPRINKLE WITH ICING SUGAR. REFRIGERATE. MAKES 2 DOZEN SQUARES.

CHEWY CHOCOLATE PEANUT BARS

TASTES LIKE ALMOND ROCA.

2 CUPS	ROLLED OATS	500 ML
I CUP	GRAHAM WAFER CRUMBS	250 ML
3/4 CUP	BROWN SUGAR	175 ML
1/4 TSP	BAKING SODA	I ML
1/2 CUP	SALTED PEANUTS	125 ML
1/2 CUP	CORN SYRUP	125 ML
1/2 CUP	BUTTER, MELTED	125 ML
I TSP	VANILLA EXTRACT	5 ML
I	PACKAGE (6 OZ/170 G) SEMISWEET CHOCOLATE CHIPS	I
1/2 CUP	PEANUT BUTTER	125 ML

PREHEAT OVEN TO 375°F (190°C). GREASE A 15- BY 10-INCH (38 BY 25 CM) RIMMED COOKIE SHEET. IN A LARGE BOWL, COMBINE OATS, CRUMBS, SUGAR, BAKING SODA AND PEANUTS. MIX WELL. COMBINE CORN SYRUP WITH MELTED BUTTER AND VANILLA. STIR INTO OAT MIXTURE AND MIX WELL. PRESS INTO PAN AND BAKE FOR 15 MINUTES. MELT CHOCOLATE CHIPS AND PEANUT BUTTER TOGETHER IN A DOUBLE BOILER. SPREAD OVER WARM, BAKED BARS. COOL 10 MINUTES IN PAN AND CUT INTO 2- BY I-INCH (5 BY 2.5 CM) BARS. REFRIGERATE TO SET CHOCOLATE. MAKES 5 DOZEN BARS.

PEANUT BUTTER BROWNIES

1/2 CUP	BUTTER	125 ML
1/2 CUP	GRANULATED SUGAR	125 ML
1/2 CUP	DARK BROWN SUGAR, PACKED	125 ML
1	EGG, BEATEN	1
1/3 CUP	PEANUT BUTTER	75 ML
1/2 TSP	VANILLA EXTRACT	2 ML
1 CUP	OATMEAL	250 ML
1 CUP	ALL-PURPOSE FLOUR	250 ML
1/2 TSP	BAKING SODA	2 ML
1/4 TSP	SALT	1 ML

ICING

1 CUP	ICING SUGAR	250 ML
1/2 CUP	PEANUT BUTTER	125 ML
4 TO 6 TBSP	MILK	60 TO 90 ML

CREAM BUTTER AND SUGARS; ADD EGG, PEANUT BUTTER AND VANILLA. MIX WELL. STIR IN OATMEAL, FLOUR, BAKING SODA AND SALT. BAKE AT 350°F (180°C) FOR 25 TO 30 MINUTES IN A GREASED 9-INCH (23 CM) SQUARE PAN. COMBINE INGREDIENTS FOR ICING; BLEND WELL. ICE BROWNIES WHILE WARM. COOL AND ENJOY! MAKES 2 DOZEN BROWNIES.

IT COSTS NO MORE TO GO FIRST CLASS — YOU JUST CAN'T STAY AS LONG.

MATRIMONIAL BARS

AT LAST, THE VERY THING FOR ALL THAT
RHUBARB YOU FROZE LAST FALL. OR USE THE
TRADITIONAL DATE FILLING.

RHUBARB FILLING

3 CUPS	CHOPPED RHUBARB	750 ML
1 1/2 CUPS	GRANULATED SUGAR	375 ML
2 TBSP	CORNSTARCH	30 ML
1 TSP	VANILLA EXTRACT	5 ML

DATE FILLING

8 OZ	CHOPPED DATES	250 G
1/2 CUP	WATER	125 ML
2 TBSP	BROWN SUGAR	30 ML
1 TSP	GRATED ORANGE ZEST	5 ML
2 TBSP	ORANGE JUICE	30 ML
1 TSP	LEMON JUICE	5 ML

CRUST

1 1/2 CUPS	ROLLED OATS	375 ML
1 1/2 CUPS	ALL-PURPOSE FLOUR	375 ML
1/2 TSP	BAKING SODA	2 ML
1 TSP	BAKING POWDER	5 ML
1/4 TSP	SALT	1 ML
1 CUP	BROWN SUGAR	250 ML
1 CUP	BUTTER	250 ML

FILLING: DECIDE WHETHER YOU WANT TO MAKE RHUBARB
FILLING OR DATE FILLING. COMBINE FILLING INGREDIENTS
AND COOK UNTIL THICK. IF MAKING DATE FILLING, ADD
FRUIT JUICES AFTER COOKING. COOL COMPLETELY.

CONTINUED ON NEXT PAGE...

CRUST: PREHEAT OVEN TO 350°F (180°C). COMBINE INGREDIENTS AND PAT TWO-THIRDS OF THE MIXTURE INTO A GREASED 9-INCH (23 CM) SQUARE PAN. SPREAD FILLING AND SPRINKLE WITH REMAINING CRUMBS. BAKE FOR 30 TO 35 MINUTES. CHILL BEFORE CUTTING. MAKES 16 SQUARES.

SHORTCUT ALMOND ROCA

THE SECRET TO THIS POPULAR TREAT IS OWNING A CANDY THERMOMETER.

1 TBSP	CORN SYRUP	15 ML
1¼ CUPS	GRANULATED SUGAR	300 ML
1 CUP	BUTTER	250 ML
¼ CUP	WATER	60 ML
1¼ CUPS	TOASTED SLIVERED ALMONDS	300 ML
¾ CUP	CHOCOLATE CHIPS	175 ML

IN A HEAVY SAUCEPAN, GENTLY BOIL SYRUP, SUGAR, BUTTER AND WATER FOR 20 MINUTES OR UNTIL "HARD CRACK" APPEARS ON CANDY THERMOMETER, 300°F (150°C). DO NOT STIR. REMOVE FROM HEAT, ADD ALMONDS AND STIR WELL. IMMEDIATELY SPREAD ON AN UNGREASED COOKIE SHEET AND SPRINKLE WITH CHOCOLATE CHIPS. AS THEY MELT, SPREAD THE CHOCOLATE CHIPS EVENLY OVER THE CANDY. COOL IN REFRIGERATOR OR FREEZER. BREAK INTO BITE-SIZE PIECES AND HIDE SOME. WHATEVER YOU LEAVE OUT DISAPPEARS! (THIS DOES NOT DOUBLE WELL.) MAKES ABOUT 2 DOZEN PIECES.

ALMOND FLORENTINES

EVERYONE WANTS THIS RECIPE! A REAL SLEEPER.

GRAHAM WAFERS

I CUP	BUTTER	250 ML
I CUP	BROWN SUGAR	250 ML
I CUP	FLAKED ALMONDS	250 ML

OIL A 15- BY 10-INCH (38 BY 25 CM) RIMMED BAKING SHEET. ARRANGE WAFERS TO COVER PAN. MELT BUTTER AND BROWN SUGAR AND COOK OVER MEDIUM HEAT FOR 5 MINUTES. DO NOT BOIL. SPOON MIXTURE OVER WAFERS. SPRINKLE FLAKED ALMONDS OVER TOP. BAKE AT 375°F (190°C) FOR 7 MINUTES. TURN OVEN OFF, OPEN DOOR (DO THE DISHES, TAKE OUT THE GARBAGE, SIT UP STRAIGHT, DON'T PICK AT IT) AND COOL FOR ABOUT I HOUR. CUT WHILE STILL WARM, OTHERWISE THEY WILL STICK TO THE PAN. YUMMY! MAKES ABOUT 3 DOZEN PIECES.

THE FIRST HALF OF OUR LIVES IS RUINED BY OUR PARENTS AND THE SECOND HALF BY OUR CHILDREN.
— CLARENCE DARROW

MICROWAVE PEANUT BRITTLE

TRAVELS WELL AND MAKES A GREAT GIFT.

1 CUP	SALTED PEANUTS, PECANS OR CASHEWS	250 ML
1 CUP	GRANULATED SUGAR	250 ML
1/2 CUP	CORN SYRUP	125 ML
PINCH	SALT	PINCH
1 TSP	BUTTER	5 ML
1 TSP	VANILLA EXTRACT	5 ML
1 TSP	BAKING SODA	5 ML

STIR FIRST FOUR INGREDIENTS TOGETHER IN AN 8-CUP (2 L) MEASURING CUP OR VERY LARGE MICROWAVE-SAFE BOWL. COOK ON HIGH FOR 3 TO 4 MINUTES. STIR WELL. COOK FOR 4 MORE MINUTES. STIR IN BUTTER AND VANILLA. COOK FOR 1 MINUTE MORE. ADD BAKING SODA AND GENTLY STIR UNTIL LIGHT AND FOAMY. SPREAD MIXTURE QUICKLY ON LIGHTLY GREASED COOKIE SHEET. COOL FOR AN HOUR. BREAK INTO PIECES. MAKES ABOUT 3 DOZEN PIECES.

MEN WHO THINK WOMEN ARE THE WEAKER SEX
HAVE NEVER GONE SHOPPING WITH ONE.

BOURBON BALLS

AN ELEGANT CHOCOLATE GOODIE — GREAT FOR GIFTS.

FILLING

1 1/2 CUPS	BUTTER	375 ML
1	CAN (14 OZ OR 300 ML) SWEETENED CONDENSED MILK	1
3 LBS	ICING SUGAR	1.5 KG
1 TSP	VANILLA EXTRACT	5 ML
1/2 CUP	BOURBON	125 ML
1 CUP	NUTS, CHOPPED	250 ML

CHOCOLATE DIP

1	PACKAGE (8 OZ/225 G) UNSWEETENED CHOCOLATE SQUARES	1
1	PACKAGE (8 OZ/225 G) SEMISWEET CHOCOLATE SQUARES	1
1 CUP	WALNUTS, LARGE PIECES	250 ML

FILLING: BROWN BUTTER IN SAUCEPAN. CREAM MILK AND HALF THE SUGAR. ADD VANILLA AND BOURBON TO THE CREAMED MIXTURE. ADD BROWNED MARGARINE TO REMAINING SUGAR AND BEAT THE TWO MIXTURES TOGETHER UNTIL SMOOTH. ADD NUTS. PUT MIXTURE IN FREEZER UNTIL HARD ENOUGH TO FORM BITE-SIZE BALLS. ROLL INTO BALLS AND PLACE ON COOKIE SHEET. PLACE BACK IN FREEZER OR FRIDGE TO HOLD SHAPE.

DIP: MELT ALL INGREDIENTS, EXCEPT NUTS, IN DOUBLE BOILER. DIP BALLS IN THE CHOCOLATE USING TOOTHPICK, ALLOWING EXCESS CHOCOLATE TO DRIP OFF. PLACE ON WAX PAPER-LINED COOKIE SHEET AND IMMEDIATELY PLACE

CONTINUED ON NEXT PAGE...

WALNUT ON TOOTHPICK HOLE. REFRIGERATE OR FREEZE IF MAKING AHEAD. MAKES ABOUT 150 CANDIES.

TIP: THESE ARE BEST MADE WITH A FRIEND OR A SON/ DAUGHTER FOR THAT YULETIDE SPIRIT. IF WORKING ALONE, THE FILLING MAY HAVE TO BE RETURNED TO THE FREEZER WHENEVER IT BECOMES TOO STICKY TO ROLL. CHOCOLATE ALSO MAY HAVE TO BE REHEATED DURING DIPPING.

FRESH FRUIT SUCH AS STRAWBERRIES, CHERRIES OR BANANAS MAY BE DIPPED IN THE CHOCOLATE FOR A SPECIAL TREAT.

MONEY DOES NOT BRING HAPPINESS... BUT IT HAS BEEN KNOWN TO BRING AN OCCASIONAL SMILE.

CHOCOLATE PEANUT BUTTER BALLS

A CHRISTMAS FAVORITE!

1 CUP	PEANUT BUTTER	250 ML
1 CUP	ICING SUGAR	250 ML
1/2 CUP	NUTS, CHOPPED	125 ML
1/2 CUP	RICE KRISPIES	125 ML
4 OZ	SEMISWEET CHOCOLATE CHIPS	120 G
1 TBSP	BUTTER	15 ML

MIX TOGETHER FIRST FOUR INGREDIENTS AND CHILL IN FRIDGE FOR 10 TO 15 MINUTES. ROLL INTO BALLS. MELT CHOCOLATE CHIPS WITH BUTTER. DIP BALLS IN CHOCOLATE AND CHILL. MAKES ABOUT 3 DOZEN.

PUMPKIN CHEESECAKE

A GRAND FINALE FOR THANKSGIVING DINNER.

GINGER SNAP CRUST

I CUP	CRUSHED GINGER SNAPS	250 ML
3 TBSP	BUTTER, MELTED	45 ML
I TSP	GROUND CINNAMON	5 ML
2 TBSP	BROWN SUGAR	30 ML

FILLING

4	PACKAGES (EACH 8 OZ/250 G) CREAM CHEESE, SOFTENED	4
I $\frac{1}{2}$ CUPS	GRANULATED SUGAR	375 ML
5	EGGS	5
$\frac{1}{4}$ CUP	ALL-PURPOSE FLOUR	60 ML
2 TSP	PUMPKIN PIE SPICE OR EQUAL PARTS GINGER, CINNAMON AND NUTMEG	10 ML
I	CAN (14 OZ/398 ML) PUMPKIN	I
2 TBSP	RUM	30 ML
I CUP	WHIPPING (35%) CREAM, WHIPPED	250 ML

CRUST: COMBINE INGREDIENTS. LIGHTLY GREASE A 10-INCH (25 CM) SPRINGFORM PAN AND LINE BOTTOM WITH CRUMB MIXTURE. PAT FIRM AND CHILL.

FILLING: PREHEAT OVEN TO 325°F (160°C). BEAT SOFTENED CREAM CHEESE TILL FLUFFY. SLOWLY BEAT IN SUGAR. ADD EGGS, ONE AT A TIME, BEATING WELL AFTER EACH ADDITION. GRADUALLY BEAT IN FLOUR, SPICES, PUMPKIN AND RUM. POUR BATTER OVER CRUST. BAKE FOR I $\frac{1}{2}$ TO I $\frac{3}{4}$ HOURS OR UNTIL FILLING IS SET. COOL FOR AN HOUR. REFRIGERATE SEVERAL HOURS. GARNISH WITH WHIPPED CREAM AND A SPRINKLE OF CINNAMON. SERVES 10 TO 12.

POPPY SEED CAKE

THE DAY WE BROUGHT THIS TO THE OFFICE,
WE ATE SO MUCH WE HAD TO SKIP LUNCH!

1/4 CUP	POPPY SEEDS	60 ML
1/4 CUP	MILK	60 ML
1	BOX (18 1/4 OZ/515 G) LEMON CAKE MIX	1
1	PACKAGE (4 OZ/114 G) INSTANT VANILLA PUDDING MIX	1
4	EGGS	4
1/2 CUP	VEGETABLE OIL	125 ML
1 CUP	WARM WATER	250 ML

SPICE MIXTURE

1 TBSP	UNSWEETENED COCOA POWDER	15 ML
1 TBSP	GROUND CINNAMON	15 ML
1 TBSP	GRANULATED SUGAR	15 ML

GLAZE

3 TBSP	FRESHLY SQUEEZED LEMON JUICE	45 ML
6 TBSP	ICING SUGAR	90 ML

SOAK POPPY SEEDS IN MILK FOR AT LEAST 1 HOUR. MIX TOGETHER CAKE MIX, PUDDING, EGGS, OIL AND WATER. ADD POPPY SEED MIXTURE. IN A SMALL BOWL, COMBINE SPICE MIXTURE INGREDIENTS. GREASE AND FLOUR A 10-INCH (25 CM) BUNDT PAN. POUR IN A LAYER OF CAKE MIXTURE AND SPRINKLE WITH SPICE MIXTURE, REPEATING UNTIL ALL IS USED. BAKE AT 350°F (180°C) FOR 1 HOUR. COMBINE GLAZE INGREDIENTS. TURN CAKE OUT AND, WHILE STILL WARM, DRIZZLE GLAZE MIXTURE OVER CAKE. SERVES 12 TO 16.

POPPY SEED CHIFFON CAKE

1/2 CUP	POPPY SEEDS	125 ML
1 CUP	BOILING WATER	250 ML
2 CUPS	ALL-PURPOSE FLOUR	500 ML
1 1/2 CUPS	GRANULATED SUGAR	375 ML
1 TBSP	BAKING POWDER	15 ML
1 TSP	SALT	5 ML
1/2 CUP	SALAD OIL	125 ML
2 TSP	VANILLA EXTRACT	10 ML
7	EGGS, SEPARATED	7
1/4 TSP	BAKING SODA	1 ML
1/2 TSP	CREAM OF TARTAR	2 ML

ICING

2 CUPS	WHIPPING (35%) CREAM	500 ML
1/2 CUP	GRANULATED SUGAR	125 ML
2 TSP	VANILLA EXTRACT	10 ML
2 TO 3 TSP	UNSWEETENED COCOA POWDER, SIFTED	10 TO 15 ML

SOAK POPPY SEEDS IN BOILING WATER UNTIL LUKEWARM.
IN A BOWL, SIFT TOGETHER FLOUR, SUGAR, BAKING
POWDER AND SALT. FORM A WELL IN CENTER AND ADD
OIL, POPPY SEEDS WITH WATER, VANILLA, EGG YOLKS AND
BAKING SODA. BEAT UNTIL SMOOTH. IN ANOTHER BOWL,
BEAT EGG WHITES WITH CREAM OF TARTAR UNTIL STIFF
PEAKS FORM. POUR YOLK MIXTURE OVER EGG WHITES
AND GENTLY FOLD (DO NOT STIR). POUR INTO UNGREASED
10-INCH (25 CM) TUBE PAN. BAKE AT 350°F (180°C) FOR
60 MINUTES. INVERT PAN TO COOL.

CONTINUED ON NEXT PAGE...

ICING: WHIP CREAM. ADD SUGAR, THEN ADD VANILLA AND COCOA. BLEND WELL. STORE IN FRIDGE AND ICE CAKE AS CLOSE TO SERVING TIME AS POSSIBLE! SERVES 12 TO 16.

DO UNTO OTHERS — THEN RUN!

APPLE KUCHEN

ANYTHING THIS EASY SHOULDN'T TASTE THIS GOOD!

1/2 CUP	BUTTER	125 ML
1	BOX (18 1/4 OZ/515 G) YELLOW CAKE MIX	1
1/2 CUP	FLAKED COCONUT	125 ML
2	CANS (EACH 14 OZ/398 ML) APPLESAUCE	2
1/2 CUP	GRANULATED SUGAR	125 ML
1 TSP	GROUND CINNAMON	5 ML
1 CUP	SOUR CREAM	250 ML
2	EGG YOLKS	2

CUT BUTTER INTO CAKE MIX UNTIL CRUMBLY. MIX IN COCONUT. PAT INTO A GREASED 13- BY 9-INCH (33 BY 23 CM) CAKE PAN, BUILDING UP EDGES SLIGHTLY. BAKE AT 350°F (180°C) FOR 10 MINUTES. SPREAD APPLESAUCE OVER WARM CRUST. MIX SUGAR AND CINNAMON AND SPRINKLE OVER APPLES. BLEND SOUR CREAM AND EGG YOLKS AND DRIZZLE OVER APPLES. BAKE AT 350°F (180°C) FOR 25 MINUTES. SERVE WARM. FREEZES WELL. SERVES 12.

NOTE: SOUR CREAM AND YOLK MIXTURE DOESN'T COMPLETELY COVER APPLES.

HAZELNUT TORTE

*HAZEL MIGHT BE A NUT, BUT SHE KNOWS HER TORTES.
A GOURMET BREEZE — AND BEST OF ALL, YOU CAN MAKE
IT AND FREEZE UP TO 2 WEEKS IN ADVANCE.*

1/4 CUP	ALL-PURPOSE FLOUR	60 ML
1/2 TSP	BAKING POWDER	2 ML
1/4 TSP	GROUND CINNAMON	1 ML
1/2 CUP	BUTTER	125 ML
2/3 CUP	GRANULATED SUGAR	150 ML
3	EGGS, SEPARATED	3
1 CUP	HAZELNUTS (FILBERTS), TOASTED, FINELY GROUND	250 ML
3 TBSP	HAZELNUT LIQUEUR (FRANGELICO) OR GRAND MARNIER	45 ML
1 1/2 CUPS	WHIPPING (35%) CREAM	375 ML
1/4 CUP	GRANULATED SUGAR	60 ML
2 TBSP	HAZELNUTS (FILBERTS), TOASTED, FINELY GROUND	30 ML

GREASE AN 8-INCH (20 CM) ROUND CAKE PAN. LINE
BOTTOM WITH GREASED WAX PAPER. IN A BOWL, STIR
TOGETHER FLOUR, BAKING POWDER AND CINNAMON. SET
ASIDE. IN A LARGE BOWL, BEAT BUTTER AND 2/3 CUP
(150 ML) SUGAR UNTIL FLUFFY. BEAT IN EGG YOLKS. ADD
FLOUR MIXTURE; BEAT WELL. STIR IN 1/2 CUP (125 ML) OF
GROUND NUTS. IN A BOWL (USING CLEAN BEATERS),
BEAT EGG WHITES TILL STIFF PEAKS FORM. FOLD INTO
CAKE BATTER. TURN BATTER INTO PAN (IT WON'T BE
RUNNY). BAKE AT 350°F (180°C) FOR 35 MINUTES OR UNTIL
TOOTHPICK COMES OUT CLEAN. COOL ON WIRE RACK FOR

CONTINUED ON NEXT PAGE...

10 MINUTES. REMOVE CAKE FROM PAN; REMOVE WAXED PAPER. DON'T PANIC; IT'S A SHALLOW CAKE. DRIZZLE LIQUEUR OVER TOP. SET IN FRIDGE TO CHILL. WHEN THOROUGHLY CHILLED, SLICE HORIZONTALLY IN 2 LAYERS. TRANSFER ONE LAYER TO CAKE PLATE. WHIP CREAM WITH $1/4$ CUP (60 ML) SUGAR. MIX REMAINING $1/2$ CUP (125 ML) NUTS WITH HALF THE CREAM AND USE AS FILLING BETWEEN CAKE LAYERS. SPREAD RESERVED CREAM OVER TOP AND SIDES OF CAKE. SPRINKLE 2 TBSP (30 ML) OF NUTS ON TOP. SERVES 12.

TO FREEZE: PLACE UNCOVERED CAKE IN FREEZER FOR 30 MINUTES TILL CREAM FROSTING IS FROZEN. WRAP CAKE IN 3 LAYERS OF PLASTIC WRAP AND FREEZE UNTIL READY TO USE. THAW WRAPPED CAKE IN FRIDGE OVERNIGHT.

BUDGET: A MATHEMATICAL CONFIRMATION
OF YOUR SUSPICIONS.

BANANA GINGER LOAF

YOU CAN USE A GINGERBREAD CAKE MIX INSTEAD OF
MAKING THE CAKE FROM SCRATCH.

CAKE

1/2 CUP	BUTTER	125 ML
1/2 CUP	BROWN SUGAR, LIGHTLY PACKED	125 ML
1	EGG	1
1 1/2 CUPS	ALL-PURPOSE FLOUR	375 ML
1 TSP	BAKING SODA	5 ML
1/4 TSP	SALT	1 ML
1 TSP	GROUND GINGER	5 ML
1/2 TSP	GROUND CINNAMON	2 ML
1/2 CUP	LIGHT (FANCY) MOLASSES	125 ML
1/2 CUP	HOT WATER	125 ML

FILLING

1	BOX (3 1/2 OZ/100 G) LEMON PUDDING MIX	1
1 CUP	MILK	250 ML
1/2 CUP	WHIPPING (35%) CREAM, WHIPPED	125 ML
3	LARGE BANANAS	3
1/4 CUP	LIGHT CORN SYRUP	60 ML

CREAM BUTTER AND SUGAR TOGETHER. ADD EGG AND BEAT
UNTIL LIGHT AND FLUFFY. COMBINE FLOUR, BAKING SODA,
SALT, GINGER AND CINNAMON. COMBINE MOLASSES AND
HOT WATER. ADD THE DRY INGREDIENTS ALTERNATELY
WITH THE MOLASSES MIXTURE. BLEND UNTIL WELL
COMBINED. POUR BATTER INTO A WELL-GREASED, FLOURED
AND WAX PAPER-LINED 15- BY 10-INCH (38 BY 25 CM)

RIMMED BAKING SHEET. BAKE AT 350°F (180°C) FOR
15 TO 20 MINUTES OR UNTIL TOOTHPICK INSERTED IN
CENTER COMES OUT CLEAN. COOL IN PAN ON WIRE RACK
FOR 10 MINUTES, THEN REMOVE FROM PAN AND COOL
COMPLETELY, ABOUT 1 HOUR.

PREPARE LEMON PUDDING MIX AS PACKAGE DIRECTS,
BUT USE ONLY 1 CUP (250 ML) MILK. FOLD IN WHIPPED
CREAM. CUT GINGERBREAD CROSSWISE IN THIRDS.
PLACE 1 PIECE ON PLATTER. THINLY SLICE 1 BANANA AND
PLACE SLICES ON GINGERBREAD. TOP WITH HALF THE
PUDDING. REPEAT ONCE. TOP WITH REMAINING PIECE OF
GINGERBREAD. COVER AND REFRIGERATE FOR 1 HOUR. JUST
BEFORE SERVING, SLICE REMAINING BANANA AND PLACE ON
TOP OF CAKE. BRUSH BANANA SLICES WITH CORN SYRUP.
SERVES 10.

THE LORD GIVETH AND THE GOVERNMENT TAKETH AWAY.

EASY PEACH TORTE

A FAVORITE SUMMER DESSERT — THE SPONGE CAKE IS ALSO TERRIFIC FOR TRIFLE.

3	EGGS	3
3/4 CUP	GRANULATED SUGAR	175 ML
1/4 CUP	VEGETABLE OIL	60 ML
1/2 TSP	SALT	2 ML
1/2 TSP	ALMOND OR VANILLA FLAVORING	2 ML
3/4 CUP	ALL-PURPOSE FLOUR	175 ML
1	CAN (19 OZ/540 ML) PEACH PIE FILLING	1
3 OR 4	PEACHES, SLICED	3 OR 4
1 CUP	WHIPPING (35%) CREAM, WHIPPED	250 ML
1/2 CUP	TOASTED SLIVERED ALMONDS	125 ML

BEAT EGGS WITH ELECTRIC BEATER FOR 2 MINUTES. ADD SUGAR AND BEAT UNTIL THICK. ADD OIL, SALT, FLAVORING AND FLOUR; MIX WELL. POUR INTO A WELL-GREASED 9-INCH (23 CM) SPRINGFORM PAN. BAKE AT 350°F (180°C) FOR 25 MINUTES. (THIS CAKE FREEZES WELL. WHY NOT DOUBLE THE RECIPE AND HAVE AN EXTRA ON HAND?)

TO ASSEMBLE: SPREAD PIE FILLING ON CAKE. TOP WITH PEACHES, THEN WHIPPED CREAM. SPRINKLE WITH TOASTED ALMONDS AND A FEW MORE PEACH SLICES. SERVES 8.

COCONUT WHIP CAKE

THIS GETS BETTER IN THE FRIDGE —
EVEN A WEEK LATER, IF IT LASTS!

1	BOX (18 1/2 OZ/520 G) YELLOW CAKE MIX	1
1 1/2 CUPS	MILK	375 ML
1/2 CUP	GRANULATED SUGAR	125 ML
2 CUPS	FLAKED COCONUT	500 ML
1	CONTAINER (4 CUPS/1 L) COOL WHIP	1

PREPARE CAKE MIX AS DIRECTED AND BAKE IN A 13- BY 9-INCH (33 BY 23 CM) PAN. COOL 15 MINUTES, THEN PRICK HOLES ALL OVER WITH MEAT FORK. MEANWHILE, COMBINE MILK, SUGAR AND 1/2 CUP (125 ML) COCONUT IN SAUCEPAN. BRING TO A BOIL AND SIMMER FOR 1 MINUTE. CAREFULLY SPOON OVER WARM CAKE. COOL COMPLETELY. FOLD 1/2 CUP (125 ML) COCONUT INTO COOL WHIP AND SPREAD OVER CAKE. SPRINKLE REMAINING COCONUT ON TOP. REFRIGERATE OVERNIGHT. SERVES 12 TO 16.

WHAT WILL TODAY'S GENERATION BE ABLE TO TELL THEIR CHILDREN THEY HAD TO DO WITHOUT?

MOCHA WHIPPED CREAM CAKE

EASY AND SHOWY.

CAKE

5	EGGS, SEPARATED (SHOULD BE ROOM TEMPERATURE)	5
I CUP	GRANULATED SUGAR	250 ML
I TSP	VANILLA EXTRACT	5 ML
1/2 TSP	INSTANT COFFEE GRANULES, DISSOLVED IN 3 TBSP (45 ML) BOILING WATER	2 ML
I CUP	ALL-PURPOSE FLOUR	250 ML
I TSP	BAKING POWDER	5 ML

FROSTING

2 CUPS	WHIPPING (35%) CREAM	500 ML
2 TBSP	BROWN SUGAR	30 ML
1/4 CUP	STRONG COLD COFFEE	60 ML
2 TBSP	COFFEE LIQUEUR	30 ML
1/4 CUP	TOASTED ALMONDS FOR GARNISH	60 ML

CAKE: PREHEAT OVEN TO 350°F (180°C). COMBINE EGG YOLKS AND SUGAR IN A LARGE BOWL AND BEAT UNTIL THICK AND LEMON-COLORED (5 MINUTES). BLEND IN VANILLA AND COFFEE MIXTURE. COMBINE FLOUR AND BAKING POWDER AND BLEND INTO BATTER. BEAT EGG WHITES UNTIL STIFF. FOLD INTO BATTER. TURN INTO UNGREASED 10-INCH (25 CM) TUBE PAN. BAKE FOR 30 MINUTES. INVERT ONTO RACK AND LET STAND UNTIL COMPLETELY COOL.

FROSTING: WHIP CREAM WITH SUGAR UNTIL SOFT PEAKS FORM. ADD COFFEE AND LIQUEUR AND BEAT UNTIL STIFF.

CONTINUED ON NEXT PAGE...

CUT CAKE INTO 3 LAYERS. USE ABOUT ONE-THIRD OF THE FROSTING TO FILL LAYERS AND REMAINDER TO FROST ENTIRE CAKE. SPRINKLE WITH TOASTED ALMONDS. CHILL FOR 4 HOURS BEFORE SERVING. SERVES 12 TO 16.

DARK CHOCOLATE CAKE

PARDON THE PACKAGES — YOUR GUESTS CERTAINLY WILL!

1	PACKAGE (18 1/4 OZ/515 G) DARK DEVIL'S FOOD CAKE MIX	1
1	PACKAGE (3 3/4 OZ/113 G) INSTANT CHOCOLATE PUDDING MIX	1
1 CUP	SOUR CREAM	250 ML
1/2 CUP	COOKING OIL	125 ML
1/2 CUP	WARM WATER	125 ML
4	EGGS, BEATEN	4
1 1/2 CUPS	SEMISWEET CHOCOLATE CHIPS	375 ML
	ICING SUGAR (OPTIONAL)	

IN A LARGE BOWL, COMBINE ALL INGREDIENTS EXCEPT CHOCOLATE CHIPS. BEAT 4 MINUTES. FOLD IN CHIPS. BAKE IN A GREASED AND FLOURED 10-INCH (25 CM) BUNDT PAN AT 350°F (180°C) FOR 50 TO 60 MINUTES OR UNTIL TOOTHPICK COMES OUT CLEAN. COOL IN PAN FOR 15 MINUTES, THEN TURN OUT ONTO SERVING PLATE. DUST WITH ICING SUGAR, IF YOU REALLY WANT TO MAKE THINGS DIFFICULT. SERVES 12 TO 16.

CRATER CAKE

THE CHILDREN NAMED THIS CAKE AND WHEN IT'S FINISHED, YOU'LL SEE WHY.

I CUP	BUTTER	250 ML
2 CUPS	GRANULATED SUGAR	500 ML
2	EGGS, BEATEN	2
I TSP	VANILLA EXTRACT	5 ML
3	RIPE MASHED BANANAS	3
3 CUPS	ALL-PURPOSE FLOUR	750 ML
2 TSP	BAKING POWDER	10 ML
2 TSP	BAKING SODA	10 ML
I CUP	SOUR CREAM	250 ML
I TSP	GROUND CINNAMON	5 ML
1/2 CUP	BROWN SUGAR	125 ML
1 1/2 CUPS	CHOCOLATE CHIPS (OR TO TASTE)	375 ML

CREAM TOGETHER BUTTER AND SUGAR. ADD BEATEN EGGS AND BEAT UNTIL SMOOTH. ADD VANILLA AND MASHED BANANAS; MIX UNTIL SMOOTH. SIFT FLOUR, BAKING POWDER AND BAKING SODA; ADD TO BANANA MIXTURE ALTERNATELY WITH SOUR CREAM, ENDING WITH DRY INGREDIENTS. POUR HALF THE BATTER INTO A GREASED 13- BY 9-INCH (33 BY 23 CM) PAN. COMBINE CINNAMON AND BROWN SUGAR. SPRINKLE HALF THE MIXTURE OVER THE BATTER IN PAN. TOP WITH HALF THE CHOCOLATE CHIPS. REPEAT LAYERS. BAKE AT 350°F (180°C) FOR 45 TO 50 MINUTES. SERVES 12 TO 16.

CHOCOLATE ZUCCHINI CAKE

1/4 CUP	BUTTER	60 ML
1/2 CUP	VEGETABLE OIL	125 ML
1 3/4 CUPS	GRANULATED SUGAR	425 ML
2	EGGS	2
1 TSP	VANILLA EXTRACT	5 ML
1/2 CUP	BUTTERMILK OR SOUR MILK	125 ML
2 1/2 CUPS	ALL-PURPOSE FLOUR	625 ML
1/4 CUP	UNSWEETENED COCOA POWDER	60 ML
1/2 TSP	BAKING POWDER	2 ML
1 TSP	BAKING SODA	5 ML
1/2 TSP	GROUND CINNAMON	2 ML
1/2 TSP	GROUND CLOVES	2 ML
2 CUPS	GRATED ZUCCHINI	500 ML
1/4 CUP	CHOCOLATE CHIPS	60 ML

CREAM TOGETHER BUTTER, OIL, SUGAR, EGGS, VANILLA AND BUTTERMILK. SIFT DRY INGREDIENTS AND ADD TO CREAMED MIXTURE. MIX IN ZUCCHINI AND CHOCOLATE CHIPS. BAKE IN A GREASED AND FLOURED 10-INCH (25 CM) BUNDT PAN OR A GREASED 13- BY 9-INCH (33 BY 23 CM) PAN AT 325°F (160°C) FOR 45 MINUTES. DELICIOUS! SERVES 12 TO 16.

THE TROUBLE WITH BEING PUNCTUAL IS THAT NOBODY'S THERE TO APPRECIATE IT!

CHOCOLATE MOUSSE CAKE

TOTALLY DECADENT!

<u>CAKE</u>

7	SQUARES (EACH 1 OZ/30 G) SEMISWEET CHOCOLATE	7
4 OZ	BUTTER	125 G
7	EGGS, SEPARATED	7
1 CUP	GRANULATED SUGAR	250 ML
1 TSP	VANILLA EXTRACT	5 ML
1 OZ	KAHLÚA	30 ML
1 OZ	TIA MARIA	30 ML

<u>FROSTING</u>

1 CUP	WHIPPING (35%) CREAM	250 ML
1/3 CUP	ICING SUGAR	75 ML
1 TSP	KAHLÚA	5 ML

CAKE: PREHEAT OVEN TO 325°F (160°C). MELT CHOCOLATE AND BUTTER OVER LOW HEAT. IN A BOWL, BEAT EGG YOLKS AND 3/4 CUP (175 ML) OF THE SUGAR UNTIL VERY LIGHT AND FLUFFY, AT LEAST 5 MINUTES. SLOWLY BEAT IN WARM CHOCOLATE MIXTURE AND VANILLA. IN ANOTHER LARGE BOWL, BEAT EGG WHITES UNTIL SOFT PEAKS FORM. ADD 1/4 CUP (60 ML) OF SUGAR, 1 TBSP (15 ML) AT A TIME, BEATING CONSTANTLY FOR 10 MINUTES. CAREFULLY FOLD CHOCOLATE MIXTURE INTO THE EGG WHITES. RESERVE 1 1/2 CUPS (375 ML) BATTER, COVER AND REFRIGERATE. POUR THE REST OF THE BATTER INTO A 9-INCH (23 CM) SPRINGFORM PAN. BAKE CAKE FOR 35 MINUTES AND COOL. CAKE WILL DROP AND PULL AWAY FROM THE SIDES OF THE

CONTINUED ON NEXT PAGE...

PAN. REMOVE OUTSIDE RING OF PAN. SPRINKLE LIQUEURS OVER CAKE, THEN SPREAD RESERVED BATTER ON TOP OF CAKE. REFRIGERATE UNTIL FIRM.

FROSTING: BEAT WHIPPING CREAM UNTIL SOFT PEAKS FORM. ADD ICING SUGAR AND KAHLÚA. SPREAD FROSTING OVER TOP AND SIDES OF CAKE. FREEZE UNCOVERED TILL FROZEN, THEN WRAP WITH FOIL. REMOVE FROM FREEZER 15 MINUTES BEFORE SERVING. SERVES 8 TO 10.

NOTE: THIS RECIPE CONTAINS RAW EGGS. IF THE FOOD SAFETY OF RAW EGGS IS A CONCERN FOR YOU, USE PASTEURIZED WHOLE EGGS, SEPARATED.

ONE OF LIFE'S GREATEST DISAPPOINTMENTS IS FINDING THAT THE GUY WHO WRITES THE ADS FOR THE BANK IS NOT THE SAME GUY WHO MAKES THE LOANS.

CHOCOLATE RASPBERRY TORTE

GOD MADE CHOCOLATE AND THE DEVIL THREW THE
CALORIES IN! THIS TASTES AS GOOD AS IT LOOKS.

CAKE

2 CUPS	ALL-PURPOSE FLOUR	500 ML
2 TSP	BAKING SODA	10 ML
1/2 TSP	SALT	2 ML
1/2 TSP	BAKING POWDER	2 ML
3	SQUARES (EACH 1 OZ/30 G) UNSWEETENED CHOCOLATE	3
1/2 CUP	BUTTER	125 ML
2 CUPS	BROWN SUGAR, PACKED	500 ML
3	EGGS	3
1 1/2 TSP	VANILLA EXTRACT	7 ML
3/4 CUP	SOUR CREAM	175 ML
1/2 CUP	STRONG COFFEE	125 ML
1/2 CUP	COFFEE-FLAVORED LIQUEUR (KAHLÚA)	125 ML

FILLING

1 CUP	WHIPPING (35%) CREAM	250 ML
2 TBSP	ICING SUGAR	30 ML
1	JAR (12 OZ/341 ML) RASPBERRY OR STRAWBERRY JAM	1

FROSTING

1 1/2 CUPS	CHOCOLATE CHIPS	375 ML
3/4 CUP	SOUR CREAM	175 ML
PINCH	SALT	PINCH
	CHOCOLATE CURLS	
	RASPBERRIES OR STRAWBERRIES	

CONTINUED ON NEXT PAGE...

CAKE: PREHEAT OVEN TO 350°F (180°C). GREASE AND FLOUR TWO 9-INCH (23 CM) CAKE PANS. MIX FLOUR, BAKING SODA, SALT AND BAKING POWDER. MELT CHOCOLATE AND LET COOL. IN A LARGE BOWL, BEAT BUTTER, BROWN SUGAR AND EGGS AT HIGH SPEED UNTIL LIGHT AND FLUFFY, ABOUT 5 MINUTES. BEAT IN MELTED CHOCOLATE AND VANILLA. AT LOW SPEED, BEAT IN FLOUR MIXTURE (IN FOURTHS), ALTERNATING WITH SOUR CREAM (IN THIRDS). ADD COFFEE AND LIQUEUR, BLENDING UNTIL SMOOTH. POUR BATTER INTO PANS AND BAKE FOR 30 TO 35 MINUTES OR UNTIL SURFACE SPRINGS BACK. COOL IN PANS FOR 10 MINUTES, THEN REMOVE FROM PANS AND COOL ON WIRE RACKS.

FILLING: BEAT CREAM UNTIL IT BEGINS TO THICKEN. SPRINKLE IN ICING SUGAR AND BEAT UNTIL STIFF. REFRIGERATE. SLICE CAKE LAYERS IN HALF HORIZONTALLY TO MAKE FOUR LAYERS (CAKE LAYERS CUT MORE EASILY IF FROZEN FIRST). PLACE ONE LAYER, CUT SIDE UP, ON CAKE PLATE. SPREAD WITH $1/2$ CUP (125 ML) RASPBERRY JAM AND $1/2$ CUP (125 ML) WHIPPED CREAM. REPEAT WITH REMAINING LAYERS, ENDING WITH TOP LAYER CUT SIDE DOWN.

FROSTING: MELT CHOCOLATE CHIPS IN TOP OF DOUBLE BOILER. ADD SOUR CREAM AND SALT AND BEAT UNTIL FROSTING IS CREAMY AND SMOOTH. FROST TOP AND SIDES OF CAKE. GARNISH WITH CHOCOLATE CURLS AND FRESH BERRIES. SERVES 10 TO 12.

TIP: TO MAKE CHOCOLATE CURLS, WARM A GOOD-QUALITY CHOCOLATE BAR TO ROOM TEMPERATURE, THEN USE A VEGETABLE PEELER TO SHAVE OFF CURLS.

CHOCOLATE CHIFFON CAKE

1/2 CUP	UNSWEETENED COCOA POWDER	125 ML
3/4 CUP	BOILING WATER	175 ML
1 3/4 CUPS	CAKE FLOUR	425 ML
1 3/4 CUPS	GRANULATED SUGAR	425 ML
1 1/2 TSP	BAKING SODA	7 ML
1 TSP	SALT	5 ML
1/2 CUP	SALAD OIL	125 ML
7	UNBEATEN EGG YOLKS	7
2 TSP	VANILLA EXTRACT	10 ML
1 CUP	EGG WHITES (7 WHITES)	250 ML
1/2 TSP	CREAM OF TARTAR	2 ML

IN A SMALL BOWL, MIX COCOA AND BOILING WATER
TOGETHER AND LET COOL. IN A LARGE BOWL, MIX FLOUR,
SUGAR, BAKING SODA AND SALT. MAKE A WELL OR HOLE
IN CENTER OF DRY INGREDIENTS. COMBINE SALAD OIL,
EGG YOLKS, COCOA MIXTURE AND VANILLA. POUR INTO
CENTER OF DRY INGREDIENTS. BEAT UNTIL VERY SMOOTH.
BEAT EGG WHITES AND CREAM OF TARTAR UNTIL STIFF
AND FOLD GENTLY INTO MIXTURE USING A SPATULA.
POUR INTO A 10-INCH (25 CM) TUBE PAN AND BAKE AT
325°F (160°C) FOR 55 MINUTES, THEN 350°F (180°C) FOR
10 MINUTES. SERVES 12 TO 16.

BLACK BOTTOM CUPCAKES

WICKED!

I	PACKAGE (8 OZ/250 G) CREAM CHEESE, SOFTENED	I
I	EGG, SLIGHTLY BEATEN	I
1/3 CUP	GRANULATED SUGAR	75 ML
PINCH	SALT	PINCH
I	PACKAGE (6 OZ/170 G) CHOCOLATE CHIPS	I
I CUP	GRANULATED SUGAR	250 ML
1 1/2 CUPS	ALL-PURPOSE FLOUR	375 ML
1/4 CUP	UNSWEETENED COCOA POWDER	60 ML
I TSP	BAKING SODA	5 ML
1/2 TSP	SALT	2 ML
I CUP	WATER	250 ML
1/2 CUP	VEGETABLE OIL	125 ML
I TBSP	VINEGAR	15 ML
I TSP	VANILLA EXTRACT	5 ML

IN A SMALL BOWL, COMBINE FIRST FOUR INGREDIENTS. ADD CHOCOLATE CHIPS AND SET ASIDE. MIX REMAINING INGREDIENTS WELL. FILL MUFFIN TINS, LINED WITH PAPER CUPS, ONE-THIRD TO HALF FULL WITH THIS MIXTURE. DROP A LARGE SPOONFUL OF CHEESE MIXTURE ON TOP. BAKE FOR 20 TO 25 MINUTES AT 350°F (180°C). MAKES 20 CUPCAKES.

THE TROUBLE WITH LIPSTICK IS THAT IT DOESN'T.

FAIL-PROOF PASTRY

5 CUPS	ALL-PURPOSE FLOUR	1.25 L
1 TSP	BAKING POWDER	5 ML
1 TSP	SALT	5 ML
1 LB	LARD	500 G
1	EGG	1
1 TBSP	VINEGAR	15 ML
	COLD WATER	

MIX FLOUR, BAKING POWDER AND SALT TOGETHER. CUT IN LARD WITH 2 KNIVES OR A PASTRY CUTTER. MIX EGG IN A 1-CUP (250 ML) MEASURING CUP, ADD VINEGAR AND FILL TO $\frac{3}{4}$ MARK WITH COLD WATER. ADD LIQUID MIXTURE SLOWLY TO BLEND MIXTURE TO FORM A BALL. HANDLE DOUGH AS LITTLE AS POSSIBLE. CHILL FOR 1 TO 2 HOURS IN REFRIGERATOR BEFORE ROLLING. MAKES ENOUGH PASTRY FOR 4 TO 5 DOUBLE-CRUST PIES.

HAVING CHILDREN IS AN EXAMPLE OF A HEREDITARY TRAIT;
IF YOUR PARENTS DIDN'T HAVE ANY CHILDREN,
CHANCES ARE YOU WON'T EITHER.

SHOO-FLY PIE

*MAKES YOUR EYES LIGHT UP AND YOUR HIPS
SAY "HOWDY." I NEVER GET ENOUGH OF
THAT WONDERFUL STUFF.*

2/3 CUP	LIGHT BROWN SUGAR, FIRMLY PACKED	150 ML
1/2 CUP	ALL-PURPOSE FLOUR	125 ML
1 1/2 TSP	GROUND CINNAMON	7 ML
1/2 TSP	GROUND NUTMEG	2 ML
1/4 CUP	BUTTER, SOFTENED	60 ML
2	EGGS	2
2/3 CUP	LIGHT CORN SYRUP	150 ML
1/3 CUP	LIGHT (FANCY) MOLASSES	75 ML
1/2 TSP	BAKING SODA	2 ML
1 CUP	WARM WATER	250 ML
1 CUP	RAISINS	250 ML
1	UNBAKED 9-INCH (23 CM) PIE SHELL	1

COMBINE SUGAR, FLOUR, CINNAMON AND NUTMEG IN
A BOWL. USING A PASTRY BLENDER OR FORK, WORK IN
BUTTER UNTIL MIXTURE IS THE TEXTURE OF COARSE
MEAL. IN A SEPARATE BOWL, WHISK EGGS, CORN SYRUP
AND MOLASSES UNTIL WELL BLENDED. DISSOLVE BAKING
SODA IN WARM WATER AND ADD TO EGG MIXTURE.
SPRINKLE RAISINS IN THE PIE SHELL AND POUR MOLASSES
MIXTURE INTO SHELL. TOP WITH ONE-THIRD OF THE SUGAR
MIXTURE, SPRINKLING AS EVENLY AS POSSIBLE. BAKE FOR
25 MINUTES AT 400°F (200°C). FILLING WILL BE SOFT BUT
SLIGHTLY CRUSTY. SPRINKLE WITH REMAINING SUGAR AND
BAKE FOR ANOTHER 5 MINUTES. SERVES 8 TO 10.

FLAPPER PIE

PEOPLE "FLIP" FOR IT!

10	DOUBLE GRAHAM WAFERS, CRUSHED	10
8	SODA BISCUITS, CRUSHED	8
1 TBSP	GRANULATED SUGAR	15 ML
1/2 CUP	BUTTER	125 ML

CREAM FILLING

2 CUPS	MILK	500 ML
1 TBSP	CORNSTARCH	15 ML
1/2 CUP	GRANULATED SUGAR	125 ML
3	EGG YOLKS (SAVE WHITES FOR LATER)	3
1/2 TSP	VANILLA EXTRACT	2 ML
6 TBSP	GRANULATED SUGAR	90 ML

COMBINE GRAHAM WAFERS, SODA BISCUIT CRUMBS, SUGAR AND BUTTER. RESERVE 1 CUP (250 ML) FOR TOPPING. PAT REMAINDER OF THE CRUMBS IN A 9-INCH (23 CM) PIE PLATE AND BAKE AT 350°F (180°C) FOR 5 MINUTES. SET ASIDE TO COOL.

FILLING: POUR MILK INTO TOP OF DOUBLE BOILER OR HEAVY SAUCEPAN. MIX CORNSTARCH AND SUGAR AND STIR INTO MILK. ADD SLIGHTLY BEATEN EGG YOLKS AND VANILLA. COOK, STIRRING CONSTANTLY UNTIL MIXTURE COMES TO A BOIL AND BECOMES THICK. POUR INTO PIE CRUST. LET COOL.

CONTINUED ON NEXT PAGE...

NOW, BEAT 3 EGG WHITES, GRADUALLY ADDING SUGAR UNTIL EGG WHITES ARE FIRM AND FORM PEAKS. PILE GENTLY INTO COOLED PIE FILLING. SPREAD TO EDGE OF CRUST. SWIRL THE WHITES FOR AN ATTRACTIVE TOPPING. SPRINKLE WITH REMAINING CRUMBS. BAKE AT 350°F (180°C) FOR 7 TO 10 MINUTES OR UNTIL LIGHTLY BROWNED. SERVES 6 TO 8.

*I FINALLY GOT IT ALL TOGETHER —
NOW I FORGET WHERE I PUT IT!*

IRISH COFFEE CREAM PIE

A LURE FOR LEPRECHAUNS.

CRUST

1 1/4 CUPS	VANILLA WAFER CRUMBS	300 ML
1/3 CUP	GRANULATED SUGAR	75 ML
PINCH	GROUND CINNAMON	PINCH
1/3 CUP	MELTED BUTTER	75 ML
1/2 CUP	FLAKED TOASTED ALMONDS	125 ML

FILLING

1	ENVELOPE (1/4 OZ/7 G) UNFLAVORED GELATIN POWDER (ABOUT 1 TBSP/15 ML)	1
1/4 CUP	COLD WATER	60 ML
1 TBSP	INSTANT COFFEE	15 ML
2	EGGS, SEPARATED	2
1/4 CUP	IRISH WHISKEY OR SCOTCH	60 ML
1/2 CUP	BROWN SUGAR	125 ML
1/2 TSP	VANILLA EXTRACT	2 ML
1/2 TSP	GROUND CINNAMON	2 ML
PINCH	SALT	PINCH
1 CUP	WHIPPING (35%) CREAM, WHIPPED	250 ML
1/4 CUP	FLAKED TOASTED ALMONDS	60 ML

CRUST: COMBINE INGREDIENTS AND PRESS INTO A GREASED 9-INCH (23 CM) PIE PLATE. BAKE AT 425°F (220°C) FOR 8 MINUTES. COOL IN FRIDGE.

FILLING: SPRINKLE GELATIN OVER WATER IN A SMALL HEAVY-BOTTOMED SAUCEPAN. ADD INSTANT COFFEE AND COOK OVER LOW HEAT UNTIL GELATIN AND COFFEE ARE DISSOLVED, ABOUT 1 MINUTE. REMOVE FROM HEAT

CONTINUED ON NEXT PAGE...

AND KEEP WARM. BEAT EGG WHITES UNTIL STIFF AND SET ASIDE. BEAT EGG YOLKS, WHISKEY, SUGAR, VANILLA, CINNAMON AND SALT IN A LARGE BOWL UNTIL LIGHT. GRADUALLY STIR IN WARM COFFEE-GELATIN MIXTURE. FOLD IN WHIPPED CREAM, THEN FOLD IN BEATEN EGG WHITES. POUR INTO COLD CRUST AND SPRINKLE WITH TOASTED ALMONDS. REFRIGERATE AT LEAST 2 HOURS. SERVES 6 TO 8.

NOTE: THIS RECIPE CONTAINS RAW EGGS. IF THE FOOD SAFETY OF RAW EGGS IS A CONCERN FOR YOU, USE PASTEURIZED WHOLE EGGS, SEPARATED, OR SUBSTITUTE $1/4$ CUP (60 ML) PASTEURIZED LIQUID WHOLE EGGS FOR THE YOLKS AND USE $1/4$ CUP (60 ML) PASTEURIZED LIQUID EGG WHITES.

BACHELOR'S DEFINITION OF GOURMET:
ANYTHING ABOVE ROOM TEMPERATURE.

SPIKED APPLE BETTY

AN OLD FAVORITE WITH A COMPANY TOUCH.
SERVE WARM WITH CREAM, WHIPPED CREAM OR
VANILLA OR CINNAMON ICE CREAM.

5 CUPS	SLICED PEELED APPLES	1.25 L
1/2 TSP	CINNAMON SUGAR	2 ML
1 TSP	GRATED LEMON ZEST	5 ML
1 TSP	GRATED ORANGE ZEST	5 ML
2 TBSP	GRAND MARNIER	30 ML
2 TBSP	AMARETTO	30 ML
3/4 CUP	GRANULATED SUGAR	175 ML
1/4 CUP	BROWN SUGAR	60 ML
3/4 CUP	ALL-PURPOSE FLOUR	175 ML
1/4 TSP	SALT	1 ML
1/2 CUP	BUTTER	125 ML

SLICE APPLES INTO A GREASED 8-CUP (2 L) CASSEROLE
DISH. SPRINKLE SUGAR, LEMON AND ORANGE ZEST AND
LIQUEURS ON TOP OF APPLES. IN ANOTHER BOWL, MIX
REMAINING INGREDIENTS WITH A PASTRY BLENDER UNTIL
CRUMBLY. PAT MIXTURE OVER APPLES. BAKE, UNCOVERED,
AT 350°F (180°C) UNTIL TOP IS LIGHTLY BROWNED, ABOUT
1 HOUR. SERVES 8.

FRENCH LEMON PIE

4	EGGS	4
I CUP	LIGHT CORN SYRUP	250 ML
I TSP	GRATED LEMON ZEST	5 ML
1/3 CUP	LEMON JUICE	75 ML
2 TBSP	MELTED BUTTER	30 ML
1/2 CUP	GRANULATED SUGAR	125 ML
2 TBSP	ALL-PURPOSE FLOUR	30 ML
I	UNBAKED 9-INCH (23 CM) PIE SHELL	I
1/2 CUP	WHIPPING (35%) CREAM	125 ML

IN A MEDIUM BOWL, BEAT EGGS; ADD CORN SYRUP, LEMON ZEST, LEMON JUICE AND MELTED BUTTER. MIX SUGAR AND FLOUR TOGETHER, THEN STIR INTO EGG MIXTURE. POUR INTO UNBAKED PIE SHELL AND BAKE AT 350°F (180°C) FOR 50 MINUTES. CHILL. JUST BEFORE SERVING, WHIP CREAM AND MOUND IT ON TOP OF THE PIE. SERVES 6 TO 8.

A MAN CLAIMS HIS WIFE LOST HER CREDIT CARDS BUT HE HASN'T REPORTED IT BECAUSE WHOEVER STOLE THEM SPENDS LESS THAN SHE DID.

PEACHES AND CREAM PIE

3 CUPS	SLICED PEELED PEACHES	750 ML
1	9-INCH (23 CM) PIE SHELL, UNBAKED	1
1/2 CUP	GRANULATED SUGAR	125 ML
3 TBSP	ALL-PURPOSE FLOUR	45 ML
1/4 TSP	GROUND CINNAMON	1 ML
PINCH	SALT	PINCH
1 CUP	SOUR CREAM	250 ML
1/4 CUP	BROWN SUGAR	60 ML

ARRANGE PEACHES IN PASTRY SHELL. COMBINE SUGAR, FLOUR, CINNAMON, SALT AND SOUR CREAM. BEAT MIXTURE UNTIL SMOOTH AND POUR OVER PEACHES. BAKE AT 425°F (220°C) FOR 15 MINUTES. REDUCE HEAT TO 350°F (180°C) AND BAKE FOR 35 MINUTES LONGER OR UNTIL FILLING IS SET. SPRINKLE BROWN SUGAR OVER TOP AND PLACE UNDER BROILER UNTIL MELTED. COOL SLIGHTLY BEFORE SERVING. SERVES 6 TO 8.

LIFE DOES NOT BEGIN AT THE MOMENT OF CONCEPTION OR BIRTH. IT BEGINS WHEN THE KIDS LEAVE HOME AND THE DOG DIES.

RHUBARB CRISP WITH BOURBON SAUCE

RUM OR BRANDY CAN BE SUBSTITUTED.

RHUBARB CRISP

3/4 CUP	BROWN SUGAR, FIRMLY PACKED	175 ML
3/4 CUP	ALL-PURPOSE FLOUR	175 ML
1/3 CUP	BUTTER, SOFTENED	75 ML
1 TSP	GROUND CINNAMON	5 ML
6 CUPS	DICED FRESH OR FROZEN RHUBARB	1.5 KG
1/3 TO 2/3 CUP	GRANULATED SUGAR	75 TO 150 ML
	GRATED ZEST OF 1 LEMON	

BOURBON SAUCE

3	EGG YOLKS	3
1/3 CUP	GRANULATED SUGAR	75 ML
1 CUP	WHIPPING (35%) CREAM	250 ML
1/3 CUP	MILK	75 ML
1/4 CUP	BOURBON	60 ML
PINCH	SALT	PINCH

CRISP: COMBINE FIRST FOUR INGREDIENTS UNTIL CRUMBLY. IN AN 8-CUP (2 L) CASSEROLE DISH, COMBINE RHUBARB, SUGAR AND LEMON ZEST. COVER WITH FIRST MIXTURE. BAKE FOR 1 HOUR AT 350°F (180°C).

SAUCE: IN TOP OF DOUBLE BOILER, BEAT YOLKS AND SUGAR UNTIL LIGHT AND LEMON-COLORED. WHISK IN CREAM AND MILK. COOK OVER HOT WATER (NOT BOILING) UNTIL MIXTURE COATS A SPOON. STIR IN BOURBON AND SALT. COOK FOR 5 MINUTES. SERVE WARM OVER SCOOPS OF RHUBARB CRISP. SERVES 8.

RHUBARB MERINGUE PIE

4 CUPS	FINELY CHOPPED RHUBARB	1 L
3	EGGS, SEPARATED	3
1 CUP	GRANULATED SUGAR	250 ML
2 TBSP	ALL-PURPOSE FLOUR	30 ML
2 TBSP	MELTED BUTTER	30 ML
1	9-INCH (23 CM) UNBAKED PIE SHELL	1
1/3 CUP	GRANULATED SUGAR	75 ML

COMBINE RHUBARB AND EGG YOLKS. ADD SUGAR AND FLOUR AND MIX WELL. STIR IN BUTTER AND SPOON INTO PIE SHELL. BAKE AT 350°F (180°C) FOR 30 MINUTES OR UNTIL SET. TO MAKE MERINGUE, BEAT EGG WHITES UNTIL SOFT PEAKS FORM. CONTINUE BEATING AND SLOWLY ADD SUGAR UNTIL MIXTURE IS THICK AND GLOSSY. HEAP LIGHTLY OVER PIE AND SPREAD TO EDGES OF THE CRUST. BROWN IN A 350°F (180°C) OVEN FOR ABOUT 10 MINUTES. SERVES 6 TO 8.

I KNOW AN EXECUTIVE ASSISTANT WHO CAN TYPE TWENTY LETTERS IN AN HOUR. HER BOSS IS STILL WAITING FOR HER TO LEARN THE OTHER SIX.

PALACE PIE

A ROYAL TREAT!

1	EGG, SLIGHTLY BEATEN	1
1 CUP	ICING SUGAR	250 ML
1/4 CUP	BUTTER OR MARGARINE, SOFTENED	60 ML
1/4 TSP	VANILLA EXTRACT	1 ML
1	9-INCH (23 CM) BAKED PIE CRUST	1
1 1/2 CUPS	WHIPPING (35%) CREAM	375 ML
1/2 CUP	SLICED STRAWBERRIES (OR 2/3 CUP/ 150 ML CRUSHED PINEAPPLE, WELL DRAINED)	125 ML
1/4 CUP	CHOPPED MARASCHINO CHERRIES, WELL DRAINED	60 ML
1/4 CUP	CHOPPED PECANS OR SLIVERED ALMONDS	60 ML
	MARASCHINO CHERRY HALVES, WELL DRAINED	

IN A SMALL BOWL, COMBINE EGG, ICING SUGAR, BUTTER AND VANILLA. BEAT WITH AN ELECTRIC MIXER UNTIL LIGHT AND CREAMY. SPREAD EVENLY IN BAKED PIE CRUST. IN A MEDIUM BOWL, WHIP CREAM UNTIL SOFT PEAKS FORM. FOLD IN STRAWBERRIES OR PINEAPPLE, MARASCHINO CHERRIES AND NUTS. SPREAD EVENLY OVER ICING SUGAR MIXTURE. REFRIGERATE FOR 2 HOURS. GARNISH WITH MARASCHINO CHERRY HALVES. SERVES 8.

NOTE: THIS RECIPE CONTAINS A RAW EGG. IF THE FOOD SAFETY OF RAW EGGS IS A CONCERN FOR YOU, SUBSTITUTE A PASTEURIZED WHOLE EGG OR 1/4 CUP (60 ML) PASTEURIZED LIQUID WHOLE EGGS.

PUMPKIN CHIFFON PIE

YOU'LL BE THANKFUL FOR THIS ONE.

1	ENVELOPE (¼ OZ/7 G) UNFLAVORED GELATIN POWDER (ABOUT 1 TBSP/15 ML)	1
½ CUP	COLD WATER	125 ML
4	EGGS, SEPARATED	4
1 CUP	EVAPORATED MILK	250 ML
1 CUP	CANNED PUMPKIN	250 ML
½ CUP	BROWN SUGAR	125 ML
½ TSP	SALT	2 ML
½ TSP	GROUND NUTMEG	2 ML
½ TSP	GROUND CINNAMON	2 ML
¼ TSP	GROUND GINGER	1 ML
¼ CUP	BROWN SUGAR	60 ML
1	9-INCH (23 CM) BAKED PIE SHELL	1
1 CUP	WHIPPING (35%) CREAM, WHIPPED	250 ML

SOFTEN GELATIN IN COLD WATER. SET ASIDE. IN DOUBLE BOILER, HEAT EGG YOLKS, MILK, PUMPKIN, ½ CUP (125 ML) BROWN SUGAR AND SPICES. COOK, STIRRING, FOR 10 MINUTES. REMOVE FROM HEAT, ADD GELATIN, STIRRING UNTIL DISSOLVED. REFRIGERATE UNTIL THICK. BEAT EGG WHITES AND ¼ CUP (50 ML) BROWN SUGAR UNTIL THICK. FOLD INTO PUMPKIN MIXTURE. TURN INTO PIE SHELL, TOP WITH WHIPPED CREAM AND REFRIGERATE UNTIL READY TO SERVE. SERVES 6 TO 8.

NOTE: THIS RECIPE CONTAINS RAW EGG WHITES. IF THE FOOD SAFETY OF RAW EGGS IS A CONCERN FOR YOU, SUBSTITUTE ½ CUP (125 ML) PASTEURIZED LIQUID EGG WHITES.

PUMPKIN PECAN PIE

WE THOUGHT WE'D CALL THIS "PI R SQUARED"
BUT THEN WE REMEMBERED "PIE ARE ROUND"!

4	EGGS	4
2 CUPS	CANNED OR MASHED COOKED PUMPKIN	500 ML
1 CUP	GRANULATED SUGAR	250 ML
1/2 CUP	DARK CORN SYRUP	125 ML
1 TSP	VANILLA EXTRACT	5 ML
1/2 TSP	GROUND CINNAMON	2 ML
1/4 TSP	SALT	1 ML
1	UNBAKED 9-INCH (23 CM) PIE SHELL	1
1 CUP	CHOPPED PECANS	250 ML
1 CUP	WHIPPING (35%) CREAM, WHIPPED (OPTIONAL... JUST KIDDING!)	250 ML

BREAK EGGS INTO A LARGE BOWL. BEAT WITH A WIRE WHISK OR FORK. ADD PUMPKIN, SUGAR, CORN SYRUP, VANILLA, CINNAMON AND SALT. STIR UNTIL SUGAR IS DISSOLVED AND INGREDIENTS ARE WELL BLENDED. POUR INTO PIE SHELL AND SPRINKLE WITH PECANS. BAKE IN 350°F (180°C) OVEN FOR 40 MINUTES OR UNTIL FILLING IS SET. DELICIOUS AS IS, OR TOPPED WITH WHIPPED CREAM. SERVES 6 TO 8.

TIME WOUNDS ALL HEELS.

CHOCOLATE PECAN PIE

BEWARE! RICH AND APPEALING TO
TRUE CHOCOLATE LOVERS.

3	EGGS, SLIGHTLY BEATEN	3
I CUP	CORN SYRUP	250 ML
4	SQUARES (EACH I OZ/30 G) SEMISWEET CHOCOLATE, MELTED AND COOLED	4
$1/3$ CUP	GRANULATED SUGAR	75 ML
2 TBSP	BUTTER, MELTED	30 ML
I TSP	VANILLA EXTRACT	5 ML
$1\frac{1}{2}$ CUPS	PECAN HALVES	375 ML
I	9-INCH (23 CM) PASTRY SHELL, UNBAKED	I
I CUP	WHIPPING (35%) CREAM, WHIPPED, OR ICE CREAM	250 ML

IN A LARGE BOWL, STIR EGGS, CORN SYRUP, CHOCOLATE, SUGAR, MELTED BUTTER AND VANILLA UNTIL WELL BLENDED. STIR IN PECANS. POUR INTO PASTRY SHELL. BAKE AT 450°F (230°C) FOR 15 MINUTES. REDUCE HEAT TO 350°F (180°C) AND BAKE FOR 50 TO 60 MINUTES OR UNTIL KNIFE COMES OUT CLEAN. TOP WITH WHIPPED CREAM OR ICE CREAM (GILDING THE LILY). SERVES 6 TO 8.

A LOT OF GOOD ARGUMENTS ARE SPOILED BY
SOME GUY WHO KNOWS WHAT HE'S TALKING ABOUT!

CHOCOLATE MOUSSE PIE

CRUST

1 1/4 CUPS	GRAHAM WAFER CRUMBS	300 ML
1/4 CUP	BROWN SUGAR	60 ML
1/3 CUP	BUTTER, MELTED	75

FILLING

4 OZ	SEMISWEET CHOCOLATE	120 G
1/3 CUP	MILK	75 ML
2 TBSP	GRANULATED SUGAR	30 ML
4 OZ	CREAM CHEESE	125 G
1	ENVELOPE (1 1/2 OZ/40 G) WHIPPED TOPPING	1

CRUST: MIX CRUST INGREDIENTS TOGETHER AND PRESS INTO 8-INCH (20 CM) PIE PLATE. BAKE AT 300°F (150°C) FOR 5 TO 8 MINUTES. COOL.

FILLING: HEAT CHOCOLATE AND 2 TBSP (30 ML) OF MILK UNTIL CHOCOLATE MELTS. BEAT SUGAR INTO CREAM CHEESE. ADD REMAINING MILK AND CHOCOLATE MIXTURE AND BEAT UNTIL SMOOTH. PREPARE TOPPING ACCORDING TO PACKAGE DIRECTIONS AND FOLD INTO CHOCOLATE MIXTURE, MIXING WELL UNTIL SMOOTH. SPOON INTO CRUST AND REFRIGERATE AT LEAST 3 HOURS. SERVES 6 TO 8.

TO MAKE YOUR DREAMS COME TRUE,
YOU HAVE TO STAY AWAKE!

FUDGE PIE WITH CUSTARD SAUCE

RICH AND DELICIOUS!

FUDGE PIE

1/2 CUP	BUTTER	125 ML
2 OZ	UNSWEETENED CHOCOLATE	60 G
2	EGGS	2
1 CUP	GRANULATED SUGAR	250 ML
1/4 CUP	ALL-PURPOSE FLOUR	60 ML
1/4 TSP	SALT	1 ML
1 TSP	VANILLA EXTRACT	5 ML
3/4 CUP	PECAN HALVES, CHOPPED (OPTIONAL)	175 ML

CUSTARD SAUCE

1 CUP	MILK	250 ML
1 CUP	WHIPPING (35%) CREAM	250 ML
3/4 CUP	GRANULATED SUGAR	175 ML
6	EGG YOLKS, SLIGHTLY BEATEN	6
2 TBSP	GRAND MARNIER OR ANY ORANGE-FLAVORED LIQUEUR	30 ML

PIE: MELT BUTTER AND CHOCOLATE OVER LOW HEAT. COMBINE REMAINING INGREDIENTS. ADD CHOCOLATE MIXTURE AND BEAT UNTIL SMOOTH. POUR INTO A WELL-BUTTERED 8-INCH (20 CM) PIE PLATE. BAKE AT 350°F (180°C) FOR 25 TO 30 MINUTES.

SAUCE: IN A HEAVY SAUCEPAN OVER MEDIUM-HIGH HEAT, BRING MILK, CREAM AND SUGAR TO A FULL BOIL. WHISKING CONSTANTLY, ADD ONE-QUARTER OF THE HOT CREAM MIXTURE IN A SLOW, STEADY STREAM TO EGG YOLKS. REDUCE HEAT TO MEDIUM. WHISK WARM

CONTINUED ON NEXT PAGE...

EGG YOLK MIXTURE SLOWLY INTO REMAINING CREAM MIXTURE. WHISKING CONSTANTLY, COOK UNTIL MIXTURE THICKENS AND COATS BACK OF A METAL SPOON (ABOUT 3 MINUTES — THIS HAPPENS ALL OF A SUDDEN). DO NOT OVERCOOK OR EGGS WILL SCRAMBLE. REMOVE SAUCE FROM HEAT; WHISK 3 MINUTES UNTIL SLIGHTLY COOL. WHISK IN LIQUEUR (THAT IS, IF YOUR WHISK ISN'T BROKEN YET), THEN STRAIN. PLACE PLASTIC WRAP OVER CUSTARD; REFRIGERATE UNTIL CHILLED.

TO SERVE: PUT SAUCE ON PLATE FIRST, THEN A SLICE OF PIE ON TOP. AT ANY RATE, THAT'S THE WAY WE WOULD DO IT! SERVES 6 TO 8.

NO FOOD TASTES AS GOOD AS THE FOOD YOU EAT WHEN YOU'RE CHEATING ON A DIET.

PECAN CRUST ICE CREAM PIE WITH CARAMEL SAUCE

WELL WORTH THE EFFORT!

CRUST

1	EGG WHITE (SAVE YOLK FOR CARAMEL SAUCE)	1
1/2 TSP	SALT	2 ML
1/4 CUP	GRANULATED SUGAR	60 ML
1 1/2 CUPS	PECANS OR WALNUTS, FINELY CHOPPED	375 ML
1 PINT	COFFEE ICE CREAM	500 ML
1 PINT	VANILLA ICE CREAM	500 ML

CARAMEL SAUCE

2/3 CUP	DARK BROWN SUGAR	150 ML
1/4 CUP	EVAPORATED MILK	60 ML
1/4 CUP	BUTTER	60 ML
1/3 CUP	LIGHT CORN SYRUP	75 ML
1	EGG YOLK	1
1 TSP	VANILLA EXTRACT	5 ML

CRUST: BEAT EGG WHITE WITH SALT UNTIL STIFF. ADD SUGAR GRADUALLY AND FOLD IN NUTS. POUR INTO A WELL-BUTTERED 9-INCH (23 CM) PIE PAN. SPREAD EVENLY ON SIDES AND BOTTOM. PRICK BOTTOM IN 8 OR 10 PLACES. (DO NOT PRICK SIDES.) BAKE AT 400°F (200°C) FOR 10 TO 12 MINUTES. COOL, THEN CHILL. SOFTEN ICE CREAM AND SPREAD ON CRUST. MORE ICE CREAM CAN BE USED IF DESIRED. FREEZE.

SAUCE: MIX ALL INGREDIENTS IN DOUBLE BOILER. COOK FOR 5 MINUTES UNTIL THICKENED. STIR CONSTANTLY. SERVE HOT OVER PIE. SERVES 6 TO 8.

TIN ROOF PIE

*TAKES ONLY MINUTES — AND THEY'LL
ASK FOR SECONDS.*

1/4 CUP	PEANUT BUTTER	60 ML
1/4 CUP	LIGHT CORN SYRUP	60 ML
2 CUPS	CORN FLAKES CEREAL, CRUSHED	500 ML
I QUART	VANILLA ICE CREAM, SOFTENED	I L
3 TBSP	UNSALTED PEANUTS, CHOPPED	45 ML
	CHOCOLATE SYRUP, HEATED	

IN A 9-INCH (23 CM) PIE PLATE, COMBINE PEANUT BUTTER
AND CORN SYRUP. ADD CEREAL AND MIX UNTIL WELL
COMBINED. PRESS INTO BOTTOM AND SIDES OF PLATE.
CHILL. SPOON SOFTENED ICE CREAM INTO SHELL. SPRINKLE
WITH CHOPPED NUTS. FREEZE. REMOVE FROM FREEZER
I HOUR BEFORE SERVING. SERVE WITH WARM CHOCOLATE
SYRUP. SERVES 6 TO 8, IF YOU DON'T INVITE ELEPHANTS.

*I DON'T CARE WHAT THE WORLD KNOWS ABOUT ME,
I JUST HOPE MY MOTHER NEVER FINDS OUT.*

SHORTBREAD TARTS WITH CHEESE 'N' FRUIT OR LEMON FILLING

SO PRETTY TO LOOK AT, AND FUN TO EAT!

CHEESE 'N' FRUIT FILLING

8 OZ	CREAM CHEESE, SOFTENED	250 G
I	CAN (14 OZ OR 300 ML) SWEETENED CONDENSED MILK (EAGLE BRAND)	I
1/3 CUP	LEMON JUICE	75 ML
I TSP	VANILLA EXTRACT	5 ML
	KIWI AND STRAWBERRY PIECES	

LEMON FILLING

1/2 CUP	FRESHLY SQUEEZED LEMON JUICE	125 ML
I TBSP	GRATED LEMON ZEST	15 ML
I CUP	GRANULATED SUGAR	250 ML
3	EGGS, WELL BEATEN	3
1/2 CUP	BUTTER, ROOM TEMPERATURE	125 ML

SHORTBREAD TART SHELLS

I CUP	BUTTER	250 ML
1/2 CUP	ICING SUGAR	125 ML
1 1/2 CUPS	ALL-PURPOSE FLOUR	375 ML
I TBSP	CORNSTARCH	15 ML

CHEESE 'N' FRUIT FILLING: IN A LARGE BOWL, BEAT CHEESE UNTIL FLUFFY. GRADUALLY BEAT IN MILK. STIR IN LEMON JUICE AND VANILLA. CHILL FOR SEVERAL HOURS. KEEPS WELL IN THE REFRIGERATOR.

LEMON FILLING: PUT JUICE AND ZEST IN DOUBLE BOILER. WHISK IN SUGAR, EGGS AND BUTTER AND BLEND WELL.

CONTINUED ON NEXT PAGE...

PLACE OVER GENTLY BOILING WATER AND WHISK CONSTANTLY UNTIL MIXTURE BECOMES CLEAR AND THICKENS. COOL BEFORE FILLING TARTS. KEEPS WELL IN THE REFRIGERATOR.

TART SHELLS: MIX INGREDIENTS. WITH YOUR FINGERS; PAT INTO $1\frac{1}{2}$-INCH (4 CM) TART TINS TO FORM SHELLS. PRICK THE BOTTOMS WITH A FORK AND BAKE FOR 20 MINUTES AT 300°F (150°C). AFTER 10 MINUTES, PRICK BOTTOMS AGAIN AS SHELLS PUFF UP. (THIS RECIPE DOUBLES WELL, AND THEY FREEZE BEAUTIFULLY.)

TO ASSEMBLE: FILL TARTS WITH CHEESE MIXTURE AND DECORATE WITH SMALL PIECES OF KIWI AND STRAWBERRIES, OR FILL TARTS WITH LEMON FILLING. MAKES ABOUT 2 DOZEN TARTS.

A FRIEND IN NEED IS A — DAMN NUISANCE!

PECAN CUPS

SHELLS

I CUP	BUTTER	250 ML
I	PACKAGE (8 OZ/250 G) CREAM CHEESE	I
PINCH	SALT	PINCH
2 CUPS	ALL-PURPOSE FLOUR	500 ML

FILLING

2	EGGS	2
I$\frac{1}{2}$ CUPS	BROWN SUGAR, PACKED	375 ML
2 TBSP	BUTTER, MELTED	30 ML
I$\frac{1}{2}$ CUPS	PECANS, CHOPPED	375 ML
$\frac{1}{2}$ TSP	VANILLA EXTRACT	2 ML

SHELLS: BEAT BUTTER, CREAM CHEESE AND SALT UNTIL FLUFFY. ADD FLOUR AND CONTINUE TO MIX. PUT DOUGH IN REFRIGERATOR UNTIL FIRM TO HANDLE. AFTER CHILLING, FORM DOUGH INTO LITTLE BALLS AND PRESS INTO BOTTOM AND SIDES OF SMALL, LIGHTLY GREASED 2-INCH (5 CM) TART TINS.

FILLING: BEAT EGGS AND ADD ALL REMAINING INGREDIENTS AND SPOON INTO SHELLS. BAKE AT 350°F (180°C) FOR 30 MINUTES. MAKES 48 TARTS.

ENGLISH COOKING: IF IT'S WARM IT'S BEER,
IF IT'S COLD IT'S FOOD!

CHERRY BERRIES ON A CLOUD

MERINGUE

6	EGG WHITES	6
1/2 TSP	CREAM OF TARTAR	2 ML
1/4 TSP	SALT	1 ML
1 1/2 CUPS	GRANULATED SUGAR	375 ML

FILLING

8 OZ	CREAM CHEESE, SOFTENED	250 G
1 CUP	GRANULATED SUGAR	250 ML
1 TSP	VANILLA EXTRACT	5 ML
2 CUPS	WHIPPING (35%) CREAM, WHIPPED	500 ML
2 CUPS	MINIATURE MARSHMALLOWS	500 ML

TOPPING

1	CAN (19 OZ/540 ML) CHERRY PIE FILLING	1
1 TSP	LEMON JUICE	5 ML
2 CUPS	SLICED FROZEN STRAWBERRIES	500 ML

MERINGUE: HEAT OVEN TO 275°F (140°C). GREASE A 13- BY 9-INCH (33 BY 23 CM) PAN. BEAT EGG WHITES, CREAM OF TARTAR AND SALT UNTIL FROTHY. GRADUALLY BEAT IN SUGAR. BEAT UNTIL VERY STIFF, ABOUT 15 MINUTES. SPREAD IN PAN. BAKE FOR 1 HOUR. TURN OFF OVEN AND LEAVE MERINGUE IN OVEN OVERNIGHT OR 12 HOURS.

FILLING: MIX CREAM CHEESE WITH SUGAR AND VANILLA. GENTLY FOLD IN WHIPPED CREAM AND MARSHMALLOWS. SPREAD OVER MERINGUE. REFRIGERATE OVERNIGHT OR 12 HOURS. CUT INTO SERVING PIECES. ADD TOPPING.

TOPPING: STIR PIE FILLING AND LEMON JUICE INTO THAWED STRAWBERRIES. WHEW! IT'S DONE. SERVES 12.

GRAND SLAM FINALE

A BEST OF BRIDGE TRADITION!

I CUP	VANILLA WAFER COOKIE CRUMBS (30 WAFERS)	250 ML
1/2 CUP	TOASTED ALMONDS, FINELY CHOPPED	125 ML
1/4 CUP	BUTTER, MELTED	60 ML
4 CUPS	STRAWBERRIES	I L
12 OZ	GOOD-QUALITY WHITE CHOCOLATE	375 G
4 OZ	CREAM CHEESE	125 G
1/4 CUP	GRANULATED SUGAR	60 ML
1/4 CUP	ORANGE LIQUEUR OR FROZEN ORANGE JUICE CONCENTRATE	60 ML
I TSP	VANILLA EXTRACT	5 ML
2 CUPS	WHIPPING (35%) CREAM	500 ML
	UNSWEETENED COCOA POWDER	

COMBINE WAFER CRUMBS, ALMONDS AND BUTTER. PRESS INTO BOTTOM OF A 9-INCH (23 CM) SPRINGFORM PAN. WASH, DRY AND HULL BERRIES. RESERVE A COUPLE FOR GARNISH. CUT A FEW STRAWBERRIES IN HALF, LENGTHWISE, AND PRESS FLAT SIDES ALL AROUND SIDE OF SPRINGFORM PAN. ARRANGE WHOLE BERRIES, POINTS UP, ON CRUST. CHOP CHOCOLATE AND MELT IN DOUBLE BOILER OR MICROWAVE. COOL SLIGHTLY. BEAT CHEESE UNTIL SMOOTH, THEN BEAT IN SUGAR. MIX IN LIQUEUR (OR JUICE) AND VANILLA. SLOWLY BEAT IN CHOCOLATE. WHIP THE CREAM. STIR ABOUT ONE-THIRD OF THE CREAM INTO CHOCOLATE MIXTURE AND FOLD IN THE REMAINDER. POUR OVER BERRIES, SHAKING PAN GENTLY TO FILL IN BETWEEN BERRIES. REFRIGERATE FOR AT LEAST 3 HOURS

CONTINUED ON NEXT PAGE...

(OVERNIGHT IS FINE). REMOVE SIDES AND BOTTOM OF SPRINGFORM PAN. DUST WITH COCOA AND GARNISH WITH RESERVED STRAWBERRIES. SERVES 12.

IT'S TRUE THAT MONEY TALKS... MINE JUST SAID GOODBYE.

RHUBARB CREAM DESSERT

4 CUPS	SLICED RHUBARB	1 L
1/4 CUP	WATER	60 ML
1	PACKAGE (3 OZ/85 G) RASPBERRY JELL-O	1
1	ENVELOPE (1/4 OZ/7 G) UNFLAVORED GELATIN POWDER (ABOUT 1 TBSP/15 ML)	1
1/4 CUP	GRANULATED SUGAR	60 ML
1	PACKAGE (15 OZ/425 G) FROZEN RASPBERRIES	1
1 PINT	VANILLA ICE CREAM	500 G
1 CUP	WHIPPING (35%) CREAM, WHIPPED	250 ML

BRING RHUBARB AND WATER TO A BOIL; SIMMER, COVERED, FOR 20 MINUTES, UNTIL TENDER. REMOVE FROM HEAT. ADD JELL-O, GELATIN AND SUGAR, STIRRING UNTIL DISSOLVED. ADD FROZEN RASPBERRIES AND ICE CREAM. ALLOW TO THAW, STIRRING OCCASIONALLY. POUR INTO STEMMED GLASSES. REFRIGERATE UNTIL SET, ABOUT 3 HOURS. GARNISH WITH WHIPPED CREAM. SERVES 4.

RHUBARB DELIGHT

CRUST

1 CUP	ALL-PURPOSE FLOUR	250 ML
1/4 TSP	SALT	1 ML
2 TBSP	GRANULATED SUGAR	30 ML
1/2 CUP	BUTTER	125 ML

FILLING

1 CUP	GRANULATED SUGAR	250 ML
2 TBSP	ALL-PURPOSE FLOUR	30 ML
1/3 CUP	CREAM	75 ML
3	EGG YOLKS	3
2 1/4 CUPS	RED RHUBARB, CUT VERY FINE	560 ML

MERINGUE

3	EGG WHITES	3
1/4 TSP	CREAM OF TARTAR	1 ML
6 TBSP	GRANULATED SUGAR	90 ML

CRUST: MIX TOGETHER INGREDIENTS AND PUT INTO AN 8-INCH (20 CM) SQUARE CAKE PAN. BAKE AT 325°F (160°C) FOR 10 MINUTES OR UNTIL LIGHTLY BROWNED.

FILLING: MIX ALL INGREDIENTS AND COOK OVER LOW HEAT UNTIL THICK. POUR INTO CRUST.

MERINGUE: BEAT EGG WHITES AND CREAM OF TARTAR UNTIL FOAMY. GRADUALLY BEAT IN SUGAR, ABOUT 2 TBSP (30 ML) AT A TIME. BEAT UNTIL MERINGUE IS THICK AND GLOSSY AND SUGAR IS DISSOLVED. MERINGUE SHOULD BE SMOOTH AND STAND IN STIFF PEAKS. SPREAD MERINGUE OVER FILLING. BAKE AT 400°F (200°C) UNTIL LIGHTLY BROWNED. SERVES 6 TO 8.

TIRAMISU

4	EGGS, SEPARATED	4
3/4 CUP	GRANULATED SUGAR	175 ML
2	PACKAGES (EACH 8 OZ/250 G) CREAM CHEESE, ROOM TEMPERATURE	2
1/4 CUP	KAHLÚA OR RUM	60 ML
1/2 CUP	STRONG COFFEE	125 ML
1	PACKAGE (8 OZ/250 G) LADYFINGERS OR VANILLA WAFERS	1
2	SQUARES (EACH 1 OZ/30 G) SEMISWEET CHOCOLATE, FINELY GRATED	2

BEAT EGG YOLKS IN A MEDIUM BOWL. ADD SUGAR GRADUALLY UNTIL WELL MIXED. ADD CREAM CHEESE AND MIX WELL. IN A DEEP BOWL, BEAT EGG WHITES UNTIL SOFT PEAKS FORM. FOLD INTO CHEESE MIXTURE. SPREAD ONE-QUARTER OF THE CHEESE MIXTURE INTO A LARGE GLASS SERVING BOWL. DIP LADYFINGERS IN MIXTURE OF KAHLÚA AND COFFEE AND COVER CHEESE LAYER. REPEAT 3 TIMES, SPRINKLING CHOCOLATE ON EACH AND ENDING WITH CHEESE AND CHOCOLATE. REFRIGERATE FOR 6 HOURS OR OVERNIGHT. SERVES 8 TO 10.

NOTE: THIS RECIPE CONTAINS RAW EGGS. IF THE FOOD SAFETY OF RAW EGGS IS A CONCERN FOR YOU, USE PASTEURIZED WHOLE EGGS, SEPARATED, OR SUBSTITUTE 1/2 CUP (125 ML) PASTEURIZED LIQUID WHOLE EGGS FOR THE EGG YOLKS AND USE 1/2 CUP (125 ML) PASTEURIZED LIQUID EGG WHITES.

FRUIT POOF

YOU SHOWOFF YOU!

<u>PUFF</u>

2/3 CUP	WATER	150 ML
1/3 CUP	BUTTER	75 ML
2/3 CUP	ALL-PURPOSE FLOUR	150 ML

<u>CRUST</u>

2/3 CUP	ALL-PURPOSE FLOUR	150 ML
1 TBSP	GRANULATED SUGAR	15 ML
1/4 CUP	BUTTER	60 ML
3	EGGS	3

<u>FILLING</u>

1	BOX (3 1/2 OZ/100 G) INSTANT VANILLA PUDDING	102 G
1 1/2 CUPS	MILK	375 ML
1/2 CUP	WHIPPING (35%) CREAM	125 ML
2 CUPS	SLICED PEACHES, SLICED KIWIS, HALVED STRAWBERRIES, HALVED GRAPES, BLUEBERRIES AND/OR RASPBERRIES	500 ML
1/4 CUP	APPLE JELLY, MELTED	60 ML

PUFF: COMBINE WATER AND BUTTER IN A MEDIUM SAUCEPAN AND BRING TO A BOIL, STIRRING TO MELT BUTTER. ADD FLOUR ALL AT ONCE. COOK AND STIR UNTIL MIXTURE FORMS A BALL THAT DOESN'T SEPARATE. SET ASIDE TO COOL FOR 15 MINUTES.

CONTINUED ON NEXT PAGE...

CRUST: COMBINE FLOUR WITH SUGAR. CUT IN BUTTER UNTIL CRUMBLY. FIRMLY PRESS CRUMBS INTO AN 8-INCH (20 CM) CIRCLE ON AN UNGREASED BAKING SHEET. SET ASIDE. PREHEAT OVEN TO 400°F (200°C). ADD EGGS TO DOUGH IN SAUCEPAN, ONE AT A TIME, BEATING WELL AFTER EACH ADDITION. GENTLY SPREAD ONE-QUARTER OF THE DOUGH OVER CRUST, FORMING A 5-INCH (13 CM) CIRCLE. DROP SPOONFULS OF DOUGH AROUND EDGE OF SMALLER CIRCLE. BAKE FOR 15 MINUTES, THEN REDUCE HEAT TO 350°F (180°C) AND CONTINUE BAKING FOR 35 TO 40 MINUTES. COOL.

FILLING: PREPARE PUDDING, USING MILK. BEAT CREAM AND FOLD INTO PUDDING. SPOON FILLING INTO CENTER OF PUFF. ARRANGE FRUIT ON TOP AND BRUSH FRUIT WITH MELTED JELLY. CHILL FOR 2 HOURS. SERVES 8.

BEING OF SOUND MIND, I'M SPENDING MY MONEY AS FAST AS I CAN!

FROSTY PEACH DESSERT

COOL, CREAMY AND SMOOTH.

I CUP	ALL-PURPOSE FLOUR	250 ML
1/3 CUP	BROWN SUGAR	75 ML
1/4 TSP	GROUND CINNAMON	I ML
1/2 CUP	BUTTER, MELTED	125 ML
10	PEACHES	10
I CUP	GRANULATED SUGAR	250 ML
1/4 CUP	PASTEURIZED LIQUID EGG WHITES	60 ML
2 TBSP	LEMON JUICE	30 ML
I CUP	WHIPPING (35%) CREAM, WHIPPED	250 ML

IN SHALLOW PAN, COMBINE FLOUR, BROWN SUGAR, CINNAMON AND MELTED BUTTER, MIXING WELL. BAKE IN 350°F (180°C) OVEN FOR 20 MINUTES, STIRRING 2 TO 3 TIMES TO KEEP MIXTURE CRUMBLY. LET COOL. RESERVE I CUP (250 ML) FOR TOPPING. SPREAD REMAINDER IN 9-INCH (23 CM) SPRINGFORM PAN OR IN A 13- BY 9-INCH (33 BY 23 CM) BAKING PAN. PEEL AND STONE 4 PEACHES. SLICE THINLY AND PLACE IN A LARGE, DEEP BOWL AND MASH WELL. ADD SUGAR, EGG WHITES AND LEMON JUICE. BEAT AT MEDIUM SPEED UNTIL FOAMY, THEN AT HIGH SPEED UNTIL DOUBLED IN VOLUME AND MIXTURE HAS THICKENED, ABOUT 10 MINUTES. FOLD WHIPPED CREAM INTO PEACH MIXTURE. SPREAD OVER CRUMB MIXTURE. SPRINKLE RESERVED CRUMBS ON TOP. COVER AND FREEZE FOR AT LEAST 6 HOURS. TRANSFER TO FRIDGE 30 MINUTES BEFORE SERVING. TO SERVE, PEEL AND SLICE REMAINING PEACHES AND ARRANGE OVER EACH SERVING. SERVES 10.

Chocolate Raspberry Torte (page 318)

French Lemon Pie (page 329)

Pavlova (page 353)

Sangria à la Moe (page 368)

PAVLOVA

NEW ZEALAND'S NATIONAL DESSERT.

4	EGG WHITES	4
I CUP	GRANULATED SUGAR	250 ML
½ TSP	VANILLA EXTRACT	2 ML
I TSP	VINEGAR	5 ML
2 CUPS	WHIPPING (35%) CREAM	500 ML
	FRESH FRUIT: KIWI, BLUEBERRIES AND STRAWBERRIES ARE PERFECT	
½ CUP	TOASTED SLIVERED ALMONDS	125 ML

BEAT EGG WHITES UNTIL SOFT PEAKS FORM. CONTINUE BEATING WHILE ADDING SUGAR SLOWLY, I TBSP (15 ML) AT A TIME. ADD VANILLA AND VINEGAR. BEAT UNTIL VERY STIFF. PLACE WAXED OR BROWN PAPER ON A COOKIE SHEET AND SPREAD MIXTURE IN A CIRCLE, SLIGHTLY SMALLER THAN DESIRED SIZE. BAKE FOR I HOUR AT 275°F (140°C). TURN OVEN OFF AND LEAVE MERINGUE IN OVEN OVERNIGHT TO DRY. PEEL OFF PAPER. TOP WITH WHIPPED CREAM, FRESH FRUIT AND TOASTED ALMONDS. SERVES 6 TO 8.

A DIPLOMAT IS A PERSON WHO CAN TELL YOU TO GO TO HELL IN SUCH A WAY THAT YOU ACTUALLY LOOK FORWARD TO THE TRIP.

TOFFEE MERINGUE

MAKE MERINGUES IN ADVANCE AND
YOU WILL HAVE AN EASY DESSERT.

2	PACKAGES (EACH 2 OZ/56 G) MACKINTOSH'S TOFFEE	2
4	EGG WHITES	4
I CUP	GRANULATED SUGAR	250 ML
1/2 TSP	VANILLA EXTRACT	2 ML
I TSP	VINEGAR	5 ML
2 CUPS	WHIPPING (35%) CREAM, SWEETENED TO TASTE	500 ML
	CHOCOLATE CURLS	

PREHEAT OVEN TO 275°F (140°C). PUT TOFFEE IN FREEZER
TILL FROZEN. CUT OUT TWO 9-INCH (23 CM) BROWN
PAPER CIRCLES AND PLACE ON A COOKIE SHEET. WHIP
EGG WHITES UNTIL THEY FORM PEAKS. GRADUALLY ADD
SUGAR, VANILLA AND VINEGAR AND CONTINUE BEATING
UNTIL STIFF. SPREAD EGG MIXTURE IN TWO 8-INCH (20 CM)
CIRCLES. (MIXTURE WILL EXPAND DURING BAKING.) BAKE FOR
I HOUR. TURN OVEN OFF AND LEAVE MERINGUES TO DRY
FOR SEVERAL HOURS. DO NOT OPEN OVEN. WHEN READY
TO SERVE, CRUSH TOFFEE — A HAMMER WORKS WELL! ADD
TO WHIPPED CREAM. SPREAD HALF THE MIXTURE BETWEEN
FIRST AND SECOND MERINGUE. TOP WITH REMAINING
CREAM. GARNISH WITH CHOCOLATE CURLS. SERVES
8 TO 10.

GRAND MARNIER CRÈME

A LIGHT DELIGHT ON THE PATH OF NO RESISTANCE!

3	EGG YOLKS	3
1/4 CUP	GRANULATED SUGAR	60 ML
1 CUP	WHIPPING (35%) CREAM	250 ML
1/4 CUP	GRAND MARNIER	60 ML
	SHAVED CHOCOLATE	

COMBINE YOLKS AND SUGAR. BEAT UNTIL THICK. WHIP CREAM TO FORM STIFF PEAKS. FOLD WHIPPED CREAM INTO YOLK AND SUGAR MIXTURE. FOLD GRAND MARNIER INTO MIXTURE. POUR INTO YOUR PRETTIEST SHERBET GLASSES AND PLACE IN FREEZER FOR AT LEAST 3 HOURS. JUST BEFORE SERVING, GARNISH WITH SHAVED CHOCOLATE. SERVES 4 TO 6.

NOTE: THIS RECIPE CONTAINS RAW EGG YOLKS. IF THE FOOD SAFETY OF RAW EGGS IS A CONCERN FOR YOU, SUBSTITUTE PASTEURIZED EGG YOLKS OR 6 TBSP (90 ML) PASTEURIZED LIQUID WHOLE EGGS.

MIDDLE AGE: WHEN A BROAD MIND AND A NARROW WAIST CHANGE PLACES.

CRÈME CARAMEL

A GOURMET TOUCH THAT CAN BE MADE
THE DAY BEFORE.

CARAMEL

3/4 CUP	WATER	175 ML
I CUP	GRANULATED SUGAR	250 ML

CUSTARD

4	WHOLE EGGS	4
3	EGG YOLKS	3
I TSP	VANILLA EXTRACT	5 ML
1/2 CUP	GRANULATED SUGAR	125 ML
3 CUPS	CREAM	750 ML

CARAMEL: PLACE WATER AND SUGAR IN SAUCEPAN; STIR OVER LOW HEAT UNTIL SUGAR DISSOLVES; INCREASE HEAT AND BRING TO A BOIL. BOIL FOR ABOUT 10 TO 15 MINUTES UNTIL MIXTURE TURNS GOLDEN BROWN AND CARAMELIZES. WATCH CLOSELY AS IT WILL BURN VERY EASILY. POUR CARAMEL INTO 8 INDIVIDUAL SOUFFLÉ DISHES (RAMEKINS). ROTATE DISHES QUICKLY SO CARAMEL EVENLY COATS SIDES AND BASE OF DISH.

CUSTARD: IN A LARGE BOWL, BEAT TOGETHER WHOLE EGGS, EGG YOLKS, VANILLA AND SUGAR UNTIL LEMON-COLORED. SCALD CREAM IN SAUCEPAN AND ALLOW TO COOL SLIGHTLY. POUR CREAM INTO EGG MIXTURE, STIRRING CONSTANTLY. POUR CUSTARD MIXTURE EVENLY INTO EACH DISH. SET DISHES IN SHALLOW BAKING PAN CONTAINING I INCH (2.5 CM) WATER. BAKE CUSTARDS AT 325°F (160°C) FOR 35 TO 40 MINUTES UNTIL CUSTARD IS

CONTINUED ON NEXT PAGE...

SET. COOL IN REFRIGERATOR FOR SEVERAL HOURS. JUST
BEFORE SERVING, SET DISHES IN HOT WATER AND EASE
CUSTARDS AWAY FROM SIDES OF DISH. INVERT ONTO
SERVING PLATES. SERVES 8.

OVERWEIGHT: LIVING BEYOND YOUR SEAMS.

STELLA BY STARLIGHT

*A SIMPLE, DELICATE SABAYON. BEAUTIFUL
WITHOUT BEING FLAMBOYANT.*

6	EGG YOLKS	6
1/3 CUP	GRANULATED SUGAR	75 ML
8 OZ	WHITE WINE (ANY KIND WILL DO)	250 ML
	LEMON ZEST FOR GARNISH	

STELLA JUST PUTS ALL THIS IN A HEAVY 4-QUART (4 L)
POT OVER MEDIUM-HIGH HEAT AND BEATS THE DAYLIGHTS
OUT OF IT. (USE AN ELECTRIC BEATER.) THIS TAKES ABOUT
5 MINUTES. IT SHOULD BE LIGHT AND FLUFFY AND FILL
THE POT. SERVE IMMEDIATELY, TOPPED WITH LEMON
ZEST. MAY BE SPOONED OVER FRESH FRUIT. SERVES
8 TO 10.

CHOCOLATE SABAYON

4	EGG YOLKS	4
1/2 CUP	GRANULATED SUGAR	125 ML
1/2 CUP	WHITE WINE	125 ML
1/4 CUP	UNSWEETENED COCOA, SIFTED	60 ML
1 CUP	WHIPPING (35%) CREAM	250 ML
2 TBSP	COFFEE LIQUEUR	30 ML

IN A DOUBLE BOILER (NOT ALUMINUM), BEAT EGG YOLKS
AND SUGAR WITH ELECTRIC BEATER OVER MEDIUM HEAT
FOR 2 MINUTES OR UNTIL SLIGHTLY THICKENED. IN
A SMALL BOWL, WHISK WINE AND COCOA. ADD TO EGG
MIXTURE AND BEAT FOR 2 TO 3 MINUTES ON HIGH UNTIL
MIXTURE HAS TRIPLED IN VOLUME AND COATS BACK OF
SPOON. REMOVE FROM HEAT AND PLACE IN A LARGE BOWL;
LET COOL. WHIP OCCASIONALLY. WHIP CREAM AND FOLD IN
LIQUEUR. GENTLY FOLD INTO CHOCOLATE MIXTURE. SPOON
INTO YOUR PRETTIEST SHERBET DISHES. SERVES 8.

LEMON SORBET

THIS IS A DELIGHTFUL FINALE TO A SUMPTUOUS MEAL.
IF YOU REALLY WANT TO SHOW OFF, SERVE BETWEEN
COURSES TO "CLEANSE" THE PALATE. LAH-DE-DAH!

I CUP	MILK (2% OR SKIM WILL DO)	250 ML
I CUP	WHIPPING (35%) CREAM	250 ML
	JUICE OF 5 LEMONS (I CUP/250 ML), RESERVE SHELLS	
2/3 CUP	BERRY SUGAR (FINE GRANULATED)	150 ML

MIX ALL INGREDIENTS TOGETHER IN A SHALLOW DISH AND
FREEZE FOR 4 HOURS. STIR OCCASIONALLY TO BREAK
UP ICE CRYSTALS. SPOON INTO LEMON SHELLS, COVER
AND RETURN TO FREEZER UNTIL READY TO SERVE. (HINT:
CUT ENDS OFF RINDS SO THEY WON'T "ROCK AND ROLL"
WHEN YOU SERVE THEM.) GARNISH WITH A MINT LEAF.
SERVES 10.

BE LIKE A DUCK: ABOVE THE SURFACE, LOOK COMPOSED AND
UNRUFFLED; BELOW THE SURFACE, PADDLE LIKE CRAZY.

FROZEN LEMON MOUSSE WITH RASPBERRY SAUCE

LIGHT AND COOL.

LEMON MOUSSE

1 1/2 TSP	UNFLAVORED GELATIN POWDER (1/2 PACKAGE)	7 ML
1/2 CUP	LEMON JUICE	125 ML
3	EGGS, SEPARATED	3
2/3 CUP	GRANULATED SUGAR	150 ML
	GRATED ZEST OF 1 LEMON	
PINCH	SALT	PINCH
1 CUP	WHIPPING (35%) CREAM	250 ML
3	STALE MACAROONS (OPTIONAL)	3

RASPBERRY SAUCE

1	PACKAGE (15 OZ/425 G) FROZEN RASPBERRIES WITH JUICE	1
	JUICE OF 1/2 LEMON	
1/2 CUP	GRANULATED SUGAR	125 ML
1/2 TSP	CORNSTARCH	2 ML
1/4 CUP	FRAMBOISE, KIRSCH OR GRAND MARNIER	60 ML

MOUSSE: DISSOLVE GELATIN IN LEMON JUICE IN TOP OF A DOUBLE BOILER SET OVER SIMMERING WATER. BEAT EGG YOLKS WITH 1/3 CUP (75 ML) SUGAR UNTIL MIXTURE IS LEMON-COLORED. FOLD LEMON GELATIN MIXTURE AND ZEST INTO BEATEN YOLKS.

GRADUALLY ADDING REMAINING 1/3 CUP (75 ML) SUGAR, BEAT EGG WHITES WITH PINCH OF SALT UNTIL THEY

CONTINUED ON NEXT PAGE...

FORM STIFF PEAKS. BLEND LARGE SPOONFUL OF BEATEN WHITES IN LEMON-EGG YOLK MIXTURE. WHIP CREAM AND FOLD REMAINING WHITES AND CREAM INTO LEMON-EGG MIXTURE; DON'T OVERBLEND — ALLOW SOME WHITE TO SHOW. FILL SOUFFLÉ DISH OR INDIVIDUAL GLASS DISHES TWO-THIRDS FULL. IF USING MACAROONS, CRUSH AND SPRINKLE OVER DESSERT, THEN FILL DISH WITH REMAINING MIXTURE. FREEZE FOR 2 TO 3 HOURS.

SAUCE: COMBINE THAWED RASPBERRIES AND JUICE WITH LEMON JUICE IN BLENDER. PURÉE UNTIL SMOOTH AND STRAIN TO REMOVE ALL SEEDS. POUR RASPBERRY MIXTURE INTO SAUCEPAN AND ADD SUGAR. BRING TO A BOIL OVER MEDIUM-HIGH HEAT, THEN SIMMER FOR 15 MINUTES. DISSOLVE CORNSTARCH IN LIQUEUR AND STIR INTO RASPBERRY MIXTURE. REMOVE FROM HEAT AND COOL. COVER AND REFRIGERATE. SERVE OVER LEMON MOUSSE. SERVES 4.

NOTE: THIS RECIPE CONTAINS RAW EGGS. IF THE FOOD SAFETY OF RAW EGGS IS A CONCERN FOR YOU, USE PASTEURIZED WHOLE EGGS, SEPARATED, OR SUBSTITUTE 6 TBSP (90 ML) PASTEURIZED LIQUID WHOLE EGGS FOR THE YOLKS AND USE 6 TBSP (90 ML) PASTEURIZED LIQUID EGG WHITES.

TELLING YOUR TEENAGER THE FACTS OF LIFE IS LIKE GIVING A FISH A BATH!

FRUIT DIP

RICH AND WONDERFUL.

1 CUP	SOUR CREAM	250 ML
1 CUP	WHIPPING (35%) CREAM, WHIPPED	250 ML
1/4 CUP	BROWN SUGAR	60 ML
1 TBSP	DARK RUM	15 ML
1 TBSP	GRAND MARNIER	15 ML

MIX INGREDIENTS TOGETHER AND SERVE WITH SLICED FRUIT AS A DIP OR TOPPING. MAKES ABOUT 3 CUPS (750 ML).

A YOUTHFUL FIGURE IS WHAT YOU GET WHEN YOU ASK A WOMAN HER AGE.

HOT FUDGE SAUCE

DOES WONDERS FOR STALE CAKE.
HOW ABOUT A HOT FUDGE SUNDAE?

2	SQUARES (EACH 1 OZ/30 G) BITTERSWEET CHOCOLATE	2
1/2 CUP	BUTTER	125 ML
1 1/2 CUPS	GRANULATED SUGAR	375 ML
1/2 TSP	SALT	2 ML
3/4 CUP	EVAPORATED MILK	175 ML
1/2 TSP	VANILLA EXTRACT	2 ML

HEAT INGREDIENTS ALL TOGETHER IN A HEAVY SAUCEPAN AND BRING TO A BOIL. REMOVE FROM HEAT AND COOL. POUR INTO AIRTIGHT CONTAINER AND STORE IN FRIDGE. DON'T PANIC: THIS IS A THIN SAUCE — TO MAKE *YOU* THICK. MAKES ABOUT 2 1/2 CUPS (625 ML).

FROTHY ORANGE SLUSHY

INSTANT BREAKFAST!

1 CUP	WATER	250 ML
1 CUP	MILK	250 ML
1	CAN (6 OZ/170 ML) FROZEN ORANGE JUICE CONCENTRATE	1
2 TBSP	GRANULATED SUGAR	30 ML
1 TSP	VANILLA EXTRACT	5 ML
2	EGGS	2
10 TO 12	ICE CUBES	10 TO 12

PUT ALL INGREDIENTS IN A BLENDER AND WHIRL AWAY. SERVES 4.

NOTE: THIS RECIPE CONTAINS RAW EGGS. IF THE FOOD SAFETY OF RAW EGGS IS A CONCERN FOR YOU, SUBSTITUTE PASTEURIZED EGGS OR 1/2 CUP (125 ML) PASTEURIZED LIQUID WHOLE EGGS.

A REAL SMOOTHIE

LOW-CAL AND HEALTHY — BUT IT TASTES LIKE YOU'RE CHEATING.

1	BANANA	1
1/2 CUP	APPLE OR ORANGE JUICE	125 ML
1/2 CUP	FROZEN BLUEBERRIES, THAWED	125 ML
3/4 CUP	YOGURT, PLAIN	175 ML
1/2 TSP	VANILLA EXTRACT	2 ML

BLEND ALL INGREDIENTS. SERVES 2.

GRADUATION PUNCH

IF YOUR CHILD SHOULD HAPPEN TO GRADUATE, SERVE THIS! (IF THEY DON'T GRADUATE, ADD THE VODKA.)

4 CUPS	PINEAPPLE JUICE	1 L
4 CUPS	LIMEADE	1 L
4 CUPS	ORANGE JUICE	1 L
4 CUPS	ORANGE POP	1 L
2	BOTTLES (26 OZ/750 ML) VODKA (OPTIONAL)	2
8 CUPS	GINGER ALE	2 L
	ORANGE SLICES	
	STRAWBERRIES	

MIX ALL LIQUIDS TOGETHER, ADDING GINGER ALE LAST, IN A LARGE PUNCH BOWL. FLOAT ORANGE SLICES AND STRAWBERRIES ON TOP FOR A FESTIVE TOUCH. SERVES 30.

REMEMBER WHEN "FREEZE-DRIED" MEANT THAT THE LAUNDRY HAD HUNG TOO LONG ON THE CLOTHESLINE?

MARGARITAS MUCHO GRANDE

3/4 CUP	FROZEN LIMEADE	175 ML
3/4 CUP	WATER	175 ML
3/4 CUP	TEQUILA	175 ML
1/3 CUP	TRIPLE SEC	75 ML
	ICE TO FILL BLENDER	

POUR ABOVE INGREDIENTS INTO BLENDER AND BLEND
UNTIL FROTHY. OLÉ! SERVES 6.

FUZZY NAVELS

THIS IS HOW WE SPELL RELIEF.

9 OZ	PEACH SCHNAPPS	275 ML
3 OZ	VODKA	75 ML
2 CUPS	ORANGE JUICE	500 ML
8	ICE CUBES	8

COMBINE ALL INGREDIENTS IN A BLENDER. HURRY AND
BLEND UNTIL FROTHY. SERVES 6.

LONG ISLAND ICED TEA

HIGH TEA! WITH A LITTLE HELP FROM YOUR FRIENDS!

3 OZ	VODKA	75 ML
3 OZ	GIN	75 ML
3 OZ	TEQUILA	75 ML
3 OZ	SOUTHERN COMFORT	75 ML
1	CAN (12 OZ/341 ML) COKE	1
1	CAN (12 OZ/341 ML) SODA WATER	1
1/2 CUP	LIME CORDIAL	125 ML

MIX ALL INGREDIENTS IN A LARGE PITCHER AND FILL WITH ICE CUBES. STIR, DRINK, ENJOY! SERVES 6.

AFTER 40, IT'S PATCH, PATCH, PATCH.

SANGRIA À LA MOE

4	BOTTLES (EACH 750 ML) RED SANGRIA WINE	4
1	BOTTLE (750 ML) GOOD DRY RED WINE	1
1	BOTTLE (750 ML) GOOD DRY WHITE WINE	1
12 OZ	INEXPENSIVE BRANDY	375 ML
3 CUPS	GINGER ALE	750 ML
3	ORANGES	3
3	LIMES	3
3	LEMONS	3

THE DAY BEFORE SERVING, COMBINE ALL LIQUID INGREDIENTS IN A LARGE PLASTIC OR GLASS CONTAINER (DO NOT USE ALUMINUM). SLICE FRUIT THINLY AND ADD TO LIQUID. REFRIGERATE OVERNIGHT TO ALLOW FLAVORS TO MELLOW (THE WAY YOU AND YOUR FRIENDS WILL FEEL WHEN IMBIBING THIS BREW). WE HAVE NO IDEA HOW MANY THIS WILL SERVE — YOU KNOW YOUR FRIENDS BETTER THAN WE DO!

GLØGG

*OUR DANISH FRIEND SERVES THIS WONDERFUL
SPICED WINE AT SKATING PARTIES.*

3	CINNAMON STICKS	3
1 TBSP	WHOLE CLOVES	15 ML
1	BOTTLE (750 ML) RED WINE	1
1 CUP	BRANDY	250 ML
1	BOTTLE (12 OZ/341 ML) BEER	1
1	ORANGE, THINLY SLICED WITH RIND ON	1
1	SLICE LEMON	1
3/4 CUP	GRANULATED SUGAR	175 ML
1 CUP	RAISINS	250 ML
1/3 CUP	SLIVERED ALMONDS	75 ML

MAKE A SPICE BAG WITH CINNAMON AND CLOVES. COMBINE
EVERYTHING IN A LARGE POT; BRING TO A BOIL; SIMMER
FOR 1 1/2 HOURS, COVERED. REMOVE ORANGE AND LEMON
SLICES AND SPICE BAG BEFORE SERVING. SERVES 12 TO 16.

*THE CLOSEST TO PERFECTION A PERSON EVER COMES
IS WHEN HE FILLS OUT A JOB APPLICATION.*

TERRY'S PUNCH

TERRY MOORE, OUR FAVORITE VANCOUVER RADIO PERSONALITY, INVENTED THIS LIBATION.

1	BOTTLE (750 ML) CHAMPAGNE	1
1 CUP	GRAND MARNIER	250 ML
4 CUPS	ORANGE JUICE (FRESH IS BEST)	1 L

COMBINE ALL INGREDIENTS IN A LARGE BOWL. IF IT'S A THIRSTY PARTY, MIX MORE AS REQUIRED. SERVES 12 TO 16.

STICKS FLOAT. THEY WOOD.

MIDSUMMER MADNESS

THIS MAKES A WHOLE BUNCH OF FROZEN SLUSH. SERVE YOUR GUESTS 2 PARTS SLUSH TO 1 PART 7-UP, GINGER ALE OR SODA WATER. TOP WITH A SLICE OF LIME, THEN HEAD FOR THE PATIO!

2 CUPS	APRICOT BRANDY	500 ML
1 CUP	VODKA OR RUM	250 ML
1	CAN (48 OZ/1.36 L) PINEAPPLE JUICE	1
1	CAN (48 OZ/1.36 L) APRICOT NECTAR	1
1	CAN (12 OZ/341 ML) FROZEN ORANGE JUICE	1
1	CAN (12 OZ/341 ML) FROZEN LEMONADE	1

MIX ALL TOGETHER IN A LARGE FREEZABLE CONTAINER. FREEZE UNTIL SLUSHY. SERVES 20 TO 30.

HOT BUTTERED RUM

STORE IN YOUR FREEZER IN SMALL CONTAINERS.
GREAT FOR GIFTS.

HOT RUM BASE

1 LB	BUTTER, ROOM TEMPERATURE	500 G
4 CUPS	VANILLA ICE CREAM, SOFTENED	1 L
3 1/2 CUPS	ICING (CONFECTIONER'S) SUGAR	875 ML
2 CUPS	BROWN SUGAR	500 ML
1 1/2 TSP	GROUND CINNAMON	7 ML
1/2 TSP	GROUND ALLSPICE	2 ML

IN A LARGE BOWL, MIX BUTTER AND ICE CREAM TOGETHER.
BLEND IN ALL OTHER INGREDIENTS. STORE IN FREEZER.
MAKES ABOUT 9 CUPS (2.25 L).

HOT BUTTERED RUM

2 TBSP	HOT RUM BASE	30 ML
1 1/2 OZ	DARK RUM	45 ML
	CINNAMON STICK	

IN A LARGE MUG, ADD HOT RUM BASE AND DARK RUM. FILL
MUG WITH BOILING WATER AND STIR WITH CINNAMON
STICK UNTIL MIXTURE IS BLENDED. SERVES 1.

Library and Archives Canada Cataloguing in Publication

The complete Best of Bridge cookbooks volume 2: all 350 recipes from Winners and Grand slam.

Originally published under titles: Winners and Grand slam.

ISBN 978-0-7788-0253-2

1. Cookery.   I. Title: Best of Bridge.

TX715.6.C65143 2010   641.5   C2010-903193-8

INDEX

A

After Angel Food Cookies, 277
alcohol. *See* beer; liqueur; wine; *specific beverages*
Alfredo Sauce, 264
almonds
 Almond Florentines, 298
 Almond Orange Pheasant (or Cornish Hens), 166
 Chicken Tetrazzini, 160
 Committee Salad, 104
 Korean Chicken Salad, 112
 Shortcut Almond Roca, 297
 Zucchini Cookies, 283
antipasto, 91–92
appetizers, 62–92
apples
 Apple Kuchen, 305
 Cranberry Stuffing, 259
 Mulligatawny Soup, 137
 Spiked Apple Betty, 328
 Swiss Apple Quiche, 12
 Yammy Apples, 247
apricots
 Barbecued Pork Roast, 188
 Chicken Mandalay, 153
 Health Nut Muffins, 24
Arizona Fruit Salad, 116
artichokes
 Artichoke and Zucchini Salad, 94
 Chicken Artichoke Casserole, 158
 Crab-Stuffed Artichoke Hearts, 79
 Hot Artichoke Dip, 45
 Marinated Artichoke and Mushroom Salad, 96
 Tomato and Artichoke Casserole, 239
 Viva! Veggies, 217
 Wild Rice and Artichoke Hearts, 255
asparagus
 Asparagus Chicken Puffs, 83
 Asparagus Noodle Bake, 201
 Asparagus Pasta Salad, 106
 Baked Asparagus, 218
 Classy Chicken, 149
 "Death to Dieters" Chicken Lasagna, 213
 Noodle Maker's Chop Suey, 190
 Pasta Primavera, 202
 Tisdale Annie's Asparagus Puff, 219
Aunty Lil's Simple Antipasto, 91
Avgolemono, 134

avocado
 Arizona Fruit Salad, 116
 Avocado Soup, 123
 Committee Salad, 104
 Guacamole Cherry Tomato Halves, 75
 Mexicana Antipasto, 92
 Super Nachos, 90

B

bacon
 Baked Beans, 220
 Cheese and Bacon Muffins, 33
 A Different Spinach Salad, 99
 Fried Cabbage, 225
 Ham and Cheese Puffs, 88
 Linguine with Red Clam Sauce, 207
 Peachtree Plaza Salad, 105
 Quiche Lorraine, 11
 Sensational Sausage Roll, 22
 Spaghetti Carbonara, 208
 The Utmost Grilled Cheese, 16
 Weekender Special, 8
Baked Asparagus, 218
Baked Bananas in Orange and Lemon Juice, 216
Baked Beans, 220
Baked Cheese and Tomato Strata, 14
Baked Fish Mozzarella, 142
bananas
 Baked Bananas in Orange and Lemon Juice, 216
 Banana Ginger Loaf, 308
 Banana Muffins, 26
 Best-Ever Banana Bread, 35
 Blueberry Banana Bread, 36
 Crater Cake, 314
 Going Bananas, 34
 A Real Smoothie, 364
Barbecued Pork Roast, 188
bars and squares, 288–96
basil (fresh)
 Cream of Parsley and Basil Soup, 129
 Marinated Fish Fillets with Basil Butter, 143
 Pasta with Crab and Basil, 205
 Pesto Sauce, 263
beans. *See also* beans, green; bean sprouts
 Baked Beans, 220
 Calico Bean Pot, 222
 Speedy Baked Beans, 221
 Super Nachos, 90

beans, green
  Calico Bean Pot, 222
  Mandarin Green Beans, 231
  Pasta Primavera, 202
  Sudden Valley Green Beans, 230
bean sprouts
  A Different Spinach Salad, 99
  Korean Chicken Salad, 112
  Layered Chicken Salad, 114
  Oriental Garden Toss, 103
beef
  Beef Extraordinaire with Sauce Diane,
    169
  Beef-on-a-Stick, 174
  Burritos, 181
  Cabbage Roll Casserole, 179
  Family Favorite Meatloaf, 177
  Ginger-Fried Beef, 172
  Jelly Balls, 89
  Mad about Cabbage Rolls, 178
  Manicotti, 210
  Moussaka, 196
  Pasta Pot, 204
  Shortcut Stroganoff, 176
  Simply Sauerbraten, 173
  Steak and Mushroom Kabobs, 175
  Super Nachos, 90
  Super Tender Flank Steak, 171
  Taco Pie, 180
  Unattended Roast Beef, 170
beer
  Gløgg, 369
  Ham Baked in Beer, 185
  Rarebit in a Hole, 64
Beet Salad, Russian, 97
bell peppers. See peppers, bell
Best-Ever Banana Bread, 35
beverages, 364–71
Black Bottom Cupcakes, 321
B.L.'s Cookies, 279
blueberries
  Blueberry Banana Bread, 36
  Fruit and Lime Chicken Salad, 115
  Fruit Poof, 350
  Pavlova, 353
  A Real Smoothie, 364
Bomb Shelter Croustades, 74
Boozy Onions, 231
Bourbon Balls, 300
brandy
  Brandy-Nut Brie, 69
  Gløgg, 369
  Midsummer Madness, 370
  Sam's Brandied Chicken, 150
  Sangria à la Mode, 368

breads, 51–61
  quick, 34–38
broccoli
  Broccoli Lasagna au Gratin, 211
  Broccoli Soup, 124
  Classy Chicken, 149
  Onions Stuffed with Broccoli, 233
  Pasta Primavera, 202
  Pasta Vegetable Salad, 107
  Sicilian Broccoli, 223
  Spaghetti Squash Primavera, 244
  Spinach or Broccoli Timbales, 237
  Viva! Veggies, 217
Brown Bagger's Special, 291
brunch dishes, 6–21
Brussels Sprouts, Tolerable, 224
Burritos, 181
Butter-Baked Taters, 250
Buttermilk Biscuits, 59
Butter Tart Slice, 290

C

cabbage
  Cabbage Roll Casserole, 179
  Fried Cabbage, 225
  Killer Coleslaw, 93
  Mad about Cabbage Rolls, 178
  Oriental Garden Toss, 103
Cadillac Oysters, 77
cakes, 302–21
Calico Bean Pot, 222
candies, 297–301
cantaloupe. See melon
carrots
  Carrot and Raisin Muffins, 29
  Carrots l'Orange, 227
  Épinards, Eh!, 236
  Korean Chicken Salad, 112
  Nifty Carrots, 226
  Perfect Parsnips, 234
  Spaghetti Squash Primavera, 244
cashews
  Brandy-Nut Brie, 69
  Cashew Pork Tenderloin, 187
  Microwave Peanut Brittle, 299
  Sweet and Spicy Cashew Chicken, 156
cauliflower
  Cauliflower Soup with Blue Cheese, 125
  Curried Cauliflower, 228
  Pasta Vegetable Salad, 107
celery
  Mulligatawny Soup, 137
  Pasta Vegetable Salad, 107
  Perfect Parsnips, 234
  Wild Rice Casserole, 258

Chart House Blue Cheese Dressing, 121
cheese. *See also* cream cheese; *specific types of cheese (below)*
  Baked Cheese and Tomato Strata, 14
  Baked Fish Mozzarella, 142
  Brandy-Nut Brie, 69
  Broccoli Lasagna au Gratin, 211
  Cauliflower Soup with Blue Cheese, 125
  Chart House Blue Cheese Dressing, 121
  Cheese Marinated Onions, 232
  Chicken Enchilada Casserole, 165
  Chicken Parmesan, 152
  Chiles Rellenos, 229
  Christmas Cheese Balls, 68
  Cocktail Spread, 49
  "Death to Dieters" Chicken Lasagna, 213
  Eggs Florentine, 7
  Épinards, Eh!, 236
  French Onion Soup au Gratin, 128
  Gourmet Macaroni and Cheese, 198
  How Cheesy Do You Want It?, 63
  "The Ladies" Seafood Casserole, 148
  Manicotti, 210
  Pasta Pot, 204
  Sausage Pie, 20
  Spanakopita, 73
  Spinach Lasagna, 212
  Stuffed Camembert Appetizer, 70
  Super Nachos, 90
  Swiss Apple Quiche, 12
  Tisdale Annie's Asparagus Puff, 219
  Tomato Cheese Bake, 240
  Tomatoes Florentine, 241
  The Utmost Grilled Cheese, 16
  Weekender Special, 8
cheese, Cheddar
  Asparagus Noodle Bake, 201
  Cheddar Dill Muffins, 32
  Cheese and Bacon Muffins, 33
  Cheesy Acorn Squash, 246
  Chicken Enchiladas, 164
  Chippy Knees Bites, 71
  Cocktail Crisps, 67
  Crab Tartlets, 81
  Ham and Cheese Puffs, 88
  Jalapeño Corn Muffins, 30
  Railroad Dip, 44
  Rarebit in a Hole, 64
  Sunday Eggs and Ham, 9
  Zucchini Cheese Pie, 15
cheese, Monterey Jack
  Burritos, 181
  Eggs Olé!, 6
  Hot Mushroom Salad, 95
  Moussaka, 196

cheese, Parmesan
  Alfredo Sauce, 264
  Cheese-Fried Zucchini, 242
  Dill and Parmesan Tomatoes, 238
  Ham and Mushroom Lasagna, 214
  Pesto Sauce, 263
  Spaghetti Squash Primavera, 244
Chef Toner's Mussels Creole, 78
cherries
  Cherry Berries on a Cloud, 345
  Palace Pie, 333
Chewy Chocolate Peanut Bars, 294
Chewy Kids' Cookies, 278
chicken
  Asparagus Chicken Puffs, 83
  Chicken Artichoke Casserole, 158
  Chicken Atlanta, 110
  Chicken Cacciatore, 159
  Chicken Enchilada Casserole, 165
  Chicken Enchiladas, 164
  Chicken Mandalay, 153
  Chicken Mexicana, 163
  Chicken Parmesan, 152
  Chicken Pot Pie, 161
  Chicken Tetrazzini, 160
  Classy Chicken, 149
  Crispy Sesame Chicken, 155
  "Death to Dieters" Chicken Lasagna, 213
  Fruit and Lime Chicken Salad, 115
  Hot 'n' Spicy Wings, 87
  Korean Chicken Salad, 112
  Layered Chicken Salad, 114
  Mulligatawny Soup, 137
  Sam's Brandied Chicken, 150
  Sortas, 86
  Sweet and Spicy Cashew Chicken, 156
  "Talk about Easy" Chicken Wings, 85
  Tangy Chicken Tidbits, 84
  Whip-Lash Chicken, 162
  Yummy Chicken, 154
Chiles Rellenos, 229
Chippy Knees Bites, 71
chocolate
  Black Bottom Cupcakes, 321
  Bourbon Balls, 300
  Chewy Chocolate Peanut Bars, 294
  Chocolate Chiffon Cake, 320
  Chocolate Chip Slab Cookies, 293
  Chocolate Mousse Cake, 316
  Chocolate Mousse Pie, 337
  Chocolate Peanut Butter Balls, 301
  Chocolate Pecan Pie, 336
  Chocolate Raspberry Torte, 318
  Chocolate Sabayon, 358
  Chocolate Zucchini Cake, 315

chocolate (*continued*)
Crater Cake, 314
Dark Chocolate Cake, 313
Fatal Attractions, 287
Fudge Pie with Custard Sauce, 338
Grand Slam Finale, 346
Hot Fudge Sauce, 363
Rocky Mountain Squares, 293
Shortcut Almond Roca, 297
Tiramisu, 349
Zucchini Cookies, 283
Christmas Cheese Balls, 68
Classy Chicken, 149
Cocktail Crisps, 67
Cocktail Spread, 49
coconut and coconut milk
Apple Kuchen, 305
B.L.'s Cookies, 279
Brown Bagger's Special, 291
Butter Tart Slice, 290
Coconut Bars, 289
Coconut Whip Cake, 311
Peanut Sauce, 265
coffee
Irish Coffee Cream Pie, 326
Mocha Whipped Cream Cake, 312
Tiramisu, 349
Cold Dilled Peas, 235
Committee Salad, 104
condiments, 266–71. *See also* jellies
cookies, 277–87
corn
Corn Relish, 269
Jalapeño Corn Muffins, 30
Country Cornbread, 55
crabmeat
Aunty Lil's Simple Antipasto, 91
Crab-Stuffed Artichoke Hearts, 79
Crab Tartlets, 81
Fisherman's Chowder, 135
"The Ladies" Seafood Casserole, 148
Layered Crab Dip, 45
Luncheon Soufflé Roll, 144
Pasta with Crab and Basil, 205
Snow Peas with Crab, 80
Crackers, Dilled Cocktail, 66
cranberries
Cranberry Stuffing, 259
Gourmet Cranberry Sauce, 261
Sunshine Muffins (update), 23
Terrific Turkey Stuffing, 260
Crater Cake, 314
cream. *See also* cream cheese; milk
Alfredo Sauce, 264
Avocado Soup, 123

Broccoli Soup, 124
Cauliflower Soup with Blue Cheese, 125
Cherry Berries on a Cloud, 345
Chicken Atlanta, 110
Chocolate Sabayon, 358
Cream of Curry Soup, 133
Cream of Parsley and Basil Soup, 129
Cream of Spinach Soup, 131
Crème Caramel, 356
Frozen Lemon Mousse with Raspberry
Sauce, 360
Fruit Dip, 362
Grand Marnier Crème, 355
Grand Slam Finale, 346
Irish Coffee Cream Pie, 326
Lemon Sorbet, 359
Mocha Whipped Cream Cake, 312
Mushroom Soup, 126
Mussels and Scallops in Cream, 146
Palace Pie, 333
Pavlova, 353
Quiche Lorraine, 11
Toffee Meringue, 354
cream cheese
Black Bottom Cupcakes, 321
Chocolate Mousse Pie, 337
Christmas Cheese Balls, 68
Cocktail Spread, 49
Cream Cheese Muffins, 31
Grand Slam Finale, 346
Hot Mushroom Turnovers, 72
Layered Crab Dip, 45
Linguine with White Clam Sauce, 206
Luncheon Soufflé Roll, 144
Mexicana Antipasto, 92
Pecan Cups, 344
Pumpkin Cheesecake, 302
Russian Beet Salad, 97
Shortbread Tarts with Cheese 'n' Fruit or
Lemon Filling, 342
Smoked Oyster Dip, 46
Stuffed Camembert Appetizer, 70
Tiramisu, 349
Creamy Dilled Snapper, 141
Crème Caramel, 356
Crispy Sesame Chicken, 155
Crustless Quiche, 10
cucumber
Greek Salad, 102
Korean Chicken Salad, 112
Layered Chicken Salad, 114
Salmon Pasta Salad, 108
Cumberland Sauce, 262
currants (dried)
Chewy Kids' Cookies, 278

Tea Scones, 61
Welsh Cakes, 60
Curried Cauliflower, 228

D

Dark Chocolate Cake, 313
dates
   After Angel Food Cookies, 277
   Health Nut Muffins, 24
   Matrimonial Bars, 296
"Death to Dieters" Chicken Lasagna, 213
A Different Spinach Salad, 99
dill
   Cheddar Dill Muffins, 32
   Dill and Parmesan Tomatoes, 238
   Dilled Cocktail Crackers, 66
   Easy Salmon Pâté, 47
   Marinated Fish Fillets with Basil Butter,
     143
   Perfect Parsnips, 234
dips and spreads, 44–50
Doctored Mayo Dressing, 119
Dressed-Up French Bread, 62
Duck Breasts en Casserole, 168

E

Easy Peach Torte, 310
Easy Salmon Pâté, 47
eggs
   After Angel Food Cookies, 277
   Baked Cheese and Tomato Strata, 14
   Cherry Berries on a Cloud, 345
   Chippy Knees Bites, 71
   Chocolate Chiffon Cake, 320
   Chocolate Mousse Cake, 316
   Chocolate Sabayon, 358
   Crustless Quiche, 10
   Egg Drop Soup, 133
   Eggs Florentine, 7
   Eggs Olé!, 6
   Luncheon Soufflé Roll, 144
   Midnight French Toast, 17
   Pavlova, 353
   Poppy Seed Chiffon Cake, 304
   Potato Latkes, 18
   Pumpkin Chiffon Pie, 334
   Quiche Lorraine, 11
   Rhubarb Delight, 348
   Rhubarb Meringue Pie, 332
   Stella by Starlight, 357
   Sunday Eggs and Ham, 9
   Swiss Apple Quiche, 12
   Tisdale Annie's Asparagus Puff, 219
   Toffee Meringue, 354
   Weekender Special, 8

Zucchini Cheese Pie, 15
Épinards, Eh!, 236

F

Fail-Proof Pastry, 322
Family Favorite Meatloaf, 177
Fatal Attractions, 287
Fettuccine Verde, 199
fish and seafood. *See also* crabmeat; salmon;
   shrimp
   Aunty Lil's Simple Antipasto, 91
   Baked Fish Mozzarella, 142
   Cadillac Oysters, 77
   Chef Toner's Mussels Creole, 78
   Creamy Dilled Snapper, 141
   Fisherman's Chowder, 135
   Linguine with Red Clam Sauce, 207
   Linguine with White Clam Sauce, 206
   Marinated Fish Fillets with Basil Butter, 143
   Mussels and Scallops in Cream, 146
   O-Sole-O-Mio, 139
   Seafood in Wine, 82
   Seafood Kabobs, 147
   Smoked Oyster Dip, 46
   Wine-Poached Halibut, 138
Flapper Pie, 324
Flour, Seasoned, 273
Fluffy Baked Potatoes, 249
French Lemon Pie, 329
French Onion Soup au Gratin, 128
Fresh Fruit Dressing, 117
Fresh Tomato Bisque, 132
Fried Cabbage, 225
Frosty Peach Dessert, 352
Frothy Orange Slushy, 364
Frozen Lemon Mousse with Raspberry Sauce,
   360
fruit. *See also* fruit juices; *specific fruits*
   Arizona Fruit Salad, 116
   Fruit and Lime Chicken Salad, 115
   Fruit Poof, 350
   Marinated Fruit Salad, 118
   Papaya with Shrimp and Curry Mayonnaise,
     109
   Pavlova, 353
   Shortbread Tarts with Cheese 'n' Fruit or
     Lemon Filling, 342
Fruit Dip, 362
fruit juices. *See also* orange juice
   Gingered Melon Soup, 122
   Graduation Punch, 365
   Midsummer Madness, 370
   A Real Smoothie, 364
Fudge Pie with Custard Sauce, 338
Fuzzy Navels, 366

G

ginger
  Gingered Melon Soup, 122
  Ginger-Fried Beef, 172
  Ginger Snaps, 281
  Sour Cream Ginger Buns, 58
  Sweet and Spicy Cashew Chicken, 156
Glazed Cinnamon Bars, 288
Gløgg, 369
Going Bananas, 34
Gourmet Cranberry Sauce, 261
Gourmet Macaroni and Cheese, 198
Graduation Punch, 365
Grand Marnier Crème, 355
Grand Slam Finale, 346
grapes
  Fruit and Lime Chicken Salad, 115
  Fruit Poof, 350
  Marinated Fruit Salad, 118
Greek Ribs, 189
Greek Salad, 102
Green Tomato Marmalade, 271
Guacamole Cherry Tomato Halves, 75

H

ham
  Ham and Cheese Puffs, 88
  Ham and Mushroom Lasagna, 214
  Ham Baked in Beer, 185
  Holy Ham Loaf with Marvelous Mustard
    Sauce, 186
  Spaghetti Carbonara, 208
  Sunday Eggs and Ham, 9
Hazelnut Torte, 306
Health Nut Muffins, 24
herbs (fresh). See also basil; dill; parsley
  Marinated Fish Fillets with Basil Butter, 143
  Pasta Primavera, 202
Herb's Soup with Shrimp, 136
Holy Ham Loaf with Marvelous Mustard Sauce,
    186
Hot Artichoke Dip, 45
Hot Buttered Rum, 371
Hot Fudge Sauce, 363
Hot Mushroom Salad, 95
Hot Mushroom Turnovers, 72
Hot 'n' Spicy Wings, 87
How Cheesy Do You Want It?, 63

I

ice cream (as ingredient)
  Hot Buttered Rum, 371
  Pecan Crust Ice Cream Pie with Caramel
    Sauce, 340

  Rhubarb Cream Dessert, 347
  Tin Roof Pie, 341
Irish Coffee Cream Pie, 326
Italian Sausage and Pasta, 209
Italian Zucchini, 243

J

Jalapeño Corn Muffins, 30
Jalapeño Pepper Jelly with Lumps, 48
jellies, 48, 50, 272
Jelly Balls, 89

K

Killer Coleslaw, 93
kiwis
  Fruit Poof, 350
  Pavlova, 353
  Shortbread Tarts with Cheese 'n' Fruit or
    Lemon Filling, 342
Korean Chicken Salad, 112

L

"The Ladies" Seafood Casserole, 148
lamb
  Leg of Lamb with Red Currant Sauce, 195
  Marinated Barbecued Lamb, 194
  Moussaka, 196
lasagna, 211–15
Layered Chicken Salad, 114
Layered Crab Dip, 45
Leek Soup, Mushroom and, 127
Leg of Lamb with Red Currant Sauce, 195
lemon
  Avgolemono, 134
  French Lemon Pie, 329
  Frozen Lemon Mousse with Raspberry
    Sauce, 360
  Green Tomato Marmalade, 271
  Lemon Sorbet, 359
  Midsummer Madness, 370
  Sangria à la Mode, 368
  Shortbread Tarts with Cheese 'n' Fruit or
    Lemon Filling, 342
lettuce
  Arizona Fruit Salad, 116
  Artichoke and Zucchini Salad, 94
  Committee Salad, 104
  A Different Spinach Salad, 99
  Fruit and Lime Chicken Salad, 115
  Greek Salad, 102
  Hot Mushroom Salad, 95
  Korean Chicken Salad, 112
  Layered Chicken Salad, 114
  Marinated Artichoke and Mushroom Salad,
    96

Oriental Garden Toss, 103
Papaya with Shrimp and Curry Mayonnaise, 109
Peachtree Plaza Salad, 105
Romaine with Oranges and Pecans, 98
lime
    Graduation Punch, 365
    Long Island Iced Tea, 367
    Margaritas Mucho Grande, 366
    Sangria à la Mode, 368
Linguine with Red Clam Sauce, 207
Linguine with White Clam Sauce, 206
liqueur
    Chocolate Mousse Cake, 316
    Chocolate Raspberry Torte, 318
    Frozen Lemon Mousse with Raspberry Sauce, 360
    Fuzzy Navels, 366
    Gourmet Cranberry Sauce, 261
    Grand Marnier Crème, 355
    Grand Slam Finale, 346
    Long Island Iced Tea, 367
    Margaritas Mucho Grande, 366
    Marinated Fruit Salad, 118
    Miss Scarlett's Wine Cordial, 272
    Spiked Apple Betty, 328
    Terry's Punch, 370
    Tiramisu, 349
liquor. *See* beer; liqueur; wine; *specific beverages*
liver
    Liver Stir-Fry, 182
    Sam's Brandied Chicken, 150
Long Island Iced Tea, 367
Luncheon Soufflé Roll, 144

M

Macaroni and Cheese, Gourmet, 198
Mad about Cabbage Rolls, 178
Mandarin Green Beans, 231
Mandarin Orange Muffins, 27
Manicotti, 210
Maple Syrup Graham Bread, 52
Margaritas Mucho Grande, 366
Marinated Artichoke and Mushroom Salad, 96
Marinated Barbecued Lamb, 194
Marinated Fish Fillets with Basil Butter, 143
Marinated Fruit Salad, 118
marshmallows
    Cherry Berries on a Cloud, 345
    Rocky Mountain Squares, 293
Matrimonial Bars, 296
meat, 169–96. *See also specific meats*
melon
    Fruit and Lime Chicken Salad, 115
    Gingered Melon Soup, 122

Marinated Fruit Salad, 118
Seafood Kabobs, 147
Mexicana Antipasto, 92
Mexican Rice, 253
Microwave Peanut Brittle, 299
Midnight French Toast, 17
Midsummer Madness, 370
milk (fresh and canned)
    Baked Cheese and Tomato Strata, 14
    Bourbon Balls, 300
    Fisherman's Chowder, 135
    Flapper Pie, 324
    Frothy Orange Slushy, 364
    Fruit Poof, 350
    Ham and Mushroom Lasagna, 214
    Hot Fudge Sauce, 363
    "The Ladies" Seafood Casserole, 148
    Luncheon Soufflé Roll, 144
    Mushroom and Leek Soup, 127
    Potato Soup, 130
    Pumpkin Chiffon Pie, 334
    Shortbread Tarts with Cheese 'n' Fruit or Lemon Filling, 342
Mincemeat Muffins, 25
Miss Scarlett's Wine Cordial, 272
Mocha Whipped Cream Cake, 312
Monk's Mustard, 266
Moussaka, 196
muffins, 23–33
Mulligatawny Soup, 137
mushrooms
    Beef Extraordinaire with Sauce Diane, 169
    Bomb Shelter Croustades, 74
    Cashew Pork Tenderloin, 187
    Cheesy Acorn Squash, 246
    Chicken Mexicana, 163
    Chicken Pot Pie, 161
    Chicken Tetrazzini, 160
    "Death to Dieters" Chicken Lasagna, 213
    Ham and Mushroom Lasagna, 214
    Hot Mushroom Salad, 95
    Hot Mushroom Turnovers, 72
    Liver Stir-Fry, 182
    Marinated Artichoke and Mushroom Salad, 96
    Mushroom and Leek Soup, 127
    Mushroom Soup, 126
    Noodle Maker's Chop Suey, 190
    Oven-Baked Wild Rice, 257
    Rice with Mushrooms and Pine Nuts, 254
    Sam's Brandied Chicken, 150
    Sensational Sausage Roll, 22
    Shortcut Stroganoff, 176
    Spaghetti Squash Primavera, 244
    Spinach-Stuffed Mushroom Caps, 71

mushrooms (*continued*)
    Steak and Mushroom Kabobs, 175
    Sudden Valley Green Beans, 230
    Veal Scaloppini and Mushrooms, 183
    Viva! Veggies, 217
    Weekender Special, 8
    Wild Buffet Rice!, 256
    Wild Rice Casserole, 258
Mussels Creole, Chef Toner's, 78
mustards, 266–67

N

Naan, 56
Nifty Carrots, 226
Noodle Maker's Chop Suey, 190
noodles. *See also* pasta
    Asparagus Noodle Bake, 201
    Chicken Tetrazzini, 160
    Killer Coleslaw, 93
    Simply Sauerbraten, 173
nuts. *See also specific types of nuts*
    Bourbon Balls, 300
    Chocolate Peanut Butter Balls, 301
    Glazed Cinnamon Bars, 288
    Rice with Mushrooms and Pine Nuts, 254
    Zucchini Cookies, 283
Nuts and Bolts, 65

O

oats
    B.L.'s Cookies, 279
    Blueberry Banana Bread, 36
    Brown Bagger's Special, 291
    Chewy Chocolate Peanut Bars, 294
    Chewy Kids' Cookies, 278
    Coconut Bars, 289
    Health Nut Muffins, 24
    Matrimonial Bars, 296
    Oatmeal Bread, 51
    Peanut Butter Brownies, 295
    Scotch Squares, 292
olives
    Aunty Lil's Simple Antipasto, 91
    Dressed-Up French Bread, 62
    Greek Salad, 102
    Mexicana Antipasto, 92
    Sicilian Broccoli, 223
onions
    Beef Extraordinaire with Sauce Diane, 169
    Boozy Onions, 231
    Cheese Marinated Onions, 232
    Corn Relish, 269
    Fettuccine Verde, 199
    French Onion Soup au Gratin, 128
    Italian Zucchini, 243

Mulligatawny Soup, 137
    Onions Stuffed with Broccoli, 233
    Pasta Primavera, 202
    Piccalilli, 268
    Railroad Dip, 44
    Spanakopita, 73
    Zucchini Relish, 270
orange. *See also* orange juice
    Almond Orange Pheasant (or Cornish Hens),
        166
    Arizona Fruit Salad, 116
    Baked Bananas in Orange and Lemon Juice, 216
    Carrot and Raisin Muffins, 29
    Chicken Atlanta, 110
    Committee Salad, 104
    Cumberland Sauce, 262
    Fresh Fruit Dressing, 117
    Gløgg, 369
    Gourmet Cranberry Sauce, 261
    Mandarin Green Beans, 231
    Mandarin Orange Muffins, 27
    Midnight French Toast, 17
    Pineapple Loaf, 37
    Romaine with Oranges and Pecans, 98
    Sangria à la Mode, 368
    Sunshine Muffins, 23
    Sweet Potatoes in Orange Sauce, 248
orange juice
    Carrots l'Orange, 227
    Frothy Orange Slushy, 364
    Fuzzy Navels, 366
    Graduation Punch, 365
    Grand Slam Finale, 346
    Midsummer Madness, 370
    O-Sole-O-Mio, 139
    A Real Smoothie, 364
    Speedy Baked Beans, 221
    Spunky Orange Ribs, 191
    Terry's Punch, 370
Oriental Garden Toss, 103
O-Sole-O-Mio, 139
Oven-Baked Wild Rice, 257

P

Palace Pie, 333
Papaya with Shrimp and Curry Mayonnaise, 109
parsley (fresh)
    Barbecued Pork Roast, 188
    Cream of Parsley and Basil Soup, 129
Parsnips, Perfect, 234
pasta. *See also* noodles
    Alfredo Sauce, 264
    Asparagus Pasta Salad, 106
    Broccoli Lasagna au Gratin, 211
    "Death to Dieters" Chicken Lasagna, 213

Fettuccine Verde, 199
Gourmet Macaroni and Cheese, 198
Ham and Mushroom Lasagna, 214
Italian Sausage and Pasta, 209
Linguine with Red Clam Sauce, 207
Linguine with White Clam Sauce, 206
Manicotti, 210
Pasta Pot, 204
Pasta Primavera, 202
Pasta Vegetable Salad, 107
Pasta with Crab and Basil, 205
Salmon Pasta Salad, 108
Spaghetti Carbonara, 208
Spicy Penne, 200
Spinach Lasagna, 212
pastry (as ingredient)
Asparagus Chicken Puffs, 83
Chicken Pot Pie, 161
Quiche Lorraine, 11
Sensational Sausage Roll, 22
Spanakopita, 73
Pastry, Fail-Proof, 322
Pavlova, 353
peaches
Easy Peach Torte, 310
Frosty Peach Dessert, 352
Fruit Poof, 350
Peaches and Cream Pie, 330
Peachtree Plaza Salad, 105
peanuts and peanut butter
Chewy Chocolate Peanut Bars, 294
Chocolate Peanut Butter Balls, 301
Microwave Peanut Brittle, 299
Nuts and Bolts, 65
Peanut Butter Brownies, 295
Peanut Butter Cookies, 284
Peanut Sauce, 265
Tin Roof Pie, 341
Whip-Lash Chicken, 162
peas (green)
Chicken Pot Pie, 161
Cold Dilled Peas, 235
Layered Chicken Salad, 114
Oriental Garden Toss, 103
Pasta Primavera, 202
Snow Peas with Crab, 80
Spaghetti Squash Primavera, 244
Sweet and Spicy Cashew Chicken, 156
pecans
Brandy-Nut Brie, 69
Brown Bagger's Special, 291
Chocolate Pecan Pie, 336
Christmas Cheese Balls, 68
Fruit and Lime Chicken Salad, 115
Microwave Peanut Brittle, 299

Palace Pie, 333
Peachtree Plaza Salad, 105
Pecan Crisps, 285
Pecan Crust Ice Cream Pie with Caramel
   Sauce, 340
Pecan Cups, 344
Pineapple Loaf, 37
Pumpkin Pecan Pie, 335
Romaine with Oranges and Pecans, 98
Strawberry Bread, 38
Peppernuts, 282
peppers, bell (sweet)
Corn Relish, 269
Eggs Olé!, 6
Jalapeño Pepper Jelly with Lumps, 48
Pepper Relish, 50
Piccalilli, 268
Sweet and Spicy Cashew Chicken,
   156
Whip-Lash Chicken, 162
peppers, chile (hot)
Chicken Enchilada Casserole, 165
Chiles Rellenos, 229
Chippy Knees Bites, 71
Crustless Quiche, 10
Ham and Cheese Puffs, 88
Jalapeño Corn Muffins, 30
Jalapeño Pepper Jelly with Lumps, 48
Mexicana Antipasto, 92
Salsa, 262
Super Nachos, 90
Taco Pie, 180
Perfect Parsnips, 234
Pesto Dressing, 120
Pesto Sauce, 263
Phantom Rhubarb Muffins, 28
Piccalilli, 268
pies and tarts, 322–44
pineapple
Holy Ham Loaf with Marvelous Mustard
   Sauce, 186
Marinated Fruit Salad, 118
Palace Pie, 333
Pineapple Loaf, 37
Pita Toasts, 57
Plum Sauce, 261
poppy seeds
Poppy Seed Cake, 303
Poppy Seed Chiffon Cake, 304
Poppy Seed Cookies, 286
pork. See also bacon; ham; sausage
Baked Beans, 220
Barbecued Pork Roast, 188
Cashew Pork Tenderloin, 187
Greek Ribs, 189

pork (*continued*)
  Holy Ham Loaf with Marvelous Mustard
    Sauce, 186
  Mad about Cabbage Rolls, 178
  Noodle Maker's Chop Suey, 190
  Pork Dumplings, 192
  Spunky Orange Ribs, 191
  Tomato Cantonese Pork, 184
potatoes
  Butter-Baked Taters, 250
  Chicken Pot Pie, 161
  Cream of Parsley and Basil Soup, 129
  Fluffy Baked Potatoes, 249
  Mulligatawny Soup, 137
  Potatoes Rösti, 252
  Potato Latkes, 18
  Potato Skins, 251
  Potato Soup, 130
Potlatch Salmon, 140
poultry. *See* chicken; duck; turkey
prosciutto. *See* ham
pumpkin
  Pumpkin Cheesecake, 302
  Pumpkin Chiffon Pie, 334
  Pumpkin Pecan Pie, 335

Q

Quiche Lorraine, 11
quick breads, 34–38
Quick Molasses Brown Bread, 53

R

Railroad Dip, 44
raisins
  After Angel Food Cookies, 277
  Brown Bagger's Special, 291
  Butter Tart Slice, 290
  Carrot and Raisin Muffins, 29
  Chewy Kids' Cookies, 278
  Gløgg, 369
  Going Bananas, 34
  Health Nut Muffins, 24
  Mincemeat Muffins, 25
  Quick Molasses Brown Bread, 53
  Rice with Mushrooms and Pine Nuts, 254
  Shoo-Fly Pie, 323
  Steamed Brown Bread for Beans, 54
  Tea Scones, 61
Rarebit in a Hole, 64
raspberries
  Frozen Lemon Mousse with Raspberry
    Sauce, 360
  Fruit Poof, 350
  Rhubarb Cream Dessert, 347
A Real Smoothie, 364

rhubarb
  Matrimonial Bars, 296
  Phantom Rhubarb Muffins, 28
  Rhubarb Cream Dessert, 347
  Rhubarb Crisp with Bourbon Sauce, 331
  Rhubarb Delight, 348
  Rhubarb Meringue Pie, 332
rice. *See also* wild rice
  Almond Orange Pheasant (or Cornish Hens),
    166
  Avgolemono, 134
  Cabbage Roll Casserole, 179
  Mad about Cabbage Rolls, 178
  Mexican Rice, 253
  Mulligatawny Soup, 137
  Rice with Mushrooms and Pine Nuts, 254
Rocky Mountain Squares, 293
Romaine with Oranges and Pecans, 98
rum
  Fruit Dip, 362
  Hot Buttered Rum, 371
  Midsummer Madness, 370
  Tiramisu, 349
Russian Beet Salad, 97

S

salads and dressings, 93–121
salmon
  Easy Salmon Pâté, 47
  Potlatch Salmon, 140
  Salmon Pasta Salad, 108
  Smoked Salmon Superb, 76
  Teriyaki Barbecued Salmon Steaks, 139
Salsa, 262
Salt Substitute, 274
Sam's Brandied Chicken, 150
Sangria à la Mode, 368
sauces, 261–65
sausage
  Italian Sausage and Pasta, 209
  Sausage 'n' Johnny Cake, 19
  Sausage Pie, 20
  Sensational Sausage Roll, 22
  Terrific Turkey Stuffing, 260
  Wild Buffet Rice!, 256
Scotch Squares, 292
seafood. *See* fish and seafood
Seasoned Flour, 273
seasonings, 272–74
Sensational Sausage Roll, 22
sesame seeds
  Crispy Sesame Chicken, 155
  Killer Coleslaw, 93
  Korean Chicken Salad, 112
  Sortas, 86

Shoo-Fly Pie, 323
Shortbread Tarts with Cheese 'n' Fruit or
    Lemon Filling, 342
Shortcut Almond Roca, 297
Shortcut Stroganoff, 176
shrimp
    Cocktail Spread, 49
    Fisherman's Chowder, 135
    Herb's Soup with Shrimp, 136
    "The Ladies" Seafood Casserole, 148
    Papaya with Shrimp and Curry Mayonnaise,
        109
    Seafood Kabobs, 147
    Smoked Salmon Superb, 76
Sicilian Broccoli, 223
side dishes, 216–60
Simply Sauerbraten, 173
Smoked Oyster Dip, 46
Smoked Salmon Superb, 76
snow peas
    Layered Chicken Salad, 114
    Snow Peas with Crab, 80
    Sweet and Spicy Cashew Chicken, 156
Sortas, 86
soups, 122–37
Sour Cream Ginger Buns, 58
Spaghetti Carbonara, 208
Spaghetti Squash Primavera, 244
Spanakopita, 73
Speedy Baked Beans, 221
Spicy Penne, 200
Spiked Apple Betty, 328
spinach
    Cream of Spinach Soup, 131
    A Different Spinach Salad, 99
    Eggs Florentine, 7
    Épinards, Eh!, 236
    Luncheon Soufflé Roll (variation), 144
    Spanakopita, 73
    Spinach Lasagna, 212
    Spinach or Broccoli Timbales, 237
    Spinach Salad with Sour Cream Dressing, 100
    Spinach-Stuffed Mushroom Caps, 71
    Springtime Spinach Dip, 44
    Tomatoes Florentine, 241
spreads and dips, 44–50
Springtime Spinach Dip, 44
Spunky Orange Ribs, 191
squares and bars, 288–96
squash. See also pumpkin; zucchini
    Cheesy Acorn Squash, 246
    Spaghetti Squash Primavera, 244
Steak and Mushroom Kabobs, 175
Steamed Brown Bread for Beans, 54
Stella by Starlight, 357

strawberries
    Cherry Berries on a Cloud, 345
    Fruit and Lime Chicken Salad, 115
    Fruit Poof, 350
    Grand Slam Finale, 346
    Palace Pie, 333
    Pavlova, 353
    Shortbread Tarts with Cheese 'n' Fruit or
        Lemon Filling, 342
    Strawberry Bread, 38
Stuffed Camembert Appetizer, 70
Sudden Valley Green Beans, 230
Sunday Eggs and Ham, 9
sunflower seeds
    Committee Salad, 104
    Killer Coleslaw, 93
Sunshine Muffins, 23
Super Nachos, 90
Super Tender Flank Steak, 171
Sweet and Spicy Cashew Chicken, 156
Sweet Potatoes in Orange Sauce, 248
Swiss Apple Quiche, 12

T

Taco Pie, 180
"Talk about Easy" Chicken Wings, 85
Tangy Chicken Tidbits, 84
Tarragon Mustard, 267
Tea Scones, 61
tequila
    Long Island Iced Tea, 367
    Margaritas Mucho Grande, 366
Teriyaki Barbecued Salmon Steaks, 139
Terrific Turkey Stuffing, 260
Terry's Punch, 370
Thousand Island Dressing, 120
Tin Roof Pie, 341
Tiramisu, 349
Tisdale Annie's Asparagus Puff, 219
Toffee Meringue, 354
Tolerable Brussels Sprouts, 224
tomatoes. See also tomato sauce
    Baked Cheese and Tomato Strata, 14
    Chicken Cacciatore, 159
    Chicken Mexicana, 163
    Dill and Parmesan Tomatoes, 238
    Fresh Tomato Bisque, 132
    Green Tomato Marmalade, 271
    Guacamole Cherry Tomato Halves, 75
    Ham and Mushroom Lasagna, 214
    Herb's Soup with Shrimp, 136
    Italian Sausage and Pasta, 209
    Italian Zucchini, 243
    Linguine with Red Clam Sauce, 207
    Mad about Cabbage Rolls, 178

tomatoes (*continued*)
Mexican Rice, 253
Pasta Pot, 204
Pasta Primavera, 202
Pasta with Crab and Basil, 205
Piccalilli, 268
Salsa, 262
Sausage Pie, 20
Spicy Penne, 200
Taco Pie, 180
Tomato and Artichoke Casserole, 239
Tomato Cantonese Pork, 184
Tomato Cheese Bake, 240
Tomatoes Florentine, 241
Viva! Veggies, 217
Whip-Lash Chicken, 162
tomato sauce (as ingredient)
Cabbage Roll Casserole, 179
Chicken Parmesan, 152
Chiles Rellenos, 229
Duck Breasts en Casserole, 168
Manicotti, 210
Moussaka, 196
tortillas
Burritos, 181
Chicken Enchilada Casserole, 165
Chicken Enchiladas, 164
turkey
Chicken Atlanta, 110
"Death to Dieters" Chicken Lasagna, 213
Mulligatawny Soup, 137

U

Unattended Roast Beef, 170
The Utmost Grilled Cheese, 16

V

Veal Scaloppini and Mushrooms, 183
vegetables. *See also specific vegetables*
Moussaka, 196
Viva! Veggies, 217
vodka
Fuzzy Navels, 366
Long Island Iced Tea, 367
Midsummer Madness, 370

W

Wafer Puffs, 280
walnuts
After Angel Food Cookies, 277
Bourbon Balls, 300
Brown Bagger's Special, 291
Green Tomato Marmalade, 271
Health Nut Muffins, 24
Pecan Crust Ice Cream Pie with Caramel
Sauce, 340
Scotch Squares, 292
water chestnuts

Chicken Mandalay, 153
A Different Spinach Salad, 99
Layered Chicken Salad, 114
Oven-Baked Wild Rice, 257
Weekender Special, 8
Welsh Cakes, 60
Whip-Lash Chicken, 162
whiskey
Bourbon Balls, 300
Brandy-Nut Brie, 69
Irish Coffee Cream Pie, 326
Rhubarb Crisp with Bourbon Sauce, 331
wild rice
Oven-Baked Wild Rice, 257
Terrific Turkey Stuffing, 260
Wild Buffet Rice!, 256
Wild Rice and Artichoke Hearts, 255
Wild Rice Casserole, 258
wine
Almond Orange Pheasant (or Cornish Hens),
166
Boozy Onions, 231
Cadillac Oysters, 77
Chocolate Sabayon, 358
Gløgg, 369
Marinated Barbecued Lamb, 194
Miss Scarlett's Wine Cordial, 272
Mussels and Scallops in Cream, 146
Sangria à la Mode, 368
Stella by Starlight, 357
"Talk about Easy" Chicken Wings, 85
Terry's Punch, 370
Wine-Poached Halibut, 138

Y

Yammy Apples, 247
yogurt
Cheddar Dill Muffins, 32
Creamy Dilled Snapper, 141
Fresh Fruit Dressing, 117
Mulligatawny Soup, 137
A Real Smoothie, 364
Yummy Chicken, 154

Z

zucchini
Artichoke and Zucchini Salad, 94
Cheese-Fried Zucchini, 242
Chocolate Zucchini Cake, 315
Eggs Olé!, 6
Italian Zucchini, 243
Moussaka, 196
Pasta Primavera, 202
Spaghetti Squash Primavera, 244
Zucchini Cheese Pie, 15
Zucchini Cookies, 283
Zucchini Relish, 270
Zucchini Salad, 101